India Studies in Business and Economics

The Indian economy is considered to be one of the fastest growing economies of the world with India amongst the most important G-20 economies. Ever since the Indian economy made its presence felt on the global platform, the research community is now even more interested in studying and analyzing what India has to offer. This series aims to bring forth the latest studies and research about India from the areas of economics, business, and management science. The titles featured in this series will present rigorous empirical research, often accompanied by policy recommendations, evoke and evaluate various aspects of the economy and the business and management landscape in India, with a special focus on India's relationship with the world in terms of business and trade.

More information about this series at http://www.springer.com/series/11234

Ajay Bhaskarabhatla

Regulating Pharmaceutical Prices in India

Policy Design, Implementation and Compliance

Springer

Ajay Bhaskarabhatla
Erasmus School of Economics
Erasmus University Rotterdam
Rotterdam, The Netherlands

ISSN 2198-0012 ISSN 2198-0020 (electronic)
India Studies in Business and Economics
ISBN 978-3-030-06652-9 ISBN 978-3-319-93393-1 (eBook)
https://doi.org/10.1007/978-3-319-93393-1

Printed on acid-free paper

This Springer imprint is published by the registered company Springer International Publishing AG part of Springer Nature.
The registered company address is: Gewerbestrasse 11, 6330 Cham, Switzerland

To my mother

Acknowledgements

I thank the AIOCD for generously sharing the data. I also thank a number of students at Erasmus School of Economics, who have assisted in writing the book. In particular, I would like to thank Andreea Beznea, Sophie de Clercq, Farhan Haider, Huibert van der Hart, David November, Matej Opatrny, Henning Sökeland, and Clément Staner. I would also like to thank my coauthors on research papers based on the Indian pharmaceutical industry, Priyatam Anurag, Chirantan Chatterjee, Bas Karreman, and Enrico Pennings. I would like to thank Erasmus Research Institute of Management for financial support. I also thank S. Srinivasan, Malini Aisola, and T. Srikrisna for their insights into the Indian pharmaceutical industry. Finally, I would like to thank my wife, brother, and sister-in-law for their encouragement and support.

Contents

Chapter 1
Introduction

Providing affordable access to essential medicines in developing countries remains a significant challenge, and it is an integral part of the global efforts to achieve Millennium Development Goals (Pécoul et al. 1999, UN.org 2015). Recent surveys show that essential medicines are available in only 58% of the healthcare facilities in the public sector and 67% in the private sector in developing countries. Also, the median prices of essential medicines are, on average, 2.92 and 4.62 times higher than international reference prices in public and private sectors respectively (UN Report 2015).[1] To improve access to essential medicines, many developing countries regulate the prices of country-specific lists of essential medicines, adapted from the World Health Organization's (WHO) model list to suit the local needs (IMS Health 2015). The impact of such regulations depends as much on the design of the policy as on implementation. Rarely if ever studies examine, in detail, the design, enforcement and compliance aspects of such price control regulations (see, for an exception, Bhaskarabhatla et al. 2016).

In this book, we examine these issues by focusing on the case study of the Indian pharmaceutical industry. India is a useful context to explore the impact of regulations on the pricing of medicines for several reasons. First, India is an emerging economy that has increasingly adopted policies of economic liberalization and deregulated several sectors and industries. At the same time, India expanded the decades-old policy of price control regulations on essential medicines, providing an opportunity to study the design, implementation, and enforcement of such policies.

Second, India's price control regulation on medicines affects hundreds of millions of uninsured people spending money out-of-pocket on healthcare needs, including the 20% of its population that lives below the poverty line (The World Bank 2017, Selvaraj et al. 2018). Ensuring the success of such regulations and learning from

[1]International reference prices (IRPs) are median prices of quality multi-source medicines offered to low- and middle-income countries by not-for-profit and for-profit suppliers, as available from Management Sciences for Health (MSH) International Drug Price Indicator Guide (MDC Gap Task Force 2015).

A. Bhaskarabhatla, *Regulating Pharmaceutical Prices in India*, India Studies in Business and Economics, https://doi.org/10.1007/978-3-319-93393-1_1

their limitations is useful for India as well as for other countries around the world undergoing similar policy changes (Selvaraj 2013).

Third, several civil society groups have successfully argued before the Supreme Court of India that the prices of essential medicines, which form a significant component of the healthcare expenses, are soaring, reflecting the need for a government response in the form of price control regulations to make medicines more accessible and affordable. Although India expanded price control regulations recently, these groups continue to argue for a further expansion of the scope of regulation. They demand the inclusion of substitute medicines under the price control regime, greater alignment of price controls with India's public health needs, an improvement of the methodology for determining the ceiling price, and a mechanism to control the exorbitant margins on several essential medicines (Shankar 2014). There is also a concern among the civil society organizations that, under pressure from the pharmaceutical companies, pharmaceutical policies and price control laws that protect access to affordable medicines will quickly erode (Chatterjee 2013). As a cautionary note, they point to the challenges in access to essential medicines for chronic diseases such as diabetes and asthma (e.g., Kotwani 2010).

Fourth, the pharmaceutical firms and their trade associations argue that price control regulations have led to a significant loss of revenue, that the price control regulations have been ineffective, and that better alternatives, such as bulk public procurement, exist to make medicines more affordable and accessible (McLain 2014; Silverman 2015; IMS Health 2015).

Fifth, the Indian pharmaceutical industry is considered an extremely competitive market with tens or hundreds of firms competing with each other in narrowly-defined medicine markets, reflecting a thriving entrepreneurial culture and raising concerns among many as to why price control regulations are necessary (Saberwal 2006). The presence of price control regulations, some argue, leads to the delay in the launch of new, patented medicines into India, exacerbating the negative consequences. However, others argue that although India is a net exporter of cheap generic medicines, many medicines are either out-of-stock or too expensive in the domestic market (Selvaraj 2007). Also, the price control policies apply mainly to out-of-patent medicines and a policy to control the prices of patented medicines has not been finalized in over a decade (Francis 2016). While prior research on pharmaceutical regulation is focused on intellectual property protection in developing countries, few studies examine the capacity to regulate pharmaceutical markets, most of which are out of patent protection (Pezzola and Sweet 2016; Sell 2003).

Finally, the regulator responsible for implementing the price control regulation on essential medicines, the National Pharmaceutical Pricing Authority (NPPA) itself is fighting a battle for relevance and survival (Francis 2014a). Some observers have expressed concern that the government is attempting to dismantle the NPPA and dilute price controls (Shankar 2014). The NPPA is also concerned about the potential shortages of medicines that enter price control regulations, one of the many ways in which firms can mitigate and circumvent the regulations. For example, the NPPA received reports of shortages of several essential medicines such as anti-malarial medicines and considered invoking special powers to instruct pharmaceutical firms to produce human albumin (Nautiyal 2014, 2015a). The NPPA is also in need of greater investment to improve monitoring and enforcement of the price control regulations. We document the successes and failures of the NPPA in designing and enforcing price control regulations, which can help regulators in other low- and middle-income countries.

Many economists question the usefulness of price control regulations, as such regulations can introduce inefficiency in the market and also allow firms to respond in a manner that often defeats the intended purpose of the regulation. We argue that some level of regulation is essential in these medicine markets for several reasons unique to the Indian context. They include but not limited to: (i) the branding of generic medicines; (ii) the cartelization of the pharmaceutical distribution system; (iii) the use of restrictive vertical trade practices; (iv) the opposition to retail chains and online sale of medicines; (v) the promotion of more expensive brands of a medicine by retail pharmacies and physicians when less expensive substitutes are available; (vi) the weaknesses in drug approval processes that lead to the introduction of irrational fixed-dose combinations; (vii) the lack of enforcement mechanisms for ensuring transparency in pricing and profit margins of pharmaceutical firms; (viii) and the inexplicably high variation in prices of medicines. Although some of these issues are being addressed through the enforcement of India's newly reformed competition laws, these efforts have not translated into lower prices or margins. Previous literature suggests that a decline in the scope of price controls in India in the 1990s and early 2000s increased medicine prices, sometimes surpassing prices in Canada and the UK and that the market mechanisms at the time were ineffective in stabilizing the prices of medicines (Mehta 2005). Prior studies also suggest that pharmacists and hospitals in India receive substantial margins, sometimes as high as 1000%, indicating the need for regulation (e.g., Mathew 2004; Nautiyal 2015b).

Previous analyses of the 2013 price control regulation on essential medicines in India are mostly anecdotal and conducted by activists and journalists, and often contain far-reaching conclusions. For example, in examining the potential impact of the 2013 price control regulation, Ray (2013) stated,

> Indian consumers will undoubtedly be the biggest beneficiaries of the new DPCO [Drug Price Control Order], as ceiling prices will now be based on roughly 91% of the pharmaceutical market by value, resulting in up to 20% price reduction in 60% of the NLEM [National List of Essential Medicines] medicines. The prices of some drugs will fall by even up to 70%.

By contrast, a study sponsored by the Organization of Pharmaceutical Producers of India (OPPI), an association of research-based pharmaceutical firms in India, claims that the 2013 price control regulation has little effect on access to essential medicines compared to a matched set of unregulated medicines in the same therapeutic area. The study is conducted by IMS Health, whose market data on pharmaceutical firms formed the basis for the NPPA to fix the ceiling prices in 2013. The study proposes alternatives to price control regulation such as taxing alcohol and tobacco to subsidize essential medicines. As PharmaBiz.com (2015) notes:

> Some key findings of the study are[:] primary beneficiaries of the DPCO 2013 price controls have been high-income patient populations, rather than the low-income targets; the consumption of price-controlled drugs in rural areas has decreased by 7% over the past two years, while that of non-price controlled products has risen by 5%; and the DPCO 2013 has resulted in an increase in market concentration (fewer brands are now listed) and a decrease in competitive intensity (the average number of new brands has gone down since 2013).

In this book, we address the need for a systematic and comprehensive analysis of the nature and impact of the 2013 price control regulation on several essential medicines in India. Our study is based on an analysis of the data collected by the AIOCD, known among the industry observers in India by its product name, Pharmatrac data. The NPPA used the IMS data in 2013 but, under criticism from several firms and disputes arising from fixing ceiling prices using the IMS data, the NPPA switched to the Pharmatrac data in 2015 (Francis 2014b). We exploit Pharmatrac data to examine quantitatively the method used by the NPPA to fix ceiling prices, and the challenges that arose in fixing them. Pharmatrac data cover the period from January 2011 until July 2016, which makes it possible to analyze the trends before and after the DPCO 2013. The data are disaggregated at the level of the stock keeping unit, which allows us to compare different brands and dosages of the same medicine as well as different medicines within the same therapeutic category. Moreover, the data distinguish between different delivery forms of the same medicine, such as a tablet, injection, capsule or syrup. Such disaggregation along with the partial nature of the regulation allows us to study the impact of the regulation by comparing regulated and unregulated dosages of the same medicine.

The book is divided into four parts. In the first part, we provide a historical account of the price control regulations on pharmaceuticals in India. We examine the efforts leading up to the 2013 regulation and elaborate on the policy process that unfolded. We also document the essential characteristics of the Indian pharmaceutical industry that motivates the need for introducing price control regulation. We illustrate, using Pharmatrac data on medicines, the extent of margins firms obtain for essential medicines and the need for controlling them. The second part of the book focuses on the design of the 2013 price control regulation. We examine the details of the design and highlight the inherent challenges and shortcomings. We also study how firms have used the slowly unfolding policy process to their advantage. The third part of the book examines the effectiveness of these regulations. In particular, we focus on the many ways in which pharmaceutical firms have mitigated the impact of the regulations. We discuss, using several case studies of individual medicines, as well as analyses of comprehensive lists of price-controlled medicines, the nature, and extent of coverage of price regulations, their effectiveness, and impact. The fourth part describes the nature of enforcement and compliance. In particular, we examine the extent of compliance with price ceilings imposed on essential medicines in India in 2013 and how it has changed in response to enforcement efforts. We estimate how much firms overcharged above the ceiling price and the total overcharged amount. We also reflect on whether the regulator has followed a targeted approach to enforcement to induce compliance and whether such targeting has had any impact on overall compliance. The book concludes in Chap. 9, which examines recent developments to strengthen price control regulation by expanding the scope to include medical devices such as stents.

Overall, our analysis identifies several limitations of the design of the regulation due to its partial nature. The exclusion of closely related substitutes and dosages of the same medicine has weakened the effectiveness of the regulation. We also identify limitations due to the weaknesses in the existing enforcement regime to regulate pharmaceutical prices in India. The powers to regulate pharmaceutical prices are distributed across different organizations, often with competing interests. The pharmaceutical industry falls under the supervision of the Ministry of Chemicals and Fertilizers, which, naturally, attempts to promote industry-related interests. However, the Ministry of Health, responsible for access to healthcare and affordable medicines does not oversee the regulation of pharmaceutical prices in India. A proposal to consolidate the multiplicity of regulatory authorities and unify them under a new Ministry of Pharmaceuticals exists, but strict enforcement of pharmaceutical price controls may not happen even after such a reorganization if there is no clear enforcement strategy (Business Standard 2015). Chief among the reasons for the lack of enforcement is perhaps the limited political mandate to pursue enforcement vigorously. Another important limitation is that the regulator at the national level has a limited enforcement budget of Rs. 100 million for the year 2015–2016, minimal presence across various states in the country, and seemingly receives little cooperation from the state drug controllers. Compounding these issues is the regulator's decision to allocate Rs. 50 million for consumer awareness schemes, such as building mobile applications to solicit complaints from the citizens, rather than streamlining data collection and enforcement. A third limitation is that the regulatory authority likely underestimates the extent of the violations of price ceilings. An internal study of the regulator shows that in January 2015, 99.4% of the medicines sold in India are in compliance, which is at variance with our estimates of the potential fines based on Pharmatrac data. A vital contribution of our study is to identify the firms and markets in which the most flagrant violations of the ceiling prices have occurred. The regulator can build on these results to focus its enforcement rupees.

As our study shows, even with minimal resources, it is possible to document, to the fullest extent, price ceiling violations in each month during the 3 years of the implementation of price control regulations. The prices and unit sales are easy to monitor, as they are displayed on medicine packs, and sales data are compiled monthly in several readily available databases such as IMS Health and AIOCD Pharmatrac. If these data are appropriate to determine the ceiling prices, surely they must also be valid for detecting cases of overcharging. The sale of medicines through online platforms has meant that the prices of several brands of medicines are displayed online. Bringing in retailers, hospitals, online platforms, and dealers into the ambit of enforcement can potentially improve compliance. The regulator currently reports the price of a regulated medicine per tablet or injection. As we will discuss later, pharmaceutical firms are creative in their design of stock keeping units (SKU), which makes determining whether or not a given brand of medicine is in violation of the price ceiling regulation challenging for the average citizen.[2] The regulator's efforts to publish a searchable list of the SKU-specific ceiling prices rather than per-tablet ceiling prices is a useful step, as it becomes easier for the more than 750,000 pharmacists in the country to know whether the medicine brands they sell are in violation of the regulations.

As noted earlier, one of the challenges in effective regulation of medicine prices in India is the manner in which the regulatory system is currently organized. The task of providing affordable healthcare is distributed among the ministry of health and family welfare, the ministry of chemicals and fertilizers, which oversees the department of pharmaceuticals, and the ministry of commerce. The administration and regulation are distributed over the Central Drug Standards Control Organization (CDSCO), the National Pharmaceutical Pricing Authority (NPPA), and various state drug controllers. In recent years, there has been a vocal criticism of the manner in which some of the regulators have operated and the Drug Technical Advisory Board (DTAB) and proposed to rename the CDSCO as the "Indian Drug Administration," which would ensure a dedicated pool of qualified workforce to enforce the regulations (Vijay 2017). While the book does not offer solutions to improving the organization of the pharmaceutical regulatory system in India, it provides a context for the debate by documenting the limitations of the current efforts to design, implement, and enforce price control regulations in India.

References

Business Standard. (2015, December 10). Govt to create a separate ministry for pharma in one year: Ananth Kumar, Business Standard.

Bhaskarabhatla, A. S., Chatterjee, C., Anurag, P., & Pennings, H. P. G. (2016). Mitigating regulatory impact: The case of partial price controls on metformin in India. *Health Policy and Planning, 32*(2), 194–204.

Chatterjee, P. (2013). India's patent case victory rattles Big Pharma. *Lancet, 381*(9874), 1263.

Francis, P. (2014a, October 22). Patented Drugs & DPCO. PharmaBiz.com

Francis, P. (2014b, July 02). Modifying DPCO 2013. PharmaBiz.com

Francis, P. (2016, November 22). Do not dismantle NPPA. PharmaBiz.com

IMS Health. (2015), Assessing the impact of price control measures on access to medicines in India. IMS Health India Report.

Kotwani, A. (2010). Access to essential medicines and standard treatment for chronic diseases. *Indian Journal of Pharmacology, 42*(3), 127–128.

Mathew, J. C. (2004). Paswan in favor of same profit margins for branded & generic drugs. *PharmaBiz* [online]. Available from http://www.pharmabiz.com/NewsDetails.aspx?aid=24757&sid=2

[2]An SKU is a particular brand of medicine sold by a firm for a particular delivery and dosage form. For example, "CROCIN ADVANCE 500 MG TABLET 10" is an SKU indicating that Crocin, a popular brand of Paracetamol manufactured by GSK, contains 500 mg of the active ingredient and ten tablets in the pack.

Mehta, P. S. (2005). *Towards a functional competition policy for India.* New Delhi: Academic Foundation.

McLain, S. (2014, July 15). India's new drug-price controls: Unintended consequences? *Wall Street Journal.*

Nautiyal, S. (2014, September 26). Human albumin serum not available across India post NPPA price cut. PharmaBiz.com

Nautiyal, S. (2015a, March 23). NPPA may invoke para 3 of DPCO to address shortage of human albumin. PharmaBiz.com

Nautiyal, S. (2015b, May 29). Maharashtra FDA detects 5 distributors involved in overpricing of cardiac stents. PharmaBiz.com

Pécoul, B., Chirac, P., Trouiller, P., & Pinel, J. (1999). Access to essential drugs in poor countries: A lost battle? *Journal of the American Medical Association, 281*(4), 361–367.

Pezzola, A., & Sweet, C. M. (2016). Global pharmaceutical regulation: The challenge of integration for developing states. *Globalization and Health, 12*, 85.

PharmaBiz.com. (2015, July 15). Price control unlikely to improve access to medicines in India: IMS study.

Ray, T. J. (2013). *New drug price control order of India: Is it directionally right improving access to medicines?* [online]. Available from http://www.tapanray.in/new-drug-price-control-order-of-india-is-it-directionally-right-improving-access-to-medicines/

Saberwal, G. (2006). New pharma-biotech company formation in India. *Nature Biotechnology, 24* (5), 499–501.

Sell, S. (2003). *Private power, public law: The globalization of intellectual property rights.* Cambridge: Cambridge University Press.

Selvaraj, S. (2007). *How effective is India's drug price control regime.* Boston: Harvard School of Public Health [online]. Available from https://cdn1.sph.harvard.edu/wp-content/uploads/sites/114/2012/10/RP256.pdf

Selvaraj, S. (2013, August 2). Africa could learn from India's burgeoning pharma sector. *British Medical Journal, 347*, f4235.

Selvaraj, S., Farooqui, H., & Karan, A. (2018). Quantifying the financial burden of households' out-of-pocket payments on medicines in India: A repeated cross-sectional analysis of national sample survey data, 1994–2014. *BMJ Open, 8*, e018020. https://doi.org/10.1136/bmjopen-2017-018020.

Shankar, R. (2014, August 21). NGOs ask government to bring more essential and lifesaving drugs under price control. PharmaBiz.com

Silverman, E. (2015, July 20). Price controls for drugs in India fail to improve access for patients: Report. *Wall Street Journal.*

UN Report. (2015). MDC gap task force report 2015: taking stock of global partnership for development. Economic Analysis & Policy Division. United Nations.

Vijay, N. (2017, January 18). Change to IDA from CDSCO will usher in fresh wave of accountability & professionalism: Dr Jagashetty. PharmaBiz.com

Part I
Historical Context and the Motivation for Regulation

Chapter 2
Brief History of Regulating Pharmaceutical Prices

2.1 Introduction

In this chapter, we begin with a historical overview of India's efforts to design a price regulation mechanism for essential medicines and how such efforts culminated in the latest episode of price controls in 2013. The chapter documents how India began regulating nearly 350 medicines in 1970, steadily lowered the scope of regulation to 74 in 1995, and then expanded the number again to nearly 350 in 2013, completing the full circle. The historical account shows how the same set of issues have arisen during the design, implementation, and enforcement of each of the episodes of price control regulations.

Price controls have been commonplace in India since its independence in 1947. They were part of a broader set of 'command-and-control' policies that regulated almost all areas of economic activity in the country to strengthen the economy and promote local investment and production (Mehta 2005). Price controls on several commodities instituted by the British before independence continued to exist even afterward, and they were made permanent through the Essential Commodities Act of 1955. Under the act, India regulated the prices of a wide variety of products such as petroleum and related derivatives, food grains and seeds, textiles, and fertilizers (see, for an overview, De 2014). The regulation of medicine prices, however, did not begin under the Essential Commodities Act. Instead, India started to control the prices of medicines in the backdrop of the national emergency created by the Sino-Indian war in 1962, under the 1915 Defense of India Act.

India introduced the Drugs Display of Prices Order of 1962 and the Drugs Control of Prices Order of 1963, effectively freezing medicine prices as an emergency measure. The government replaced the 1962 and 1963 drug control orders with the Drugs Prices Display and Control of 1966. On the one hand, the 1966 order strengthened the control regime by mandating pharmaceutical firms to obtain prior approval from the government before increasing the prices of any medicine formulation (Basak 2008; Mehta 2005). On the other hand, however, the order introduced

A. Bhaskarabhatla, *Regulating Pharmaceutical Prices in India*, India Studies in Business and Economics, https://doi.org/10.1007/978-3-319-93393-1_2

exceptions to the price control regime by keeping newly developed medicines outside the ambit of price control. By mandating that pharmaceutical firms request an authorization to increase prices of new drugs, the government sought to manage the upward trend of prices in the industry. What followed was a system of greater bureaucratic control over the price control regime and myriad exceptions. India implemented a series of price control regimes through various orders, in an attempt to institutionalize the affordability and availability of 'essential' medicines.[1]

2.2 Deregulation of Pharmaceutical Prices from the 1970s to the 1990s

The next revision of the order in 1970 issued under Section 3 of the 1955 Essential Commodities Act, enabled India to control the production, distribution, and supply of essential medicines. The government hoped that the revised order would ensure equitable distribution and availability of essential medicines at fair prices (Joseph 2015; Government of India 1955). The 1970 DPCO allowed the government to regulate the prices of essential bulk drugs and their formulations by restricting excessive profiteering, which was intended to ensure greater supply, distribution, and availability of essential drugs. As shown in Table 2.1, most bulk drugs and their formulations sold on the market were either directly or indirectly affected by the 1970 DPCO, indicating a shift towards increased control and protectionism in India (Malhotra 2010). The 1970 DPCO stipulated that a company's pre-tax profit from its pharmaceutical activity should not exceed 15% of its pharmaceutical sales, net of excise duty and sales tax (Mehta 2005). The 1970 order targeted only 18 bulk drugs and their formulations, while the prices of the remaining bulk drugs were frozen. The order allocated a healthy markup of 75% on the material, conversion and packaging costs. Also, the markup was set higher for new combinations of existing drugs at 100% and new drugs at 150%. Alternatively, companies could fix prices within the ceiling of a 75% mark-up for essential drugs and 150% for other drugs, as long as their gross profit did not exceed 15% of sales (Joseph 2015).

The 1970 DPCO represented the introduction of cost-based regulation of drug pricing in India, which is sometimes also referred to as 'rate-of-return' or 'cost-plus' regulation. This kind of regulation targeted firms' profit margins, limiting profit-maximizing behavior and the abuse of market power (Cowan 2002). The government considered cost-based regulation as a way to balance the need for controlling drug prices while at the same time providing sufficient profits to manufacturers to

[1]'Essential drugs' are defined as drugs that meet the priority healthcare needs of the population (WHO 2017). Today, priority healthcare needs are established based on disease prevalence and public health relevance, as well as clinical efficacy and safety and cost considerations.

Table 2.1 Overview of the DPCOs leading up to 2002

DPCO	Framework	Number of drugs under regulation	Market coverage	Pricing mechanism	Categories and their respective markup/MAPE
DPCO 1970	Essential Commodities Act 1955	Almost **all** bulk drugs and their formulations	Indirectly, the entire market	Cost-based	
DPCO 1979	Drug Policy 1977	**347** bulk drugs and their formulations	80%	Cost-based	Cat. I 40% Cat. II 55% Cat. III 100%
DPCO 1987	Drug Policy 1986	**142** bulk drugs and their formulations	60%	Cost-based	Cat. I 75% Cat. II 100%
DPCO 1995	Drug Policy 1994	**74** bulk drugs and their formulations	~40% at the time of implementation	Cost-based	Cat. I 100%
DPCO 2004 (proposed but not implemented)	Pharmaceutical Policy 2002	**34** bulk drugs and their formulations	~20%	Cost-based	Cat. I 100%

incentivize production (Mehta 2005). Consequently, the 1970 order involved direct control on the profits of pharmaceutical firms and indirect control on the prices of 18 essential medicines and capping of the remaining medicines at their prevailing price. The product-wise margins under the 1970 DPCO were flexible, and companies had the freedom to set the prices of their products without the approval of the government as long as their overall profit margin did not exceed the stipulated norm. However, the cost-based approach to pricing had some downsides. In particular, determining actual costs as opposed to claimed costs proved to be a difficult task for the regulatory authorities. Until the establishment of the National Pharmaceutical Pricing Authority (NPPA) in 1997, there was no dedicated regulatory authority to monitor the market activity and enforce pharmaceutical price controls. The Drug Controllers at the state-level monitored the prices in addition to shouldering a range of other responsibilities. Moreover, since imported products were priced based on their landing costs, the policy made room for loopholes on imported products and indirectly encouraged the sale of relatively more expensive medicines produced in foreign countries (Malhotra 2010).

Following the 'command-and-control' policies of the 1970s, the government appointed the Hathi Committee to find ways to make India self-sufficient in producing medicines (Joseph 2015). The government asked the committee to analyze the pharmaceutical industry and make recommendations for the rapid growth of the small-scale sector, high-quality production of drugs, lowering of prices, and equitable distribution of basic medicines. The committee's final report promoted the wholesale nationalization of the pharmaceutical industry, the introduction of a list of essential medicines, the creation of a national drug administration authority, and the use of generic names for single-ingredient drugs, among others (Government of India 1975). Although the pharmaceutical industry strongly opposed a number of these recommendations, the report remained the basis for the new framework for placing drugs under price control for the next few decades (Malhotra 2010).

The 1970 Indian Patents Act enabled the domestic pharmaceutical industry to become self-sufficient (Malhotra 2010). Under the Indian Patents Act, substances used in food and pharmaceuticals could not be granted product patents but could obtain process patents for 5 years from the date of the grant of the patent (Mehta 2005). The Act played an important role in promoting the Indian pharmaceutical industry, as several domestic firms began to produce several bulk drugs and formulations at a lower cost. The government aimed to create opportunities for smaller, local firms, and to rely less on imports of medicines. The growth of the domestic industry also helped turn the country into an exporter of high-quality, affordable generic drugs over the next decades (KPMG 2006). However, despite the growth in the number of small-scale manufacturers, large pharmaceutical firms continue to sell more expensive branded versions of generic medicines. Industry leaders, characterized by their strong marketing power, often engage in promotional competition rather than price competition and nudge doctors to prescribe brand names rather than cost-effective generic medicines (Blech 2006; *Medico Friends Circle* 2006). Although the Hathi Committee recommended generic prescribing as a means to increasing availability and affordability of essential drugs, the industry remains opposed to the concept of generic prescribing and continues to fight against it even today.[2] The pharmaceutical industry was opposed to price regulation and pushed for liberalization. The 1979 DPCO incorporated some of Hathi Committee recommendations, but many were either excluded or not implemented.

The 1979 DPCO decreased the number of regulated drugs, but the mark-ups on certain drugs were lower than in the previous version of the DPCO. The 1979 order classified medicines into three categories and restricted markups at 40, 55 and 100% respectively[3] (Government of India 1979). Meanwhile, it was still mandatory for both pharmaceutical manufacturers and importers to obtain approval from the government before introducing a new formulation, dosage, or pack size. Moreover, in 1979, the prices of bulk drugs used in the production of essential medicines were also placed under price control (Government of India 1979). Anecdotal evidence shows that firms responded to the 1979 DPCO by exiting from the regulated markets, causing an 'artificial' shortage of essential medicines in the country (Bal 1986a, b, p. 1029):

[2]The idea of generic prescribing was once again recommended by the Sen Committee in 2005, but it was not implemented (Malhotra 2010).

[3]The 1979 DPCO defined markup as the sum of distribution costs, outward freight, manufacturer's margin, promotional expenses and trade commissions, calculated as a percentage value of the cost of production (Government of India 1979).

> The pharmaceutical industry reacted to the DPCO of 1979 in peculiar ways. The production of category I and II drugs started falling markedly while the production of categories III and IV drugs showed an upward rise. The production of drugs in category I dropped from 4.5 percent in 1978 to 3.6 percent in 1980 and that of drugs in category II from 16.7 percent in 1978 to 13.2 percent in 1980. However, in the case of drugs in category III the production increased from 67.1 percent in 1978 to 68.6 percent in 1980. Thus an artificial scarcity of essential drugs was being created.

The regulators in India attributed the shortage of essential medicines to inadequate incentives for pharmaceutical firms and decided to adopt a policy of steady deregulation. The government appointed the Kelkar Committee to provide further recommendations for the revision of the drug policy. In 1984, the committee established the need for liberalizing the strict profitability curbs that seemingly affected the industry's growth. The Drug Policy of 1986, entitled 'Measures for Rationalization, Quality Control and Growth of Drugs and Pharmaceuticals Industry in India,' therefore represented a clear regulatory shift away from protectionism. The revised 1987 DPCO reduced the category of drugs under price control to two and increased the margins for both. The margins or Maximum Allowed Post-manufacturing Expenses (MAPE) grew from 40 to 75% for Category I drugs and from 55 to 100% for Category II drugs (Government of India 1987).[4] More importantly, the number of price-controlled medicines dropped from 347 to 142 in 1987, as shown in Table 2.1.

In the mid-1980s, India started introducing measures towards industrial liberalization across all sectors of the economy, including the pharmaceutical industry. Liberalization continued in the 1990s, in part influenced by the international context and in part driven by industry pressures.[5] Consequently, the drug policy of 1994 and the 1995 DPCO were introduced in an era of economic liberalization, abolishment of industrial licensing, and reduction of barriers to foreign direct investment (FDI) (Government of India 2012). Despite the drop in drug prices throughout the 1970s resulting from the introduction of price control and the modified patents regime, prices started rising again when the price control regime became weaker in the mid-1980s (Rane 1996).

The 1995 DPCO classified medicines into scheduled and unscheduled categories and capped the MAPE for formulation drugs at 100% for all indigenously

[4]The term 'Maximum Allowed Post-manufacturing Expenses' (MAPE) replaced the concept of 'mark-up' in the 1987 DPCO to incorporate all costs incurred after production, as well as trade margins (Government of India 1987).

[5]The Uruguay Round of Multilateral Trade Negotiations concluded in 1994, establishing the World Trade Organization (WTO). The Organization aims to facilitate the free flow of goods and services across nations and to promote multilateral negotiations for further liberalization of trade (WTO 2017). One of the principal agreements that were signed by all members of the WTO in 1994 was the Agreement on Trade-Related Aspects of Intellectual Property Rights (TRIPS), requiring member states to provide a set of minimum standards of protection of intellectual property rights, including patent protection for pharmaceuticals (WTO 1994). Developing countries such as India that had previously abolished product patents were given several years to change their patent regime. Consequently, India became compliant with the agreement in 2005 (Malhotra 2010).

manufactured formulations of the medicines in the scheduled category (Government of India 1995). The medicines that were deemed to be not sufficiently competitive were kept under the ambit of price control. They included medicines markets with an annual turnover (sales) of Rs. 10–40 million and featuring a dominant firm accounting for over 90% of the market share or medicine markets with more than Rs. 40 million annual sales and featuring a small number of firms or firm with 10% market share for single formulators (Selvaraj 2007). As such, the number of medicines under regulation fell from 142 to 74, meaning that approximately 40% of the market was covered by the DPCO (see Table 2.1). However, the share of the pharmaceutical industry under regulation continued to decline over the years, as the number of bulk drugs and their formulations continued to grow and the pharmaceutical policy moved further towards deregulation. As a result, while 25% of the market was covered by the DPCO in 2006, only 12% was covered in 2010 (Malhotra 2010).[6] Moreover, according to civil society organizations such as LOCOST (2006), the drop in the number of price-controlled medicines in the revised DPCO resulted in the exclusion of important medicines related to anemia, diarrhea, cancer, tuberculosis, hypertension, and diabetes from the list of price-controlled medicines. Although the regulators and industry leaders argued that removing price controls would lead to lower prices through stronger competition among manufacturers, evidence showed that the prices of decontrolled medicines increased, sometimes by more than ten percent (Selvaraj 2007).

2.3 The Demand More Price Controls After 2002 Leading to the 2013 DPCO

2.3.1 2002–2003: The Bangalore High Court Ruling and the Supreme Court Order

The shift from protectionism to liberalization in the Indian pharmaceutical industry reached its high point in February 2002, when the Ministry of Chemicals and Fertilizers announced a new pharmaceutical pricing policy (see for timeline, Table 2.2). The new pricing policy aimed to open the market to foreign investment and to reduce the number of price-controlled drugs from 76 in 1995 to 38 (Mehta 2005).[7] In response, several healthcare activists argued that, over time, price controls on medicines would completely disappear if the 2002 policy is implemented (LOCOST

[6]According to Selvaraj (2007), the 2006 DPCO affected only ten percent of the drug market in 2007. According to Malhotra (2010), the 74 drugs that were on the 1995 DPCO represented less than 15% of the medicines defined as 'essential' by the new NLEM (Malhotra 2010).

[7]The number of price-controlled drugs reduced to 74 in 1997. Meanwhile, the list for the 2002 DPCO initially covered 38 drugs but was later reduced to 34 drugs.

Table 2.2 Chronology of events

Date	Event
February 2002	Government announces the draft 2002 Pharmaceutical Policy. The number of bulk drugs under price regulation are reduced from 74 (under DPCO 1995) to 34
November 2002	Civil society groups file a Public Interest Litigation against the government's policy, and the Karnataka High Court (HC) issues stay order on the policy, ultimately marking it as unconstitutional
March 2003	The government denounces the HC ruling and takes the matter to the Supreme Court of India (SC). The SC also stays the implementation of the 2002 National Pharmaceutical Policy and directs the government to bring all essential medicines under price regulation
August 2004	The Ministry of Chemicals and Fertilizers constitutes the Sandhu Committee to review the span of price control and to suggest reasonable trade margins on the sale of drugs
November 2004	The Sandhu Committee's preliminary recommendations are to lower trade margins and to implement an intensive monitoring system for all essential drugs that are not under price control. It also suggests that the span of price controls should not be increased. The committee did not reach conclusions on the issue of criteria
November 2004	The Prime Minister's Office constitutes the Sen Committee to explore options other than price control for achieving the objective of making available life-saving drugs at reasonable prices
September 2005	The final Sen Committee Report states that active government intervention is necessary for the pharmaceutical industry and recommends price cap regulation of formulations
December 2005	The government releases the draft 2006 Pharmaceutical Policy (Part A) without the section on price regulation
August 2006	The government constitutes a Joint Review Committee comprising of three government representatives and fourteen industry representatives to look into the matter of price regulation (i.e., Part B of the policy)
November 2006	The joint review committee submits its report, but the government and industry fail to reach a consensus on price regulation
November 2006	The Minister-in-charge announces a self-regulation initiative of the industry to reduce the price of 886 medicines
February 2006	The government forms the Pharma Advisory Committee with 160 members to look into the issue of pricing
January 2007	The draft Pharmaceutical Policy is referred to an Empowered Group of Ministers
August 2007	The voluntary self-regulation initiative fails. Companies are found to be overcharging on medicines
October 2011	The draft 2011 National Pharmaceutical Pricing Policy is released for public comments but receives heavy criticism from key stakeholders
September 2012	The Supreme Court gives a final opportunity to the Group of Ministers to submit their report
November 2012	The Group of Minister recommends ceiling price based regulation of formulations
December 2012	The 2012 Pharmaceutical Policy is announced by the government

2006). Moreover, they argued that the medicines under regulation were increasingly older formulations and were increasingly becoming 'irrelevant.' Alarmed by the challenges posed by fading price controls on access to medicines for poor consumers, civil society organizations such as the All India Drug Action Network (AIDAN) brought the matter to the Karnataka (Bangalore) High Court (Basak 2008).[8] Under the proposed pharmaceutical policy of 2002, the sales of medicines (that is, the moving annual turnover value) became an essential criterion for determining the ceiling price of bulk drugs. The idea was to identify markets for bulk drugs of mass consumption, which did not feature sufficient levels of competition to lower prices (Government of India 2002). Therefore, the concerns raised by citizen groups in the Public Interest Litigation (PIL) against the government's policy were that price controls were determined based on sales rather than the volume of sales, thereby putting in danger the availability and affordability of essential drugs (Mathew 2002). Moreover, according to Amit Sen Gupta, the co-convener of Jan Swasthya Abhiyan, a network of healthcare organizations, the drug pricing policy was not contingent on the country's health policy, the availability of healthcare, or the prevalence of diseases. Medicine such as quinine and primaquinine, used to battle malaria, were not under price control, while analgin (also known as Metamizole), a drug banned in many countries since the 1970s, was listed as essential (Narrain 2004).

Concerned by the rising prices of life-saving medicines, the Karnataka High Court granted a stay order for the new Pharmaceutical Policy on November 12, 2002, compelling the government to stop implementing the policy (Ray 2013).[9] By August 2002, the High Court lifted the stay order on all aspects of the policy such as those concerning pharmaceutical R&D, the changes to the regulatory infrastructure and education, except for the part concerning the pricing of drugs (Mathew 2002). After further analysis, a 2002 High Court verdict challenged the validity of the policy, terming it (Mathew 2003a): "arbitrary and unreasonable and violative of relevant provisions of Essential Commodities Act, 1955 and Article 14 and 21 of the Constitutions only to the extent of the price control mechanism adopted in the policy to determine drugs under price control." Opposing the High Court decision, the government took the case to the Supreme Court of India. On March 10, 2003, the Supreme Court reversed the Karnataka High Court's stay order on the 2002 Pharmaceutical Policy but stipulated that the Government "shall consider and formulate appropriate criteria for ensuring essential and life-saving drugs not to fall out of price control" (Nair 2006).

The Supreme Court judgment directed the Department of Chemicals and Fertilizers to revise its policy and to revise the list of drugs that were considered essential and life-saving by May 2003 (Arthapedia 2015). However, this led to some

[8]The All India Drug Action Network (AIDAN), the Medico Friends Circle (MFC), the Low Cost Standard Therapeutics (LOCOST) and the Jan Swasthya Sahyog filed the petition (Narrain 2004).

[9]'Life-saving' drugs are defined as drugs that are used in life-threatening situations or for emergency care (The Sen Committee 2005).

confusion, as the government had accepted to revise its list of essential medicines, but not the entire policy (Mathew 2003b). Nonetheless, following further Supreme Court directives, the Department of Chemicals and Fertilizers drafted a revised list of essential medicines, which included 354 essential drugs that satisfied the country's priority healthcare needs (Arthapedia 2015b; Government of India 2003). They became part of the first National List of Essential Medicines (NLEM) in 2003, overriding the previous National Essential Drugs List in 1996. The drug pricing policy remained a matter of debate among different sections of the government, which had opposing views on the scope of drug price controls. The Ministry of Health and Family Welfare and the Ministry of Chemicals and Fertilizers preferred to bring all medicines listed in the NLEM under the price control regime, while the Prime Minister's office and the Planning Commission sought alternatives to the expansion of price controls (Malhotra 2010). Over the years, various committees were therefore constituted to look into the issue of price controls and search for options other than price controls.

This episode marked the beginning of a protracted series of debates surrounding the design of price control regulation. Several stakeholders such as associations of the pharmaceutical firms lobbied for a reduction in the number of medicines under price control while the government sought to ensure the affordability of life-saving drugs. The pharmaceutical firms argued that reducing the number of drugs under price control would increase competition and therefore lower drug prices. However, a closer look at drug prices throughout the 1980s, 1990s and early 2000s showed that this was not the case (Rane 1996; Selvaraj 2007). Brand leaders were often price leaders, maintaining prices that were not affordable for poor consumers (Narrain 2004). Throughout this period of debate, the 1994 Pharmaceutical Policy remained the principal mechanism for price controls on medicines.

2.3.2 *2004–2005: Investigating Ways to Make Life-Saving Drugs Available at Reasonable Prices (the Sandhu Committee and the Pronab Sen Committee Reports)*

In the wake of the Supreme Court's March 2003 order, several committees were constituted to make recommendations for a revised pharmaceutical policy that could satisfy the expectations of the various interest groups involved in the debate surrounding price controls. The process began with the revision of the NLEM in 2003, based on the World Health Organization's Model List of Essential Medicines. The committee responsible for drafting the list used the following criteria: (i) the priority health care needs of the Indian population; (ii) the country's prevailing diseases; (iii) safety and efficacy; (iv) comparative cost-effectiveness; and (v) infrastructure for delivery (Government of India 2003). However, the pharmaceutical policy covered only a small fraction of the medicines included in the NLEM, which did not keep pace with the dynamics of public health (Malhotra 2010). Civil society organizations stressed the importance of making essential drugs available to the broader public at affordable prices. Particularly, India struggled with managing disease burdens for HIV/AIDS, diabetes, and cardiovascular problems but their medications remained outside the price control regime (LOCOST 2006).[10] The discussion on drug pricing also gained momentum following changes to the patent regime in India in 2005. India introduced product patents on the 1st of January 2005, to meet the international commitments made during the Uruguay Round of Multilateral Trade Negotiations. The prevailing patents regime established by the 1970 Patents Act had enabled India to grow as a producer of generic medicines on the strength of process patents. Beginning in 2005, India was expected to continue to benefit from the production of generics, but the freedom to reverse-engineer newer molecules was hindered (The Sen Committee Report 2005). The shift in the patent regime generated concerns of price increases and shortages of affordable drugs.

Consequently, in August 2004, the Ministry of Chemicals and Fertilizers set up a new committee under the chairmanship of G. S. Sandhu. The committee was asked to review the span of price control and to suggest reasonable trade margins on the sale of drugs, in light of the Supreme Court order and continued public debate on the issue of drug pricing. After consulting with the industry representatives, NGOs, health activists and field experts, the Sandhu Committee concluded that the current framework for price control was ineffective and endorsed a new monitoring system. The committee's interim report came out as early as November 2004 and made many recommendations, but could not make any conclusions on the issue of criteria for price controls. The findings of the report contained several observations relevant for price regulation (Mathew 2004a):

1. The NLEM 2003 was determined to be a comprehensive list of essential and life-saving drugs, which may form a basket of drugs suitable for price management (through price control and price monitoring);
2. Price control should be limited for ease of administration, improved availability and to avoid adverse effects on the growth of the pharmaceutical industry;
3. Two types of monitoring should exist (i) *intensive* monitoring for the 339 essential drugs that were in the 2003 NLEM but not under price control; and (ii) *regular* monitoring for price-controlled drugs and drugs outside the NLEM basket. A 10–15% annual price increase would apply to the drugs under price control regulation (Mathew 2004a);
4. Trade margins should be capped at 8–16% for wholesalers and retailers respectively. Meanwhile, the margins for non-scheduled drugs are restricted to 10% for

[10]LOCOST (2006) argues that many essential drugs were systematically deregulated leading up to the 2002 Pharmaceutical Policy, while many non-essential or sometimes dangerous medications remained under price control (for an overview, see Table 1, p. 135). The organization emphasizes the downfalls of using only economic criteria, such as company turnover in the 1995 DPCO, to establish what drugs should be regulated. Until 2002, economic criteria dominated essentiality of medicines, contrary to what the Kelkar Committee recommended in 1984. Therefore, the debate surrounding price control included discussions around the principles of selection for price-controlled drugs (The Sen Committee 2005).

wholesalers and 20% for retailers for branded drugs, and 15 and 35% respectively for generic drugs. The NPPA is expected to implement the rules on trade margins[11];
5. The NPPA should also interact more with State Drug Controllers, consumer organizations, NGOs and industry organizations to facilitate enforcement and compliance;
6. The government should increase public awareness about the Drug Policy and the prices fixed by the NPPA to strengthen consumer movement and keep a check on high prices;
7. Other recommendations included: negotiations at the time of launching a new patented drug, higher health insurance coverage, dedicated schemes for people below the poverty line, decreased taxes and levies on drugs in the NLEM, the use of an open-tender approach for the procurement of drugs (similar to the Rajasthan Model of Medicare Societies), compounding of offenses arising from the violation of price controls, the creation of DPCO State Cells for better enforcement and the development of a pharmaceutical price index to monitor the movement of prices.

The recommendations concerning trade margins came as a solution to the high-profit margins that existed for control-free drugs. For example, some medicines enjoyed a trade margin of 500–2000% for generic medicines (Mathew 2004b). In fact, generics were sold at almost the same price as branded drugs in India, and the huge margins were being passed on to the trade by pharmaceutical companies through high sales volumes (Francis 2005). The Minister for Chemicals and Fertilizers did not entirely agree with having different margins for branded and generics medicines since he considered that manufacturing costs should be the same. However, he supported the idea that the NPPA should play a more significant role in the price control of all drugs (Mathew 2004b). Although the proposed caps on trade margins of scheduled and non-scheduled formulations were to be implemented through the Drugs (Prices Control) Amendment Order 2004 in December 2004, the Ministry of Chemicals and Fertilizers received objections from the Prime Minister's office, the Law Ministry and from the industry and trade sectors and could not enact these changes (Mathew 2005a).[12] In the meantime, the Prime Minister's Office had initiated a different task force under the chairmanship of Pronab Sen to consider alternatives to price control (The Sen Committee 2005). Furthermore, some of the recommendations of the Sandhu Committee were ambiguous regarding their impact on the consumer. For example, the annual allowance of 10–15% price increase on these same drugs would lead to a price that would double every few years (Malhotra 2010). The NPPA's level of staffing was also a significant problem for implementing the recommended monitoring system involving

[11]Trade margins (i.e., profits) should not be confused with 'markups' or the 'MAPE,' which cover all costs incurred after production, as well as margins.

[12]The following year, trade margins of 200–300% were proposed for the retail price of generics and were found more agreeable by the industry and trade sectors (Francis 2006, 2016).

339 drugs outside the ambit of price control. Such a system would have faced significant problems with effective monitoring and with ensuring compliance.

In November 2004, the Prime Minister's office constituted the Sen Committee under the chairmanship of Pronab Sen, who was the Principal Advisor at the Planning Commission, to explore options other than price control to make life-saving drugs available at reasonable prices. The committee met with industry representatives, international agencies, health professionals, NGOs and academics and concluded in September 2005 that "the pharmaceutical industry by its very nature is non-competitive, and requires active public intervention to ensure competitive outcomes" (The Sen Committee 2005, p. 19). The final report included the following proposals (Alexander 2007; The Sen Committee 2005):

1. Price controls should only apply to formulations and not to bulk drugs or other upstream products
2. Price controls should not be based on company turnover, but on the essentiality of the drug
3. The effect of price control on the entire therapeutic class should be considered
4. Price ceilings should be implemented, and companies can place themselves anywhere below the cap—price ceilings should rise according to the Wholesale Price Index (WPI) for manufactured goods
5. A stronger central drug supervisory and regulatory system should be created—it should include the various regulatory bodies that already exist, including the NPPA, and it should support state-level regulatory bodies (the creation of DPCO state cells is also mentioned)
6. NLEM 2003 should form the basis of drugs for price control and monitoring
7. Public procurement and distribution of drugs through the public health system should mainly be for generics
8. Low-volume, high-priced drugs (e.g., for HIV/AIDS) should be exempted from excise duty, customs duty, and other levies, and this benefit should be transferred to the consumer
9. The government should improve public awareness and educate people about the scope and extent of the Drug Policy

The Sen Committee, in accordance with its mandate, recommended a switch from a cost-based pricing system to a reference pricing system (Mathew 2005b): The committee note that "no effort should be made to impose a uniform price, and only a ceiling price should be indicated" (The Sen Committee 2005, p. 4). The reference price for existing essential drugs would be the price quoted in bulk procurement by the government or other agencies and the reference price for new drugs would be the average price of the top three selling products by value in the therapeutic category. In case there are less than three brands in the respective market, the average of all existing medicines would be taken, and if no reference price were found domestically, the lowest price in the world would be established as a reference (The Sen Committee 2005). Companies could address the Price Negotiations Committee to examine the ceiling price based on superior therapeutic cost-effectiveness and all patented drugs, and their formulations would have to go through mandatory price negotiations before receiving market approval (Malhotra 2010). However, the committee noted the risk of pharmaceutical firms "circumventing price controls is extremely easy through non-standard combinations, strengths, and other such innovations. Also, there is a tendency for prescriptions to move away from controlled drugs to non-controlled drugs in the same therapeutic class. The consequence of the quality of treatment is not known, but it is almost certain that the consumers end up buying higher priced products" (The Sen Committee 2005, p. 28). Consequently, the task force recommended coverage of all formulations of the same drug under the new ceiling price regime and price monitoring of all therapeutic substitutes. It also took note of high prices of branded generics and suggested de-branding of generic drugs. Several concerns were raised by both the industry and NGOs concerning some of the recommendations put forth by the Sen Committee (Mathew 2005c). First, both sides expressed worry about the de-branding of generic drugs, feeling that brand names have a value for assuring the quality of products. They also disagreed with the committee's suggestions to define reference prices based on the institutional prices quoted by the companies in public procurement process, fearing that either quality or quantity may be compromised. Lastly, both groups agreed that there should be less or zero taxation on drugs, and the NGOs advocated for a system of trade margins based on medicines prices.

The Prime Minister's task force made some important advancements in the discussion around price controls. Although other committees were constituted throughout this period to shed light on the debate surrounding the drug policy (e.g., the National Manufacturing Competitiveness Council, the National Commission on Macroeconomics and Health, the Standing Committee on Chemicals and Fertilizers), the Sandhu and Sen Committees contributed most to the debate and consequent revisions of the pharmaceutical policy (Malhotra 2010). The proposals made by the two committees finally led to the Draft 2006 Pharmaceutical Policy and spurred discussions on ways to make the policy more impactful. The reports of the committees included some common points, namely, the need to make regulation more visible to the public, the acknowledgement of the NLEM as a comprehensive list of essential medicines that could serve as the basis for price control and monitoring, price negotiations on new patented drugs, the necessity of DPCO State Cells and the strengthening of the NPPA's role as a central drug regulatory body. Also, the Sandhu Committee attempted to bring down trade margins on all essential medicines, since consumers were burdening high margins. The Sen Committee Report highlighted the outdated nature of the cost-based system of drug price control and suggested a reference pricing system. The discussion brought by the latter also emphasized the need to regulate drugs based on essentiality and not economic criteria. Some of these recommendations, such as restrictions on trade margin restrictions, were not readily implementable due to opposition from the trade and industry lobbies. For example, the Sen Committee recommended a 50% markup to make up for the proposed trade margins and distribution costs, but industry leaders felt that without a 300–400% markup they would not be able to survive (Mathew 2005d). However, evidence shows that at that time, trade margins for wholesalers ranged from 2 to 12.4% and from 15 to 43.7% for retailers in other developed countries (Malhotra 2010). The government also considered the recommendation to strengthen the NPPA and reviewed its overall structure and working pattern and resolved to develop proper IT infrastructure that would enable the NPPA to interact with other drug regulatory authorities efficiently. The government also planned to devote more funds to the NPPA's infrastructure, increase its staff, and demand greater accountability (Mathew 2005e).

2.3.3 2006–2012: From 2006 to the 2012 National Pharmaceutical Pricing Policy

Based on the recommendations of the Sandhu and Sen Committees, the Department of Chemicals and Fertilizers published Part A of a draft of the 2006 Pharmaceutical Policy on December 28, 2005. However, the government did not release the section on price regulation, referred to as Part B. Part A of the draft served as a blueprint for future directions and included some provisions regarding drug pricing, such as mandatory price negotiations of patented drugs before granting marketing approval (Malhotra 2010). The government decided to take the full list of essential medicines included in the NLEM as the entire list of medicines for price regulation and split the 354 drugs into five categories. The rationale was to create a 'multi-dimensional' system of price regulation by following different types of pricing regulation and monitoring systems for different categories of drugs (Mathew 2005f). The government hoped that through the inclusion of all drugs under the NLEM under some form of price scrutiny, the new policy would circumvent the Supreme Court's supervision.

Under the proposed policy, only the medicines in the first category were subject to cost-based price control. These medicines were identified following the same criteria used in the National Pharmaceutical Policy of 2002 while using revised data and accounting for inflation to determine the drugs. This process resulted in about 35 medicines to be included in the first category. The policy included another 39 medicines, generally sold at low prices, in a category named 'hospital supply medicines.' This category would only be subject to price monitoring but not price control. Another category consisted of 42 medicines for life-threatening diseases like cancer and HIV/AIDS, which would be made affordable through public-private partnerships and special access arrangements. The prices of all medicines that would not be monitored, that is, the medicines that did not fall under the category or 'hospital supply,' were frozen until ceiling prices or trade margins could be calculated based on a new price control framework contained in the undisclosed Part B.

According to the Pharmaceutical Policy of 2005, the ceiling prices would be calculated based on the weighted average of the Maximum Retail Price (MRP) of the top three producers of the drug by value and volume (Mathew 2005f). As we will discuss in greater detail subsequently throughout the book, the price to the retailer (PTR) rather than MRP became the basis for determining the ceiling price eventually. However, experts warned that if the government wanted to satisfy both the Supreme Court and the industry, it would have to restrict the application of the new policy only to the specific strengths of the drugs mentioned in the NLEM and not to all formulations of the same drugs (Mathew 2006). That meant that industry and trade representatives wanted the essential drugs list to be scrutinized on purely NLEM terms, that is, regulate the strengths mentioned in the NLEM, but leave all other strengths and formulations unregulated.

In August 2006, the government formed the Joint Review Committee composed of three government representatives and fourteen industry representatives to formulate Part B of the Pharmaceutical Policy. The review committee report states, “Industry feels that all 354 drugs and their formulations under NLEM 2003 need not be subjected to price control. There are several categories of these drugs whose prices are reasonable, or these may not directly affect the consumer, or the drugs are critical but the number of manufacturers is too few, or the drugs are subsidized through public health programmes. These can be excluded from price control and placed under the prevailing price monitoring system, i.e., no increase beyond 20% per annum” (PharmaBiz 2006b). On the other hand, members of the government desired to keep open the possibility of cost-based pricing. Following the deliberations of the Joint Review Committee, the Pharma Advisory Forum comprised of 160 members was created. The forum included stakeholders such as chemist associations, consumer representatives, state drug controllers, the Drugs Controller General of India, the NPPA, pharmaceutical associations, central and state health ministry officials and representatives from the Ministry of Chemicals and Fertilizers. Industry associations protested that the forum leaned too much in favor of the regulator and the ministry.

Following the formation of the Advisory Forum, industry associations proposed voluntary self-regulation. In line with this initiative, 11 pharmaceutical companies agreed to reduce the price of 886 medicines by October 1st, 2006 (Malhotra 2010). According to the Ministry of Chemicals and Fertilizers, the list of medicines included a wide range of therapeutic categories and several commonly used medicines like analgesics, cough syrups, tonics and drugs meant to treat infectious diseases, bronchial disorders and antibiotics, as well as antihypertensives, dermatological medicines, eye drops, disinfectants, gastrointestinal medicines and anti-diabetic medicines (PharmaBiz 2006a). Self-regulation by industry can, under certain conditions, result in increased social welfare (Maxwell et al. 2000; Toffel and Short 2011). However, a closer study by Malhotra (2010, p. 121) highlighted the following: "The 886 items included a pregnancy test card, 7 Ayurvedic medicines, at least 31 forms of iron, vitamins, or other nutritional supplements. Notwithstanding the positive role the preceding items play in healthcare, it is argued that these items could not be viewed as (allopathic) formulations. It was found that from the 886 items, only 134 or 15.1% were listed in CIMS9 (July–October 2007), Drug Today (October–December 2007), or IDR (November 2007–January 2008)." Naturally, the 752 drugs not listed on the three reference books were likely to have insignificant sales since doctors did not usually prescribe items that were excluded from these reference books. Moreover, out of the 134 drugs that were listed, 103 items had a price higher than the agreed price, 16 had a lower price, nine had a price lower than or equal to the agreed price in at least one out of the three reference books, and only six had a reduced price in all three reference books (Malhotra 2010). Further investigation illustrated that out of the 134 drugs; an important proportion was not widely available in all states. Therefore, despite widely publicized price reductions, many of the 886 formulations were either not accessible or sold at higher prices.

After further revisions, the Group of Ministers began deliberating on the draft Pharmaceutical Policy 2006 in January 2007. The draft policy remained with the group for several years until 2011 when the National Pharmaceutical Pricing Policy 2011 (NPPP 2011) became available for public comments in October 2011 (Joseph 2015). News reports indicated that heightened lobbying efforts by the industry delayed the deliberations, creating differences of opinion among the ministries (PharmaQuest 2009). The 2011 NLEM and the recommendations of the Sen Committee 2005 became the basis for NPPP 2011 (Government of India 2011a, b). The Group of Ministers recommended a market-based approach to drug pricing, as was advocated by the Sen Committee in 2005. It also overruled the Health Ministry's proposal to set the ceiling price as the average of the three lowest priced medicines and suggested to fix the ceiling price according to the average price of the top three selling brands (of single-ingredient formulations) by value (Joseph 2015). Additionally, the draft policy excluded essential medicines with price less than Rs. 3 per tablet from price regulation.

Several stakeholders criticized the government's new draft pharmaceutical policy. The draft, described as a 'flawed' document, was once again taken to the Supreme Court by the All India Drug Action Network (AIDAN), an independent network of NGOs (Ray 2012a). AIDAN argued against the market-based pricing methodology calculated as the weighted average price of the top three brands and appealed for the cost-based pricing approach as a way to contain high prices. Furthermore, AIDAN criticized the lack of control mechanisms to prevent manufacturers from avoiding price control by modifying their formulations. Global policy actors such as the WHO also disagreed with the proposed mechanism to fix the ceiling price based on the top three selling brands, stating that the policy was "virtually topping off the price of top brands" (Economic Times 2011). Other experts condemned the exclusion of certain medicines and the formulation-level control (Selvaraj et al. 2012; Selvaraj and Farooqui 2012). The pharmaceutical industry was in favor of a market-based method for price regulation but advocated against increasing the span of regulation. Moreover, industry associations refused to accept the possible mitigation of the adverse impact of price control caused by the partial regulation of formulations. The Indian Pharmaceutical Alliance maintained that partial regulation would not necessarily benefit pharmaceutical firms, as "price control of specified strength will affect all strengths of the drug. You can't price a 10 mg drug disproportionately to a 5 mg strength under price control" (The Hindu Business Line 2007). The industry associations also expressed their disappointment with the proposed method: "the decision to reach retail prices based on a simple average is very damaging to the industry, and our profit margins will erode considerably" (The Hindu Business Line 2007).

In September 2012, the Supreme Court gave a final opportunity to the Group of Ministers to communicate its decision (Rajagopal 2012). It was clear that the Group of Ministers had the difficult task of putting in place a robust pharmaceutical pricing policy that could satisfy both the consumers and the industry, as well as reconciling short-term interests with long-term goals and concerns (Arthapedia 2015; Ray 2012b). The government revised the draft policy, following the criticisms from several key stakeholders. The final version of the policy document was notified in December 2012 and formed the blueprint for the 2013 DPCO. The mechanism for fixing the ceiling price was modified to incorporate the mean price of all brands with more than one percent market share. It also withdrew the proposed exclusion of medicines based on medicine prices. The NPPP regulated formulations only, based on essentiality criteria as specified under the 2011 NLEM (Government of India 2012). Although the NLEM contains 348 drugs with various dosages and strengths, formulations based on a combination of these drugs can potentially be subject to price regulation. The government also decided to use the market-based pricing approach to fixing ceiling prices.

2.3.4 Amendments After the Implementation of the 2013 DPCO Regulation

The Department of Pharmaceuticals notified the government's decision to implement the price control regulation in December 2012 and published the revised DPCO on May 15th, 2013, authorizing the NPPA to regulate the prices of all 348 medicines on the NLEM corresponding to 652 formulations under 27 therapeutic categories. The DPCO received little support from stakeholders, regardless of their views on price regulation. Multinational firms were worried that price controls would diminish their margins to the degree that would not permit them to launch new medicines and to maintain their sales in existing markets. The domestic pharmaceutical industry and the retail trade associations portrayed the DPCO as unnecessary and argued that the industry did not need regulation, as it remained competitive (Nautiyal 2013). Moreover, both the activist judiciary that called for legislative action and the NGOs that lobbied for price regulation described the new DPCO as inadequate and ineffective (Times of India 2015). The order, therefore, prompted a patchwork of amendments.

In May 2014, the NPPA notified new guidelines, highlighting that certain legislative clauses gave it wider powers to control drug prices (Kamath 2014). Under paragraph 19 of the 2013 DPCO, the NPPA could monitor and, if necessary, regulate prices of drugs currently not under price control regulation, but considered essential. Soon afterward, in July 2014, the NPPA announced that 108 new anti-diabetic and cardiovascular drugs would be added to the list of controlled formulations, in addition to the 348 existing ones (NPPA 2014). The NPPA felt that although these medicines differed from similar price-controlled medicines regarding binders, fillers, dyes, preservatives, coating agents and dissolution agents, they did not differ in their therapeutic value. However, the order was revoked by September 2014 due to non-compliance and discontent from pharmaceutical firms and directives from the government. Although the order was revoked, the potential for expanded price control pushed the pharmaceutical industry to file lawsuits (Kamath 2014).

The 2013 DPCO, in theory, has several advantages over the 1995 DPCO. The 1995 DPCO used a cost-based method of controlling medicine prices but collecting cost information proved to be difficult for regulators. By contrast, the market-based approach adopted in the 2013 DPCO allows for determining the ceiling price based on the prevailing prices in the market. The price ceiling regulation is also considered better than cost-based regulation as price ceilings preserve the incentives for completion on prices. The 2013 DPCO also allows for a continuous revision of the price cap, which again preserves the incentive to improve production efficiency (Cowan 2002). Also, the 2013 DPCO contained support for research and development (R&D) by exempting new drugs from price control for five years (Kumar et al. 2014), a step necessitated by India's implementation India's introduction of pharmaceutical product patents in 2005. The patent regime in 2013 was different from the one in 1995 when only process patents were allowed. This shift gave more strength to MNCs, which had been discouraged by India's previous protectionist policies (KPMG 2006). However, this also resulted in a different kind of lobbying power. Although Kumar et al. (2014) state that the 1995 DPCO was a 'win-win' situation for manufacturers, since the government could not fix prices, and that the 2013 DPCO addressed this problem in favor of the consumer, the analysis that is presented in the following chapters shows that pharmaceutical firms found ways to avoid regulation or mitigate its impact.

References

Alexander, J. (2007, September 25). Chemicals ministry to set up price monitoring cells in all states under new policy. PharmaBiz.com

Arthapedia. (2015a). *Drug Price Control Orders (DPCO)* [online]. Available from http://www.arthapedia.in/index.php?title=Drug_Price_Control_Orders_(DPCO)

Arthapedia. (2015b). *National list of essential medicines of India 2011* [online]. Available from: http://www.arthapedia.in/index.php?title=National_List_of_Essential_Medicines_of_India_2011

Bal, A. (1986a). Distortions in drug policy: Who is to be blamed? *Economic and Political Weekly, 21*(23), 1029–1032.

Bal, A. (1986b). Drug policy. *Economic and Political Weekly, 21*, 2009–2014.

Basak, S. C. (2008). The genesis of drug price control. *PharmaBiz* [online]. Available from http://pharmabiz.com/ArticleDetails.aspx?aid=42905&sid=9

Blech, J. (2006). *Inventing disease and pushing pills: Pharmaceutical companies and the medicalisation of normal life*. London: Routledge.

Cowan, S. (2002). Price-cap regulation. *Swedish Economic Policy Review, 9*, 167–188.

De, R. (2014). 'Commodities must be controlled': Economic crimes and market discipline in India (1939–1955). *International Journal of Law in Context, 10*(3), 277–294.

Economic Times. (2011). New drug policy draft faces public heat. *Economic Times* [online]. Available from http://articles.economictimes.indiatimes.com/2011-12-19/news/30534341_1_price-control-pricing-policy-pricing-formula

Francis, P. A. (2005). Margin control on generics. *PharmaBiz* [online]. Available from http://www.pharmabiz.com/ArticleDetails.aspx?aid=25563&sid=3

Francis, P. A. (2006). Fixing generics margin. *PharmaBiz* [online] Available from http://www.pharmabiz.com/ArticleDetails.aspx?aid=32909&sid=3

Francis, P. A. (2016). Capping margins on medicines. *PharmaBiz* [online] Available from http://www.pharmabiz.com/NewsDetails.aspx?aid=92965&sid=3

Government of India. (1955). *Essential Commodities Act, 1955.*

Government of India. (1975). *Report of the committee on drugs and pharmaceutical industry (Hathi Committee Report) 1975*. New Delhi: Ministry of Petroleum & Chemicals.

Government of India. (1979). *The drugs (prices control) order 1979.*

Government of India. (1987). *The drugs (prices control) order 1987.*

Government of India. (1995). *The drugs (prices control) order*. New Delhi: Ministry of Chemicals and Fertilizers.

Government of India. (2002). *Pharmaceutical policy of India*. New Delhi: Ministry of Chemicals and Fertilizers.

Government of India. (2003). *National list of essential medicines 2003*. New Delhi: Ministry of Chemicals and Fertilizers.

Government of India. (2011a). *National list of essential medicines, 2011*. New Delhi: Ministry of Chemicals and Fertilizers.

Government of India. (2011b). *National pharmaceutical pricing policy, 2011 (NPPP-2011)*. New Delhi: Ministry of Chemicals and Fertilizers.

Government of India. (2012). *National pharmaceutical pricing policy, 2012*. New Delhi: Ministry of Chemicals and Fertilizers.

Joseph, R. K. (2015). *Pharmaceutical industry and public policy in post-reform India*. Abingdon: Routledge.

Kamath, G. (2014). India's drug price control regime just pulled off a logic defying move. *Quartz India* [online]. Available from https://qz.com/270321/indias-drug-price-control-regime-just-pulled-off-a-logic-defying-move/

KPMG. (2006). *The Indian pharmaceutical industry: Collaboration for growth*. Available from https://www.kpmg.de/media/20060501_The_Indian_pharmaceutical__industry.pdf

Kumar, V., Gupta, N. V., & Kumar, K. A. (2014). A comparison between old and latest systems in DPCO. *International Journal of Pharmacy and Pharmaceutical Sciences, 6*(2), 19–20.

LOCOST. (2006). *A lay person's guide to medicines: What is in them and what is behind them* (Revised ed.). Baroda: LOCOST.

Malhotra, P. (2010). *The impact of TRIPS on India: An access to medicines perspective*. Basingstoke: Palgrave Macmillan.

Mathew, J. C. (2002). Bangalore HC partially vacates stay on Pharma Policy 2002, next hearing on Sept 23. *PharmaBiz* [online]. Available from http://www.pharmabiz.com/NewsDetails.aspx?aid=9500&sid=2

Mathew, J. C. (2003a). SC admits govt appeal against HC ruling on Pharma Policy, hearing to begin by month end. *PharmaBiz* [online]. Available from http://pharmabiz.com/NewsDetails.aspx?aid=14547&sid=2

Mathew, J. C. (2003b). SC directive to redraft Pharma Policy, 2002 baffles the Dept of Chemicals. *PharmaBiz* [online]. Available from http://pharmabiz.com/NewsDetails.aspx?aid=15810&sid=2

Mathew, J. C. (2004a). Sandhu Committee recommends "Price management" of drugs. *PharmaBiz* [online]. Available from http://www.pharmabiz.com/NewsDetails.aspx?aid=24864&sid=2

Mathew, J. C. (2004b). Paswan in favor of same profit margins for branded & generic drugs. *PharmaBiz* [online]. Available from http://www.pharmabiz.com/NewsDetails.aspx?aid=24757&sid=2

Mathew, J. C. (2005a). Centre puts off plan for fixing trade margins for generic drugs by amending DPCO. *PharmaBiz* [online] Available from http://www.pharmabiz.com/NewsDetails.aspx?aid=25609&sid=2

Mathew, J. C. (2005b). Industry unhappy over reference price plans. *PharmaBiz* [online]. Available from http://pharmabiz.com/NewsDetails.aspx?aid=28314&sid=2

Mathew, J. C. (2005c). NGOs disagree with task force plans for de-branding, reference price. *PharmaBiz* [online]. Available from http://pharmabiz.com/NewsDetails.aspx?aid=28406&sid=2

Mathew, J. C. (2005e). Major revamp of NPPA on anvil to make it effective in controlling drug prices. *PharmaBiz* [online]. Available from http://www.pharmabiz.com/NewsDetails.aspx?aid=30519&sid=2

Mathew, J. C. (2005f). Price control to be brought down to 35 drugs in Pharma Policy 2005, monitoring on 319 others. *PharmaBiz* [online]. Available from http://www.pharmabiz.com/NewsDetails.aspx?aid=30592&sid=2

Mathew, J. C. (2006). Technical approach to NLEM in new Pharma policy may benefit drug industry. *PharmaBiz* [online]. Available from http://www.pharmabiz.com/NewsDetails.aspx?aid=33202&sid=2

Maxwell, J. W., Lyon, T. P., & Hackett, S. C. (2000). Self-regulation and social welfare: The political economy of corporate environmentalism. *Journal of Law and Economics, 43*, 583–617.

Medico Friends Circle (2006). Submission to the Government of India: A balanced pharmaceutical policy. Available from http://www.mfcindia.org/PMdrugpricing.html

Mehta, P. S. (2005). *Towards a functional competition policy for India*. New Delhi: Academic Foundation.

Nair, M. D. (2006). National pharmaceutical policy 2006. *PharmaBiz* [online]. Available from http://saffron.pharmabiz.com/article/detnews.asp?articleid=35455&sectionid=46

Narrain, S. (2004). A life-saving order. *Frontline, 21*(15). Available from http://www.frontline.in/static/html/fl2115/stories/20040730004110300.htm.

Nautiyal, S. (2013, July 4). AIOCD to move SC against DPCO 2013 to contest margin cut for retailers, wholesalers. PharmaBiz.com

NPPA. (2014). Price notification on the 10th of July 2014. Available from http://www.nppaindia.nic.in/paragraph19/press10july14/so1734e-10-7-14.html

PharmaBiz. (2006a). Paswan releases list of 886 drugs with reduced MRP provided by IPA & 2 cos. *PharmaBiz* [online]. Available from http://www.pharmabiz.com/PrintArticle.aspx?aid=36096&sid=2

PharmaBiz. (2006b). Report of the Joint Committee on Draft National Pharmaceutical Policy Submitted on Nov 30, 2006. *PharmaBiz* [online]. Available from http://saffron.pharmabiz.com/red.asp?fn=/services/docs/IDMA07.asp

PharmaQuest. (2009). Paswan blames powerful industry lobby for thwarting national pharma policy. February 9, 2009. *PharmaQuest* [online]. Available from http://www.pharmaquest.biz/paswan-blames-powerful-industry-lobby-for-thwarting-national-pharma-policy/

Rajagopal, D. (2012). Supreme Court order on drug price control upsets calculations of pharma firms. *The Economic Times* [online]. Available from http://economictimes.indiatimes.com/industry/healthcare/biotech/pharmaceuticals/supreme-court-order-on-drug-price-control-upsets-calculations-of-pharma-firms/articleshow/16676399.cms?intenttarget=no

Rane, W. (1996). Analysis of drug prices, 1980–1995. *Economic and Political Weekly, 31*, 2331–2340.

Ray, T. J. (2012a). *The new drug policy of India enters into the final lap of a Marathon Run* [online]. Available from http://www.tapanray.in/the-new-drug-policy-of-india-enters-into-the-final-lap-of-a-marathon-run/

Ray, T. J. (2012b). *The new drug policy is languishing in a labyrinth* [online]. Available from http://www.tapanray.in/the-new-drug-policy-is-languishing-in-a-labyrinth/

Ray, T. J. (2013). *New drug price control order of India: Is it directionally right improving access to medicines?* [online]. Available from http://www.tapanray.in/new-drug-price-control-order-of-india-is-it-directionally-right-improving-access-to-medicines/

Selvaraj, S. (2007). *How effective is India's drug price control regime.* Boston: Harvard School of Public Health.

Selvaraj, S., Hasan, H., Chokshi, M., Sengupta, A., Guha, A., Shiva, M., Srinivasan, S., Phadke, A., Gopakumar, K. M., Santhosh, M. R., Menghaney, L., & Bhardwaj, K. (2012). Pharmaceutical pricing policy: A critique. *Economical and Political Weekly, 47*(4), 20–23.

Selvaraj, S., & Farooqui, H. H. (2012). Draft drug price policy 2011: Legitimising unaffordable medicine prices? *Economic and Political Weekly, 47*(46), 13–17.

The Hindu Business Line. (2007). Pharma industry opposes price control mechanism. *The Hindu Business Line* [online]. Available from http://www.thehindubusinessline.com/todays-paper/pharma-industry-opposes-price-control-mechanism/article1646222.ece

The Sen Committee. (2005). *Report: Task force to explore options other than price control for achieving the objective of making available life-saving drugs at reasonable prices.* New Delhi: Department of Chemicals and Petrochemicals, Government of India.

Times of India. (2015). Drug pricing policy irrational, re-examine it, Supreme Court tells Centre. *The Times of India* [online]. Available from http://timesofindia.indiatimes.com/india/Drug-pricing-policy-irrational-re-examine-it-Supreme-Court-tells-Centre/articleshow/48092107.cms

Toffel, M., & Short, J. (2011). Coming clean and cleaning up: Does voluntary self-reporting indicate effective self-policing? *Journal of Law and Economics, 54*(3), 609–649.

WHO. (2017). Model list. *The World Health Organization* [online]. Geneva. Available from http://www.who.int/medicines/publications/essentialmedicines/20th_EML2017.pdf?ua=1

WTO. (1994). Agreement on trade-related aspects of intellectual property rights (TRIPS). *The World Trade Organization* [online]. Geneva. Available from http://www.wto.org/english/docs_e/legal_e/27-trips_01_e.htm

WTO. (2017). Overview: A navigational guide. *The World Trade Organization* [online]. Geneva. Available from https://www.wto.org/english/thewto_e/whatis_e/tif_e/agrm1_e.htm

Chapter 3
Is the 2013 Price Control Regulation Necessary?

3.1 Introduction

In this chapter, we address whether pharmaceutical price control regulations, introduced in India in the 1970s when the domestic pharmaceutical industry was still in its infancy, are relevant today. India is currently among the largest exporters of generic, low-cost pharmaceuticals to countries around the world. Also, other countries such as China have removed price caps regulations on low-cost medicines due to rising concerns about the declining quality and shortages of regulated medicines (Burkitt 2014). We complement the historical account of the policy process detailed in the previous chapter resulting in the 2013 DPCO regulation with a quantitative approach in this chapter. In particular, we use Pharmatrac data to examining whether pharmaceutical markets in India are competitive and whether greater competition is sufficient to ensure lower prices in these markets. Our goal here is neither to advocate a greater role for market forces nor call for government intervention in general, and we refer the readers to other studies for such discussions (e.g., Datta-Chaudhuri 2000). We envisage a limited role for reasonable regulations in the Indian pharmaceutical industry, given its unique characteristics.

3.2 Pharmaceuticals Are Credence Goods with High Search Costs

We begin by describing the idiosyncratic features of the pharmaceutical industry that affect the intensity of competition and prices in medicine markets. First, medicines are different from other goods we purchase. In many industries, the products can be characterized as search goods, as their utility and quality can be assessed before purchase. For example, automobiles, houses, clothing, and groceries are some examples of search goods. By contrast, the pharmaceutical industry is an excellent

A. Bhaskarabhatla, *Regulating Pharmaceutical Prices in India*, India Studies in Business and Economics, https://doi.org/10.1007/978-3-319-93393-1_3

example of a market for experience and credence goods. Unlike search goods, the consumers of credence and experience goods find it difficult to assess beforehand, and sometimes even after the purchase, the quality and utility of the products. The customers in pharmaceutical markets cannot judge the quality or utility of medicines and rely on the medical advice of their physician (Zeithaml 1981). Further complicating the nature of transactions in pharmaceutical markets is how the demand for these goods is generated and what role physicians and pharmacists play in completing these transactions. While the doctor chooses the drug and writes a prescription, the customer pays for it, typically out of pocket in India, which causes the demand for pharmaceuticals to be driven by prescriptions of doctors rather than well-informed decisions made by the final consumers. If the doctor acts as a perfect agent of the patient by making choices that the patient would have made in the absence of any information asymmetry, then there is little cause for concern. However, when the interests of physicians and pharmacists differ from those of the patients, then competition alone cannot guarantee lower prices. Such situations can lead to supplier-induced demand, a phenomenon by which the customer buys more of a good at a higher price than she would if she were fully informed. As a result, customers may end up buying more expensive substitutes and bundles of medicines, which leads to a loss of social welfare (Evans 1974).

In many countries, the presence of large institutional buyers such as health insurance companies and expert intermediaries such as public health agencies safeguards the interests of the patient. However, in a country such as India where the insurance coverage is negligible, and patients pay out of pocket for purchasing medicines, pharmaceuticals become more of a credence good than in other countries. If the physicians and pharmacists receive a percentage of the profits from the sale of medicines, then they have an incentive to promote the demand for higher-priced medicines, which yield higher profits in absolute terms, at the expense of lower-priced substitutes. As we will argue later, the cartelization of pharmacies in India, and the nexus between the physicians' clinics and pharmacies that adjoin them, the aggressive promotional practices of the pharmaceutical firms, and the unethical division of profits along the pharmaceutical distribution value chain suggest that the presence of a large number of brands of a medicine at the country-level does not necessarily translate to lower prices at the neighborhood pharmacy.

Second, the consumption of goods in general and medicines, in particular, involves switching costs. Switching costs pose an added challenge to the customers in pharmaceutical markets, and can potentially undermine the competitiveness of an industry. Switching costs are the costs incurred by the consumer as a result of switching brands, suppliers, or products (Porter 1980). Burnham et al. (2003) developed a typology of switching costs that identifies three types. First, procedural switching costs include all costs related to potential economic risk, evaluation and learning time and setup costs. Second, financial switching costs involve all costs that can be expressed in monetary value, including potential benefits and losses. Third, relational switching costs include all costs related to psychological or emotional discomfort due to the loss of identity and the ending of relationships. Burnham et al. (2003) suggest that all forms of switching costs significantly influence customer loyalty. Switching costs are associated with higher profits for incumbents (Beggs and Klemperer 1992), less elastic or inelastic demand (Farrell and Shapiro 1988), and increased barriers to entry for a supplier and higher strategic advantages for incumbents (Karakaya 1989). Switching costs are not necessarily financial but include "search costs, transaction costs, learning costs, loyal customer discounts, customer habit, emotional cost and cognitive effort, coupled with financial, social, and psychological risk on the part of the buyer" (Fornell 1992: 10).

Since the purchase of medicines involves the patient, the physician, and the pharmacist, there are switching costs for all three parties. Prior research has explored the extent to which intra-molecular, and inter-molecular substitution takes place in the pharmaceutical industry.[1] Ellison et al. (1997) find that demand for both intra- and intermolecular substitutes is price elastic. However, inter-molecular substitutes are more price elastic compared to intra-molecular substitutes. This means that doctors are more likely to prescribe a different brand of the same molecule than a completely different molecule when they prescribe a new medicine to a patient. The fact that there is some price elasticity in demand for medication leaves some space for competitive forces on the demand side to incentivize producers to become more productive and to lower their prices. However, these competitive forces are hindered when physicians allocate little effort in gathering information about brands of medicines. Since the physician is the only one judging the information on all available drugs and their relative prices, she should invest in getting to know all options available (e.g., Steele 1962; Walker 1971; Temin 1980; Ellison et al. 1997). The drug prescription decision is formed by learning effects of patients and the doctor that prescribes it (Ellison et al. 1997). This shows that information is not a universal good in the pharmaceutical industry and that demand is shaped by personal experiences of both the patient and the doctor.

Physician brand loyalty plays a key role when it comes to switching costs in the pharmaceutical industry. Pharmaceutical firms try to generate physician loyalty to maintain their market share. Waheed et al. (2011) found that the donation of tangible rewards from pharmaceuticals to physicians leads to higher prescription loyalty. Also, professional values of pharmaceutical sales representatives promote prescription loyalty; that is, recommendations of the drug by major doctors at seminars are strongly related to the high prescription loyalty of attending physicians. The brand value appears not to be related to prescription loyalty. These findings point to the prevalence of switching costs in the pharmaceutical industry. In a country such as India, where generic medicines are sold under different brand names, and pure generics account for a small fraction of the overall sales, physician brand loyalty is stronger than in other countries, leading to higher switching costs. Overall, the presence of switching costs can severely hinder the competitive functioning of markets.

[1]Intra-molecule research focuses on substitutability of different molecules for the same therapeutic therapy, inter-molecule research focuses on substitutability amongst drugs that contain the same molecule, but differ in brand, strength, pack size and price

To deepen the discussion on the competitiveness of the Indian pharmaceutical markets, we elaborate on how the pharmaceutical distribution is organized and governed. Laws regulating pharmacies in India are derived from the Drugs and Cosmetics Act (1940) and the Drugs and Cosmetics Rules (1945). The former regulates the import, manufacturing and distribution process of drugs in India, and the latter contains provisions for classifications of drugs and guidelines for the storage, sales, and prescriptions. These laws are implemented under the supervision of the Central Drug Standard Control Organization (CDSCO). However, this organization is understaffed, and it has been severely criticized for approving unsafe bundles or cocktails of medicines, which serve as expensive substitutes (Evans and Pollock 2015). The Indian government has pushed the pharmaceutical sector to de-brand generic medicines, which can intensify price competitive (PharmaBiz.com 2017). Recall that the Hathi committee's final report recommended the use of generic names for single-ingredient drugs, among others (Government of India 1975). However, pharmaceutical firms with a high brand value benefit from the increased switching costs due to brand loyalty and are therefore have strongly opposed such moves over the last four decades. Also, while the government has encouraged pharmacies to stock more generics, pharmacies have an interest in pushing the branded drugs, which yield higher trade margins. The government has also encouraged the physicians to be aware of the available generic options. However, physicians remain brand-loyal and rarely write prescriptions containing generic medicines names. Substitutability of branded drugs and generics becomes lower when doctors are unaware of the chemical compositions of drugs they prescribe, leading to higher switching costs among brands and medicines. Another problem is that the poor quality of prescriptions written by hand by many physicians, which are difficult to read. Since the patient is unaware of his prescription, he ends up buying expensive branded drugs that are given to him by the pharmacists. The Indian government as well as the Medical Council of India (MCI) have discussed guidelines ranging from the quality of prescriptions to the issue of debranding and stimulating the supply of generics. The government has also introduced a program called Jan Aushadi under which entrepreneurs can setup medicine shops exclusively for the sale of generic medicines. However, overall there has been little change in the functioning of the pharmaceutical markets in India since the formation of the union of retailers, the All India Organization of Chemists and Druggists (AIOCD), in 1975, which operates as a cartel. With branded drugs dominating the Indian industry, firms can still differentiate their otherwise homogeneous product from competitors. As a result, prices become more dispersed, varying with the familiarity of brands, and become more expensive for patients.

In summary, the idiosyncratic features of the pharmaceutical industry in general and in India, in particular, hinder competitive forces for three reasons. First, chemically identical substitutes might not be regarded as substitutes by physicians. Second, the production and prescription of generic medicines lag behind the sale of branded medicines, which severely hinders price competition. Third, physician brand loyalty increases switching costs, especially when pharmaceutical firms offer tangible rewards to the physician and the pharmacist.

3.3 Choice and Competition Are Limited in Local Pharmaceutical Markets in India

So far, we argued, largely based on the theory of credence goods and search costs, that pharmaceutical markets in India are not necessarily competitive. While, in theory, it is a possibility, it may not necessarily be the reality of the Indian medicine markets. In fact, the general impression among many is that the Indian pharmaceutical industry, featuring a large number of firms in any given medicine market, is highly competitive and the prices of medicines in India are among the lowest in the world. If it is true, then there is no necessity for imposing price ceilings on essential medicines in India. Before we examine the design, implementation, and impact of the 2013 DPCO legislation, we address questions about the necessity of 2013 regulation briefly. Our purpose here is not to argue that price controls are *per se* good or bad. Instead, we want to highlight some of the reasons advanced by various patient interest groups before the Supreme Court of India and various committees appointed by the government to convince them that price regulation is still necessary. We do so by reviewing the recent literature on the pricing and availability of medicines in India as well as on pharmaceutical marketing and prescription practices. We will complement the review of the literature in this section with a more quantitative approach in the next section.

We document several reasons for regulating the prices of essential medicines in India. First, in many medicine markets, greater choice and perceived competition at the national level does not necessarily lead to greater choice, lower prices, or greater availability in a local market. Sharma and Kaplan (2016) study the pricing and availability of insulin in the state of Delhi, which is also the capital city of India and is noted for its relatively efficient public-sector procurement system for medicines. Although 16 domestic brands and 87 foreign brands manufacture human insulin in India, in a survey of 40 pharmacy outlets in Delhi, the 40 IU/ml human insulin, considered essential under the 2013 DPCO, is available in its soluble version in only 47.5% of the outlets, in the isophane version in only 25%, and in the biphasic isophane version in 67.5%. The availability of analog insulin versions is lower in the range of 2.5–25%. The availability of 100 IU/ml human insulin, not considered essential and hence not regulated, is even lower in the range of 5–12.5%. Sharma and Kaplan (2016) find that the median consumer price of 40 IU/ml human insulin per 10 ml is 2.39 times and that of 100 IU/ml strength is 2.62 times compared to the public-sector procurement price in Delhi. In other words, the presence of more than 100 brands of insulin, a medicine on which a large number of chronically ill diabetes patients rely for daily usage, is often unavailable and competition at the local level is severely limited.

Second, in India, out-of-patent medicines are sold under brand names. Also, the prices of such "branded" generic medicines are several times higher than their cost of production. Srinivasan (1999) compares the market price of 61 medicines obtained from the October 1998 issue of the Monthly Index of Medical Specialties (MIMS, India) with the lowest prices quoted in the public-sector procurement process in the

Indian state of Tamilnadu in August 1998 for equivalent formulations and packaging. In all but one case, the public-sector procurement price, used as a proxy for the marginal cost of production, is several times higher than the market price of substitute brands. In 15 cases, the market price of a competing brand is more than ten times the public-sector procurement price. In particular, Torrent set a market price of 1190, more than 52 times the public-sector procurement price of 22.60, for 100 tablets of Albendazole 400 mg. German Remedies set a market price 43 times the procurement price for Bisacodyl 5 mg and Sun Pharma charged 40 times the procurement price for Alprazolam 0.5 mg tablets. Phadke and Srinivasan (2013) repeat the analysis for nine medicines and find that the market leader's price in each case is more than ten times the public-sector procurement price in Tamilnadu. For example, the market leader's price for Atorvastatin 10 mg is 50 times Domperidone 10 mg is 40 times the public procurement price.

Third, compounding the problem of high prices of branded medicines is the role of pharmaceutical marketing, pharmacists, and doctors. In India, physicians prescribe certain brands rather than their underlying formulation (Nalinakanthi 2014). Miller and Catherine (2016) conduct a systematic review of the literature and find that pharmacists in many low- and middle-income Asian countries employ profit-maximizing strategies that are linked to poor dispensing practices. Kamat and Nichter (1998) study the role played by pharmacists in Mumbai, the financial capital of India. They interview 75 pharmacy owners and managers, 35 medical representatives who market medicines to pharmacists and doctors, and 150 randomly-selected customers. Their analysis indicates that medicine wholesalers and medical representatives incentivize pharmacists to substitute brands prescribed by the doctor for other brands with higher margins. In their sample, 72% of the pharmacists recommend substitutes when a prescribed brand is not available, and 34% of the customers accept their recommendations. Gillian and Grills (2016) conduct a systematic review of the literature on the role of doctors and pharmacists in the misuse of medications. In their analysis of 115 articles, they find that in some cases doctors pursue profit motive and prescribe higher cost medication while pharmacists follow the doctors' lead (see, also, Kotwani et al. 2010; Kotwani et al. 2012). Analysis of prescriptions written by doctors in India reveals that in more than 96% of the cases, doctors prescribe brand names instead of the generic ingredient names, limiting the choice to the consumer (Patel et al. 2005). Seeberg (2012) studies pharmacies in a relatively underdeveloped state of India, Odisha, and finds similar conclusions. Since pharmacists receive a proportion of the price of medicine as revenue, they are incentivized to sell more expensive substitutes when low-priced alternatives exist, limiting competition in pharmaceutical markets in India.

Gulhati (2004), an editor of the Monthly Index of Medical Specialties, the most widely used reference guide for doctors in India, provides several examples of how doctors are persuaded by pharmaceutical firms to prescribe medicines to increase their private incentives and profit margins for the pharmaceutical firms and pharmacists: (i) in most cases of chlamydial genital infection, doctors in India prescribe the higher priced ofloxacin at Rs. 100, as opposed to tetracycline at Rs. 14 or doxycycline at Rs. 28; (ii) doctors in India prefer pantoprazole at Rs. 6 per tablet as opposed to omeprazole at Rs. 2 per tablet although many clinical trials indicate that there is little difference in efficacy; and (iii) similarly, doctors in India prescribe perindopril at Rs. 9.4 per tablet as opposed to enalapril at Rs. 1 per tablet. Although these are examples from 2004, there is no reason to believe that the nature of relationships between the doctors, pharmacists, and pharmaceutical firms has changed subsequently. Recent cases of pricing of medical devices indicate that hospitals have also begun collaborating with these players in administering more expensive substitutes. As Gulhati (2004) notes, if prescribers and producers collaborate to take advantage of consumers' vulnerability, the state must intervene. In its report on the pricing or medicines and trade margins, the Pant Committee noted that the pharmacists and other traders in the retail chain promote higher-priced medicines (Pant et al. 2016, p. 27):

> The trader gets bargaining leverage and when he is able to sell at the printed MRP [maximum resale price], he gets a higher trade margin. Higher MRP therefore provides an incentive to the retailer to sell those brands which have higher MRP printed on them. The patient is always at the receiving end. He cannot decide the bargaining level and most of the times he is guided by the printed MRP. Thus high MRP's is a tool to cheat the helpless consumer.

In a letter stating its opposition to calls for limiting high trade margins, the Organization of Pharmaceutical Producers of India argued against the possibility to substitute between different brands of a generic drug formulation until generic drugs are debranded. Incidentally, the OPPI stated in the same letter that it is opposed to the debranding of single-ingredient medicines as well. The OPPI stated (Pant et al. 2016, p. 67):

> OPPI feels that it is the doctor who best understands the needs of patients. Doctors take decisions on the brand to be prescribed based on their experience and conviction on quality of certain manufacturers and the varying ability of patients to pay for better quality. It is the Doctor who is solely responsible for the medical outcome of his/her patient, and there must be no move that compromises the Doctor's ability to decide on a prescription. Substitution at a chemist level may bring in competition on all aspects other than science and quality. This can also lead to potential anti-competitive vertical arrangements between retailers and manufacturers to push sales. Substituting medicines of one brand by other brand or by the generic will result in the decision-making process shifting from well-qualified professionals like doctors and physicians to sales staff in the chemists/pharmacy shops. Many of such pharmacies do not have qualified pharmacist on the premises.

The use of marketing practices to influence the prescription behavior of doctors and pharmacists is another contributing factor, limiting the competition (Oldani 2004). Joelving (2015) investigates the role of pharmaceutical sales representatives in India generating prescriptions by organizing health camps. Those who visit the health camp for a checkup have little choice but to purchase the specific brand of medicine produced by the sponsors of the health camp. Joelving (2015) notes that the practice creates new customers and allows companies to influence prescription patterns. Also, the sales representatives sometimes perform the tests on patients themselves at the health camps, and the practice is common among not only domestic firms in India but also prevalent among the Indian subsidiaries of major pharmaceutical companies such as Abbott, Bayer, GlaxoSmithKline, Roche, and Sanofi. The Organization of Pharmaceutical Producers of India (OPPI), of which these companies are members, responded to Joelving's article by noting that they have little control over how the health camps are conducted, indicating lack of accountability in marketing practices (Smetacek 2016).

Fourth, the distribution of pharmaceuticals in India is cartelized, which severely limits competition among pharmacists and incentivizes pharmaceutical firms to increase margins for retailers, pushing the prices of medicines higher (Bhaskarabhatla et al. 2017). The retailers of medicines in India are organized as a powerful union, the All India Organization of Chemists and Druggists (AIOCD), and they are found to be operating as a downstream cartel by the Competition Commission of India. The primary objective of the AIOCD is to maintain a 30% vertical trade margin. As a part of their activities, the AIOCD regulates the entry of pharmaceutical firms into district markets. As a result, even when more than a hundred different brands of Paracetamol tablets are sold in India, at any given medical store, only a small number of brands are available. Our data do not disaggregate sales by district, and we cannot document the limited nature of competition quantitatively locally. The absence of third-party agencies such as insurance companies who can bargain with pharmaceutical companies and pharmacies further contributes to the inability of consumers to limit prices or exercise choice.

Finally, there is evidence to suggest that hospitals have played an unhelpful role in lowering the cost of medicines. For example, for many drugs and devices administered in hospitals, studies find that hospitals charge exorbitantly high margins. In a study conducted by the Maharashtra Food and Drug Administration, hospitals in Mumbai routinely charged prices two to three times the wholesale price. Nautiyal (2014a) notes:

> Patients were being forced to pay double or even triple the price for medical devices at hospitals. As most of these are not available in the open market, patients can't check prices and are held hostage by the hospitals, which force them to buy at the price they quote. However, experts also opine that having an MRP has not prevented profiteering in medicines, with the MRP being fixed high enough to accommodate commissions since there is no limit on what the MRP can be. Moreover, while MRP is mandatory on everything manufactured in India, many devices are imported and escape this stipulation. In most hospitals, if two devices are more or less equal, the choice of which one is used depends on which fetches the hospital a bigger cut.

Nautiyal (2014b) reports that hospitals in collusion with wholesalers are profiteering from the sale of drugs and medical devices at hospitals:

> Over 80 medical devices under disposables category which fall under the respiratory emergency care segment are not available at retail drug stores as of today. Sources in the healthcare industry have revealed that the practice of selling these products to stockists and they in turn selling the products to hospitals at high prices and at high margin is prevalent for some time now. It has also been found that hospitals have been taking advantage of this situation as patients have no idea about either the cost or the use of such devices. Simple devices like oxygen mask, IV cannula and infusion therapy products are priced as high as 10–30 times more when it reaches the point of care.

In summary, at each level in the Indian pharmaceutical industry, starting from manufacturing down to dispensing of medicines, there is an incentive to inflate the profit margin in such a manner that the maximum resale price is several times the cost of production. While prior studies such as Sharma and Kaplan (2016) and Phadke and Srinivasan (2013) illustrate the nature of this problem comparing the market prices with those of the public-sector procurement price, a more systematic and comprehensive analysis is required to document the nature and extent of the problem.

3.4 Evidence Indicates Leading Brands Are Also the Price Leaders

We use the AIOCD's Pharmatrac data to investigate whether the prices of medicines in India are relatively higher compared to their costs of production. Naturally, in the absence of data on firm-specific costs disaggregated by individual medicines, we cannot conduct a definitive test of the proposition. Nonetheless, we will examine several aspects of the medicine markets that are revealing and consistent with the proposition. While previous analyses of the arguments involved anecdotes of select medicines, our approach is to document the reasons more comprehensively for a broad selection of medicines. We do so by examining wholesale and retail prices for the first batch of 150 medicines for whom the NPPA fixed the ceiling price on June 14, 2013. We will refer to these medicines as the "June 14, 2013 List" for the rest of the book. These medicines include tablets, injections, and syrups.

At the outset, we acknowledge that the imposition of price controls may have both positive and negative effects. For example, both multinational and domestic firms may exit medicine markets because of insufficient profit margins in regulated medicine markets. Domestic firms may shift production of the regulated medicines, leading to shortages. Similarly, innovator firms may delay the launch of newly patented medicines due to price ceilings. Although the DPCO has exemptions for newly invented medicines, we agree that multinational firms may be discouraged by the presence of regulations such as price controls and the burden associated complying with them.

We begin by examining price variation among the top-selling medicines in India. We show in Table 3.1 the lowest-priced and the highest-priced SKUs of each of the top eight medicines in their tablet form. We compute the ratio of the highest price to the lowest price and report it in the last column of Table 3.1. The price of a 5 mg tablet of Atorvastatin ranges from Rs. 0.9 to Rs. 10.87, indicating that the highest price is 12 times higher than the lowest price. Similarly, in the market for Cefixime 50 mg tablets, the highest price is five-time the lowest price. The number ranges from 5 to 120, indicating significantly large price dispersion in these markets. One may argue that the presence of price dispersion is not necessarily a sign of lack of competition. Instead, if SKUs with lower prices have larger market shares, then the presence of a few SKUs with relatively large prices is not a cause for concern.

Table 3.1 Variation in prices within medicine markets

Medicine	High priced SKU	Price	Low priced SKU	Price	Factor[a]
Atorvastatin	Azerva 5 mg tablet 10	108.70	Genxvast 5 mg tablet 10	9	12×
Cefixime	Safix 50 mg tablet 10	99	Zim 50 mg tablet 10	19.05	5×
Ranitidine	Consec 150 mg tablet 10	109	Ranitidine 150 mg tablet 10	2.56	43×
Rosuvastatin	Rosuchol 5 mg tablet 10	160.62	Rosuson 5 mg tablet 10	15	11×
Telmisartan	Micardis 40 mg tablet 10	386	Telgard 40 mg tablet 10	15.97	24×
Azithromycin	Vicon 500 mg tablet 3	240.95	Woazicin 500 mg tablet 3	25	10×
Cefpodoxime	Cedopil 100 mg tablet 10	483.47	Ceflus 100 mg tablet 10	42.26	11×
Pantoprazole	Pentagon 40 mg tablet 10	600	Pantonir 40 mg tablet 10	5	120×

Source: AIOCD Pharmatrac (2011–2015)
[a]Factor is defined as the price of highest-priced sku/price of lowest-priced sku

We examine whether firms that lead the market in terms of pricing, charging the highest price, also have the largest market share. We present in Table 3.2 the top-ten drugs in terms of sales value, sold in India from January 2011 until June 2016. We report total sales during this period in the second column and the weighted average price in column 3. The weighted average price of Atorvastatin is Rs. 6.41. The market leader charges Rs. 7.71, higher than the weighted average price, and has a market share of 14.1%. The weighted average price of the top five is Rs. 6.74 firms and they account for 57.9% of the market share. By contrast, the next five firms account for 22.9% of the market share at a weighted average price of Rs. 6.14. The top five firms account for more than half of the market share across these medicine markets and consistently charge higher prices. Moreover, in seven out of ten sub-groups, the market leader charges a price higher than the weighted average price that is charged by all firms in the market. This table clearly indicates that firms with higher market shares charge higher prices. However, this correlation might be explained by other factors, and must, therefore, be further analyzed. For example, differences in quality are often invoked to explain such vast differences in pricing and market shares of the firms operating in these markets. Nonetheless, prior studies find that the Indian pharmaceutical markets do not exhibit the kind of differences in quality that justify such large differences in prices.

Much of the differences in prices result from differences in the underlying trade margins. Singal et al. (2011) examine trade margins for five commonly used medicines, alprazolam, cetirizine, ciprofloxacin, fluoxetine, and lansoprazole, all manufactured in multiple versions by the same company. In particular, they distinguish branded and branded-generic SKUs of the same medicine manufactured by the same company. For example, Alerid and Cetcip are the branded and branded-generic versions of Cetirizine 10 mg, both manufactured by Cipla. The markup for the retailer for the branded medicine is 30% and 1016% for the branded-generic. One obvious concern is whether the quality of medicines between the two versions is different even if they are manufactured by the same company. Singal et al. (2011) conduct a quality test for each pair of branded and branded-generic medicines and find that both versions of the five medicines are "within their permissible range for all the quantitative and qualitative parameters as prescribed in Indian Pharmacopoeia."

Table 3.2 Top ten medicines sold in India by sales

Medicine	Sales (billion)	Weighted average price	Market leader's price	Market leader's share (%)	Weighted average price of top 5	Market share of top 5	Weighted average price of next 5	Market share of next 5
Atorvastatin	41.8	6.41	7.71	14.1	6.74	57.9	6.14	22.9
Cefixime	33.7	12.45	10.66	19.7	11.64	54.8	10.59	20.0
Ranitidine	25.2	0.66	0.59	34.9	0.78	98.1	0.61	1.8
Pantoprazole	23.8	8.38	8.88	30.5	7.79	86.4	6.31	5.7
Rosuvastatin	23.5	11.23	11.80	26.2	11.95	59.9	10.53	19.4
Telmisartan	22.9	6.95	7.92	30.9	6.63	54.3	6.18	19.7
Cefpodoxime	22.1	18.65	14.22	14.4	19.09	53.7	17.45	17.5
Azithromycin	22.1	25.14	29.73	24.2	26.91	57.0	22.45	15.8
Cefuroxime	20.2	57.06	87.13	34.2	56.44	66.4	26.91	11.0
Metroprolol	18.7	2.89	3.27	23.7	3.58	51.7	2.75	19.5

Source: AIOCD Pharmatrac (2011–2015)

Notes: Medicine sales are in rupees. Price is weighted by sales to obtain the weighted average price. Market leader is the leading firm in each market with the largest market share. Market leader's price is the average price charged by the market leader and market leader's share is the average market share of the market leader

We now restrict our analysis to price-controlled medicines and examine the whether leading brands of medicines among the June 14, 2013 List are also the price leaders. The suggested pattern hints at an indirect test of whether the prices in a medicine market are relatively high and whether the markets are functioning competitively. In particular, we argue that if the brands with the largest market share also happen to be the brands with the highest prices, then either the consumers remain brand-loyal despite being well-informed about the alternatives or the consumers rely on the judgments of their physicians and pharmacists. Although the presence of switching costs can cause consumers to remain brand-loyal when lower-priced alternatives exist, the discussion in the earlier section concerning the prescription behavior of the doctors and the dispensing behavior of the pharmacists suggests that the consumers of medicines in India have limited choice in practice and that pharmaceutical firms have considerable market power.

Using the AIOCD data, we examine the pricing strategies for 66 tablet medicines on the "June 14, 2013, List." We limit our analysis to tablets as comparing the relative prices across multiple brands of tablets is relatively straightforward compared injection or syrup brands. In particular, we analyze the prices of the top three SKUs of each medicine in terms of their market share from the beginning of our dataset in January 2011 until the public notification of the list of regulated medicines in December 2012. The results of the analysis are presented in Table 3.3. The names of the medicines are reported in column 1, the top three SKUs are reported in column 2, and their corresponding market shares are reported in column 3. The average price of the SKU during the 2 years is reported in column 4. The number in column 5 is obtained by dividing SKU price by the average of the minimum price during this period. The number in column 5 is generally above one, indicating that the prices charged by market leaders are several times more than the minimum price prevailing in the market. For example, in the case of Acyclovir 200 mg tablets, the leading brand with 40% market share charges Rs. 6.13 per tablet, which is 3.87 times higher than the minimum price per tablet in the market. Similarly, the brand with the second highest market share of 21% charges Rs. 6.53, which is more than four times the minimum price in the market. The top three brands of Acyclovir 200 mg tablets account for more than three-fourths of the market share, and each one of them charges a price that is a multiple of the minimum price in the market. While two of the three top SKUs of Aciclovir 200 mg, involve a time-release tablet and the third is a five-tablet pack rather than the usual ten-tablet pack, these factors do not appear to explain their relatively higher prices. The next four tablets on the list, Amiodarone, Amitriptyline, Atenolol, and Atorvastatin involve top three SKUs with an identical number of immediate-release tablets, but their prices are several times higher than the minimum in the market. Collectively, the medicines in Table 3.3 account for 44% of the "June 14, 2013, List" and support the argument that price leaders and also market leaders.

In column 6 of Table 3.3, we list the retail trade margin, calculated as the percent increase in maximum retail price (MRP) relative to price to the retailer (PTR). The trade margin is around 26%, indicating the incentive for wholesalers and retailers to push these medicines and pharmaceutical sales representatives to market these

Table 3.3 Pricing strategies of market leaders in 66 tablets regulated under DPCO 2013 and ceiling prices fixed on 14 June 2013

Medicine	SKU	Share	Price	Price/ Min Price	Margin
Acyclovir tablets 200 mg	Acivir 200 mg tablet Dt 10	40.51	6.13	3.87	26.85
	Zovirax 200 mg tablet 5	21.82	6.53	4.12	27.34
	Ocuvir 200 mg tablet Dt 10	16.29	4.7	2.97	26.9
Amiodarone tablets 100 mg	Cordarone 100 mg tablet 10	82.43	6.44	5.26	27.34
	Amiodar 100 mg tablet 10	4.8	6.06	4.95	26.11
	Amipace 100 mg tablet 10	3.36	4.96	4.05	27.35
Amiodarone tablets 200 mg	Cordarone X 200 mg tablet 10	82.76	12.83	2.03	26.87
	Amiodar 200 mg tablet 10	4.45	11.62	1.83	26.94
	Amipace 200 mg tablet 10	3.59	9.92	1.57	27.34
Amitriptyline tablets 25 mg	Tryptomer 25 mg tablet 10	72.05	2.55	2.45	27.42
	Eliwel 25 mg tablet 10	7.87	2.74	2.64	26.44
	Amitone 25 mg tablet 10	5.67	1.46	1.4	26.8
Atenolol tablets 100MG	Aten 100 mg tablet 14	37.51	3.91	4.09	26.2
	Tenormin 100 mg tablet 14	30.82	4.05	4.24	27.34
	Tenolol 100 mg tablet 14	13.09	3.05	3.19	27.33
Atorvastatin tablets 5 mg	Atorva 5 mg tablet 10	17.35	2.79	4.06	26.71
	Storvas 5 mg tablet 10	16.31	4.94	7.2	29.43
	Aztor 5 mg tablet 10	14.85	3.7	5.38	26.83
Azathioprine tablets 50 mg	Azoran 50 mg tablet 10	83.53	8.17	2.09	27.12
	Zymurine 50 mg tablet 10	7.42	6.14	1.57	28.72
	Imuran 50 mg tablet 25	3.64	14.08	3.6	26.14
Azithromycin tablets 500 mg	Azithral 500 mg tablet 3	25.81	23.68	10.25	27.34
	Azee 500 mg tablet 3	10.51	18.06	7.82	27.33
	Zathrin 500 mg tablet 3	4.5	15.81	6.84	26.87
Carbimazole tablets 10 mg	Neo Mercazole 10 mg tablet 100	88.59	2.61	1.09	26.85
	Thyrocab 10 mg tablet 60	5.85	2.88	1.21	65.49
	Anti Thyrox 10 mg tablet 100	4.92	2.39	1	27.34
Carbimazole tablets 5 mg	Neo Mercazole 5 mg tablet 100	90.92	1.58	1.11	27.34
	Anti Thyrox 5 mg tablet 100	4.72	1.43	1	26.86
	Thyrocab 5 mg tablet 100	4.03	1.46	1.02	27.13
Clomiphene citrate tablets 100 mg	Siphene 100 mg tablet 5	35.31	11.5	2.66	29.97
	Clofert 100 mg tablet 5	33.74	10.89	2.52	26.91
	Fertyl super 100 mg tablet 5	10.59	10.12	2.34	27.34
Colchicin tablets 0.5 mg	Zycolchin 0.5 mg tablet 10	83.82	3.12	3.17	26.6
	Goutnil 0.5 mg tablet 10	15.96	1.98	2.01	26.84
	Colochicine 0.5 mg tablet 10	0.22	1.64	1.67	25.98

(continued)

Table 3.3 (continued)

Medicine	SKU	Share	Price	Price/ Min Price	Margin
Diethylcarbamazine citrate tablets 50 mg	Banocide forte 50 mg tablet 30	95.34	0.74	2.62	27.35
	Banocide 50 mg tablet 10	4.42	0.48	1.71	70.43
	Banocide 50 mg tablet 100	0.14	0.36	1.26	232.96
Digoxin tablets 0.25 mg	Lanoxin 0.25 mg tablet 10	92.13	1.35	2.35	23.19
	Lanoxin 0.25 mg tablet 250	4.74	1.29	2.26	19.2
	Dixin 0.25 mg tablet 10	2.7	0.82	1.43	24.17
Diltiazem tablets 30 mg	Dilzem 30 mg tablet 10	79.65	2.52	2.81	31.1
	Angizem 30 mg tablet 10	10.96	2.69	3	26.59
	Channel 30 mg tablet 10	3.9	2.5	2.79	26.07
Enalapril Maleate tablets 2.5 mg	Envas 2.5 mg tablet 15	62.18	1.56	4.06	26.86
	Enam 2.5 mg tablet 15	23.37	1.6	4.16	27.34
	Nuril 2.5 mg tablet 10	5.69	1.62	4.22	27.69
Enalapril Maleate tablets 5 mg	Envas 5 mg tablet 15	60.67	2.53	7.92	26.84
	Enam 5 mg tablet 15	21.11	2.16	6.78	27.34
	Nuril 5 mg tablet 10	6.5	2.78	8.69	27.16
Ethambutol tablets 400 mg	Combutol 400 mg tablet 10	72.78	1.77	1.03	23.62
	Mycobutol 400 mg tablet 10	19.81	1.95	1.14	23.18
	Themibutol 400 mg tablet 10	7.4	1.72	1	23.62
Ethambutol tablets 600 mg	Combutol 600 mg tablet 10	67.47	2.6	1.39	23.63
	Mycobutol 600 mg tablet 10	24.12	2.95	1.57	23.17
	Themibutol 600 mg tablet 10	5.85	2.56	1.37	23.61
Ethambutol tablets 800 mg	Combutol 800 mg tablet 10	58.75	3.45	1.42	23.62
	Mycobutol 800 mg tablet 10	23.52	3.87	1.59	23.61
	Themibutol 800 mg tablet 10	5.8	3.4	1.4	23.62
Folic Acid tablets 5 mg	Folvite 5 mg tablet 30	84.02	1.89	12.56	26.37
	Fol 5 5 mg tablet 10	3.61	1.31	8.73	26.53
	Sysfol new 5 mg tablet 30	3.33	1.15	7.62	28.21
Glibenclamide tablets 2.5 mg	Semi Daonil 2.5 mg tablet 10	72.65	0.47	2.19	26.77
	Semi Euglucon 2.5 mg tablet 10	15.25	0.51	2.4	26.34
	Daonil 2.5 mg tablet 60	6.29	0.76	3.59	76.2
Glibenclamide tablets 5 mg	Daonil 5 mg tablet 10	84.4	0.83	2.17	26.79
	Euglucon 5 mg tablet 10	10.21	0.76	1.97	27.31
	Daonil 5 mg tablet 600	4.39	0.63	1.63	493.49
Hydrochlorthiazide tablets 12.5 mg	Aquazide 12.5 mg tablet 10	73.49	0.97	1.58	26.84
	Hydride 12.5 mg tablet 10	8.9	1.04	1.7	26.86
	Hydrazide 12.5 mg tablet 10	8	0.64	1.04	26.39

(continued)

Table 3.3 (continued)

Medicine	SKU	Share	Price	Price/ Min Price	Margin
Hydrochlorthiazide tablets 25 mg	Aquazide 25 mg tablet 10	70.03	1.63	2	26.44
	Hydrazide 25 mg tablet 10	9.7	1.1	1.35	26.07
	Hydride 25 mg tablet 10	8.63	1.7	2.08	26.9
Hydroxychloroquine phosphate tablets 200 mg	Hcqs 200 mg tablet 10	66.46	5.23	1.63	26.82
	Hydroquin 200 mg tablet 10	7.08	5.46	1.7	26.71
	Oxcq 200 mg tablet 10	6.34	5.03	1.57	26.63
Imatinib tablets 400 mg	Imat 400 mg tablet 10	21.84	182.11	1.4	96.34
	Levin(Drl) 400 mg tablet 10	18.67	329.03	2.54	28.12
	Veenat 400 mg tablet 10	18.57	265.1	2.04	30.03
Imipramine tablets 25 mg	Depsonil 25 mg tablet 10	65.73	0.99	1.72	27.32
	Antidep 25 mg tablet 10	17.04	0.77	1.34	30.92
	Depsol 25 mg tablet 10	6.98	0.59	1.03	26.31
Imipramine tablets 75 mg	Antidep 75 mg tablet 10	56.22	2.2	1.57	31.06
	Depsol 75 mg tablet 10	22.39	1.57	1.11	26.09
	Depsin 75 mg tablet 10	3.83	2.29	1.63	24.98
Isosorbide 5 Mononitrate tablets 10 mg	Monotrate 10 mg tablet 10	43.54	2.17	2.18	26.9
	Ismo 10 mg tablet 15	36.77	1.85	1.85	27.34
	Monit 10 mg tablet 15	9.54	1.23	1.24	30.35
Isosorbide 5 Mononitrate tablets 20 mg	Monotrate 20 mg tablet 10	37.99	3.49	4.65	26.9
	Ismo 20 mg tablet 15	37.66	3.08	4.1	27.34
	Monit 20 mg tablet 15	9.36	2.03	2.71	30.71
Lamivudine + Nevirapine + Stavudine tablets 150 m	Triomune 150/30/200 mg tablet 30	56.25	16.85	3.19	27.34
	Emtri 150/30/200 mg tablet 30	18.08	17.53	3.32	29.22
	Stavex Ln 150/30/200 mg tablet 30	10.04	16.73	3.17	26.23
Lamivudine + Zidovudine tablets 150 mg + 300 mg	Duovir 150/300 mg tablet 60	34.34	15.26	1	27.34
	Duovir 150/300 mg tablet 10	20.9	16.73	1.1	27.34
	Zidolam 150/300 mg tablet 10	17	16.01	1.05	27.34
Leflunomide tablets 20 mg	Lefra 20 mg tablet 10	34.03	16.99	1.93	31.25
	Lefno 20 mg tablet 10	18.47	13.59	1.55	27.19
	Cleft 20 mg tablet 10	14.18	18.02	2.05	29.06
Lithium Carbonate tablets 300 mg	Lithosun 300 mg tablet 10	51.7	2.05	2.07	26.8
	Licab 300 mg tablet 10	33.03	1.45	1.46	30.84
	Elcab 300 mg tablet 10	3.05	1.02	1.03	10.49
Losartan Potassium tablets 25 mg	Losar 25 mg tablet 10	24.39	2.47	4.17	26.31
	Repace 25 mg tablet 10	18.07	2.58	4.36	26.83
	Covance 25 mg tablet 10	9.66	3.1	5.23	30

(continued)

Table 3.3 (continued)

Medicine	SKU	Share	Price	Price/ Min Price	Margin
Losartan Potassium tablets 50 mg	Losar 50 mg tablet 10	21.4	4.61	4.19	26.04
	Repace 50 mg tablet 10	15.85	4.89	4.45	26.87
	Losar 50 mg tablet 15	10.31	4.87	4.43	29.26
Medroxy Progesterone Acetate tablets 10 mg	Deviry 10 mg tablet 10	43.98	4.12	1.28	26.87
	Meprate 10 mg tablet 10	23.46	4.07	1.26	29.95
	Modus 10 mg tablet 10	20.76	4.94	1.53	26.86
Mefloquine tablet 250 mg base	Mefque 250 mg tablet 4	28.12	47.5	1.52	26.67
	Mefloc 250 mg tablet 4	26.5	31.28	1	26.67
	Larimef 250 mg tablet 6	22.83	43.08	1.38	27.34
Methotrexate tablet 2.5 mg	Neotrexate 2.5 mg tablet 10	59.35	4.41	1.64	27.34
	Biotrexate 2.5 mg tablet 10	12.56	3.78	1.4	31.12
	Folitrax 2.5 mg tablet 10	10.86	3.73	1.38	27.34
Methotrexate tablets 5 mg	Folitrax 5 mg tablet 10	61.73	6.23	2.4	27.34
	Oncotrex 5 mg tablet 10	26.27	6.13	2.36	27.14
	Mexate 5 mg tablet 4	5.95	6.84	2.63	27.11
Methotrexate tablets 7.5 mg	Folitrax 7.5 mg tablet 10	66.82	9.3	6.74	27.12
	Mexate 7.5 mg tablet 4	11.85	12.68	9.2	27
	Oncotrex 7.5 mg tablet 10	11.21	8.85	6.42	27.03
Methyl Ergometrine tablets 0.125 mg	Methergin 0.125 mg tablet 10	81.96	8.99	17.94	26.87
	Utergin 0.125 mg tablet 10	11.97	6.15	12.26	27
	Ergolin 0.125 mg tablet 10	5.52	3.71	7.39	26.95
Metoclopramide tablets 10 mg	Perinorm 10 mg tablet 10	79.34	1.26	5.62	26.82
	Reglan 10 mg tablet 10	15.26	1.19	5.33	27.31
	Maxeron 10 mg tablet 10	4.36	0.94	4.19	26.9
Misoprostol tablets 100ug	Misoprost 100 mcg tablet 4	42.24	9.1	2.52	26.86
	Cytolog 100 mcg tablet 10	23.84	5.97	1.66	31.69
	Cytolog 100 mcg tablet 4	23.81	6.45	1.79	26.61
Nifedipine tablets 10 mg	Nicardia retard 10 mg tablet 10	70.78	1.3	2.26	26.88
	Calcigard retard 10 mg tablet 10	13.75	1.07	1.86	31.21
	Nifedine 10 mg tablet 10	6.19	1.05	1.83	27.31
Norethisterone tablets 5 mg	Primolut N 5 mg tablet 10	44.3	4.62	2.46	24.99
	Regestrone 5 mg tablet 10	34.05	5.21	2.77	26.85
	Cycloreg 5 mg tablet 10	4.78	5.77	3.07	27.93
Olanzapine tablets 10 mg	Oleanz 10 mg tablet 10	25.36	5.31	2.79	26.88
	Olimelt 10 mg tablet 10	17.38	5.25	2.75	27.01
	Oliza 10 mg tablet 10	8.43	4.71	2.47	26.51
Olanzapine tablets 5 mg	Oleanz 5 mg tablet 10	29.37	2.7	1.98	26.56
	Olimelt 5 mg tablet 10	14.77	2.65	1.94	27.02
	Oliza 5 mg tablet 10	10.12	2.41	1.77	26.96

(continued)

Table 3.3 (continued)

Medicine	SKU	Share	Price	Price/ Min Price	Margin
Ondansetron tablets 8 mg	Emeset 8 mg tablet 10	34.79	12.56	5.09	27.34
	Ondem 8 mg tablet md 10	15.71	8.38	3.39	27.34
	Ondem 8 mg tablet 10	14.72	6.2	2.51	27.34
Paracetamol tablets 500MG	Calpol 500 mg tablet 15	52.96	0.91	7.02	26.82
	Crocin 500 mg tablet 15	10.31	1.06	8.18	25.4
	Calpol 500 mg tablet 1000	6.73	0.32	2.48	39.1
Phenobarbitone tablets 60 mg	Gardenal 60 mg tablet 20	98.89	1.96	4.19	27.34
	Phenobarb 60 mg tablet 10	0.69	0.67	1.44	24.64
	Emgard 60 mg tablet 10	0.35	1.91	4.08	26.86
Phenytoin Sodium Capsules or tablets 50 mg	Eptoin 50 mg tablet 150	90.89	0.82	7.91	21.52
	Epsolin 50 mg tablet 100	5.97	0.57	5.51	26.7
	C Toin 50 mg tablet 90	1.68	0.68	6.57	27.34
Primaquine tablets 7.5 mg	Malirid 7.5 mg tablet 10	91.16	1.66	1.37	32.54
	Pmq Inga 7.5 mg tablet 10	5.99	1.72	1.42	26.37
	Leoprime forte 7.5 mg tablet 14	1.61	2.97	2.45	26.08
Promethazine tablets 25 mg	Avomine 25 mg tablet 10	85.32	2.29	3.71	27.33
	Phenergan 25 mg tablet 10	14.15	1.6	2.59	27.32
	Regan (A.N. Pharmacia) 25 mg tablet 10	0.32	1.37	2.22	19.74
Pyrazinamide tablets 1000 mg	Pyzina 1000 mg tablet 10	41.49	7.34	1.4	23.62
	P Zide 1000 mg tablet 10	23.06	8.4	1.6	23.62
	Pza Ciba 1000 mg tablet 10	15.39	7.69	1.47	23.15
Pyrazinamide tablets 500 mg	Pyzina 500 mg tablet 10	40.02	3.7	3.15	23.62
	Pza Ciba 500 mg tablet 10	26.86	3.96	3.38	23.63
	P Zide 500 mg tablet 10	20.75	3.82	3.26	23.16
Pyrazinamide tablets 750 mg	Pyzina 750 mg tablet 10	40.24	5.49	3.98	23.62
	P Zide 750 mg tablet 10	28.82	6.37	4.62	23.16
	Pza Ciba 750 mg tablet 10	23.63	5.92	4.29	23.19
Quinine Sulphate tablets 300 mg	Rez Q 300 mg tablet 10	46.41	5.36	2.93	27.34
	Qinarsol 300 mg tablet 10	20.31	4.54	2.48	26.41
	Cinkona 300 mg tablet 10	8.13	4.91	2.68	25.86
Raloxifene tablets 60 mg	Fiona 60 mg tablet 10	54.98	9.76	1.73	27.34
	Ralista 60 mg tablet 10	36.43	8.39	1.49	26.85
	Fiona 60 mg tablet 7	6.55	13.95	2.47	27.35
Sodium Valproate tablets 200 mg	Valparin 200 mg tablet 10	57	2.37	1.56	26.83
	Epilex 200 mg tablet 10	19.24	3.12	2.06	27.34
	Encorate 200 mg tablet 10	10.41	2.43	1.61	26.91
Stavudine + Lamivudine tablets 30 mg + 150 mg	Lamivir S 150/30 mg tablet 60	51.82	8.44	1.06	27.34
	Lamistar 150/30 mg tablet 10	20.68	8.77	1.1	27.34
	Emduo 150/30 mg tablet 60	13.9	8	1	27.44

(continued)

Table 3.3 (continued)

Medicine	SKU	Share	Price	Price/ Min Price	Margin
Tamoxifen Citrate tablets 20 mg	Tamodex 20 mg tablet 10	45.85	2.75	1.6	30.73
	Tamoxifen 20 mg tablet 10	36.9	2.83	1.65	21.1
	Tamoxifen (Het) citrate 20 mg tablet 10	14.61	2.74	1.59	27.57
Terbutaline Sulphate tablets 2.5 mg	Bricanyl 2.5 mg tablet 20	98.06	0.75	1.23	26.89
	Tetrasma 2.5 mg tablet 10	1.59	4.22	6.86	25.07
	Bricanyl 2.5 mg tablet 60	0.35	0.62	1	24.87
Trihexyphenidyl Hydrochloride tablets 2 mg	Pacitane 2 mg tablet 10	75.7	2.2	5.13	26.4
	Parkin 2 mg tablet 10	9.69	1.62	3.78	27.33
	Bexol 2 mg tablet 10	3.82	0.83	1.93	26.77
Zidovudine + Lamivudine + Nevirapine tablets 300	Duovir N 150/300/200 mg tablet 30	57.56	18.36	3.44	27.34
	Lazid—N 150/300/200 mg tablet 30	18.3	19.72	3.69	27.44
	Zidolam N 150/300/ 200 mg tablet 10	13.67	18.3	3.43	27.34

brands. To elaborate on this point, consider the case of retail margins for Amiodarone 100 mg tablets. The Cordarone 100 mg brand, which explains 82.43% of the market, is priced at Rs. 64.4 per ten tablets at 5.26 times the minimum price. The retailer margin on Cordarone brand is 26.87% or Rs. 17.3 for a pack of ten tablets. In comparison, the price of the lowest price brand is Rs. 12.24, with a retailer trade margin of Rs. 3.7, estimated at 30%. Therefore, a retailer is incentivized to market Cordarone relative to a cheaper alternative aggressively. Such retail trade margins are relatively higher compared margins for pharmaceuticals in other countries.

3.5 Evidence of High Trade Margins on Several Brands

While a trade margin of 30% for higher priced brands results in a larger absolute profit margin, pharmaceutical firms have the option to increase the trade margin from 30% to 40 or even 50%, thus increasing the net benefit to the retailer in return for retailer patronage. Srinivasan (1999) suggests that manufacturers giving exorbitant trade margins remains a major problem in the Indian pharmaceutical industry. We examine the extent of trade margins for medicines on the June 14, 2013 List. We report in Table 3.4 the retail trade margins for 125 brands of medicines with at least 100% in high trade margins, as computed in December 2012, when the 2013 DPCO list of medicines was released publicly. These brands represent 7.3% of the overall number of brands of the medicines in the June 14, 2013, List. In some medicine markets, there are multiple brands with more than 100% margin, indicating that it is

Table 3.4 Brands with more than 100% vertical trade margin in December 2012 among the 150 medicines whose ceiling price was fixed on June 14 2013

Medicine	SKU	MRP	PTR	Margin
Acyclovir tablets 200 mg	Lovir (Eli Lilly) 200 mg tablet 5	365	57.79	531.6
Ampicillin powder for suspension 125 mg/5 ml	Ampurin 125 mg dry syrup 30 ml	20	9	122.2
Atenolol tablets 100 mg	Obeta 100 mg tablet 14	30	12	150
	Hipres 100 mg tablet 14	55	11	400
Atropine Sulphate injection 0.6 mg/ml	Atrowok 0.60 mg injection 1 ml	8.5	4	112.5
Azathioprine tablets 50 mg	Azathioprine 50 mg tablet 10	442.47	41.12	976
Azithromycin tablets 500 mg	Azikem (Alkem) 500 mg tablet 3	75	27	177.8
	Azax 500 mg tablet 3	70.88	30	136.3
	Azilup 500 mg tablet 3	73.12	26	181.2
	Azivista 500 mg tablet 3	79	29	172.4
	Azitol 500 mg tablet 3	72	28.3	154.4
	Jocin 500 mg tablet 10	218	49.95	336.4
	Zithrokem 500 mg tablet 3	75	31.43	138.6
	Azicip 500 mg tablet 3	69.3	32.57	112.8
	Gerimac 500 mg tablet 3	85	35.82	137.3
Carbimazole tablets 10 mg	Thyrocab 10 mg tablet 60	428	170.31	151.3
Cyclosporine capsules 50 mg	Consiral 50 mg capsule 5	390	180	116.7
Diethylcarbamazine citrate tablets 50 mg	Banocide 50 mg tablet 10	12.75	4.46	185.9
	Banocide 50 mg tablet 100	56.25	9	525
Domperidone syrup 1 mg/ml	Stopvom 1 mg suspension 30 ml	24	9	166.7
	Vomistop 1 mg suspension 30 ml	30.5	9.7	214.4
Dopamine Hydrochloride injection 40 mg/ml	Dopacef 40 mg injection 5 ml	150	33.75	344.4
Doxorubicin injection 50 mg	Adrosal 50 mg injection 1	895	290	208.6
	Zodox 50 mg injection 1	962	450	113.8
Enalapril Maleate tablets 2.5 mg	Dilvas 2.5 mg tablet 10	18.4	3.55	418.3
Enalapril Maleate tablets 5 mg	Enalapril(Cip) 5 mg tablet 10	19.8	8	147.5
	Minipril 5 mg tablet 10	16.1	4.82	234
	Dilvas 5 mg tablet 10	29.4	3.85	663.6
Folic Acid tablets 5 mg	Folly 5 mg tablet 10	8	2	300
	Folitab 5 mg tablet 30	59.35	7	747.9
	Vitafol(Cip) 5 mg tablet 10	17.3	2.5	592
	Foldivit 5 mg tablet 10	8.33	1.9	338.4
Gemcitabine hydrochloride injection 1 gm	Gemciglan 1000 mg injection 1	5999	1809.52	231.5
	Gembin 1000 mg injection 1	6390	1993.85	220.5
Gemcitabine hydrochloride injection 200 mg	Gembin 200 mg injection 1	1440	600	140
Glibenclamide tablets 2.5 mg	Semi Daonil 2.5 mg tablet 40	29	4.87	495.5
	Daonil 2.5 mg tablet 60	65.46	9.24	608.4
Glibenclamide tablets 5 mg	Daonil 5 mg tablet 600	168	8.4	1900
Imatinib tablets 400 mg	Imanib 400 mg tablet 30	10,200	5000	104

(continued)

Table 3.4 (continued)

Medicine	SKU	MRP	PTR	Margin
Losartan Potassium tablets 25 mg	Omnitan 25 mg tablet 10	39.75	10.73	270.5
	Cosart 25 mg tablet 10	30.5	9	238.9
Losartan Potassium tablets 50 mg	Losa 50 mg tablet 10	30.18	9.24	226.6
	Cosart 50 mg tablet 10	57.5	24	139.6
Methotrexate tablets 7.5 mg	Mext 7.5 mg tablet 10	118	38.88	203.5
Methyl Ergometrine tablets 0.125 mg	Metharmed 0.125 mg tablet 10	42.6	7	508.6
	Methastar 0.125 mg tablet 10	56.25	6.98	705.9
	Methygin 0.125 mg tablet 10	57	6.5	776.9
	Methercip 0.125 mg tablet 10	69	5	1280
Metoclopramide injection 5 mg/ml	Emenorm 5 mg injection 2 ml	8	3	166.7
Metoclopramide tablets 10 mg	Vominorm 10 mg tablet 10	8.4	4	110
Midazolam injection 1 mg/ml	Mezolam 1 mg injection 10 ml	83	38	118.4
	Medzol 1 mg injection 5 ml	50	25	100
	Mezolam 1 mg injection 5 ml	49.5	22	125
Midazolam injection 5 mg/ml	Midfast 5 mg injection 5 ml	50	20	150
	Mezolam 5 mg injection 1 ml	41	20	105
Neostigmine injection 0.5 mg/ml	Tilstigmin 0.5 mg injection 5 ml	93.5	15.77	492.9
Nifedipine tablets 10 mg	Depicor 10 mg tablet Sr 10	29.4	11.41	157.7
	Calnif retard 10 mg tablet 10	126.07	11.42	1003.9
Norethisterone tablets 5 mg	Norlut N 5 mg tablet 10	53.5	19	181.6
	Dubogen 5 mg tablet 10	55	22.27	147
Ofloxacin syrup 50 mg/5 ml	Woflox 50 mg syrup 30 ml	31.65	9	251.7
	Oflokem 50 mg suspension 30 ml	34	10	240
	Eufox 50 mg suspension 30 ml	28.6	10	186
	Oflostar(Cdl) 50 mg suspension 30 ml	27	11	145.5
	Otox 50 mg suspension 60 ml	36	14.59	146.7
	Nicoflox(Phc) 50 mg suspension 30 ml	26	10	160
	Oxo 50 mg suspension 30 ml	26	8.44	208.1
Olanzapine tablets 10 mg	Tolaz 10 mg tablet 10	61.76	19.23	221.2
Olanzapine tablets 5 mg	Tolaz 5 mg tablet 10	30.71	13.64	125.1
Ondansetron tablets 8 mg	Emeset md 8 mg tablet md 10	164	43.84	274.1
Pantoprazole injection 40 mg	Pantosec iv 40 mg injection 10 ml	72	18.9	281
	Panplus 40 mg injection 10 ml	48	21.71	121.1
	Peptilcer 40 mg injection 1	65	14.45	349.8
	Pentowok 40 mg injection 10 ml	93	15	520
	Pazom iv 40 mg injection 1	65	15	333.3
	Panprazole 40 mg injection 10 ml	85	23	269.6
	Panomp 40 mg injection 10 ml	75	12	525
	Pentab 40 mg injection 10 ml	62.25	17	266.2
	P Ppi 40 mg injection 10 ml	55.4	18	207.8
	Zepoxin 40 mg injection 10 ml	72	16	350
	Pazo (Algen) 40 mg injection 10 ml	64	18	255.6

(continued)

Table 3.4 (continued)

Medicine	SKU	MRP	PTR	Margin
Paracetamol injection 150 mg/ml	Paracip 150 mg injection 2 ml	59	2.95	1900
Paracetamol syrup 125 mg/5 ml	Paracip 125 mg syrup 60 ml	26.6	11	141.8
	Pfc 125 mg syrup 60 ml	28.8	13.75	109.5
	Jagcin 125 mg syrup 60 ml	24	11.82	103
	Dolomol 125 mg syrup 60 ml	24	9.95	141.2
	Lupipara 125 mg syrup 60 ml	26.5	11.43	131.8
Paracetamol tablets 500 mg	Pyricool 500 mg tablet 15	17.5	4	337.5
	Anglopar 500 mg tablet 10	9.66	2.9	233.1
	Paracin(Trq) 500 mg tablet 100	238.28	15.22	1465.6
	Actiflu 500 mg tablet 10	38	8.42	351.3
	Cipmol 500 mg tablet 10	10.2	3.88	162.9
	Pyremol 500 mg tablet 10	8.5	4	112.5
	Pyrakem 500 mg tablet 15	20	4.8	316.7
	Temfix 500 mg tablet 10	8	3.25	146.2
	Lupipara 500 mg tablet 10	9	3.6	150
	Paracip 500 mg tablet 10	11	3.8	189.5
	Welset 500 mg tablet 10	7.56	3.35	125.7
	Doliprane 500 mg tablet 10	5.9	2.95	100
	Pyrakem 500 mg tablet 10	7.5	2.8	167.9
	Flumol 500 mg tablet 10	10.5	2.98	252.3
Permethrin lotion 5%	Scabepil 5% lotion 50 ml	65	16.92	284.2
Povidone Iodine solution 5%	Cipladine 5% solution 100 ml	90.46	25	261.8
	Antidon 5% solution 100 ml	55	16.91	225.3
	Cipladine 5% solution 500 ml	189	81.98	130.5
	Bectosept 5% solution 500 ml	152.71	70	118.2
	Lupidine 5% solution 100 ml	62.7	12.5	401.6
	Povicidal 5% solution 100 ml	62.5	15.85	294.3
	Bectosept 5% solution 100 ml	77.49	21	269
Propofol injectable 1% oil suspension	Neorof 1% injection 10 ml	138	53.26	159.1
	Profol 1% infusion 50 ml	390	175	122.9
	Neorof 1% injection 20 ml	198	74.57	165.5
	Neorof 1% infusion 50 ml	445	177.55	150.6
Pyrazinamide tablets 750 mg	Zypara 750 mg tablet 10	51	14	264.3
Quinine sulphate tablets 300 mg	Bactiquin 300 mg tablet 10	60.12	27.39	119.5
Streptokinase injection 1,500,000 IU	Stpase 1,500,000 Iu injection 10 ml	2864.59	1000	186.5
Streptokinase injection 750,000 IU	Thrombosolv 750,000 Iu injection 1	1483	527.78	181
Tamoxifen Citrate tablets 20 mg	Tomifen 20 mg tablet 10	45	22.49	100.1
Tetanus Toxoid injection	Abhay Tox injection 0.5 ml	22	10	120
Tetanus Toxoid injection	Sii Hibro injection 0.5 ml	375	136.05	175.6

(continued)

Table 3.4 (continued)

Medicine	SKU	MRP	PTR	Margin
Thiopentone Sodium injectable 0.5 G powder	Thiosol 500 mg injection 0.5 ml	62	30	106.7
Vancomycin Hydrochloride injection 1 g	Vanking 1 Gm injection 10 ml	756	160	372.5
	Vancogram 1000 mg injection 1	639	242.5	163.5
Vancomycin Hydrochloride injection 500 mg	G Vanc 500 mg injection 10 ml	385	125	208
	Vanking 500 mg injection 10 ml	425	100	325

not an uncommon practice. For example, in the market for Paracetamol 500 mg tablets, there are 14 brands with more than 100% trade margin. Similarly, in the market for Paracetamol 125 mg/5 ml syrup, five different brands have more than 100% trade margin. Closer inspection reveals that the trade margin is much higher than 100% for dispensing packs, that is, SKUs containing a large number of units for use at a hospital. For example, the trade margin for 100 tablets of Paracin 500 mg is 1465%, indicating that the brand sells each tablet at Rs. 0.15 per tablet to the retailer, presumably at a profit, indicating that their marginal cost of production is lower than Rs. 0.15. The ceiling price for Paracetamol is fixed at around Rs. 1 per tablet, more than six times the price-to-the-retailer for a dispensing pack. The MRP for Paracin 500 mg is 238, indicating that the per-tablet price to the consumer is 2.38, creating an incentive for the pharmacist and the hospitals for profiting from the inexplicably high trade margin.

Next, using data on all the 150 medicines present in the June 14, 2013 List, we examine the variation in prices for different brands of the same medicine manufactured by the same company. We found 64 cases of companies in 25 medicine markets where one or more companies sell at least three versions of the same medicine and dosage. Cipla tops the list by producing multiple brands in 16 different medicine markets. Alkem and Lupin produce multiple brands of the same medicine in six and five medicine markets respectively. The list also contains several domestic and multinational firms such as Cadila, GSK, Abbott, Indoco, Indswift, Ipca Lab, Mankind, Micro, Ranbaxy, and Zydus. Our analysis expands on the study of five medicines by Singal et al. (2011), which finds large differences in prices, but little differences in quality.

We present a partial list of firms manufacturing three or more brands within a medicine in Table 3.5. We use pricing data for May 2012, which formed the basis for fixing the ceiling price for the chosen medicines a year later in Jun 2013 (we will elaborate on the design and timing issues surrounding the 2013 DPCO in the next two chapters). The brand name and dosage of the medicine are shown in column 1, company name in column 2, and the detailed SKU in column 3. The PTR, MRP, and SKU's share of the sales within the company's medicine sales are shown in columns 4–6. The retailer trade margin is shown in column 7 and how expensive is the most expensive SKU relative to the least expensive SKU of the same company in May 2012 is shown in column 8. We find that the more expensive SKU is uniformly several times more expensive than the least expensive SKU and that it is also the

Table 3.5 Examples of price variation for medicines of a company in May 2012 for the same dosage formulation

Medicine	Company	SKU	PTR	MRP	SKU share in company	Margin	PTR/Min PTR
Albendazole (400 mg)	Cipla	Bendex 400 mg tablet 1	12.07	15.7	98.39	30.07	7.32
		Tiobend 400 mg tablet 1	3.3	12	0.07	263.64	7.32
		X worm 400 mg tablet 1	1.65	15	1.54	809.09	7.32
	Indoco	Abz 400 mg tablet 10	1.37	1.8	93.58	31.29	10
		Abz 400 mg tablet 2	13.71	18	2.59	31.29	10
		Olban 400 mg tablet 1	12.8	16.65	3.83	30.08	10
	Klar Sehen	Odal 400 mg tablet 1	9.22	10	81.62	8.46	15.36
		Odal 400 mg tablet 2	9.23	12	17.44	30.08	15.36
		Odal 400 mg tablet 20	0.6	0.75	0.95	24.98	15.36
	Lupin	Lupibend 400 mg tablet 1	1.75	12	16.7	585.71	10
		Lupiworm 400 mg tablet 1	11.43	15	72.26	31.23	10
		Lupiworm 400 mg tablet 10	1.14	1.5	11.04	31.23	10
Allopurinol (100 mg)	Cipla	Alrik 100 mg tablet 10	1.9	2.4	0.54	25.98	2.49
		Ciploric 100 mg tablet 10	1.97	2.59	67.68	31.22	2.49
		Ciprolic 100 mg tablet 10	1.99	2.59	2.12	29.96	2.49
		Zyrik 100 mg tablet 10	0.8	2.3	29.66	187.5	2.49
Alprazolam (0.25 mg)	Cipla	Restyl 0.25 mg tablet 10	1.19	1.49	3.59	25	5.96
		Restyl 0.25 mg tablet 15	0.86	1.13	96.21	31.27	5.96
		Restyl 0.5 mg tablet 10	2.14	2.67	15.59	24.96	7.13
		Restyl 0.5 mg tablet 15	1.55	2.03	84.22	31.24	7.13
		Tranax 0.25 mg tablet 10	0.2	1.24	0.14	520	5.96
		Tranax 0.5 mg tablet 10	0.3	2.2	0.18	633.33	7.13
		Tranquil 0.25 mg tablet 10	0.2	1.24	0.07	520	5.96

(continued)

Table 3.5 (continued)

Medicine	Company	SKU	PTR	MRP	SKU share in company	Margin	PTR/Min PTR
Amlodipine (5 mg)	Alkem	Amlogen 5 mg tablet 10	6.62	8.28	1.12	25	3.1
		Amlogen 5 mg tablet 7	2.13	2.79	0.98	30.52	3.1
		Amlokem 5 mg tablet 10	4.8	5	2.97	4.17	3.1
		Dip (Alkem) 5 mg tablet 10	2.25	2.9	94.93	29	3.1
	Cipla	Amlip 5 mg tablet 10	0.4	2.77	0.65	592.5	8.61
		Amlopres 5 mg tablet 10	3.44	4.48	11.53	30.08	8.61
		Amlopres 5 mg tablet 15	2.3	2.99	87.82	30.08	8.61
Amoxycillin (250 mg)	Alkem	Almox 250 mg capsule 10	1	4.34	96.06	334	2.3
		Almox 250 mg capsule 1000	0.44	1.4	3.19	221.84	2.3
		Moxikem 250 mg capsule 10	0.9	4.34	0.76	382.22	2.3
	Cipla	Cipmox 250 mg capsule 10	1.58	6.3	0.29	300	13.53
		Novamox 250 mg capsule 15	4.51	5.87	99.68	30.1	13.53
Amoxycillin (500 mg)		Cipmox 500 mg capsule 10	2.8	10.39	0.44	271.25	5.68
		Novamox 250 mg capsule 3	21.3	26.42	0.03	24	13.53
		Novamox 500 mg capsule 10	4.73	6.15	0.43	30.1	5.68
		Novamox 500 mg capsule 3	15.91	19.88	1.61	25	5.68
		Novamox 500 mg capsule 6	7.88	10.25	97.52	30.1	5.68
	Ranbaxy	Amx 500 mg capsule 10	1.89	2.34	0.03	24.02	3.89
		Mox 500 mg capsule 15	7.35	9.26	99.94	26	3.89
		Roscillin Amx 500 mg capsule 10	2.29	2.84	0.02	24.02	3.89
Amoxycillin + Clavulanic acid (500/125 mg)	Cadila	Lmx forte 500/125 mg tablet 6	16.65	21.85	95.93	31.24	2.01
		Mokcan cv 500/125 mg tablet 6	8.28	41.67	0.15	403.02	2.01
		Symbiotik xl plus 500/125 mg tablet 6	16.57	19.95	3.92	20.39	2.01
	Cipla	Advent 500/125 mg tablet 6	13.84	18	50.09	30.1	2.78
		Cipclav 500/125 mg tablet 6	28.8	36	1.74	25	2.78
		Cipmox cv 500/125 mg tablet 6	10.37	42	0.09	305.01	2.78

		Clavmox 500/125 mg tablet 6	13.81	18	0.21	30.32	2.78
		Novaclav 500/125 mg tablet 6	28	42	4.37	50	2.78
		Novamox cv 500/125 mg tablet 10	13.08	16.09	3.96	23	2.78
		Novamox cv 500/125 mg tablet 6	13.84	18	35.77	30.1	2.78
		Omniclav 500/125 mg tablet 6	13.81	18	3.76	30.32	2.78
	Dr. Johns Lab	Jonclav 500/125 mg tablet 10	21.81	27.48	38.58	26	3.72
		Jonclav 500/125 mg tablet 6	36.64	45.8	9.55	25	3.72
		Navclav 500/125 mg tablet 10	9.85	23.95	1.88	143.05	3.72
		Roclav 500/125 mg tablet 10	20.94	27.49	31.09	31.25	3.72
		Roclav 500/125 mg tablet 6	34.91	45.82	18.9	31.25	3.72
	Morepen	Cvmox 500/125 mg tablet 6	20.95	27.5	19.18	31.24	2.48
		Eradiclav 500/125 mg tablet 10	8.46	11.1	24.43	31.24	2.48
		Eradiclav 500/125 mg tablet 6	14.1	18.5	56.38	31.25	2.48
	Ozone	Clavcare 500/125 mg tablet 6	11.43	15	46.49	31.25	2.54
		Xpand 500/125 mg tablet 6	11.43	15	43.05	31.25	2.54
		Xtend 500/125 mg tablet 6	28.98	36.22	10.46	25	2.54
Atorvastatin (10 mg)	Abbott	Caat 10 mg tablet 10	7.36	9.66	26.29	31.26	2.29
		Lipigoal 10 mg tablet 10	3.23	3.86	6.23	19.44	2.29
		Stator 10 mg tablet 10	3.22	4.22	67.47	31.26	2.29
	Cipla	Atorlip 10 mg tablet 10	7.16	9.4	99.06	31.25	6.51
		Lipvas 10 mg tablet 10	1.1	7.7	0.48	600	6.51
		Omnitor 10 mg tablet 10	1.1	7.53	0.46	584.09	6.51
	Lupin	Tonact 10 mg tablet 15	6.56	8.54	99.76	30.12	2
		Tonact 10 mg tablet 30	3.28	6.63	0.24	102.13	2
		Tonact-Mp 10 mg tablet 30	5.17	6.63	0	28.22	2
	Systopic	Orvas 10 mg tablet 10	2.83	3.71	20.6	31.23	2.8
		Orvas 10 mg tablet 14	2.02	2.65	69.55	31.23	2.8
		Orvas 10 mg tablet 5	5.65	7.12	9.85	26	2.8

(continued)

Table 3.5 (continued)

Medicine	Company	SKU	PTR	MRP	SKU share in company	Margin	PTR/Min PTR
Azithromycin (250 mg)	Alkem	Azento 250 mg tablet 6	7.97	10.46	14.79	31.25	2.61
		Azikem (Alkem) 250 mg tablet 10	3.05	7.5	0.24	145.9	2.61
		Azikem (Alkem) 250 mg tablet 6	5.5	12.5	6.85	127.27	2.61
		Pratham 250 mg tablet 6	7.27	9.54	44.03	31.25	2.61
		Zithium 250 mg tablet 6	7.39	9.7	33.46	31.24	2.61
		Zithrokem 250 mg tablet 6	4.14	12.5	0.64	201.81	2.61
	Cadila	Azivista 250 mg tablet 6	4.83	13.42	4.86	177.92	4.36
		Zycin(Cdl) 250 mg tablet 3	21.05	25.11	2.2	19.32	4.36
		Zycin(Cdl) 250 mg tablet 6	9.65	12.47	92.94	29.17	4.36
	Indswift	Azithro 500 mg tablet 3	13.68	18.63	93.89	36.21	2.09
		Azovid 500 mg tablet 3	8.33	40	1.09	380	2.09
		Swithro 500 mg tablet 3	17.45	22.78	5.02	30.57	2.09
	Ipca Lab	Azibact 250 mg tablet 6	9.99	13	83.71	30.09	2.02
		Azifast 250 mg tablet 3	20	24.33	0.56	21.67	2.02
		Azifast 250 mg tablet 6	9.9	13	15.74	31.25	2.02
	Lupin	Azilup 250 mg tablet 6	4.2	12.19	0.22	190.16	2.21
		Aziswift 250 mg tablet 6	9.2	11	31.61	19.52	2.21
		Z-1250 mg tablet 10	5.57	12.9	2.27	131.56	2.21
		Z-1250 mg tablet 6	9.28	12.08	65.91	30.1	2.21
Azithromycin (500 mg)		Azilup 500 mg tablet 3	8.67	24.37	0.13	181.23	2.08
		Aziswift 500 mg tablet 3	17.84	23.42	43.64	31.25	2.08
		Z-1500 mg tablet 3	18	23.42	56.23	30.11	2.08
Cefalexin (500 mg)	Cipla	Cefbact 500 mg capsule 10	2.89	3.8	26.22	31.26	4.1
		Cephadex 500 mg capsule 10	3.28	16.5	71.44	403.05	4.1
		Fixobact 500 mg capsule 10	11.88	15	2.34	26.27	4.1

Cefixime (200 mg)	Alembic	Cifadin 200 mg tablet 10	4	19.02	0.72	375.5	3.13
		Cifadin 200 mg tablet 4	12.5	21.25	0.38	70	3.13
		Zofix 200 mg tablet 10	9.07	11.33	98.91	24.99	3.13
	Cachet Pharm	Traxol O 200 mg tablet 10	8.14	10.59	88.09	30.11	2.5
		Traxol O 200 mg tablet 4	20.38	24.95	0.93	22.45	2.5
		Traxol O 200 mg tablet 6	13.45	16.57	10.98	23.19	2.5
	Micro	Alcef O 200 mg tablet 10	4.3	22	0.28	411.63	5.81
		Gramocef O 200 mg tablet 10	9.99	13	61.05	30.1	5.81
		Rite O Cef 200 mg tablet 10	9.99	13	38.61	30.1	5.81
		Rite O Cef 200 mg tablet 4	24.98	31.23	0.06	25	5.81
	Pfizer	Jetex 200 mg tablet Dt 10	7.62	10	4.98	31.25	2.14
		Vibazime 200 mg tablet Dt 15	5.08	6.67	6.73	31.25	2.14
		Vibazime 200 mg tablet Dt 7	10.88	14.29	88.29	31.25	2.14
Cefixime (100 mg)	Indoco	Fevorit 100 mg tablet Dt 10	4.23	5.55	34.88	31.26	2.1
		Vcef O 100 mg tablet Dt 10	4.23	5.55	58.94	31.26	2.1
		Vexim 100 mg tablet Dt 10	8.87	27	6.18	204.4	2.1
Cetirizine (10 mg)	Cipla	Alerid 10 mg tablet 10	2.99	3.93	93.44	31.26	13.61
		Cetcip 10 mg tablet 10	0.3	3.47	0.72	1055	13.61
		Cetcip 10 mg tablet 100	0.24	0.3	0.29	26	13.61
		Okacet 10 mg tablet 10	0.22	3.47	5.55	1475	13.61
	Intas	Histacet 10 mg tablet 10	0.3	2.8	0.75	833.33	3.43
		Intazin 10 mg tablet 10	0.15	2.6	0.36	1633.33	3.43
		Intazin 10 mg tablet 100	0.09	0.25	98.89	185.71	3.43
	Menarini	Cezin 10 mg tablet 10	0.41	0.54	66.28	31.39	6.65
		Cezin 10 mg tablet 1000	0.18	0.23	28.12	25	6.65
		Mcet 10 mg tablet 10	1.21	1.5	5.61	24.48	6.65
Ciprofloxacin (250 mg)	Cipla	Ciplox 250 mg tablet 10	4.18	5.44	99.83	30.12	4.64
		Medicip 250 mg tablet 10	2.43	3.16	0	29.87	4.64
		Neocip 250 mg tablet 10	0.9	3.16	0.17	251.22	4.64

(continued)

Table 3.5 (continued)

Medicine	Company	SKU	PTR	MRP	SKU share in company	Margin	PTR/Min PTR
Ciprofloxacin (500 mg)		Ciplox 500 mg tablet 10	7.12	9.27	99.75	30.1	5.09
		Ciprofloxacin (Cipla) 500 mg tablet 10	4.99	6.19	0.01	24	5.09
		Ciptec 500 mg tablet 10	1.4	6.13	0.01	337.57	5.09
		Medicip (Cipla) 500 mg tablet 10	4.86	6.13	0.03	26.02	5.09
		Neocip 500 mg tablet 10	1.88	6.13	0.2	224.99	5.09
	Ranbaxy	Cifran 500 mg tablet 10	7.58	9.55	97.9	26	5.09
		Cifran od 500 mg tablet 5	7.63	9.54	1.97	25.01	5.09
		Cipract 500 mg tablet 10	1.5	1.86	0.14	24	5.09
Clopidogrel (75 mg)	Cipla	Clopigard 75 mg tablet 10	1.3	18.05	0.08	1288.46	2.39
		Clopivas 75 mg tablet 10	3.11	6.12	28.7	96.85	2.39
		Clopivas 75 mg tablet 15	3.11	4.08	71.22	31.25	2.39
Diclofenac (50 mg)	Lupin	Defenac 50 mg tablet 10	0.26	1.4	2.19	430.3	5.9
		Diclonac 50 mg tablet 10	1.43	1.86	97.7	29.85	5.9
		Diclonova 50 mg tablet 10	1.56	2.25	0.11	44.42	5.9
	Zydus	Inac 50 mg tablet 10	1.29	1.53	76.34	18.66	3.45
		Inac 50 mg tablet 4	2.96	3.82	1.98	28.78	3.45
		Jonac 50 mg tablet 10	0.86	1.07	21.68	25.03	3.45
Diethylcarbamazine	GSK	Banocide 50 mg tablet 10	0.89	1.17	3.44	31.31	10
		Banocide 50 mg tablet 100	0.09	0.56	0.03	531.31	10
		Banocide forte 50 mg tablet 30	0.77	1.02	96.53	31.3	10
Griseofulvin (250 mg)	GSK	Griseofulvin Fp (Glaxo) 250 mg tablet 10	1.25	1.54	0.16	23.14	4
		Grisovin 250 mg tablet 10	1.24	1.54	14.05	24.24	4
		Grisovin Fp 250 mg tablet 10	1.24	1.54	85.67	24.24	4
		Grisovin Fp 250 mg tablet 40	0.31	1.56	0.12	396.81	4

Lamivudine + Stavudine + Nevirapine (150/30/200 mg)	Cipla	Triomune 150/30/200 mg tablet 30	16.83	22.1	98.17	31.25	7.12
		Triomune 150/30/200 mg tablet 60	8.42	10.52	0.06	25	7.12
		Triomune junior 150/30/200 mg tablet 10	59.92	74.9	0.04	25	7.12
		Triomune Junr 150/30/200 mg tablet 60	9.99	12.48	1.73	25	7.12
	Hetero	Nevilast 150/30/200 mg tablet 10	17.52	23	80.94	31.25	3.25
		Nevilast 150/30/200 mg tablet 30	16.76	22	18.83	31.25	3.25
		Nevilast baby 150/30/200 mg tablet 30	5.39	7	0.23	29.99	3.25
		Zidolam N 150/300/200 mg tablet 10	18.29	24	76.61	31.25	6.03
		Zidolam N 150/300/200 mg tablet 60	3.03	11.5	3.46	279.14	6.03
		Zidolam N Ecopack 150/300/200 mg tablet 30	17.52	23	19.93	31.25	6.03
Losartan (50 mg)	Unichem	Losar 50 mg tablet 10	4.78	6.28	78.02	31.27	3.05
		Losar 50 mg tablet 15	4.87	6.09	19.98	24.99	3.05
		Losar 50 mg tablet 20	4.78	6.28	1.51	31.27	3.05
		Losar 50 mg tablet 30	1.59	5.2	0.48	226.09	3.05
	Zydus	Losacar 50 mg tablet 10	3.71	4.52	92.75	21.8	2.15
		Losacar 50 mg tablet 7	7.97	10.35	0.89	29.88	2.15
		Losacar Wp 50 mg tablet 30	4.74	6.17	6.36	30.11	2.15
Losartan (25 mg)		Losacar 25 mg tablet 10	2.15	2.63	92.28	21.81	2.08
		Losacar 25 mg tablet 7	4.48	5.83	2.9	30.11	2.08
		Losacar Wp 25 mg tablet 30	2.66	3.47	4.83	30.11	2.08
Metformin (500 mg)	Cipla	Diacip 500 mg tablet 10	0.96	1.2	0.05	24.74	2.88
		Exermet 500 mg tablet 10	1.52	2	95.47	31.23	2.88
		Glumet 500 mg tablet 10	0.53	0.7	1.89	31.32	2.88
		Metfor 500 mg tablet 10	0.8	1.15	0.02	43.75	2.88
		Okamet 500 mg tablet 10	0.8	1.64	2.58	105	2.88

(continued)

Table 3.5 (continued)

Medicine	Company	SKU	PTR	MRP	SKU share in company	Margin	PTR/Min PTR
Ofloxacin (200 mg)	Abbott	Chekmet 200 mg tablet 10	2.1	3.67	40.44	74.9	3.24
		Floxid (Nicholas) 200 mg tablet 10	0.77	5.5	0.14	609.68	3.24
		Nicoflox(Phc) 200 mg tablet 10	0.88	6.5	0.23	642.86	3.24
		Piraflox 200 mg tablet 10	2.51	3.3	59.19	31.26	3.24
	Alkem	Oflokem 200 mg tablet 10	1	6.5	10.58	550	2.68
		Qmax 200 mg tablet 10	0.75	7.1	0.99	846.67	2.68
		Ronflox 200 mg tablet 10	2.01	2.63	88.42	31.23	2.68
	Cipla	Oflox 200 mg tablet 10	6.71	8.8	98.82	31.25	6.73
		Okaflox 200 mg tablet 10	1.1	8.3	0.48	654.55	6.73
		Olox 200 mg tablet 10	5.71	7.49	0.24	31.27	6.73
		Tariflox 200 mg tablet 10	1	7.56	0.31	659.04	6.73
		Zocare 200 mg tablet 10	4	5	0.15	25	6.73
	Elder	Aoxin 200 mg tablet 10	3.62	4.75	2.46	31.25	3.62
		Eldeflox 200 mg tablet 10	1	8.75	0.28	775	3.62
		Ofvista 200 mg tablet 10	2.68	3.5	97.26	30.35	3.62
Omeprazole (20 mg)	Alkem	Omee 20 mg capsule 15	0.6	4.17	57.11	594.44	5.04
		Omepraz 20 mg capsule 10	0.77	4.6	0.34	499.74	5.04
		Omepraz 20 mg capsule 15	3.03	3.93	42.55	30.01	5.04
	Cadila	Nogacid 20 mg capsule 10	0.9	6.29	3.2	601.45	5.59
		Nogacid 20 mg capsule 15	0.67	4.17	5.95	525	5.59
		Olit 20 mg capsule 10	3.72	4.85	90.86	30.13	5.59
	Cipla	Lomac 20 mg capsule 10	5.41	7.05	1.01	30.34	9.01
		Lomac 20 mg capsule 15	3.61	4.7	56.46	30.34	9.01
		Okacid 20 mg capsule 10	0.8	3.82	0.21	378	9.01
		Okacid 20 mg capsule 15	0.63	3.67	33.25	485.11	9.01
		Omecip 20 mg capsule 15	0.6	3.67	8.34	511.11	9.01

		Omeprazole(Cip) 20 mg capsule 10	1.57	3.3	0.73	109.79	9.01
	Mankind	Oskar 20 mg capsule 10	1.51	1.98	77.68	31.21	2
		Oskar 20 mg capsule 12	1.26	1.65	19.68	31.21	2
		Oskar 20 mg capsule 6	2.52	3.3	2.64	31.21	2
	Micro	Fact 20 mg capsule 10	3.05	4	1.05	31.23	11.9
		Omicap 20 mg capsule 10	9.52	12.5	98.94	31.25	11.9
		Ozec 20 mg capsule 10	0.8	6.8	0.01	750	11.9
Ondansetron (4 mg)	Indswift	Ondisolv 4 mg tablet 10	5.26	6.9	60.42	31.25	6.92
		Onswift 4 mg tablet 10	6.78	8.9	38.88	31.25	6.92
		Vomigo 4 mg tablet 10	0.98	7.15	0.69	629.59	6.92
Paracetamol (500 mg)	Alkem	P U C 500 mg tablet 10	0.81	1.06	36.8	31.19	4.9
		Paracetamol(Alkem) 500 mg tablet 10	0.19	0.55	0.17	189.47	4.9
		Pyrakem (oval) 500 mg tablet 1000	0.17	0.25	24.37	51.52	4.9
		Pyrakem 500 mg tablet 10	0.28	0.75	3.14	167.86	4.9
		Pyrakem 500 mg tablet 1000	0.17	0.21	25.24	20	4.9
		Pyricool 500 mg tablet 15	0.27	1.17	10.27	337.5	4.9
	Cipla	Actiflu 500 mg tablet 10	0.9	3.8	0.25	322.22	7.48
		Cipmol 500 mg tablet 10	0.39	1.02	1.32	161.54	7.48
		Panacip 500 mg tablet 10	0.81	1.02	0.2	26.08	7.48
		Paracetamol (Cipla) 500 mg tablet 10	0.28	0.6	3.87	114.29	7.48
		Paracip 500 mg tablet 10	0.36	1.1	72.32	205.56	7.48
		Parafast 500 mg tablet 10	0.84	1.1	0.36	31.26	7.48
		Parafast 500 mg tablet 4	2.1	2.75	21.68	31.26	7.48
	Exotic Lab	Eboo (Exotic lab) 500 mg tablet 10	2.7	3.5	64.97	29.58	9.61
		Eboo (Exotic lab) kid 500 mg tablet 10	0.76	0.99	16.98	29.75	9.61
		Eboo plus (Exotic lab) 500 mg tablet 10	7.33	9.5	8.79	29.62	9.61

(continued)

Table 3.5 (continued)

Medicine	Company	SKU	PTR	MRP	SKU share in company	Margin	PTR/Min PTR
		Eboo spaz (Exotic lab) 500 mg tablet 10	1.85	2.4	0.38	29.52	9.61
		Primol 500 mg tablet 10	0.93	1.2	7.69	29.59	9.61
		Primol plus (Exotic lab) 500 mg tablet 10	1.31	1.7	1.2	29.67	9.61
	GSK	Calpol 500 mg tablet 1000	0.32	0.45	9.9	41.57	4.98
		Calpol 500 mg tablet 15	0.92	1.2	74.85	30.15	4.98
		Calpol 500 mg tablet 500	0.34	0.47	0.67	36.98	4.98
		Crocin 500 mg tablet 15	1.05	1.36	13.95	28.96	4.98
		Crocin advance 500 mg tablet 15	1.59	2	0.64	26	4.98
	Ipca Lab	Pacimol 500 mg tablet 10	0.94	1.22	42.23	29.93	5.29
		Pacimol 500 mg tablet 1000	0.23	0.3	31.73	30.11	5.29
		Pacimol Xp 500 mg tablet 10	1.23	1.62	26.04	31.3	5.29
	Lupin	Lupicin 500 mg tablet 10	0.76	1	57.2	31.23	10.58
		Lupicin 500 mg tablet 4	1.9	2.5	5.71	31.23	10.58
		Lupipara 500 mg tablet 10	0.39	0.9	29.81	129.59	10.58
		Lupipara round 500 mg tablet 1000	0.18	0.3	7.28	66.67	10.58
Phenytoin (100 mg)	Mankind	Epiforce 100 mg tablet 10	13.33	16.67	12.75	25	11.68
		Epiforce 100 mg tablet 100	1.33	1.35	53.23	1.25	11.68
		Eptokind 100 mg tablet 100	1.52	1.9	32.79	25	11.68
		Neptoin 100 mg tablet 100	1.14	1.51	1.22	31.82	11.68
Primaquine (7.5 mg)	Leo	Leoprime 7.5 mg tablet 14	1.77	2.29	17.02	29.45	2.46
		Leoprime Forte 7.5 mg tablet 14	2.99	3.71	76.15	24.11	2.46
		Leoprime Kid 7.5 mg tablet 14	1.21	1.57	4.25	29.41	2.46
		Primelife 7.5 mg tablet 14	2.18	2.74	2.58	25.98	2.46

leading SKU when ranked by market share. For example, in the market for Albendazole 400 mg, Cipla produces three SKUs, Bendex, Tiobend, and X Worm with PTRs of Rs. 12.07, 3.3, and 1.65 respectively. The relatively more expensive brand, Bendex accounts for 98% of the sales of Albendazole 400 mg for Cipla, and it is more than seven times the price of X Worm. The retail margin for many of the medicines with lower PTR is exorbitantly high. For example, the retail margin for X Worm is 809%. The presence of such multiple versions reveals two insights. First, the marginal cost of production is closer to the lowest PTR, which is several times lower than the highest PTR. For Cipla, the marginal cost of production for Albendazole 400 mg is likely to be closer to Rs. 1.65 rather than Rs. 12.07. Second, the consumer does not benefit from the relatively lower PTR for an alternative brand, as the manufacturer sets similar MRPs across the multiple brands. For example, the MRPs of Bendex and X Worm are nearly identical at Rs. 15.7 and Rs. 15 although there is a huge discrepancy in their PTRs.

In summary, although pharmaceutical companies often complain that price control regulations are not necessary and that competition would lower prices, the nature of competition in the Indian pharmaceutical markets is limited, strengthening the case for a well-designed regulation (Basak 2008).

References

Basak, S. C. (2008). The genesis of drug price control. *PharmaBiz* [online]. Available from http://pharmabiz.com/ArticleDetails.aspx?aid=42905&sid=9

Beggs, A., & Klemperer, P. (1992). Multi-period competition with switching costs. *Econometrica: Journal of the Econometric Society, 60*, 651–666.

Bhaskarabhatla, A., Chatterjee, C., Anurag, P., & Pennings, E. (2017). Mitigating regulatory impact: The case of partial price controls on metformin in India. *Health Policy and Planning, 32*, 194–204.

Burkitt, L. (2014, May 8). China Scraps Price Caps on Low-Cost Drugs. *Wall Street Journal* [online]. Available from https://www.wsj.com/articles/china-scraps-price-caps-on-low-cost-drugs-1399525903

Burnham, T. A., Frels, J. K., & Mahajan, V. (2003). Consumer switching costs: A typology, antecedents, and consequences. *Journal of the Academy of Marketing Science, 31*(2), 109–126.

Datta-Chaudhuri, M. (2000). Market failure and government failure. *Journal of Economic Perspectives, 4*(3), 25–29.

Ellison, S. F., Cockburn, I., Griliches, Z., & Hausman, J. (1997). Characteristics of demand for pharmaceutical products: An examination of four cephalosporins. *The Rand Journal of Economics, 28*(3), 426–446.

Evans, R. (1974). *Supplier-induced demand: Some empirical evidence and implications*. London: Palgrave Macmillan.

Evans, V., & Pollock, A. (2015). The proliferation of irrational metformin fixed-dose combinations in India. *The Lancet Diabetes and Endocrinology, 3*(2), 98–100.

Farrell, J., & Shapiro, C. (1988). Dynamic competition with switching costs. *RAND Journal of Economics, 19*(1), 123–137.

Fornell, C. (1992). A national customer satisfaction barometer: The Swedish experience. *Journal of Marketing, 56*(1), 6–21.

Gillian, P., & Grills, N. (2016). Medication misuse in India: A major public health issue in India. *Journal of Public Health, 38*(2), 150–157.
Government of India. (1975). *Report of the committee on drugs and pharmaceutical industry (Hathi Committee Report) 1975*. New Delhi: Ministry of Petroleum & Chemicals.
Gulhati, C. M. (2004, December 2). Why drug price regulation? PharmaBiz.com
Joelving, F. (2015). India's "health camps": The drug rep will see you now. *British Medical Journal, 351*, h6413.
Kamat, V., & Nichter, M. (1998). Pharmacies, self-medication, and pharmaceutical marketing in Bombay, India. *Social Science and Medicine, 47*(6), 779–794.
Karakaya, F. (1989). Barriers to entry and market entry decisions in consumer and industrial goods markets. *Journal of Marketing, 53*(2), 80–91.
Kotwani, A., Wattal, C., Katewa, S., et al. (2010). Factors influencing primary care physicians to prescribe antibiotics in Delhi India. *Family Practice, 27*(6), 684–690.
Kotwani, A., Wattal, C., Joshi, P. C., et al. (2012). Irrational use of antibiotics and role of the pharmacist: An insight from a qualitative study in New Delhi, India. *Journal of Clinical Pharmacy and Therapeutics, 37*(3), 308–312.
Miller, R., & Catherine, G. (2016). Performance of retail pharmacies in low- and middle-income Asian settings: A systematic review. *Health Policy and Planning, 31*(7), 940–953.
Nalinakanthi, V. (2014). All you wanted to know about: DPCO. *The Hindu Business Line* [online]. Available from http://www.thehindubusinessline.com/opinion/all-you-wanted-to-know-about-dpco/article6458442.ece
Nautiyal, S. (2014a, July 22). Maha FDA writes to NPPA to bring medical devices under DPCO to curb profiteering. PharmaBiz.com
Nautiyal, S. (2014b, July 3). Hospitals making huge profit on simple disposables in collusion with stockists. PharmaBiz.com
Oldani, M. (2004). Thick prescriptions: Toward an interpretation of pharmaceutical sales practices. *Medical Anthropology Quarterly, 18*(3), 325–356.
Pant, S., Sah, A. K., & Khurana, A. K. (2016). *Report of the committee on high trade margins in sale of drugs*. Department of Pharmaceuticals, Government of India. Available online https://ideas.repec.org/p/ess/wpaper/id10219.html
Patel, V., Vaidya, R., Naik, D., et al. (2005). Irrational drug use in India: A prescription survey from Goa. *Journal of Postgraduate Medicine, 51*(1), 9–12.
Phadke, A., & Srinivasan, S. (2013). Pharma policy 2012 and its discontents. *Economic and Political Weekly, 48*(1), 38–42.
Pharmabiz. (2017, May 11). *Generics prescription: Stakeholders co-operation crucial*. Retrieved December 6, 2017, from http://pharmabiz.com/ArticleDetails.aspx?aid=102758&sid=21
Porter, M. E. (1980). *Competitive strategy* (p. 300). New York: Free Press.
Seeberg, J. (2012). Connecting pills and people: An ethnography of the pharmaceutical Nexus in Odisha, India. *Medical Anthropology Quarterly, 26*(2), 182–200.
Sharma, A., & Kaplan, W. (2016). Challenges constraining access to insulin in the private-sector market of Delhi, India. *BMJ Global Health, 1*(3), 1–13.
Singal, G., Nanda, A., & Kotwani, A. (2011). A comparative evaluation of price and quality of some branded versus branded-generic medicines of the same manufacturer in India. *Indian Journal of Pharmacology, 43*(2), 131–136.
Smetacek, R. (2016). Organisation of pharmaceutical producers of India replies to article on India's health camps. *British Medical Journal, 352*, i238.
Srinivasan, S. (1999). How many aspirins to the rupee? *Economical and Political Weekly, 34*(9), 514–518.
Steele, H. (1962). Monopoly and competition in the ethical drug market. *Journal of Law and Economics, 5*, 142–143.
Temin, P. (1980). *Taking your medicine*. Cambridge: Harvard University Press.

Waheed, A., Jaleel, M., & Laeequddin, M. (2011). Prescription loyalty behavior of physicians: an empirical study in India. *International Journal of Pharmaceutical and Healthcare Marketing, 5* (4), 279–298.
Walker, H. (1971). *Market power and price levels in the ethical drug industry*. Bloomington: Indiana University Press.
Zeithaml, V. A. (1981). How consumer evaluation pro cesses differ between goods and services. In J. Donnelly & W. George (Eds.), *Marketing of Services* (pp. 186–190). Chicago: American Marketing.

Part II
The Design of the 2013 DPCO Regulation

Chapter 4
The Proposed Design to Fix Ceiling Prices Under 2013 DPCO

4.1 Introduction

In previous chapters, we presented a brief overview of the history of pharmaceutical price regulation in India over a period of 4 decades and a case to motivate the need for regulating pharmaceutical prices in India in 2013. In this chapter, we examine the details of the 2013 DPCO design before we assess its success in limiting pharmaceutical prices. We begin by recalling the key differences between the 1995 and 2013 DPCO and describing the manner in which the ceiling price is estimated by the NPPA. The chapter not only anticipates the potential problems associated with the implementation of the design but also highlights how pharmaceutical firms can circumvent price controls.

4.2 Key Differences Between the 1995 and 2013 DPCO

Unlike the 1995 DPCO, which adopted a cost-based approach, the Indian regulators agreed to implement a market-based method for fixing the prices of essential medicines under the 2013 DPCO. While a government watch list of essential medicines was used to determine the set of medicines to be controlled under the 1995 DPCO, India used the 2011 version of the National List of Essential Medicines (NLEM) as the basis for the 2013 DPCO (Government of India 2011a, b). The 74 bulk drugs regulated under the 1995 DPCO accounted for nearly 40% of the overall market initially and the coverage reduced to 10% by the late 2000s (Malhotra 2010). However, 652 formulations of 348 medicines on the 2011 NLEM were regulated under the 2013 DPCO. Some preliminary estimates suggested that the coverage of the 2013 DPCO was 18% (Ray 2013). The medicines brought under regulation were narrowly defined under the 2013 DPCO based on the active pharmaceutical ingredient, the method of administration (e.g., tablet or injection) and the

A. Bhaskarabhatla, *Regulating Pharmaceutical Prices in India*, India Studies in Business and Economics, https://doi.org/10.1007/978-3-319-93393-1_4

dosage strength (e.g., 500 mg or 1000 mg)—and excluded other formulations of the same medicine and its fixed-dose combinations from any regulation. The government's decision to implement such a partial, market-based, price-cap regulation requires a clear specification of the manner in which the ceiling price will be determined. We describe the primary method used for fixing the ceiling price and alternative methods employed when the primary method cannot be implemented due to practical difficulties.

4.3 The Primary Method for Fixing the Ceiling Price Under 2013 DPCO

Under the market-based approach, the ceiling price of a medicine is proposed, in theory, to be the simple average of the prices of brands with at least 1% market share in the market for a medicine formulation. The use of the prices of brands with at least 1% market share to determine the ceiling price, in theory, avoids the potential inflation of the ceiling price if pharmaceutical firms launch higher-priced brands in the period before regulation to influence the ceiling price. While the proposal appears reasonable, in practice, several critical questions arise concerning the determination of the actual ceiling price. Which sources of data should the National Pharmaceutical Pricing Authority (NPPA) use to identify market prices? What prices should the NPPA use to determine the ceiling price? If prices at which retailers purchase medicines are used to determine the ceiling price as opposed to the maximum retail price, then how are the retail trade margins determined for the regulated medicines? What time period should the NPPA use to determine the market shares, as the identity of firms with more than 1% market share can change from month to month? In the previous version of the DPCO, firms exploited weaknesses to undermine the regulation. For example, Gulhati (2004) argues historically India's regulatory framework focused on the maximum resale price (MRP), when they should have focused on other indicators, such as transfer prices. Anecdotal evidence suggests that there was sometimes a large gap between MRP and transfer prices, meaning that companies could take advantage of this loophole (Gulhati 2004). These are some of the many practical questions that arise during the design and implementation of the policy and significantly affect its success.

To address these questions, India published the National Pharmaceutical Pricing Policy of 2012 on December 7, 2012 (Government of India 2012). According to the policy, the calculation of ceiling prices under 2013 DPCO is proposed to be based on the IMS Health dataset. IMS Health is an American company providing information, services, and technology for the healthcare industry across the world. Its Indian subsidiary compiles monthly data on the sales and prices of major pharmaceutical firms in India, disaggregated by individual medicine brands. According to the policy, the actual calculation of the ceiling price is to be performed by the NPPA. To determine the ceiling price, the NPPA is expected to calculate market shares for the period May 2012 to April 2013, but use IMS prices for the month of May 2012 to calculate the simple average of prices with more than 1% market share. At any time, the Indian government is allowed to validate these data using an appropriate survey or evaluation. Additionally, the government also has the possibility to collect its own market-based data, and such data are considered final under all conditions. The 2012 policy also requires all manufacturers, retailers, and dealers, including those of unregulated formulations, to issue a price list and supplementary price list showing conformity with price fixation and revision. In addition, the 2012 policy determined that the price at which retailers purchase the medicine is used to determine the average price to the retailer, and then a retailer margin of 16% is proposed to be added to obtain the final ceiling price. While the policy states these design choices, the government's thinking behind these choices, and the role played by various interest groups remain unspecified and unclear.

In summary, the ceiling price is determined in two steps. First, the simple average of price to the retailer (PTR) of all branded-generic and generic versions of a certain drug formulation with a market share of at least 1% is calculated. This is done on the basis of moving annual turnover of the particular drug. As a next step, a national retailer margin of 16% is added to the average price to retailer calculated under step one, using the following formula:

$$\mathrm{P(c)} = \mathrm{P(s)} * (1 + \mathrm{M}/100) \tag{4.1}$$

where, P(c) is the ceiling price, and P(s) is the simple average of the price to retailers for brands with more than 1% market share. The brands include all existing manufacturers as well as importers and marketers. A margin (M) of 16% is added to the simple average of the PTR. The ceiling price is scheduled to come into effect within a period of 45 days after notification. All existing manufacturers of the same formulation who are selling below ceiling price are required to maintain their existing maximum resale price (MRP). The ceiling price for the regulated formulations is calculated on the basis of dosage, that is, per one tablet or per one injection, and price ceilings for stock keeping units with varying package sizes are calculated as a simple multiplication with the number of tablets, capsules or injections in the package. In India, every manufacturer of both regulated and unregulated formulations is obliged to display the MRP of a certain formulation in ineffaceable print on the package, which, in theory, can facilitate enforcement activities and compliance with the DPCO. As Gulhati (2004) notes, the use MRP to fix price ceilings is problematic, which may be a reason for why the NPPA chose to focus on the PTR. However, the internal deliberations that led to these design choices remain undisclosed to the wider public.

4.4 An Illustrative Example of the Method for Fixing the Ceiling Price Under 2013 DPCO

We illustrate the determination of the ceiling price with an example. We use the case of Paracetamol, a widely used medicine in India for treating pain and fever. Paracetamol is one of the oldest and largest medicines sold in India by volume having been launched in May 1973. One of its brands is the largest brand, by volume, of any medicine in our Pharmatrac dataset (which we introduced in the previous chapter and use throughout the rest of the book). During a period of 67 months between January 2011 and August 2016, nearly 2.5 billion tablets of the largest Paracetamol brand, Calpol, were sold. During the period from May 2012 to April 2013, the year before the implementation of the 2013 DPCO, 118 different SKUs of the 500 mg Paracetamol tablet brands were present in the market. Among them, only 14 brands had a market share of at least 1%. They are shown in Table 4.1. The first column lists the stock keeping unit (SKU) and the second column lists the month and year of its launch. The third column contains the price to the retailer, and the fourth computes the price per one tablet of the SKU.

The table illustrates the considerable variation in the price of Paracetamol price per tablet among the 14 firms with more than 1% market share. Pacimol, at the top of the table, contains 1000 tablets per SKU and it is sold at a PTR of 232.5, translating to a per-tablet price of Rs. 0.23 (=232.5/1000). The average of the column labeled Price is 0.89, and the ceiling price is determined using Eq. (4.1) as 0.89*1.16 = 1.03. The ceiling price we computed is close to 0.99, the official ceiling price determined by the NPPA based on the IMS Health dataset. The marginal difference in prices is

Table 4.1 List of Paracetamol 500 mg tablet SKUs with more than 1% market share during May 2012 and April 2013

Stock keeping unit	Launch	PTR	PTR per tablet	Margin
Pacimol 500 mg tablet 1000	Dec-97	233	0.23	30.11
Calpol 500 mg tablet 1000	Feb-95	319	0.32	41.57
T98 500 mg tablet 10	Aug-06	7.62	0.76	31.23
P 500 mg tablet 10	Mar-03	8.22	0.82	30.17
Malidens 500 mg tablet 10	Feb-84	8.77	0.88	31.13
Dolo (Micro Labs) 500 mg tablet 15	May-07	13.7	0.91	31.29
Pyrigesic 500 mg tablet 10	May-73	9.21	0.92	30.29
Calpol 500 mg tablet 15	Apr-09	13.8	0.92	30.15
Pacimol 500 mg tablet 10	Apr-89	9.39	0.94	29.93
Fepanil 500 mg tablet 10	Jun-73	9.88	0.99	30.06
Xykaa Rapid 500 mg tablet 10	Mar-10	10.1	1.01	31.21
Crocin 500 mg tablet 15	Apr-07	15.8	1.05	28.96
Metacin 500 mg tablet 8	Feb-92	8.5	1.06	31.18
Crocin Advance 500 mg tablet 15	Aug-11	23.8	1.59	26

Source: Author's calculations
Data source: All India organization of chemists and druggists

due to the differences between the IMS and Pharmatrac datasets the NPPA, and we have employed respectively, but we will return to these differences in the next chapter. It is useful to note that while many SKUs were launched years before the 2013 DPCO, the highest-priced SKU in the list was launched in August of 2011 and its introduction inflates the ceiling price by pushing up the simple average of prices. Although the NPPA provides a 16% retail margin over the PTR, each SKU has provided a margin of around 30% in the period before the 2013 DPCO, where the margin is calculated as 100*(MRP-PTR)/PTR. How these margins have changed as a result of the DPCO is examined later in the book. The proponents of the cost-based regulation point to the relatively low price of some Paracetamol brands compared to the ceiling price, which suggests that the market-based method of determining the ceiling price leads to a price cap that is several times the marginal cost of production. We will return to these aspects as well later in the book. Nonetheless, the simple method of fixing the ceiling price is not applicable in all cases. The NPPA has devised alternative methods to fix the ceiling price in cases where there are insufficient firms to calculate a simple average. We discuss these exceptions in the next section.

4.5 Alternatives to the Primary Method for Fixing the Ceiling Prices

Under some conditions, the original stepwise calculation described in Sect. 4.3 cannot be implemented. For example, in cases where competition in a market for a particular formulation is limited or even absent, the original method described above would result in little to no reduction in average price to the retailer. To address such scenarios, the NPPA has generated three alternative methods to determine the ceiling price depending on whether other regulated strengths or dosage forms of the same scheduled formulation are available (Table 4.2).

First, if there are other regulated strengths or dosage forms of the same scheduled formulation, step 2 of the original method remains similar but the formula for calculating the average price to retailer changes as follows:

$$\mathrm{P(s)} = \mathrm{Pm}\,\{1 - (\mathrm{Pi1} + \mathrm{Pi2} + \cdots)/(\mathrm{N} * 100)\}.$$

The above formula first calculates Pi1, Pi2, and so on, which represent the percentage reduction in price to the retailer that would have occurred if the price ceiling mechanism were to be imposed on the unregulated dosage strength markets of the medicine. Subsequently, an average of such price reductions across unregulated dosage strength markets of the medicine is calculated, and it is multiplied by the medicine price in the regulated dosage strength market to determine the ceiling price. Therefore, the average price to the retailer is no longer a simple average of the prices of all versions of a drug formulation but uses the percentage difference

Table 4.2 Proposed calculation methods

Calculation methods	Average price to retailer P(s)	Average price to retailer P(s)	Margin to retailer (M) %	Price ceiling P(c)
Primary method		$P(s) = (Pi1 + Pi2 + \cdots)/(N*100)$	16	$P(c) = P(s).(1 + M/100)$
Alternative 1	When other regulated strengths or dosage forms of the same scheduled formulation are available	$P(s) = Pm\{1 - (Pi1 + Pi2 + \cdots)/(N*100)\}$	16	$P(c) = P(s).(1 + M/100)$
Alternative 2	When other scheduled formulations in the same sub-therapeutic category are available	$P(s) = Pm\{1 - (Pi1 + Pi2 + \cdots)/(N*100)\}$	16	$P(c) = P(s).(1 + M/100)$
Alternative 3	When only other scheduled formulations in the same therapeutic category are available	$P(s) = Pm\{1 - (Pi1 + Pi2 + \cdots)/(N*100)\}$	16	$P(c) = P(s).(1 + M/100)$

between the average PTR of other strengths and dosage forms and the highest priced formulation within the medicine dosage market to be regulated.

Second, if no other regulated strengths or dosage forms of the medicine formulation that is to be regulated are present in the market, other regulated formulations in the same sub-therapeutic category are considered as a reference group. In such cases, the average PTR in step 1 uses the percentage difference between the average PTR of other formulations in the same category and the PTR of the highest priced formulation within the medicine market to be regulated. When a particular formulation is listed under multiple sub-therapeutic categories, the lowest average PTR across categories is used for calculating the ceiling price.

Third, where no other strengths and dosage forms are available, and no other scheduled formulations in any similar sub-therapeutic categories exist, the average PTR is calculated using data from the same therapeutic categories. As with the sub-therapeutic categories, when the regulated formulation is covered by multiple therapeutic categories, the category average of the lowest PTR is considered.

4.6 Formulations Covered Under 2013 DPCO

Although some medicines are newly regulated under the 2013 DPCO, others carry over into the revised price control regime from the earlier version in 1995. The 2013 DPCO proposes a special price ceiling calculation method for such regulated formulations (also referred to as scheduled formulations). The 1995 DPCO contains a First and Second Schedule listing specifying formulations under regulation. Additionally, the 1995 DPCO includes formulations that are fixed and notified up to and after 31st, May 2012. Based on these distinctions, scheduled drugs under the provisions of the 1995 DPCO are divided into four categories: (i) those specified in First Schedule and notified under DPCO 1995 up to 31st, May 2012; (ii) those specified in First Schedule and notified under DPCO 1995 after to 31st, May 2012; (iii) those not specified in First Schedule and notified under DPCO 1995 up to 31st, May 2012; (iv) and those not specified in First Schedule and notified under DPCO 1995 after to 31st, May 2012. In all categories, prices remain effective for 1 year from the date of notification. For example, notifications up to May 31st, 2012 are applicable until May 30th, 2013. Thereafter, the traditional calculation method for fixing ceiling prices is applied. Only manufacturers of formulations in categories (i) and (ii) are allowed to revise their prices as per the annual wholesale price index prior to price fixation under the 2013 DPCO.

4.7 Price Fixation of New Drugs

In some cases, existing manufacturers of scheduled formulations introduce a new drug. The ceiling price of the new drug is determined based on current availability of the new drug in the domestic market. If the new drug is already available in the domestic market, the traditional calculation method for price fixation is applicable. The PTR of a new medicine that is not yet for sale in the domestic market is fixed by the government based on the principles of "Pharmacoeconomics," the branch of economics that uses cost-benefit, cost-effectiveness, cost-minimization, cost-of-illness and cost-utility analyses to compare pharmaceutical products and treatment strategies. A Standing Committee of Experts was formed to advise the Government on the PTR of the new drug. Existing manufacturers launching a new drug are obliged to request price approval from the government and are not permitted to sell for prices higher than the ceiling price. For fixing the ceiling price of new drugs, market-based data available for the month ending immediately before 6 months from receipt of the application for fixing the price of the new drug is used.

4.8 Exceptions to the Standard Procedure Under Paragraph 19 of the DPCO

Notwithstanding the preceding rules and alternative methods, the Indian government reserved the right to fix the ceiling price or a specific retail price of any unregulated formulation or brand under extraordinary circumstances that concern the public interest. These circumstances are detailed under the 19th paragraph of the 2013 DPCO, and such powers were briefly invoked, albeit with mixed results, in 2014 to control the prices of 108 cardiovascular and anti-diabetic medicines. Under the Paragraph 19 provisions, the government can call for an increase or decrease in the price ceiling to ensure optimal functioning of the regulation. In addition to ensuring affordable prices, the 2013 DPCO also states as an objective adequate availability and distribution of medicines. Consequently, whenever the ceiling price of a certain formulation leads to lower production and distorted allocation, the government is free to direct manufacturers to increase production and sell their formulations to public institutions. Also, the government monitors prices of unregulated medicines so that manufacturers do not increase the MRP of such medicines by more than 10% within a period of 12 months before the start of DPCO 2013. Although these safeguards are put in place to prevent shortages and sudden prices increases in regulated or substitute medicines, the question remains whether the prices of unregulated and regulated dosages of a medicine are similar or vastly different, as the DPCO was implemented.

The provisions of the DPCO 2013 do not at all apply to new drugs that are patented under the Indian Patent Act 1970 either as a product or process patent, developed through domestic R&D and not produced elsewhere for a period of

5 years. However, manufacturers with a new and inventive delivery system of a new drug are also exempted from the 2013 DPCO regulations. As noted in the introduction, the details on how to fix the prices of patented medicines remain under discussion.

4.9 Revision of Price Ceilings in the Future

Once set, the ceiling prices do not remain constant forever. In April each year, when India's financial year begins, the Indian government is required to revise ceiling prices of the regulated formulations. Subsequently, manufacturers have 45 days to ensure that their MRP does not exceed the revised ceiling price. The list of medicines in the 2013 DPCO are referred to as the first schedule, and the list can be amended by adding an additional list of medicines, referred to as the second schedule. The revision of ceiling prices for medicines in the first schedule is based on market-based data available for "the month ending immediately before 6 months of notification of revision in the first schedule." Manufacturers may, once a year in April, also increase the MRP on the basis of the wholesale price index. Such actions do not require any approval from the government, but the manufacturers must provide information about the revised MRPs. The government has the power to amend the first schedule of the DPCO 2013 and introduce a second schedule under the condition that reasons for amendment are clearly stated. The formulations that are removed from the first schedule are categorized as non-scheduled formulations, and they are no longer subject to price control regulation.

Additionally, every time the National List of Essential Medicines is revised, ceiling prices for all medicines, including the ones that are already part of the old list, are once again fixed. That is, the ceiling prices are determined afresh based on the simple average of the prices of brands with more than 1% market share in the 1-year period before the revision of the ceiling prices. The procedure is followed once every 5 years from the date of fixing the ceiling price under the 2013 DPCO or when the NLEM is revised.

India used May 2012 prices to determine the ceiling prices initially and revised the ceiling prices using data from August 2015, following the revision of NLEM in 2015.

References

Government of India. (2011a). *National list of essential medicines, 2011*. New Delhi: Ministry of Chemicals and Fertilizers.

Government of India. (2011b). *National pharmaceutical pricing policy, 2011 (NPPP-2011)*. New Delhi: Ministry of Chemicals and Fertilizers.

Government of India. (2012). *National pharmaceutical pricing policy, 2012*. New Delhi: Ministry of Chemicals and Fertilizers.

Gulhati, C. M. (2004). Why drug price regulation. *PharmaBiz* [online]. Available from http://pharmabiz.com/ArticleDetails.aspx?aid=24980&sid=21

Malhotra, P. (2010). *The impact of TRIPS on India: An access to medicines perspective*. London: Palgrave Macmillan.

Ray, T. J. (2013). *New drug price control order of India: Is it directionally right improving access to medicines?* [online]. Available from http://www.tapanray.in/new-drug-price-control-order-of-india-is-it-directionally-right-improving-access-to-medicines/

Chapter 5
Challenges with Fixing the Ceiling Price Under the 2013 DPCO

5.1 Introduction

In the previous chapter, we elaborated on the design of the 2013 DPCO and the procedure used for fixing ceiling prices under the newly-adopted market-based approach. Although it may appear relatively simple, the determination of the ceiling prices is associated with multiple challenges related to data availability, data selection, data collection, and data analysis. The lack of sufficient data and the use of inaccurate data can result in a miscalculation of the ceiling prices and create confusion among pharmaceutical companies, NGOs, and consumers, and lead to several legal disputes. The effectiveness of the 2013 DPCO will be judged based not only on the extent to which prices of essential medicines decline but also by comparing the ceiling prices resulting from the market-based approach with those that would result from using a cost-based approach. Soon after the implementation of the 2013 DPCO, some industry observers argued that the ceiling prices set by the NPPA were much higher relative to those resulting from a cost-based pricing mechanism that was previously in place. They noted that the new policy "institutionalized the super profits" (Alexander 2013a). The profit margins under the new price ceilings were estimated to be over 1000% in some cases. Moreover, the NGOs blamed the government for not sharing the data it collects from IMS and for not collecting its own data and corroborating them with other alternative sources. Are the criticisms of the 2013 DPCO design and implementation valid? In this chapter, we take a quantitative approach to examining the challenges that arose in determining the ceiling prices based on the new design and in implementing the 2013 DPCO. We begin by documenting the cases in which the pharmaceutical firms contested the NPPA's calculations and then present analyses to characterize the nature and extent of such disputes.

A. Bhaskarabhatla, *Regulating Pharmaceutical Prices in India*, India Studies in Business and Economics, https://doi.org/10.1007/978-3-319-93393-1_5

5.2 Pharmaceutical Firms Contested the Ceiling Prices Fixed by the NPPA

Four years since the start of the DPCO 2013, several inaccuracies in determining the ceiling price, which could defeat the purpose of the policy directive, have become apparent. The Department of Pharmaceuticals received a number of review petitions challenging the manner in which the NPPA calculated the ceiling price and seeking alternative pricing for their products based on packaging or other characteristics (Shankar 2016a). The NPPA began receiving such complaints as early as 2013, and several firms have been successful in convincing the Department of Pharmaceuticals that the NPPA's calculations were incorrect, as PharmaBiz.com (2013a, b) reports:

> The Delhi High Court has sent notices to the Centre and the National Pharmaceutical Pricing Authority (NPPA) as seven more companies moved the court to question the newly revised prices of formulations as per the Drug Price Control Order (DPCO) 2013. The Court sent notices to the Centre and others including NPPA on a petition filed by the Indian Drug Manufacturers Association (IDMA) on the issue of drug pricing...The companies are Novartis, Wockhardt Limited, Lupin Limited, Intas Pharmaceuticals Limited, Alembic Pharmaceuticals Limited, Sandoz Private Limited and Chiron Behring Vaccines Private Limited. Cipla Ltd and four other companies had moved the court against the 2013 DCPO and won the similar order from the High Court recently.

The basis for contesting the NPPA's ceiling prices often involves issues about the validity of the data used for determining the ceiling prices. For example, in February 2017, the Department of Pharmaceuticals advocated a re-fixation of the retail price of a fixed-dose combination medicine, Teneligliptin 20 mg + Metformin 1000 mg extended-release tablets, produced by Glenmark, as the NPPA previously used incorrect data while fixing the retail price of these formulations. When the NPPA revised the ceiling price using Pharmatrac data, the ceiling price increased by more than 10% from Rs. 11.65 to Rs. 13.02 per tablet (Shankar 2017a).

We compile a list of 22 cases where the Department of Pharmaceuticals ordered the NPPA to revise the ceiling price (see Table 5.1). We are not certain these are all the cases that the NPPA received, but these cases have been reported in an online trade journal, PharmaBiz.com. We found four cases in 2015, eight cases in 2016, and nine cases in 2017, indicating that the number of such complaints is increasing. We preview some of the objections raised unsuccessfully by the pharmaceutical companies. First, some drug companies have criticized the NPPA for failing to differentiate the consumer and dispensing pack while calculating ceiling prices. In general, dispensing packs are for use in hospitals and are therefore of larger size, sometimes containing 1000 tablets of paracetamol as opposed to 10 tablets. Combining the PTR of consumer and dispensing packs to work out average PTR for ceiling price determination generates a lower ceiling price as packs show wide variation in PTR per tablet or injection. For example, for Metoclopramide syrup 5 mg/5 ml consumer packs have a PTR ranging between Rs. 0.38 per ml and Rs. 0.44 per ml, while the PTR per unit of the dispensing pack is only Rs. 0.16 per ml. As Shankar (2014a) notes:

> The DPCO, 2013 does not distinguish between sales through retailer shop or through hospital outlets. It is only the "Price to retailer," which is captured by IMS, that is taken

Table 5.1 Department of Pharmaceuticals directs NPPA to revalidate data, re-fix ceiling price under 2013 DPCO

Department of Pharmaceuticals' directive to the NPPA	Date	Year
Review ceiling price fixed for Azithromycin	31-Oct	2013
Revalidate data on Ciprofloxacin tablet 250 mg	16-Feb	2015
Revalidate data on Cefotaxime 250 mg and 500 mg injections	4-Mar	2015
Revise prices of Ilaprazole + Domperidone capsules	3-Jun	2015
Re-fix price of Nab Tortaxel injection	28-Jul	2015
Re-fix ceiling price of Clotrimazole cream 1%	12-Jul	2016
Examine new data to review ceiling price of Erythropoietin injection 2000 IU & 10,000 IU	18-Jul	2016
Re-fix ceiling price of Azithromycin and Dexamethasone phosphate eye drops 3 ml	30-Aug	2016
Re-fix ceiling price of coagulation factor VIII	12-Sep	2016
Revise ceiling prices of Paclitaxel injection, Carboplatin, and Cisplatin	27-Sep	2016
Re-fix and re-notify ceiling prices of Cefotaxime 1 g injection	21-Oct	2016
Adopt correct methodology in fixing ceiling price of Ciprofloxacin 500 and 250 mg tabs	12-Dec	2016
Re-fix ceiling price of levoflexacin 500 mg	24-Oct	2016
Re-fix prices of Methotrexate 2.5 mg, 7.5 mg, and 10 mg tabs	3-May	2017
Re-fix ceiling price of Ondansetron 2 mg/ml injectables	5-Jan	2017
Revise ceiling price of formulation Methyldopa 500 mg tablet	12-Jan	2017
Re-fix ceiling price of Ranitidine 25 mg/ml	1-Jun	2017
Re-fix ceiling price of N-acetylcyseine 200 mg sachet	14-Aug	2017
Re-fix the ceiling price of Furosemide injection	31-Aug	2017
Re-fix ceiling prices of clomiphene 100 mg and 50 mg tablets	18-Sep	2017
Re-fix ceiling price of Co-Trimoxazole tablet	21-Sep	2017
Seek expert committee's opinion for fixing ceiling price of methylprednisolone Inj 40 mg/ml	3-Oct	2017

Source: Alexander (2013b), Shankar (2016b, c, d, e, f, g, h, i), Shankar (2017b, c, d, e, f, g, h, i, j, k)

> into account for the calculation of ceiling price. Therefore, any such further classification or exclusion of hospital sales may not be in line with provisions of DPCO, 2013.

Second, pharmaceutical firms argued that the NPPA included SKUs with less than 1% market share in determining the ceiling price. Reacting to complaints, the Department of Pharmaceuticals ordered the NPPA to follow the correct procedure in fixing the ceiling price by averaging the prices of brands with more than 1% market share rather than using aggregated market share at the company level (Shankar 2016d):

> The Department of Pharmaceuticals (DoP) has directed the NPPA to adopt the correct methodology in all such cases of calculating the ceiling price of scheduled formulations like ciprofloxacin 500 mg and ciprofloxacin 250 mg tablets as per para 4(i) of DPCO, 2013 and provisions of existing Schedule-I by including market shares of only generic/brands and not company-wise MAT [moving average turnover] percentage.

Third, pharmaceutical firms argued that the NPPA did not follow its own rules in determining the ceiling price by excluding newly entering SKUs with more than 1% market share. Responding to one case, where Volitra AQ injection containing 75 mg/ml diclofenac produced by Sun Pharmaceuticals was excluded from the calculation of the ceiling price, the Department of Pharmaceuticals asked the NPPA to not invent its own rules (Shankar 2017j):

> Review application of the company is accepted, and NPPA is directed to re-fix the price as per the provisions of DPCO 2013 within one month of this Order, rather than deciding the prices on its own derived principles which are beyond the provisions of DPCO 2013. The calculation sheets should also be put up in the public domain.

In a similar case, Torrent Pharmaceuticals argued that it intends to market Nab Tortaxel injection 100 mg, which is being manufactured by Panacea Biotech (Shankar 2015a). Torrent markets Paclitaxel injection, but the NPPA did not take into account the new SKU in determining the ceiling price. Torrent also argued that Zydus is also marketing the formulation supplied by Panacea at a retail price of Rs. 11,640, but it is ignored.

Fourth, pharmaceutical companies argued that the PTR used by the NPPA is incorrect. For example, Alkem argued that IMS Health did not revise its data after the company revised its prices based on the wholesale price index, as stated under paragraph 10 of the 2013 DPCO (Shankar 2015b).

Fifth, many pharmaceutical companies compared IMS and Pharmatrac figures to contest the ceiling prices. For example, Zydus argued that its 250 mg ciprofloxacin tablets sold under the brand name Cirpobid were ignored by the NPPA although the Pharmatrac data show that the brand has a market share of 23% (Shankar 2015c). Similarly, Baxter India argued that its SKU with more than 80% market share was not considered in determining the ceiling price for the medicine, Coagulation Factor VIII (Shankar 2016f).

Sixth, some cases involved pharmaceutical firms questioning whether the NPPA mistakenly determined the ceiling price of some medicines using alternative methods described in Chap. 4. For example, Aristo argued that the ceiling price of the combination medicine ilaprazole + domperidone was fixed under the assumption that the market was a monopoly, but there were five SKUs with more than 1% market share (Shankar 2015d). Similarly, Glenmark argued that NPPA missed several relevant SKUs in determining the ceiling price of Clotrimazole cream (Shankar 2015e).

Seventh, in many cases the NPPA used company-level market share rather than SKU-level market share in determining the ceiling price. For example, Sun Pharmaceuticals argued that the ceiling price of Ciprofloxacin was incorrectly established by using 13 and 15 SKUs for the two different doses, but only 8 SKUs were relevant. The NPPA, it was alleged, included some SKUs no longer marketed by the company.

Eighth, several companies raised questions about the manner in which the NPPA dealt with the pricing of injections. For example, Cadila argued that liquid injection and powder injection prices should be set differently (Shankar 2017k).

Although the Department of Pharmaceuticals has directed the NPPA to revise the ceiling price in a few cases documented above, there are a large number of instances where the Department of Pharmaceuticals and the NPPA refused to revise the ceiling

Table 5.2 Department of Pharmaceuticals rejects the review petitions challenging the NPPA's method of calculating ceiling prices

Company	Medicine regulated under DPCO 2013	Date	Year
Dr. Reddy's	Omeprazole 20 mg capsules	29-Oct	2013
Abbott	Phenobabitone tablets, 60 mg, and 30 mg and promethazine injection, 25 mg/ml	29-Oct	2013
Sun Pharma	Isosorbide 5 mononitrate tablet (10 mg), pantoprazole injection (40 mg), ondansetron injection (2 mg/ml) atorvastatin tablets (10 mg) and alprazolam tablets (0.25 mg)	6-Jan	2014
Unichem	Warfarin sodium tablets (5 mg), olanzapine tablet (10 mg), albendazole tablets (400 mg), albendazole suspension (200 mg/5 ml), atorvastatin tablets (10 mg), alprazolam (0.25 mg), tramadol capsule (50 mg), cetrizine tablets (10 mg) and alprazolam (0.5 mg).	6-Jan	2014
Panacea Biotec	Oral Poliomyelitis Vaccine (LA) Solution	6-Jan	2014
Win-Medicare	Povidone iodine oinment 5%	6-Jan	2014
Modi-Mundipharma	Povidone iodine oinment 5%	6-Jan	2014
Wockhardt	Povidone iodine solution 5%, povidone iodine ointment 5% and human insulin injections	10-Jan	2014
Albert David	Glucose Injection 10%	27-Feb	2014
Baxter, etc.	Ringer lactate injection	27-Feb	2014
Indi Pharma	Clindamycin tablets (300 mg)	27-Feb	2014
Gland Pharma	Heparin sodium injection (5000 IU/ml);	27-Feb	2014
Adcock Ingram	Metoclopramide injection 5 mg/ml;	27-Feb	2014
Synchem Laboratories	Oral rehydration salts powder for solution	27-Feb	2014
Neon Laboratories	Lignocaine hydrochloride + adrenaline injection (2% + adrenaline 1:200000)	27-Feb	2014
Lifestar Pharma	Calamine Lotion	14-Mar	2014
Kedrion S.p.A	Antitetanus human immunoglobulin 250 IU/pack	14-Mar	2014
Ranbaxy	Ciprofloxacin HCl injection	27-May	2015
Parenteral Drugs	Glucose inj 10% & mannitol 20% 100 ml	8-Jun	2015
Lifecare Innovations	Amphotericin B injection	8-Jul	2015
Panacea Biotec	Amphotericin B injection (50 mg)	16-Jul	2015
Pregna	Hormone Releasing IUD	27-Jul	2016
Abbott India	Carbimazole 10 mg tablet	4-Oct	2016
Sanofi	Amiodarone tablet 200 mg	14-Nov	2016
Micro Labs	Paracetamol 500 mg tablets	24-Nov	2016
Sun Pharma	Ciprofloxacin HCl tablet 250 mg	6-Dec	2016
Sanofi India	Sodium valproate 200 and 500 mg tabs; amiodarone tablets 100 mg; leflunomide 10 and 20 mg tabs	23-Dec	2016
Sun Pharma	Volini Duo (Acetaminophen 650 mg extended-release tablets)	27-Dec	2016
Sun Pharma	Ondansetron tablet	2-Jan	2017
USV	Amlodipine 5 mg, clopidogrel 75 mg tablets	30-Jan	2017

(continued)

Table 5.2 (continued)

Company	Medicine regulated under DPCO 2013	Date	Year
IPCA	Paracetamol tablet	6-Mar	2017
Sanofi India	Enoxaparin 40 mg/0.4 ml and enoxaparin 60 mg/0.6 ml	10-Mar	2017
Boehringer Ingelheim	Hyoscine butyl bromide injection	25-Apr	2017
Wockhardt	Povidone iodine solution 5%	24-May	2017
Sun Pharma	Lithium 300 mg	23-Jun	2017

Source: PharmaBiz.com

price based on questionable claims made by the pharmaceutical firms. We list such instances in Table 5.2. These disputes also provide a window into the challenges faced by the NPPA in implementing the 2013 DPCO and the tactics and strategies employed by the pharmaceutical companies. We document relatively more complaints that were rejected by the Department of Pharmaceuticals than those that were accepted, indicating that the pharmaceutical companies used the legal process to delay compliance with the regulation and also weaken enforcement. Francis (2014) summarizes the difficulty the Department of Pharmaceuticals and the NPPA experienced in fixing the ceiling prices under the 2013 DPCO:

> As in the case of earlier DPCOs, Department of Pharmaceuticals and National Pharmaceutical Pricing Authority are finding it difficult to fix and enforce new prices for 348 drugs covered under DPCO 2013 even after several months of its notification. Wherever NPPA finds scope for a reduction or only a marginal hike in prices of products, such decisions are challenged by the pharmaceutical companies seeking higher prices. Over two dozen large companies have already disputed ceiling prices fixed for several products and approached for a review during the last six months. Some of these companies are Sun Pharma, Unichem Labs, Panacea Biotec, Win-Medicare, Albert David, Baxter (India), Indi Pharma and Gland Pharma. In many cases, DoP or NPPA rejected the claims of these companies seeking higher prices for want of justification.

In the rest of the chapter, we examine using Pharmatrac data the nature and extent of these disputes between the NPPA and the pharmaceutical firms.

5.3 Disputes Due to Lack of Authentic Data

The NPPA fixed the ceiling price of 150 medicines on June 14, 2013, and 39 medicines on June 21, 2013, using the data provided by IMS Health. The NPPA also made public the calculations it performed to arrive at the ceiling price. The NPPA's reliance on the data collected by IMS Health has been criticized by several observers. For example, Francis (2014) notes:

> Now, the leading pharmaceutical companies are pointing out that the basis of price fixation by NPPA is not accurate as they consider IMS Health data used by NPPA does not represent the real prices. Following these complaints, DoP has directed NPPA to revalidate the data

> used for capping prices of all notified medicines. NPPA accordingly started seeking cost details of drugs from individual companies. Till then drug prices notified by NPPA has to be maintained by the companies... The basic problem with the NPPA is that it does not have reliable data for finalizing prices of controlled drugs as it is solely depending on IMS Health. Out of the 348 drugs, NPPA is yet to fix prices of 100 odd drugs for want of data. Some of the pharmaceutical companies are of the view now that the basis of price fixation by NPPA is not accurate as they consider IMS Health data used by NPPA does not represent the real prices.

Similarly, Phadke and Srinivasan (2013) note:

> The datasets of IMS Health are from a provider of information related to the pharma industry, and are methodologically neither robust nor reliable, and limited in its coverage.

To study the potential discrepancy in the ceiling prices resulting from alternative data sources, we compare the ceiling prices determined by the NPPA for the first batch of medicines in June 2013 with alternative price ceilings we calculated using the AIOCD's Pharmatrac data. To illustrate the differences between the two datasets, we begin by focusing on the case of Acyclovir, as it is the first item contained in the work sheet released on the 14th of June 2013.[1] We reproduce in Table 5.3 calculations presented by the NPPA as well as the prices and market shares observed in the Pharmatrac data. Table 5.3 contains 16 SKUs from the IMS data used by the NPPA, of which eight have more than 1% market share. The average of the per tablet PTR for these eight SKUs is Rs. 5.3 and an addition 16% retailer margin results in a ceiling price of $5.3 \times 1.16 = 6.14$. However, the NPPA considers 11 SKUs to fix the ceiling price at 7.3, nearly 19% more than the ceiling price of 6.14. We will return to this discrepancy in greater detail momentarily, but seven of the 16 SKUs in the IMS data are not present in the Pharmatrac data, and six of the 15 SKUs in the Pharmatrac data are not present in the IMS data. Nonetheless, there are some similarities between the numbers obtained from the two datasets. For example, Cipla's Acivir brand has the highest market share in both datasets, although there is a 3.3% difference in market share. In fact, the top four SKUs remain the same in both datasets. In addition, the PTR per tablet also matches in several cases between the two tablets.

Many of the SKUs of Acyclovir missing from both datasets are relatively small with market shares of less than 1%, indicating that such inconsistencies between datasets do not necessarily affect the ceiling price for this medicine. However, the market shares computed using the two methods differed significantly in two of the top three SKUs. There are also some differences in PTR between the two tables. Overall, there are eight SKUs, whose average per-tablet price is 5.77 and the resulting ceiling price would be $5.77 \times 1.16 = 6.69$. Although the ceiling price determined using the AIOCD Pharmatrac data is higher than that obtained from the IMS data, it is still lower compared to the ceiling price fixed by the NPPA.

The NPPA's difficulty in fixing the ceiling prices of several medicines came to light because it was not able to put together sufficient market data. For example, at

[1]The NPPA's worksheet displaying their calculations for determining the ceiling price is available online at: http://www.nppaindia.nic.in/ceiling/press14june13/workingsheet-14-6-13.html

Table 5.3 Comparing the ceiling prices for Acyclovir 200 mg using IMS Health and AIOCD Pharmatrac prices and market shares

			PTR	Share	PTR	Share
			Data source			
No	Company	SKU	IMS		Pharmatrac	
1	Cipla	Acivir Tabs Dispers 200 mg × 10	6.19	39.8	6.19	43.1
2	Glaxosmithkline	Zovirax Tab Uncoated 200 mg × 5	6.52	21.1	6.52	20.64
3	Fdc	Ocuvir Tabs Dispers 200 mg × 10	4.84	11.7	4.84	15.75
4	Torrent Pharma	Herpex Tab Uncoated 200 mg × 10	6.72	9	6.66	6.64
5	Fdc	Ocuvir Tab Uncoated 200 mg × 10	4.84	8		
6	Micro Labs	Herperax Tab Uncoated 200 mg × 5	5.1	4.4	5.1	4.91
7	Mankind	Herpikind Tabs Dispers 200 mg × 10	3.27	3.6	4.56	4.94
8	Veritaz Healthcare Ltd	Acivex 200 mg Tablet Dt 10			6.2	1.25
9	East India	Trikase 200 mg Tablet 10	4.97	1	6.05	1.07
10	Ind-Swift	Aclovir Tabs Dispers 200 mg × 10	3.29	0.6	1.85	0.03
11	Micro Labs	Herperax Tab Uncoated 200 mg × 10	5.08	0.5	2.55	0.76
12	Samarth Pharma	Axovir Tabs 200 mg × 10	4.11	0.4		
13	Micro Labs	Herperax Tabs 200 mg × 6	14.81	0.1		
14	Agio Pharma	Aciherpin Tabs 200 mg × 10	4.57	0		
15	East India	Trinase Tab Uncoated 200 mg × 10	5.64	0		
16	Vhb Lifesciences	Zoylex Tabs Dispers 200 mg × 10	5.84	0		
17	Maneesh Pharma	Clovirax Tabs Dispers 200 mg × 5	4.68	0		
18	Ipca Laboratories Pvt Ltd.	Ocurax 200 mg Tablet 10			5.03	0.33
19	Alkem Laboratories Ltd.	Herpesafe 200 mg Tablet Dt 5			4.88	0.23
20	Monichem Healthcare Pvt Ltd	Zovistar 200 mg Tablet 10			4.58	0.15
21	Alkem Laboratories Ltd.	Herpesafe 200 mg Tablet Dt 10			2.44	0.12
22	Dial Pharmaceuticals Pvt. Ltd.	Rivol 200 mg Tablet 10			4.59	0.03

the beginning of 2017, the government responded to the public pressure to regulate the prices of coronary stents, but the NPPA faced difficulties in compiling the data on prices (Shankar 2017l). Since pharmaceutical firms want to keep their orders private, the collection data on market shares has been challenging for the NPPA even during the implementation of the 1995 DPCO. Over the years, most pharmaceutical companies and importers have been reluctant to share authentic, accurate industry data with the Indian government. If such data are compiled, the NPPA can potentially use them to improve compliance with price controls. The non-cooperation by drug companies has forced the NPPA to develop its own database of pharmaceutical prices, called the Indian Pharmaceutical Database Management System (IPDMS) in 2015. As Alexander (2013c) notes,

> With a view to further tightening the monitoring process of prices of non-scheduled formulations in the market, the National Pharmaceutical Pricing Authority (NPPA) has started collecting information directly from the drug manufacturers. "NPPA has already taken initiative to collect information directly from the manufacturers. Almost 7000 manufacturers have already been addressed to submit required information. Moreover, making a provision for filing of information online will further facilitate collection of information," sources said. Currently, the NPPA depends fully on samples collected by a single agency – IMS Health- to monitor and fix the prices as the agency has not sufficient staffed to gather samples from the market on its own. The new move is aimed at reducing the dependency on IMS in the long run.

The NPPA has also moved away from the use of data exclusively from IMS Health in its subsequent revisions of the ceiling prices. According to Shankar (2017m):

> Ceiling price has been fixed based on the data provided by IMS for the month of May, 2012 under NLEM 2011 and the data provided by [AIOCD] pharmatrac for the month of August, 2015 under NLEM 2015 as per existing practice.

The problems, however, have continued to arise even in the recent revision of ceiling prices in 2015. To illustrate further, consider the case of fixing the ceiling prices for Abbott's Clomiphene 50 mg and 100 mg tablets. Abbott argued that NPPA used Rs. 104.64 as PTR for Clome 100 mg tablet 10s, but the correct PTR from August 2015 is Rs. 107.56 (Shankar 2017h). Also, Abbott claimed that NPPA incorrectly used the same PTR for both Fertomid 100 mg Tablets 10s and Fertomid 100 mg Tablets 5s of Cipla in calculating the ceiling price but the IMS data contain only the Fertomid 100 mg tablets 5 SKU. Similarly, Abbott argued that to determine the ceiling price of Clomiphene 50 mg, the NPPA used the same PTR for Ovafar 50 mg Tablets 10s and Ovafar 50 mg Tablets 5s of Organon but IMS data contain only the 5-pack.

5.4 Challenges with Older Stocks and Labeling Price-Controlled Medicines

The NPPA's 2013 DPCO notification states that the revised prices must be implemented within 45 days from the date of fixing the ceiling price but does not address the presence of older stock of price-regulated medicines on the market. Pharmaceutical companies, as well as pharmacies, have complained that it is costly to relabel or recall stock with the older price printed on their packages. Many pharmaceutical firms did not provide a list of revised prices to retailers, which resulted in retailers charging relatively higher, older prices. The problem has persisted since the initial implementation in 2013 due to the annual revision of the ceiling prices and the issue remained unresolved 3 years later. In April 2016, the NPPA determined that recalling, re-labeling of medicine stocks before price revision is not mandatory if manufacturers submit a revised price list and ensure compliance with the revised prices at the retailer level. However, the retailer trade association, the AIOCD, argued that the responsibility of displaying accurate prices lies with manufacturers. According to the president of the AIOCD (Rana 2016):

> We have found that some of the manufacturers though have reduced the prices only in their invoices as per NPPA guideline but physically supplying the products with old MRPs to dealers and asking the distributors or retailers to sell it at lesser price. They are informing distributors to circulate this information to retail chemists. This is absolutely not acceptable, because manufacturers have failed to provide the price lists to retail chemists as mandated in DPCO-2013 and can expose retail chemists to legal action in case of oversight by them. . .We have urged NPPA to ensure that they do not force our members to accept the stocks having higher than ceiling price. We will appreciate if all such products having higher than ceiling price are recalled from the trade and re-labelled with new price. Also issue new price list up to retail chemist as well. This will remove any ambiguity and help to establish a uniform system for better compliance.

The AIOCD suggested to the NPPA that providing a window of 90 days can mitigate these practical difficulties. The secretary of the Federation of Gujarat State Chemist & Druggist Association (FGSCDA), a state affiliate of the AIOCD, pointed out (PharmaBiz.com 2013a):

> It is needless to say that the issue of 45 days time frame set by NPPA for printing new prices on the old stocks had been a contentious issue from the very beginning, creating a lot of confusion among all the stake holders. What is more disturbing is the fact that as traders we have been left clueless on what our role was in this set-up. While the pharma companies insisted that it is impossible to recall and re-label the drugs within such a short time, the drug regulators desisted us from selling drugs, putting us in a spot. This lead to a lot of chaos, as there was a fear of unavailability of life saving drugs, as recalling stocks from villages and other remote areas needed much more time and elaborate planning.

Citing difficulties in implementing the DPCO order in 45 days, companies such as Cipla and Sun Pharma received temporary relief from the Delhi high court. The Drug Controller General of India (DGCI) responded by allowing companies to re-label existing stock of unsold medicines with the new prices specified under the 2013 DPCO, instead of recalling the current stock with incorrect prices and changing the packaging (Alexander 2013d). The NPPA reacted to reports that some retailers are returning stocks that do not have revised prices by urging them not to do so (Shankar 2016j):

> Concerned over the reports that some stockists and trade associations are showing resistance in selling medicines without re-stickering/re-labelling by the manufacturers as per the revised notified prices of drugs, the National Pharmaceutical Pricing Authority (NPPA) has directed the dealers including stockists and retailers not to return any stocks in case current price list as per revised notified price has been made available to them by the manufacturers. In a veiled warning to the stockists and retailers, the national drug price regulator said that any attempt by the retailers to return the stocks to the manufacturers for not re-labelling or re-stickering will be a violation of para 28 of the DPCO, 2013 if the current price list as per the revised notified price of drugs has been provided by the manufacturers.

Eventually, the NPPA and the industry reached an agreement that allowed the sale of older stocks of regulated medicines at older prices based on the date of manufacturing. According to Yadav (2016), DoP finally agreed with the AIOCD's demand for allowing the sale of medicines at prices before the price revision comes into effect until a certain manufacturing serial number expires. The NPPA further clarified that if the manufacturers show evidence sending the revised price list to the retailers or distributors, and if they sell the medicine above the ceiling price then the burden of noncompliance falls only on the distributors and retailers (Shankar 2017k).

The NPPA undertook efforts to collaborate with the pharmaceutical industry in developing a labeling method to distinguish price-controlled medicines. The NPPA argued that such an identification mark promotes awareness among consumers about the presence of lower-priced medicines (Vijay 2015). Also, the measure was expected to increase vigilance, accountability, and self-regulation (Shankar 2014b). Shankar (2014b) reports that the NPPA invited feedback from stakeholders such as the pharmaceutical industry, trade associations, consumer groups, and state drug controllers. The pharmacists soon opposed the measure, arguing that there is already considerable information provided on the package (Shankar 2014c). The IDMA also opposed the measure suggesting that any identification mark would cause confusion, ill-will, and chaos among consumers (Nautiyal 2014). The NPPA ultimately rolled back the proposal to introduce distinguishing marks (Shankar 2015e).

5.5 Challenges with Identifying SKUs with More Than 1% Market Share

The NPPA's calculations revealed that in some cases it did not follow the rules it designed to fix the ceiling price. For example, the DoP directed the NPPA to exclusively consider the formulations with a market share of 1% or more for calculation of price ceilings. The directive to the NPPA was the result of many complaints from manufacturers arguing that the NPPA sometimes averages PTRs across multiple brands instead of the PTR for a specific formulation with more than 1% market share. As noted in Table 3.3 in Chap. 3, several companies produce multiple brands of a medicine and sell at vastly different prices, and typically the brand with more than 1% market share has the largest price. In such cases, the NPPA clubbed together the market share of multiple versions of a medicine produced by a company, while the single brand/generic version of the same medicine of this company has a market share of less than 1%. For example, in one case, the DoP asked the NPPA to reexamine IMS data on ciprofloxacin hydrochloride 0.30% drops. Responding to such mistakes by the NPPA, the Indian Pharmaceutical Alliance (IPA) secretary general D G Shah noted in a letter to NPPA chairman C P Singh (Shankar 2013):

> However, we understand that the first lot of prices being notified is calculated using brands and generic versions having less than one per cent market share for companies having more than one brand. This is contrary to the above noted provisions and could distort the balance sought to be achieved by the NPPP 2012.

We examine the NPPA's calculations for fixing the ceiling prices of several other medicines and find that the primary method described in Sect. 4.2 of the book is correctly applied. For example, the calculations for Adenosine Injection 3 mg/ml, shown in Table 5.4, involve five SKUs, each with more than 1% market share. The average of the last column of 5.4 containing PTR per unit is 98.75, and the ceiling price is calculated accurately as $98.75 \times 1.16 = 114.55$. Similarly, the calculations for fixing the ceiling price for Adrenaline Bitartrate 1 mg/ml injection, also shown in Table 5.4, appears to be accurate as well. While there are eight SKUs, only seven have a market share of more than 1% and their average PTR is 32.11, and the ceiling price is $32.11 \times 1.16 = 37.24$. Nevertheless, in several cases, the calculation of the ceiling price does not match with the procedures determined under the DPCO 2013. Similar problems arose even in the revision of ceiling prices in 2015. As Shankar (2017h) notes:

> During examination, the reviewing authority DoP noted that the NPPA has taken into account certain formulations having MAT value of less than 1%. NPPA may be directed to consider only those medicines/formulations having MAT value of more than 1% market share, as DPCO does not recognize a company for average PTR but only medicines/formulations.

Shankar (2017c) notes that the DoP asked the NPPA to re-fix the ceiling price of "Methotrexate tablets 2.5 mg, 7.5 mg and 10 mg" by considering only eight formulations with SKU-wise MAT of more than 1% market share. Similarly, Shankar (2017n) notes that Sun Pharma complained with the NPPA that Mankind Pharmaceuticals' Lubistar CMC forte 1% 10 ml eye drops with less than 1% was considered in the ceiling price calculation.

Table 5.4 The accuracy of the NPPA calculations for Adenosine Injection 3 mg/ml and Adrenaline Bitartrate Injection 1 mg/ml

No	Company	SKUs for Adenosine	Share	PTR
Adenosine				
1	Sanofi	Adenocor Inj Iv. Vial 6 mg 2 ml × 1	81.70%	163.8
2	Samarth Pharma	Carnosine Inj Iv. Amp 6 mg 2 ml × 1	9.30%	80
3	Sun	Adenoject Inj Amp 3 mg 2 ml × 1 (/1 ml)	3.80%	83.93
4	Sun	Adenoject Inj Amp 3 mg 10 ml × 1 (/1 ml)	3.80%	78.11
5	Troikaa Pharma	Tachyban Inj Amp 3 mg 2 ml × 1 (/1 ml)	1.40%	87.96
Adrenaline Bitartrate				
1	Neon Labs	Norad Inj Amp 2 mg 2 ml × 1	40%	38
2	Samarth Pharma	Adrenor Infus Amp 2 ml × 1	39%	50.05
3	Neon Labs	Vasocon Inj Amp 1 mg 1 ml × 1 (/1 ml)	16%	10.15
4	Sunways	Epitrate Inj 1 ml × 1	2%	11.71
5	Sunways	Epitrate Inj 1 ml × 10	2%	6.73
6	Alkem	Dianora Amp. 1 mg 2 ml × 1 (/1 ml)	1%	62.13
7	Neon Labs	Norad Inj Iv. Amp 1 mg 4 ml × 1 (/1 ml)	1%	45.99
8	Cipla	Infunor Infus Amp 1 mg 2 ml × 1 (/1 ml)	0%	54.22

5.6 Quantitative Analysis of the Impact of Using IMS vs. AIOCD Pharmatrac Data

Since the NPPA's reliance on the IMS data can be questioned, we have recalculated the ceiling prices of 150 medicines for which the NPPA fixed prices on June 14, 2013. We rely on the Pharmatrac data to calculate the ceiling prices. These data are collected by the pharmaceutical retailer trade association, the AOICD, which many observers claim are more reliable and exhaustive compared to the IMS Health data, as the AIOCD membership of wholesalers and retailers are more conscientious in reporting data to the AIOCD. We compare the ceiling prices obtained from the AIOCD data using the traditional approach with the ceiling prices obtained from using the IMS data. Our calculations reveal discrepancies between the ceiling prices obtained using both datasets. Not only do the final price ceilings significantly differ, but also the details of the calculation and the component SKUs that constitute the determination of the ceiling price substantially differ in several cases.

We present the results of the analysis in Table 5.5. Our determination of the ceiling price is based on the primary method described in Sect. 4.1. However, for 12 medicines such as Adenosine 3 mg/ml Injection, there is only one producer in the AIOCD data that has more than 1% market share, and alternative methods have been employed by the NPPA to determine their ceiling price, as described in Chap. 3. We exclude these medicines from the analysis in Table 5.5. We also exclude a small number of medicines for which we could not find a match in the AIOCD data.

For each medicine in Table 5.5, column 1 contains the ceiling price fixed by the NPPA using the IMS data. Column 2 contains the number of SKUs in the NPPA list, and Column 3 contains the number of SKUs in the NPPA list with more than 1% market share. Column 4 contains the ceiling price determined using the AIOCD data. Column 5 contains a hypothetical ceiling price calculated using the prices of firms with less than 1% market share, which are currently excluded from influencing the ceiling price. The total number of firms in the market is shown in Column 6, and the number of firms with more than 1% market share is shown in Column 7. The difference between the IMS and AIOCD ceiling prices is shown in Column 8. To provide a concrete example, the ceiling price of Acyclovir 200 mg Tablets is determined by the NPPA to be Rs. 7.3 per tablet. The AIOCD-based ceiling price, however, is determined to be Rs. 6.69, 8% less than the NPPA's ceiling price. While there are 15 firms present in the market, eight of them have more than 1% market share in the AIOCD data, and they account for determining the ceiling price in column 4. The difference between the two ceiling prices, shown in column 6, is Rs. 0.61 for Acyclovir 200 mg Tablets. Overall, Table 5.5 contains 129 medicines, and among them, the NPPA ceiling price is greater than the AIOCD ceiling price for 48 medicines and less for 77 medicines. The ceiling prices exactly match in the case of four medicines, Enalapril Maleate Tablets 2.5 mg, Hyoscine Butyl Bromide Injection 20 mg /ml, Metoclopramide Injection 5 mg/ml, and Permethrin Cream 5%.

The NPPA excluded the prices of SKUs with less than 1% market share during May 2012 to April 2013 from the process of determining the ceiling price. One

Table 5.5 Comparison of Ceiling Prices based on IMS and AIOCD data

Column	1	2	3	4	5	6	7	8
Composition as per NLEM	NPPA ceiling price in Rs.	N of firms in NPPA list	N of firms with > 1% market share in NPPA list	AIOCD ceiling price in Rs.	AIOCD ceiling price based firms with < 1% market share in Rs.	N of firms in AIOCD list	N of firms with > 1% market share in AIOCD list	Difference in ceiling price (1)–(2)
Acyclovir Tablets 200 mg	7.3	16	8	6.69	4.3	15	8	0.61
Alpha Interferon Injection 3 million IU	759.7	4	4	692.88	464	5	4	66.82
Amiodarone Tablets 100 mg	6.52	8	6	6.37	2.74	8	6	0.15
Amiodarone Tablets 200 mg	11.67	8	7	11.7		7	7	−0.03
Amitriptyline Tablets 25 mg	2.12	21	9	2.53	2.24	25	8	−0.41
Ampicillin Powder for suspension 125 mg/5 ml	0.63	7	3	0.15	0.07	4	3	0.48
Anti-D immunoglobin (human) Injection 300 μg	2209.8	3	2	1886.64	5046	4	3	323.16
Atenolol Tablets 100 mg	3.72	25	7	4.12	2.17	12	6	−0.4
Atorvastatin Tablets 5 mg	3.82	32	19	4.06	3.72	30	14	−0.24
Atracurium besylate Injection 10 mg/ml	45.28	13	5	48.2		6	6	−2.92
Atropine Sulphate Injection 0.6 mg/ml	4.01	4	3	5.41		3	3	−1.4
Azathioprine Tablets 50 mg	9.89	9	3	9.86	7.23	9	5	0.03
Azithromycin Injection 500 mg	182.27	8	7	47.15		6	6	135.12
Azithromycin Tablets 500 mg	19.86	149	24	20.56	18.65	185	22	−0.7
Betaxolol Hydrochloride Drops 0.5%	6.59	3	3	6.98		4	4	−0.39
Carbimazole Tablets 10 mg	3.43	4	3	3.13	2.78	4	3	0.3
Carbimazole Tablets 5 mg	1.77	3	3	1.81	1.67	4	3	−0.04
Ceftazidime Injection 250 mg	63.4	10	4	42.63	46.46	8	6	20.77
Clofazimine Capsules 100 mg	2.22	3	3	2.43	3.36	3	2	−0.21
Clofazimine Capsules 50 mg	1.28	3	2	1.21	1.49	3	2	0.07
Clomiphene citrate Tablets 100 mg	12.18	10	7	14.27	10.17	11	8	−2.09
Colchicin Tablets 0.5 mg	2.88	2	2	3.09	0.97	3	2	−0.21
Cyclophosphamide Tablets 50 mg	3.75	3	2	4.09		2	2	−0.34

Cyclosporine Capsules 25 mg	24.75	7	6	26.29		5	5	−1.54
Cyclosporine Capsules 50 mg	48.26	8	8	48.96		4	4	−0.7
Dacarbazine Injection 500 mg	1029.09	2	2	638.77		3	3	390.32
Danazol Capsules 100 mg	20.33	6	5	15.58	17.89	6	5	4.75
Danazol Capsules 50 mg	9.37	6	5	8.34	7.72	6	5	1.03
Diazepam Injection 5 mg/ml	5.59	18	5	4.79		5	5	0.8
Diethylcarbamazine citrate Tablets 50 mg	0.47	3	3	0.97	0.21	4	2	−0.5
Digoxin Tablets 0.25 mg	1.26	3	2	1.37	1.27	5	3	−0.11
Diltiazem Tablets 30 mg	2.27	17	5	2.66	1.82	11	5	−0.39
Domperidone Syrup 1 mg/ml	1.03	41	7	0.89	0.63	12	5	0.14
Dopamine Hydrochloride Injection 40 mg/ml	5.53	9	6	27.31		3	3	−21.78
Doxorubicin Injection 50 mg	1145.2	13	4	639.42	485.41	9	7	505.78
Enalapril Maleate Tablets 2.5 mg	1.78	13	5	1.78	0.99	12	6	0
Enalapril Maleate Tablets 5 mg	2.96	18	5	2.71	2.22	16	6	0.25
Ethambutol Tablets 400 mg	2.17	3	3	2.15		3	3	0.02
Ethambutol Tablets 600 mg	3.15	8	4	3.24	3.02	6	4	−0.09
Ethambutol Tablets 800 mg	3.74	23	7	4.35	4.2	15	6	−0.61
Ethinylestradiol Tablets 0.01 mg	2.12	3	3	2.8		2	2	−0.68
Folic Acid Tablets 5 mg	1.15	56	5	2.79	1.65	38	6	−1.64
Gemcitabine hydrochloride Injection 1 g	5969.16	18	10	5108.66	4623.23	12	9	860.5
Gemcitabine hydrochloride Injection 200 mg	1304.86	15	9	1198.63	1525.4	11	8	106.23
Glibenclamide Tablets 2.5 mg	0.48	5	3	0.6		5	5	−0.12
Glibenclamide Tablets 5 mg	0.96	13	2	0.64	0.91	11	3	0.32
Glucagon Injection 1 mg/ml	788.33	3	3	830.78		2	2	−42.45
Glyceryl Trinitrate Injection 5 mg/ml	7.53	9	7	8.93		2	2	−1.4
Glyceryl Trinitrate Sublingual Tablets 0.5 mg	1.85	3	2	1.69		2	2	0.16
Haloperidol Injection 5 mg/ml	5.63	9	6	16.62	7.2	7	3	−10.99
Homatropine Drops 2%	5	6	3	8.04		2	2	−3.04

(continued)

Table 5.5 (continued)

Column	1	2	3	4	5	6	7	8
Hydrochlorthiazide Tablets 12.5 mg	0.97	6	5	1.14	0.86	8	5	−0.17
Hydrochlorthiazide Tablets 25 mg	1.66	6	5	1.87	1.17	7	5	−0.21
Hydroxychloroquine phosphate Tablets 200 mg	5.64	15	11	5.58	11.14	16	10	0.06
Hyoscine Butyl Bromide Injection 20 mg/ml	9.84	9	2	9.84	9.83	3	2	0
Imatinib Tablets 400 mg	268.33	5	5	237.96	230.79	15	11	30.37
Imipramine Tablets 25 mg	0.75	13	10	1	0.94	17	7	−0.25
Imipramine Tablets 75 mg	2	12	11	2.08	2.27	12	9	−0.08
Indinavir Capsules 400 mg	19.41	3	2	16.67		2	2	2.74
Isosorbide 5 Mononitrate Tablets 10 mg	1.92	14	8	1.97	1.5	12	6	−0.05
Isosorbide 5 Mononitrate Tablets 20 mg	3.29	21	10	3.33	2.65	20	8	−0.04
Ketamine Hydrochloride Injectable 50 mg/ml	10.46	9	5	10.82	35.96	7	5	−0.36
Lamivudine + Nevirapine + Stavudine Tablets 150 mg	17.29	1	1	33.09	24.28	11	7	−15.8
Lamivudine + Zidovudine Tablets 150 mg + 300 mg	19.63	8	6	19.19		7	7	0.44
Leflunomide Tablets 20 mg	28.63	6	6	28.38		6	6	0.25
Lithium Carbonate Tablets 300 mg	1.41	13	9	1.72	1.48	16	7	−0.31
Lorazepam Injection 2 mg/ml	7.39	4	2	8.39	16.15	3	1	−1
Losartan Potassium Tablets 25 mg	2.5	55	16	2.38	2.36	54	17	0.12
Losartan Potassium Tablets 50 mg	4.3	58	16	4.54	4.33	61	19	−0.24
Medroxy Progesterone Acetate Tablets 10 mg	5.24	10	5	5.02	4.35	12	7	0.22
Mefloquine Tablet 250 mg base	50.06	4	4	51.75		4	4	−1.69
Methotrexate Tablet 2.5 mg	4.72	11	7	4.66	4.54	14	7	0.06
Methotrexate Tablets 5 mg	7.6	6	4	7.49	10.16	7	4	0.11
Methotrexate Tablets 7.5 mg	11.27	8	6	10.76	10.43	8	6	0.51
Methyl Ergometrine Tablets 0.125 mg	7.14	16	3	7.42	3.36	11	3	−0.28
Metoclopramide Injection 5 mg/ml	2.09	14	7	2.09	0.64	6	5	0

Metoclopramide Syrup 5 mg/5 ml	0.47	7	3	0.1	0.1	5	4	0.37
Metoclopramide Tablets 10 mg	1.04	13	7	1.32	3.95	9	3	−0.28
Midazolam Injection 1 mg/ml	5.79	13	5	6.67	5.53	9	8	−0.88
Midazolam Injection 5 mg/ml	24.78	7	4	19.4	27.67	5	4	5.38
Misoprostol Tablets 100 µg	9.43	4	3	8.62	7.31	6	4	0.81
Neostigmine Injection 0.5 mg/ml	4.04	11	5	6.53	84.54	6	4	−2.49
Nifedipine Capsules 10 mg	1.18	7	5	1.45	0.95	7	4	−0.27
Nifedipine Tablets 10 mg	1.13	4	2	1.37	1.06	11	6	−0.24
Norethisterone Tablets 5 mg	5.07	26	9	5.42	4.24	22	9	−0.35
Ofloxacin Syrup 50 mg/5 ml	0.67	65	17	0.13	0.13	52	10	0.54
Olanzapine Tablets 10 mg	5.32	37	17	5.58	4.89	44	17	−0.26
Olanzapine Tablets 5 mg	2.9	42	18	2.95	2.75	47	15	−0.05
Ondansetron Tablets 8 mg	11.07	21	8	10.29	10.58	18	9	0.78
Oxytocin Injection 10 iu/ml	37.7	4	2	43.15	48.15	2	1	−5.45
Pantoprazole Injection 40 mg	47.93	57	13	10.51	25.44	69	12	37.42
Paracetamol Injection 150 mg/ml	3.29	12	4	3.56	3.55	9	4	−0.27
Paracetamol Suppository 80 mg	4.88	2	2	6.95		2	2	−2.07
Paracetamol Syrup 125 mg/5 ml	0.33	68	17	0.08	0.06	58	18	0.25
Paracetamol Tablets 500 mg	0.94	103	15	1.03	1.23	91	14	−0.09
Penicillamine Tablets or Capsules 250 mg	13.12	4	4	13.82		3	3	−0.7
Permethrin Cream 5%	1.77	23	10	1.77	1.63	21	10	0
Permethrin Lotion 5%	1.07	16	14	1.19	0.87	20	13	−0.12
Phenobarbitone Tablets 60 mg	1.69	6	3	2.25	1.65	3	1	−0.56
Phenytoin Sodium Capsules or Tablets 50 mg	0.77	12	4	0.82	0.79	7	3	−0.05
Povidone Iodine Solution 10%	0.91	10	6	0.94	0.81	9	6	−0.03
Povidone Iodine Solution 5%	0.39	48	9	0.64	18.64	28	7	−0.25
Primaquine Tablets 7.5 mg	1.98	4	2	2.56	1.97	7	3	−0.58
Promethazine Syrup 5 mg/5 ml	0.21	11	4	0.05	0.07	16	5	0.16

(continued)

Table 5.5 (continued)

Column	1	2	3	4	5	6	7	8
Promethazine Tablets 25 mg	2.49	10	2	2.31	0.92	6	2	0.18
Propofol Injectable 1% oil suspension	7.94	16	10	8.48	10.77	10	9	−0.54
Pyrazinamide Tablets 1000 mg	8.3	6	6	8.37	7.48	6	5	−0.07
Pyrazinamide Tablets 500 mg	3.77	15	6	4.43	4.2	8	5	−0.66
Pyrazinamide Tablets 750 mg	6.91	17	4	6.75	4.73	8	4	0.16
Quinine sulphate Injection 300 mg/ml	9.07	5	4	10.11	10.59	9	5	−1.04
Quinine sulphate Tablets 300 mg	5.1	19	8	6.07	8.34	26	8	−0.97
Rabies Vaccine Injection	302.39	6	6	311.3	306.66	11	7	−8.91
Raloxifene Tablets 60 mg	9.89	7	3	12.49	8.99	5	3	−2.6
Sodium Valproate Syrup 200 mg/5 ml	0.58	8	3	0.12	0.12	15	5	0.46
Sodium Valproate Tablets 200 mg	3.07	10	5	2.74	3.06	8	6	0.33
Stavudine + Lamivudine Tablets 30 mg + 150 mg	9.2	9	4	9.73	55.68	6	5	−0.53
Streptokinase Injection 1,500,000 IU	2034.04	9	5	1196.51	2073.8	6	5	837.53
Sulphacetamide Sodium Drops 20%	1.73	3	2	2.51		3	3	−0.78
Tamoxifen Citrate Tablets 20 mg	2.77	9	6	2.91	2.53	5	4	−0.14
Testosterone Capsules 40 mg(as undecanoate)	10.96	6	4	13.91		4	4	−2.95
Tetanus Toxoid Injection	10.29	7	4	527.12	458.93	23	12	−516.83
Thiopentone Sodium Injectable 0.5 g Powder	41.67	4	2	48.58		2	2	−6.91
Trihexyphenidyl Hydrochloride Tablets 2 mg	1.36	21	6	1.78	1.42	27	6	−0.42
Tropicamide Eye drops 1%	9.6	5	4	11.38	10.37	6	5	−1.78
Vancomycin Hydrochloride Injection 1 g	514.44	3	2	217.95		3	3	296.49
Vancomycin Hydrochloride Injection 500 mg	330.6	13	9	139.3	269.72	12	9	191.3
Vincristine Injection 1 mg/ml	50.6	5	4	48.48	68.06	9	7	2.12
Warfarin sodium Tablets 5 mg	2.24	4	2	2.93		2	2	−0.69
Zidovudine + Lamivudine + Nevirapine Tablets 300	19.05	1	0	21.68	12.39	7	5	−2.63

reason for excluding such small SKUs, although not stated by the NPPA, is because if they were allowed to influence the ceiling price, then firms can introduce several SKUs with relatively higher prices and push the potential ceiling price upwards. For example, GlaxoSmithKline introduced a 15-pack of Crocin Advance 500 mg, an SKU of Paracetamol, in August 2011 with a per-tablet price of Rs. 1.59. In comparison, the per-tablet price of most SKUs of Paracetamol 500 mg is less than one rupee. In Table 5.5 we calculate a hypothetical ceiling price based on the prices of the neglected SKUs, that is, SKUs with less than 1% market share. Among the 129 medicines listed in Table 5.5, in 29 cases, we could not compute a ceiling price based on the neglected SKUs because such SKUs were not present in the AIOCD data. Among the remaining 100 cases, in 68 of the cases, the AIOCD-based ceiling price computed using the prices of neglected SKUs is lower compared to the AIOCD-based ceiling price computed using the prices of SKUs with more than 1% market share. Furthermore, in 63 of the 100 cases, the AIOCD-based ceiling price computed using the prices of neglected SKUs is lower compared to the IMS-based ceiling price fixed by the NPPA.

We find that the number of SKUs differs between the NPPA and AIOCD datasets. For example, among the 129 medicines listed in Table 5.5, the number of SKUs is higher in the NPPA list for 72 medicines and lower in 39 cases. When we compare the number of SKUs with more than 1% market share, the NPPA list has more SKUs for 44 medicines and fewer in 39 cases. For some medicines, the coverage as measured by the number of SKUs appears to be better in the IMS/NPPA list, and for other medicines, the AIOCD dataset appears to be more comprehensive. For example, the AIOCD dataset shows 15 different SKUs for Imatinib 400 mg tablets with 11 of them holding more than 1% market share while the IMS dataset has only five. On the contrary, IMS/NPPA list has 32 SKUs of Atorvastatin 5 mg tablets with 19 holding more than 1% market share while the AIOCD dataset contains 30 and 14 respectively.

The largest absolute difference between the NPPA and AIOCD ceiling price reported in Table 5.5 is in the case of 1000 mg Gemcitabine hydrochloride injection used for chemotherapy in treating cancer patients. The difference between the two ceiling prices is Rs. 860.5 and we examine the reasons for the discrepancy further in Table 5.6. The IMS/NPPA dataset contains 18 SKUs of Gemcitabine while the AIOCD dataset for the period May 2012 to April 2013 contains 20 SKUs. However, not every SKU with more than 1% market share during May 2012 to April 2013 has sales and price information in May 2012. Only 12 of the 20 SKUs are represented in May 2012 data of the AIOCD, whose prices can be used to determine the ceiling price in the AIOCD dataset. The SKUs of Gemcitabine drawn from IMS/NPPA and AIOCD datasets are shown in Table 5.6 along with their estimated market shares and price to the retailer per injection. While Eli Lilly's Gemcite 1000 mg SKU has the same price of Rs. 6897.6 in both datasets, the market share of the SKU differs significantly between the two datasets. Eli Lilly has a market share of 57% in the IMS/NPPA dataset but only 12% in the AIOCD dataset. Overall, in many cases, neither the prices nor the market shares match across the two datasets.

Table 5.6 Comparison of Gemcitabine SKU prices in May 2012 in IMS/NPPA and AIOCD data

Company	Stock keeping unit (SKU)	IMS/NPPA dataset		AIOCD dataset	
		Market share	Price	Market share	Price
SKUs appearing in both the IMS/NPPA and AIOCD datasets					
Eli Lilly	Gemcite Inj Iv Lyo V 1 g × 1	57.10%	6897.6	12.10%	6897.6
Dr Reddys Labs	Cytogem Infus Vial 1000 mg × 1	15.70%	4724.57	50.57%	3809.52
Fresenius Kabi	Gemita Inj Iv Lyo V 1 g × 1	4.80%	4650	3.69%	4904.8
Panacea Biotec	Gemtrust Inj Lyo Vial 1000 Mg × 1	3.80%	4905	2.78%	4100
Cipla	Oncogem Inj Dry Vial 1 g × 1	2.80%	6316.55	0.43%	5572.12
Alkem	Celgem Inj Dry Vial 1 g × 1	1.80%	4887.69	7.43%	4888.01
Intas Pharma	Gemibine Inj Iv Lyo V 1000 mg 25 ml × 1	0.90%	4358.09	1.68%	4800
Emcure	Gemizan Inj Dry Vial 1000 mg × 1	0.60%	4716.92	0.15%	4575
Rpg Life Sciences	Emcitaben Inj Lyo Vial 1000 mg 25 ml × 1	0.50%	4905	6.59%	3920
Macleods Pharma	Gemacta Inj Dry Vial 1000 mg × 1	0.30%	2846.16	1.90%	3100.95
SKUs appearing only in the IMS/NPPA dataset					
Wockhardt Ltd	Winogem Inj Dry Vial 1 g × 1	5.70%	4639.17		
United Biotech	Biogem Inj Dry Vial 1000 mg × 1	1.70%	5409.98		
Vhb Lifesciences	Gemset Inj Dry Vial 1 g 25 ml × 1	0.10%	3261.83		
SKUs appearing in the IMS/NPPA and AIOCD datasets but prices unreported in the AIOCD dataset in May 2012					
Cadila Pharma	Tabicad Inj Dry Vial 1 g × 1	2.00%	4784.63	0.06%	NA
Emcure	Citafine Inj Dry Vial 1 g × 1	1.20%	4672	3.14%	NA
Khandelwal	Gempower Inj Dry Vial 1 g × 1	0.40%	4080.96	0.58%	NA
Hetero Healthcare	Gemtero Inj Dry Vial 1 g × 1	0.40%	6316.67	0.04%	NA
Ranbaxy	Xtroz Inj Dry Vial 1 g × 1	0.30%	5242	0.42%	NA
SKUs appearing only in the AIOCD dataset					
Sun Pharma Lab. Ltd.	Gemtaz 1000 mg Injection 1			4.37%	3215.24
Gland Pharma Ltd.	Gemciglan 1000 mg Injection 1			0.85%	1809.52
SKUs appearing only in the AIOCD dataset with prices unreported in May 2012					
Zydus Cadila	Gembin 1000 mg Injection 1			2.44%	NA
Parenteral Drgus	Gemcitapar 1000 mg Injection 1			0.73%	NA
Zuventus	Gemizan 1000 mg Injection 1			0.14%	NA

(continued)

Table 5.6 (continued)

		IMS/NPPA dataset		AIOCD dataset	
Company	Stock keeping unit (SKU)	Market share	Price	Market share	Price
Indswift	Gemkerb 1000 mg Injection 1			0.01%	NA

Notes: The 20 SKUs appearing in the AIOCD data during May 2012 to April 2013 period are: Dr. Reddys Laboratories Ltd. (Cytogem); Eli Lilly And Company (India) Pvt. Ltd. (Gemcite); Alkem Laboratories Ltd. (Celgem); Rpg Life Sciences Ltd. (Emcitaben); Sun Pharma Laboratories Ltd. (Gemtaz); Fresenius Kabi India Pvt. Ltd. (Gemita); Emcure Pharmaceuticals Ltd. (Citafine); Panacea Biotec Ltd. (Gemtrust); Zydus Cadila (Gembin); Macleods Pharmaceuticals Pvt. Ltd. (Gemacta); Intas Pharmaceuticals Ltd. (Gemibine); Gland Pharma Limited (Gemciglan); Parenteral Drugs (India) Ltd. (Gemcitapar); Khandelwal Laboratories Ltd. (Gempower); Cipla Ltd. (Oncogem); Ranbaxy Laboratories Ltd. (Xtroz); Zuventus Healthcare Ltd. (Gemizan); Cadila Pharmaceuticals Ltd. (Tabicad); Hetero Healthcare Ltd. (Gemtero); Indswift Laboratories Ltd. (Gemkerb)

While the AIOCD data are likely to be relatively more accurate compared to the IMS/NPPA dataset, the extent of discrepancy between the two datasets remains a serious concern in determining the ceiling price. Among 18 to 20 SKUs present in the two datasets, 15 SKUs are common between the two datasets, only 10 SKUs have both the annual market share during the period and price information in the month of May 2012. Five SKUs by Cadila, Emcure, Khandelwal, Hetero, and Ranbaxy do not have any reported sales and price information in the month of May 2012. Among these five, Cadila and Emcure have more than 1% market share in both datasets, but they cannot influence the ceiling price because of the unavailability of their price information. Six SKUs are present exclusively in the AIOCD dataset, and two of them have more than 1% market share. While price information for Zydus Cadila with 2.44% market share is unavailable for the month of May 2012, Sun Pharma' s Gemtaz brand of Gemcitabine with a market share of 4.37% is missing in the determination of the ceiling price by the NPPA using IMS dataset.

The NPPA announced in May 2013 that it would use prices of May 2012 for calculation of the ceiling prices under the DPCO 2013. This decision would mitigate the effects of potential manipulation of prices in the period prior to the start of the regulation. We further examine how the ceiling price would have changed if the price for the months other than May 2012 had been used to determine the ceiling price. We plot in Fig. 5.1 the ceiling price based on the primary method of averaging the price to the retailers of SKUs with more than 1% market during May 2012 to April 2013 using prices of these SKUs for each month. Such an exercise reveals how the ceiling price would have changed if prices of other months are used for determining the ceiling price rather than May 2012 prices alone, which may not always be available in the IMS or AIOCD datasets. According to Fig. 5.1, the ceiling price based on May 2012 prices is 5108.66, but it drops to around 4600 in some

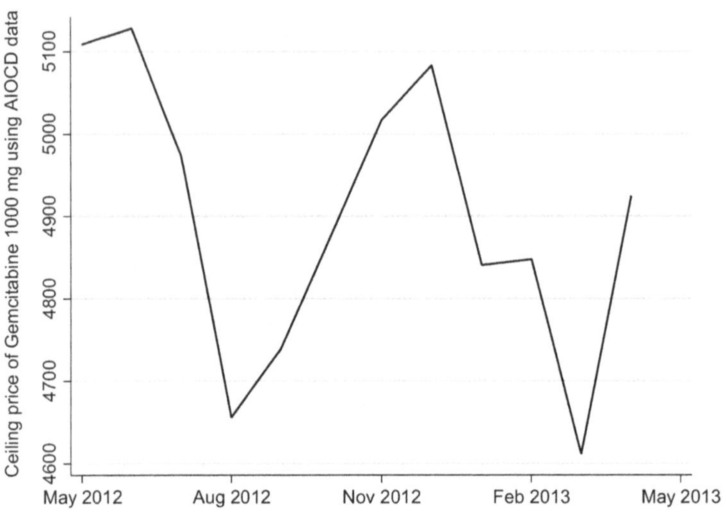

Fig. 5.1 Ceiling price of Gemcitabine using the AIOCD data, computed using prices in each month during May 2012 to April 2013

months and raises to 4900 in early 2013. These hypothetical ceiling prices, however, are lower than the ceiling price of 5969.16 computed using the IMS data.

We repeat the exercise for 39 other medicines for which the NPPA fixed the ceiling price on June 21, 2013. Table 5.7 compares the ceiling prices calculated using IMS and AOICD data. For ten medicines on the list, the AIOCD-based ceiling price is lower than the one fixed by the NPPA and higher for the remaining 25 medicines. For Ceftazidime1000 mg injection, the actual per unit ceiling price fixed under the DPCO 2013 is 20% higher than the price calculated using AOICD data. Consistent with earlier analyses, the extent of exact match between the two ceiling prices is minimal.

Differences in the choice of datasets can lead to different ceiling prices. Even while using the IMS dataset, the NPPA's implementation of the methodology for determining the ceiling price is not clear. We examine the case of Albendazole 200 mg/5 ml suspension, whose ceiling price was fixed on the 21st of June 2013. According to the NPPA Working Sheet, there are 94 different SKUs producing the medicine.[2] We estimated the market share of each SKU in the list and presented the results in Table 5.8. There are eight SKUs with more than 1% market share, but the NPPA reports using 22 SKUs in determining the ceiling price. While not explicitly mentioned, our calculations suggest that the NPPA rounded off the market share of SKUs with more than 0.50% as 1%. As a result, SKUs such as Dr. Reddy's Rediout brand of 400 mg 10 ml suspension with a market share of 0.5176% is reported by the NPPA as having 1% market share. Even under this unusual approximation, there are

[2]http://www.nppaindia.nic.in/ceiling/press21june13/workingsheet-21-6-13.html

Table 5.7 Comparison of ceiling prices for medicines NPPA fixed the ceiling price on Jun 21 2013

Medicine	IMS based ceiling price	AIOCD based ceiling price	Difference
Acetazolamide Systemic Tablet 250 mg	3.69	4.48	−0.79
Aciclovir Cream 5%	8.89	9.93	−1.04
Albendazole Solids 400 mg	1.46	12.29	−10.83
Albendazole Suspension 200 mg	1.47	1.95	−0.48
Alprazolam Tablet 0.25 mg	0.95	1.28	−0.33
Amikacin Injection 250 mg/2 ml	13.95	17.43	−3.48
Amlodipine Tablet 2.5 mg	2.03	1.71	0.32
Amlodipine Tablet 5 mg	3.06	2.7	0.36
Amoxycillin Capsule 500 mg	6.09	7.67	−1.58
Amoxycillin Suspension 125 mg	0.57	0.72	−0.15
Ampicillin Capsule 500 mg	4.76	7.25	−2.49
Ampicillin Injection 500 mg	13.41	20.39	−6.98
Artesunate Solids 50 mg	20.04	20.84	−0.8
Atenolol Solids 50 mg	2.08	2.5	−0.42
Atorvastatin Solids 10 mg	5.92	6.54	−0.62
Bromocriptine Solids 1.25 mg	7.57	9.59	−2.02
Bromocriptine Solids 2.5 mg	13.6	13.85	−0.25
Cefixime Tablet 100 mg	7.69	5.11	2.58
Ceftazidime Injection 1000 mg	229.19	190.98	38.21
Ceftriaxone Injection 250 mg	24.6	11.88	12.72
Diazepam Tablet 5 mg	1.32	2.3	−0.98
Fluconazole Capsule 200 mg	38.91	37.91	1
Fluconazole Capsule 50 mg	10.16	8.75	1.41
Fluconazole Tablet 100 mg	14.15	4.63	9.52
Fluconazole Tablet 200 mg	25.86	28.71	−2.85
Fluconazole Tablet 50 mg	7.83	6.85	0.98
Glucose Injectables 10%	0.05	0.05	0
Imatinib Mesylate Tablet 100 mg	87.59	97.11	−9.52
Levo-Thyroxine (Synthetic) Tablet 100 mcg	1.11	1.12	−0.01
Metformin Tablet 500 mg	1.57	1.92	−0.35
Omeprazole Capsule 10 mg	2.76	1.5	1.26
Omeprazole Capsule 20 mg	3.02	5.09	−2.07
Ondansetron Injection 2 mg/1 ml	7.38	7.77	−0.39
Ondansetron Syrup 2 mg/5 ml	1.03	1.08	−0.05
Primaquine Tablet 2.5 mg	1.54	2.03	−0.49

only 14 different SKUs with more than 1% market share. Yet the NPPA reports using prices for 22 packs in determining the ceiling price for the medicine at Rs. 1.48. The ceiling prices based on eight or 14 SKUs are Rs. 1.80 or Rs. 1.70 respectively.

A deeper analysis of the ceiling price reveals that the NPPA uses the listed number of packs starting from the top of the list. This means that in the case of

Table 5.8 NPPA's calculations to determine the ceiling price for Albendazole 200 mg/5 ml suspension

Company	SKU	Sales	Reported market share	Price	Market Share we Computed
Glaxosmithkline	Zentel Susp 200 mg 10 ml × 1 (/5 ml)	227,190,459	0.53	2.02	52.52817
Alkem	Noworm Susp 400 mg 10 ml × 1	42,830,864	0.1	1.95	9.902822
Mankind	Bandy Susp 200 mg 10 ml × 1 (/5 ml)	35,044,084	0.08	1.08	8.10246
Blue Cross	Womiban Susp 200 mg 10 ml ml × 1 (/5 ml)	25,375,927	0.06	1.91	5.867108
Cipla	Bendex Susp 200 mg 10 ml × 1 (/5 ml)	23,485,722	0.05	1.73	5.430078
Ranbaxy	Zeebee Susp 200 mg 10 ml × 1 (/5 ml)	12,501,945	0.03	0.53	2.890545
Indoco	Abz Susp 10 ml × 1	7,213,860	0.02	1.35	1.667899
Unichem	Wormfix Susp 200 mg 10 ml × 1 (/5 ml)	5,392,763	0.01	1.91	1.246848
Micro Labs	Xenda Susp 200 mg 10 ml × 1 (/5 ml)	3,763,669	0.01	1.70	0.870189
Albert David	Sioban Susp 200 mg 10 ml × 1 (/5 ml)	3,486,108	0.01	1.78	0.8060148
Intas Pharma	Abd Susp 200 mg 10 ml × 1 (/5 ml)	2,905,302	0.01	0.50	0.671728
Medo Pharma	Alworm Susp 200 mg 10 ml × 1 (/5 ml)	2,497,120	0.01	1.69	0.5773532
Klar Sehen	Odal Susp 200 mg 10 ml × 1 (/5 ml)	2,472,353	0.01	1.37	0.5716269
Dr Reddys Labs	Rediout Susp 400 mg 10 ml × 1	2,238,772	0.01	1.08	0.5176212
Mapra Labs	Xenith Susp 200 mg 10 ml × 1 (/5 ml)	2,151,956	0	1.49	0.4975486
Juggat Pharma	Cidazole Susp 200 mg 10 ml × 1 (/5 ml)	2,129,812	0	1.77	0.4924288
Zydus Cadila	Olworm Susp 200 mg 10 ml × 1 (/5 ml)	2,111,061	0	1.48	0.4880934
Wallace	Abwal Susp 200 mg 10 ml × 1 (/5 ml)	1,836,423	0	1.58	0.424595
Torque Pharma	Ben Plus Susp 200 mg 10 ml × 1 (/5 ml)	1,824,483	0	2.09	0.4218344
Obsurge Biotech	Ah-1 Susp 200 mg 10 ml × 1 (/5 ml)	1,740,667	0	1.33	0.4024555
Darkt Internation.	Albend Susp 200 mg 10 ml × 1	1,530,226	0	1.40	0.3537999
Shine Pharma	Albid Susp 200 mg 10 ml × 1 (/5 ml)	1,505,611	0	1.50	0.3481087
Novartis Intl.	Kealwerm Syrup 200 mg 10 ml × 1 (/5 ml)	1,475,580	0	1.69	0.3411654
Emcee	Sidose Susp 200 mg 10 ml × 1 (/5 ml)	1,413,181	0	1.54	0.3267382
Shrinivas Labs	Alvela Susp 200 mg 10 ml × 1 (/5 ml)	1,111,645	0	1.60	0.2570208

Indoco	Olban Susp 200 Mg 10 ml × 1 (/5 ml)	1,071,860	0	1.53	0.2478222
Lupin Limited	Lupibend Susp 200 Mg 10 ml × 1 (/5 ml)	1,064,667	0	0.60	0.2461591
Burnet Pharma	Ben Susp 200 mg 10 ml × 1 (/5 ml)	875,992	0	1.94	0.202536
Alembic	Worid Susp 200 mg 10 ml × 1	865,290	0	0.66	0.2000616
Alkem	Dispel Susp 200 mg 10 ml × 1 (/5 ml)	842,935	0	1.95	0.194893
Rpg Life Sciences	Exyt Susp 200 mg 10 ml × 1 (/5 ml)	777,719	0	1.88	0.1798146
Micro Labs	Albendol Susp 200 mg 10 ml × 1 (/5 ml)	761,730	0	1.58	0.1761178
Sterkem	Beworm Susp 200 mg 10 ml × 1 (/5 ml)	759,923	0	1.84	0.1757
Torrent Pharma	Alminth Susp 200 mg 10 ml × 1 (/5 ml)	686,836	0	1.31	0.1588017
Iatros Pharma	Albenmint Susp 200 mg 10 ml × 1 (/5 ml)	621,888	0	0.81	0.1437853
Wockhardt Ltd	Alzad Susp 200 mg 10 ml × 1 (/5 ml)	590,364	0	0.65	0.1364967
Makers Labs	Wintil Susp 200 mg 10 ml × 1 (/5 ml)	588,748	0	0.65	0.136123
Zydus Cadila	Zybend Susp 200 mg 10 ml × 1 (/5 ml)	534,989	0	0.64	0.1236935
Khandelwal	Alltel Susp 200 mg 10 ml × 1 (/5 ml)	514,905	0	2.04	0.11905
Abbott	Embee Susp 200 mg 10 ml × 1 (/5 ml)	472,076	0	0.50	0.1091476
Elder Pharma	Eldoben Susp 200 mg 10 ml × 1 (/5 ml)	417,818	0	1.80	0.0966027
Mars	Helmex Susp 200 mg 10 ml × 1 (/5 ml)	375,202	0	1.50	0.0867496
Alkem	Elminex Susp 200 mg 10 ml × 1 (/5 ml)	366,777	0	1.46	0.0848016
Cadila Pharma	Albendazole Syrup 200 mg 10 ml × 1 (/5 ml)	328,768	0	0.67	0.0760137
Micro Labs	Xenda Susp 200 mg 10 ml × 50 (/5 ml)	324,606	0	1.09	0.0750514
Nestor Pharma	Albest Susp 200 mg 10 ml × 1 (/5 ml)	320,270	0	1.23	0.0740489
Bestochem	Albendabest Susp 200 mg 10 ml × 1 (/5 ml)	313,789	0	1.88	0.0725504
Dales Pharma	Krumex Susp 200 mg 10 ml × 1 (/5 ml)	299,675	0	0.88	0.0692871
Mankind	Mahabend Susp 200 mg 10 ml × 1 (/5 ml)	277,092	0	0.64	0.0640658
Cadila Pharma	Vormout Susp 200 mg 10 ml × 1 (/5 ml)	226,069	0	0.51	0.0522689
Wockhardt Ltd	Wozole Susp 10 ml × 1	219,397	0	0.60	0.0507263

(continued)

Table 5.8 (continued)

Company	SKU	Sales	Reported market share	Price	Market Share we Computed
Seagull Labs	Spantel Susp 200 mg 10 ml × 1 (/5 ml)	211,310	0	1.80	0.0488565
Lincoln Pharma	Anthel Susp 200 mg 10 ml × 1 (/5 ml)	203,260	0	1.06	0.0469953
Aglowmed	Wormpel Susp 10 ml × 1	202,110	0	1.55	0.0467294
Euphoric	Pa-Pa A Susp 200 mg 10 ml × 1 (/5 ml)	199,173	0	1.30	0.0460503
Radicura Pharma	Al Susp 200 mg 10 ml × 1	178,783	0	0.92	0.041336
Libra Drugs	Zeben Susp 200 mg 10 ml × 1 (/5 ml)	128,357	0	1.13	0.0296771
Agio Pharma	Albazio Susp 200 mg 10 ml × 1 (/5 ml)	114,080	0	1.11	0.0263762
Morepen Labs	Mybend Liquid 400 mg 10 ml × 1	110,830	0	0.63	0.0256247
Orchid Chem&Pharm	Banhelmin Susp 200 mg 10 ml × 1 (/5 ml)	107,979	0	0.58	0.0249656
M M Labs	Emanthal Susp 200 mg 10 ml × 1 (/5 ml)	107,916	0	0.93	0.024951
Cipla	Tiobend Susp 200 mg 10 ml × 1 (/5 ml)	104,388	0	0.59	0.0241353
Glaxosmithkline	Zentel Susp 200 mg 50 ml × 1 (/5 ml)	97,523	0	0.96	0.0225481
Acron	Alone Syrup 10 ml × 1	95,207	0	1.45	0.0220126
Glenmark Labs	Albact Susp 200 mg 10 ml × 1 (/5 ml)	94,685	0	1.01	0.0218919
Morepen Labs	Morezole Susp 200 mg 10 ml × 1 (/5 ml)	92,755	0	2.40	0.0214457
Emcure	Sezole Susp 200 mg 10 ml × 1 (/5 ml)	92,256	0	1.27	0.0213303
Cipla	Xworm Susp 200 mg 10 ml × 1 (/5 ml)	91,113	0	0.70	0.021066
Seagull Labs	Panamint Susp 200 mg 10 ml × 1 (/5 ml)	87,317	0	1.43	0.0201884
Shreya Life Scienc	Alzist Susp 200 mg 10 ml × 1 (/5 ml)	73,921	0	1.80	0.0170911
Pharmindia	Abend Susp 200 mg 10 ml × 1 (/5 ml)	51,687	0	1.25	0.0119504
Blue Cross	Albendazole Syrup 200 mg 10 ml × 1 (/5 ml)	46,620	0	1.11	0.0107789
Medley Pharma	Odipar Susp 10 ml × 1	42,845	0	0.55	0.0099061
Indoco	Wormiknock Syrup 200 mg 10 ml × 1 (/5 ml)	39,284	0	0.57	0.0090828
Ambalal Sarabhai	Albendazole Susp 200 mg 10 ml × 1 (/5 ml)	38,072	0	0.64	0.0088025

Pfizer	Combantrin-A Susp 200 mg 10 ml × 1 (/5 ml)	28,779	0	2.09	0.0066539
Ind-Swift	Elbenol Susp 200 mg 10 ml × 1 (/5 ml)	26,019	0	0.57	0.0060158
Cadila Pharma	Wormin-A Susp 200 mg 10 ml × 1 (/5 ml)	23,534	0	1.12	0.0054412
Synchem Labs	Mintel Susp 200 mg 10 ml × 1 (/5 ml)	22,840	0	1.57	0.0052808
Moraceae Pharma	Morband Susp 200 mg 10 ml × 1 (/5 ml)	18,079	0	0.85	0.00418
Syncom	Alb Susp 200 mg 10 ml × 1 (/5 ml)	10,596	0	0.60	0.0024499
Kanpha	Bendol Susp 200 mg 10 ml × 1 (/5 ml)	8053	0	1.05	0.0018619
Zydus Cadila	Cantel Syrup 10 ml × 1	7225	0	0.50	0.0016705
Ranbaxy	Albendazole Susp 200 mg 10 ml × 1 (/5 ml)	5802	0	0.98	0.0013415
Galpha Labs	Helmanil Susp 200 mg 10 ml × 1 (/5 ml)	4500	0	1.56	0.0010404
Euphoric	Abzole Susp 200 mg 10 ml × 1 (/5 ml)	4365	0	0.98	0.0010092
Lark Labs	Toko Syrup 200 mg 10 ml × 1 (/5 ml)	3845	0	0.72	0.000889
Caryl Pharma	Alzol Susp 200 mg 10 ml × 1 (/5 ml)	3039	0	1.61	0.0007026
Zee Labs	Altec Susp 200 mg 10 ml × 1 (/5 ml)	1408	0	1.35	0.0003255
Lincoln Pharma	Bentel Susp 200 mg 10 ml × 1 (/5 ml)	989	0	1.80	0.0002287
Wings Pharma	Albazole Susp 200 mg 10 ml × 1 (/5 ml)	924	0	0.53	0.0002136
Cipla	Wormex Susp 200 mg 10 ml × 1 (/5 ml)	722	0	0.67	0.0001669
Invida India	Albrodo Susp 200 mg 10 ml × 1 (/5 ml)	410	0	0.91	0.0000948
Stadmed Private	Tagazole Susp 200 mg 10 ml × 1 (/5 ml)	110	0	1.22	0.0000254

Albendazole Suspension the first 22 packs on the working sheet are considered. It is remarkable that not all of the 22 SKUs have a market share of 1% or more. Looking closer at the companies producing the 22 packs considered, it seems that packs for fixation of the price ceilings are not chosen based on the "branded-generic and generic versions of a certain drug formulation" as stated in the DPCO 2013 having a market share of at least 1% but based on the company's total market share. In other words, once a company has a single pack that meets the market share criterion, all other packs with different retail prices produced by the same company are also used for calculating the ceiling price.

Unfortunately, this procedure is repeated for all molecules on the Working Sheet of June 21 2013, which has a significant impact on the level of the ceiling prices. We repeat our analyses for Albendazole 400 mg/5 ml suspension and find similar inconsistencies (see Table 5.9). The NPPA list contains 107 SKUs for 400 mg Albendazole. Among them, 10 SKUs have a market share of more than 1% with an estimated ceiling price of 12.71. There are 54 SKUs with more than 0.5% market share and the ceiling price based on their prices is 12.28. Yet the NPPA's ceiling price is based on 32 SKUs and fixed at 9.12.

The above analysis shows two important findings. First, it clearly demonstrates the ambiguity in the information the NPPA provides to the public. Second, it gives evidence for the claim that the fixation of ceiling prices by the NPPA is not done according to the own rules outlined in the DPCO 2013.

The inconsistencies described above are not exhaustive (Table 5.10). There are identical packages with comparable brand names included in the NPPA list and the AOICD list that match with dissimilar companies. Although it is possible that different companies offering brands are named similarly, it looks like the NPPA has confused company names sometimes leading to a lack of clarity on the type and number of brands considered for price ceiling calculation. This problem seems to apply to company Zydus Cadila in the IMS data set and company Biochem Pharmaceuticals in the AOICD dataset, as well as to company Emcure in the IMS data set and company Zuventus Healthcare in the AOICD data set. Take the case of Amikacin. Here, pack *Amicin Inj Vial 250 mg 2 ml x 1* with brand name Amicin is produced by company Zydus Cadila at a price of Rs. 13.72 per unit according to the NPPA list. The same pack *Amicin Inj Vial 250 mg 2 ml x 1* is manufactured by company Biochem according to the AOICD list at exactly the same price of Rs. 13.72 per unit. Similarly, for Ampicillin capsule the pack *Biocillin Caps 500 mg x 10* with brand name Biocillin is produced by company Zydus Cadila at a unit price of Rs. 5.24 according to the NPPA and by Biochem at the same price according to the AOICD. In the latter case, both companies also have identical market shares. Moreover, looking at molecule Cefixime, the pack *C-Tax-O Tabs Dispers 100 mg x 10* with brand name C-Tax-O is listed by the NPPA for company Emcure with a market share of 1% and a price per unit of Rs. 6.21 and by the AOICD for company Zuventus with a similar market share and price. Also in the case of Ondansetron 2 mg/5 ml the pack *Emigo 2 mg Syrup 30 ml* is produced by these same companies at comparable prices. The reason for the mismatch between companies and packages is unclear. A short search on the websites of the pharmaceutical

Table 5.9 NPPA's calculations to determine the ceiling price for Albendazole 400 mg/5 ml suspension

Company	SKU	Sales	Reported market share	Price	Market share we computed
Glaxosmithkline	Zentel Tab Uncoated 400 mg × 1	319,208,884	0.49	14.02	49.30674
Ranbaxy	Zeebee Tabs Chew 400 mg × 1	69,170,157	0.11	9.6	10.6844
Alkem	Noworm Tab Uncoated 400 mg × 1	43,831,785	0.07	12.77	6.770496
Cipla	Bendex Tabs Chew 400 mg × 1	35,547,976	0.05	12.07	5.490934
Mankind	Bandy Tabs Chew 400 mg × 1	31,024,473	0.05	6.54	4.792209
Blue Cross	Womiban Tabs 400 mg × 1	25,664,909	0.04	13.83	3.964342
Intas Pharma	Abd Tabs 400 mg × 1	8,909,485	0.01	9.84	1.376208
Mankind	Bandy Tabs 400 mg × 10	7,688,700	0.01	5.71	1.187639
Micro Labs	Xenda Tabs Chew 400 mg × 1	7,636,455	0.01	12.95	1.179568
Lupin Limited	Lupiworm Tabs Chew 400 mg × 1	7,134,612	0.01	12.26	1.102051
Indoco	Abz Tabs 400 mg × 1	6,070,724	0.01	11	0.937717
Unichem	Wormfix Tabs Chew 400 mg × 1	5,204,667	0.01	13.33	0.803941
Juggat Pharma	Cidazole Tab Uncoated 400 mg × 1	4,990,185	0.01	10.14	0.770811
Micro Labs	Xenda Tabs 400 mg × 30	4,963,188	0.01	8.96	0.766641
Zydus Cadila	Zelbend Tabs 400 mg × 1	4,725,737	0.01	9.63	0.729963
Albert David	Sioban Tabs Chew 400 mg × 1	4,543,932	0.01	12.24	0.701881
Shreya Life Scienc	Albenum Tabs 400 mg × 10	4,480,718	0.01	16.35	0.692116
Shrinivas Labs	Alvela Tabs Chew 400 mg × 1	3,881,264	0.01	12.18	0.599521
Dr Reddys Labs	Rediout Tabs Chew 400 mg × 1	3,355,741	0.01	5.77	0.518346
Alembic	Worid Tabs Chew 400 mg × 1	3,322,948	0.01	9.63	0.513281
Cipla	Xworm Tabs Chew 400 mg × 1	3,251,536	0.01	3.61	0.50225
Zydus Cadila	Olworm Tabs 400 mg × 1	2,414,483	0	10.63	0.372954
Klar Sehen	Odal Tabs Chew 400 mg × 1	2,373,826	0	8.58	0.366674
Khandelwal	Alltel Tabs Chew 400 mg × 1	2,324,107	0	14.44	0.358994
Emcee	Sidose Tabs 400 mg × 1	2,214,808	0	10.2	0.342111
Obsurge Biotech	Ah-1 Tabs Ch.Oran 400 mg × 1	2,177,641	0	6.9	0.33637

(continued)

Table 5.9 (continued)

Company	SKU	Sales	Reported market share	Price	Market share we computed
Darkt Internation.	Albend Tabs Chew 400 mg × 1	2,001,086	0	9	0.309099
Shine Pharma	Albid Tabs 400 mg × 1	1,844,490	0	10.69	0.28491
Mapra Labs	Xenith Tabs 400 mg × 1	1,796,816	0	11.26	0.277546
Ranbaxy	Albendazole Tabs 400 mg × 1	1,752,600	0	8.4	0.270716
Medo Pharma	Alworm Tabs Chew 400 mg × 1	1,745,783	0	8.99	0.269663
Glaxosmithkline	Zentel Tabs Chew 400 mg × 2	1,725,090	0	10.55	0.266467
Iatros Pharma	Albenmint Tabs 400 mg × 1	1,246,181	0	10.49	0.192492
Zydus Cadila	Albendazole Tabs 400 mg × 1	1,243,641	0	3	0.1921
Alkem	Dispel Tabs 400 mg × 1	1,195,687	0	12.45	0.184692
Sterkem	Beworm Tab Uncoated 400 mg × 1	1,127,798	0	10.82	0.174206
Palson Drug	All-In-1 Tabs 400 mg × 1	1,104,213	0	9.83	0.170563
Wallace	Abwal Tab Uncoated 400 mg × 1	1,034,127	0	11.93	0.159737
Emcee	Sidose Tabs Chew 400 mg × 10	1,025,639	0	9.73	0.158426
Burnet Pharma	Ben Tabs 400 mg × 1	915,166	0	13.17	0.141362
Lupin Limited	Lupibend Tabs Chew 400 mg × 1	717,187	0	2.66	0.110781
Glaxosmithkline	Zentel Tabs 400 mg × 5	712,550	0	11.61	0.110064
Aglowmed	Wormpel Tabs 400 mg × 1	619,344	0	9.52	0.095667
Elder Pharma	Eldoben Tab Uncoated 400 mg × 1	615,004	0	13.9	0.094997
Indoco	Olban Tabs Chew 400 mg × 1	530,345	0	11.74	0.08192
Torrent Pharma	Alminth Tabs 400 mg × 3	516,406	0	9.98	0.079767
Nestor Pharma	Albest Tabs 400 mg × 1	484,634	0	9.65	0.074859
Micro Labs	Albendol Tabs 400 mg × 1	441,812	0	9.67	0.068245
Zydus Cadila	Zybend Tabs 400 mg × 1	390,024	0	1.71	0.060245
Dales Pharma	Krumex Tab Uncoated 400 mg × 1	364,844	0	6.4	0.056356
Mars	Helmex Tabs 400 mg × 1	352,921	0	13.04	0.054514
Lincoln Pharma	Anthel Tabs Chew 400 mg × 1	342,730	0	8.11	0.05294

Laborate Pharma	Abide Tab Uncoated 400 mg × 1	339,984	0	12.26	0.052516
Emcee	Sidose Tabs 400 mg × 3	328,820	0	7.06	0.050791
Cipla	Tiobend Tabs 400 mg × 1	304,862	0	1.6	0.047091
Uni-San Pharma	Helmix Tabs Chew 400 mg × 1	304,341	0	8.43	0.04701
Satven&Mer Pharma	Low Tab Uncoated 400 mg × 10	303,459	0	0.8	0.046874
Radicura Pharma	Al Tabs 400 mg × 1	289,380	0	7.17	0.044699
Graf Labs	D Worm Tabs 400 mg × 1	287,930	0	10.73	0.044475
Makers Labs	Wintil Tabs 400 mg × 1	284,320	0	4	0.043918
Wockhardt Ltd	Alzad Tabs 400 mg × 1	282,795	0	1.4	0.043682
Wockhardt Ltd	Wozole Tabs Chew 400 mg × 1	269,132	0	1.75	0.041572
Novartis Intl.	Kealwerm Tabs 400 mg × 2	242,078	0	8.65	0.037393
Acron	Alone Tabs Chew 400 mg × 1	229,477	0	8.02	0.035446
Mankind	Mahabend Tabs 400 mg × 1	210,987	0	1.58	0.03259
Medo Pharma	Alworm Tabs Chew 400 mg × 10	196,806	0	6.97	0.0304
Klar Sehen	Odal Tabs 400 mg × 10	167,286	0	0.82	0.02584
Micro Labs	Wormal Tabs Chew 400 mg × 1	143,685	0	1.75	0.022194
Cadila Pharma	Vormout Tabs 400 mg × 1	139,855	0	1.36	0.021603
Ind-Swift	Elbenol Tabs 400 mg × 1	112,999	0	2.73	0.017454
Blue Cross	Womiban Tabs 400 mg × 4	88,964	0	6.89	0.013742
Morepen Labs	Morezole Tabs Chew 400 mg × 1	88,903	0	8.84	0.013732
Glenmark Labs	Albact Tabs 400 mg × 1	69,101	0	9.61	0.010674
Seagull Labs	Panamint Tabs 400 mg × 1	65,058	0	11.72	0.010049
Syncom	Alb Tabs 400 mg × 1	61,896	0	4	0.009561
Omega Remedies	Albee Tabs Chew 400 mg × 1	61,650	0	10.96	0.009523
Moraceae Pharma	Morband Tabs Chew 400 mg × 2	56,900	0	5.81	0.008789
Libra Drugs	X- Worm Tabs Chew 400 mg × 1	56,520	0	9	0.00873
Psychotropics	Wonil Tabs 400 mg × 5	52,490	0	2.62	0.008108
Synchem Labs	Mintel Tabs Chew 400 mg × 1	49,519	0	9.58	0.007649
Zydus Cadila	Cantel Tabs Chew 400 mg × 1	44,205	0	1.15	0.006828

(continued)

Table 5.9 (continued)

Company	SKU	Sales	Reported market share	Price	Market share we computed
M M Labs	Emanthal Tabs 400 mg × 1	42,942	0	6.14	0.006633
Libra Drugs	Zeben Tabs Chew 400 mg × 1	34,991	0	10.53	0.005405
Seagull Labs	Spantel Tabs 400 mg × 10	32,753	0	1.19	0.005059
Ashok Pharma	Envorm Tabs Chew 400 mg × 1	23,859	0	9	0.003685
Anglo French Drugs	Albendazole Tabs 400 mg × 1	22,086	0	3	0.003412
Maneesh Pharma	Goworm Tabs Chew 400 mg × 1	18,787	0	7.76	0.002902
Morepen Labs	Mybend Tabs Chew 400 mg × 1	18,168	0	1.5	0.002806
Noel Pharma	Benz Tabs 400 mg × 1	18,077	0	1.8	0.002792
Marc Laboratories	Eraworm Tabs 400 mg × 1	17,665	0	11.11	0.002729
Glenmark Pharma	Milibend Tabs 400 mg × 1	14,780	0	5.7	0.002283
Lark Labs	Toko Tabs Fort 400 mg × 1	14,055	0	4.33	0.002171
Medico Labs	Mediminth Tabs 400 mg × 1	10,649	0	4.11	0.001645
Pfizer	Combantrin-A Tabs Chew 400 mg × 1	7619	0	12.23	0.001177
Cipla	Wormex Tabs Chew 400 mg × 1	6984	0	3.25	0.001079
Unk. Generic Manf.	Albendazole Tabs 400 mg × 1	5405	0	1.09	0.000835
Indoco	Wormiknock Tabs 400 mg × 1	4880	0	1.42	0.000754
Zydus Cadila	Zelbend Tab Uncoated 400 mg × 4	2034	0	8.62	0.000314
Rpg Life Sciences	Albendazole Tabs 400 mg × 1	1476	0	2.4	0.000228
Pharmasynth Formul	Nemofex Tabs Chew 400 mg × 1	1144	0	24.34	0.000177
Syncom	Alb Tabs 400 mg × 10	1063	0	0.27	0.000164
Cadila Pharma	Wormin-A Tabs 400 mg × 1	769	0	9.05	0.000119
Mapra Labs	Xenith Tabs Chew 400 mg × 1	763	0	12.51	0.000118
Overseas	Elbend Tab Uncoated 400 mg × 2	314	0	9.81	4.85E-05
Overseas	Elbend Tab Uncoated 400 mg × 1	182	0	9.1	2.81E-05
Invida India	Albrodo Tabs 400 mg × 1	59	0	6.57	9.11E-06
Ar Ex	Saf-A Tabs 400 mg × 1	48	0	8	7.41E-06

Table 5.10 Comparison of total number of packs, packs considered and similar packs considered using IMS vs. AOICD data

Medicine with ceiling price notified on 21st June 2013	N of packs in IMS	N of packs in AOICD	N of packs used by NPPA	N of packs used in AIOCD	Common N of packs
Acetazolamide Systemic Tablet 250 mg	8	9	3	6	3
Aciclovir Cream 5%	7	8	6	5	4
Albendazole Suspension 200 mg	94	51	14	4	4
Albendazole Tablet 400 mg	107	91	32	6	6
Alprazolam Tablet 0.25 mg	84	70	17	8	7
Amikacin Injectables 250 mg	50	41	26	14	11
Amlodipine Tablet 2.5 mg	64	42	34	15	12
Amlodipine Solids 5 mg	88	71	42	17	14
Amoxycillin Suspension 125 mg	69	20	24	6	6
Amoxycillin Capsule 500 mg	105	58	18	7	5
Ampicillin Capsule 500 mg	28	11	13	4	3
Ampicillin Injection 500 mg	27	10	15	5	4
Artesunate Solids 50 mg	14	10	6	8	6
Atenolol Solids 50 mg	69	38	21	9	9
Atorvastatin Solids 10 mg	99	104	45	21	21
Bromocriptine Solids 1.25 mg	9	7	6	6	4
Bromocriptine Solids 2.5 mg	11	9	6	7	4
Cefixime Tablet 100 mg	121	125	48	20	18
Ceftazidime Injection 1000 mg	23	16	8	7	5
Ceftriaxone Injection 250 mg	67	55	28	14	11
Diazepam Tablet 5 mg	20	13	10	6	5
Fluconazole Capsule 200 mg	5	5	5	5	5
Fluconazole Capsule 50 mg	6	5	4	3	3
Fluconazole Tablet 100 mg	4	2	3	1	1
Fluconazole Tablet 200 mg	11	8	8	7	4
Fluconazole Tablet 50 mg	16	7	10	5	3
Glucose Injectables 10%	14	6	10	5	5
Imatinib Mesylate Tablet 100 mg	3	10	3	7	3
Levo-Thyroxine (Synthetic) Tablet 100 mcg	11	11	4	4	4
Metformin Tablet 500 mg	100	94	44	15	15
Omeprazole Capsule 10 mg	11	7	4	2	1
Omeprazole Capsule 20 mg	117	78	26	5	4
Ondansetron Injection 2 mg/1 ml	71	59	31	12	10
Ondansetron Syrup 2 mg/5 ml	56	40	11	7	5
Primaquine Tablet 2.5 mg	3	4	2	4	2
Ispaghula Granules	29	3	20	1	0

companies does not suggest any connection between the two, neither for Zydus Cadila and Biochem nor Emcure and Zuventus. However, since the discussed packages have a market share of more than 1%, the result is a lower number of similar packs considered for price fixation.

References

Alexander, J. (2013a). NGOs to submit comparative analysis of drug prices as SC agrees to scrutinize pricing policy. *PharmaBiz* [online]. Available from: http://pharmabiz.com/NewsDetails.aspx?aid=78097&sid=1

Alexander, J. (2013b, October 31). DoP asks NPPA to relook at ceiling price fixed for azithromycin under new DPCO. PharmaBiz.com

Alexander, J. (2013c, August 26). NPPA starts collecting info on prices of non-scheduled products directly from drug cos. Pharmabiz.com

Alexander, J. (2013d, July 3). DCGI allows cos to re-print revised prices on essential drugs already available in market. PharmaBiz.com

Francis, P. A. (2014, April 2). Editorial: IMS data and new prices. PharmaBiz.com. Available from http://www.pharmabiz.com/ArticleDetails.aspx?aid=81173&sid=3

Nautiyal, S. (2014, December 1). IDMA approaches NPPA to withdraw proposal on display of distinguishing mark for scheduled drugs. PharmaBiz.com

Phadke, A., & Srinivasan, S. (2013). Pharma policy 2012 and its discontents. *Economic and Political Weekly, 48*(1), 38–42.

PharmaBiz.com. (2013a, August 5). Delhi HC sends notice to centre on DPCO issue as more companies challenge new drug pricing. Available from http://pharmabiz.com/NewsDetails.aspx?aid=76991&sid=2

PharmaBiz.com. (2013b, September 12). Chemists, druggists for more representation. PharmaBiz.com

Rana, S. (2016, May 4). AIOCD urges NPPA to mandate cos to recall stock from trade for correction in MRPs. PharmaBiz.com

Shankar, R. (2013, June 26). NPPA formula for fixing ceiling prices of essential drugs under new DPCO confusing. PharmaBiz.com

Shankar, R. (2014a, July 15). 'Price to retailer' only basis for deciding ceiling price of a drug under DPCO: DoP. PharmaBiz.com

Shankar, R. (2014b, November 18). NPPA issues draft proposal for display of distinguishing mark & ceiling price of scheduled drugs on label. PharmaBiz.com

Shankar, R. (2014c, November 24). NPPA's move to display distinguishing mark on labels about ceiling prices of scheduled drugs opposed. PharmaBiz.com

Shankar, R. (2015a, July 28). DoP asks NPPA to fix price of Nab Tortaxel injection as per provisions of para 5(1) of DPCO 2013. PharmaBiz.com

Shankar, R. (2015b, March 4). DoP directs NPPA to revalidate data on Cefotaxime 250 mg and 500 mg injections. PharmaBiz.com

Shankar, R. (2015c, February 16). DoP directs NPPA to revalidate data on ciprofloxacin HCl tablet 250 mg. PharmaBiz.com

Shankar, R. (2015d, June 3). DoP directs NPPA to revise prices of ilaprazole + domperidone capsules. PharmaBiz.com

Shankar, R. (2015e, February 17). NPPA rolls back proposal on display of distinguishing mark & ceiling prices of scheduled drugs on labels. PharmaBiz.com

Shankar, R. (2016a, April 18). NPPA clarifies on implementation of prices fixed and notified under provisions of DPCO, 2013. PharmaBiz.com

Shankar, R. (2016b, July 12). DoP asks NPPA to re-fix ceiling price of 'Clotrimazole Cream 1%' on review petition filed by Glenmark. PharmaBiz.com
Shankar, R. (2016c, December 12). DoP directs NPPA to adopt correct methodology in fixing ceiling price of ciprofloxacin 500 & 250 mg tabs. PharmaBiz.com
Shankar, R. (2016d, July 18). DoP directs NPPA to examine new data to review ceiling price of erythropoietin Inj 2000 IU & 10000 IU. PharmaBiz.com
Shankar, R. (2016e, October 21). DoP directs NPPA to re-fix and re-notify ceiling prices of "Cefotaxime 1 gm injection". PharmaBiz.com
Shankar, R. (2016f, September 12). DoP directs NPPA to re-fix ceiling price of 'Coagulation Factor VIII'. PharmaBiz.com
Shankar, R. (2016g, August 30). DoP directs NPPA to re-fix retail price of "azithromycin and dexamethasone phosphate eye drops 3 ml vial". PharmaBiz.com
Shankar, R. (2016h, September 27). DoP directs NPPA to revise ceiling prices of "Paclitaxel injection, Carboplatin & Cisplatin" strictly as per para 4 of DPCO 2013. PharmaBiz.com
Shankar, R. (2016i, October 24). DoP quashes ceiling price of levoflexacin 500 mg by NPPA; directs to refix ceiling price as per DPCO. PharmaBiz.com
Shankar, R. (2016j, May 16). NPPA asks retailers not to return stocks if manufacturers provide current price list as per revised notified prices of drugs. PharmaBiz.com
Shankar, R. (2017a, February 6). DoP directs NPPA to re-fix retail price of teneligliptin 20 mg + metformin 1000 mg ER tablets. PharmaBiz.com
Shankar, R. (2017b, September 21). DoP asks NPPA to re-fix ceiling price of co-trimoxazole tablet after examining documentary proof submitted by Cadila Healthcare. PharmaBiz.com
Shankar, R. (2017c, May 3). DoP asks NPPA to refix prices of "Methotrexate 2.5 mg, 7.5 mg and 10 mg tabs" by considering only 8 formulations with SKU-wise MAT of more than 1% market share. PharmaBiz.com
Shankar, R. (2017d, October 3). DoP asks NPPA to take expert committee's opinion for fixing ceiling price of methylprednisolone Inj 40 mg/ml. PharmaBiz.com
Shankar, R. (2017e, August 14). DoP directs NPPA to re-fix ceiling price of N-acetylcyseine 200 mg sachet. PharmaBiz.com
Shankar, R. (2017f, January 5). DoP directs NPPA to re-fix ceiling price of ondansetron 2 mg/ml injectables. PharmaBiz.com
Shankar, R. (2017g, June 1). DoP directs NPPA to re-fix ceiling price of Ranitidine 25 mg/ml. PharmaBiz.com
Shankar, R. (2017h, September 18). DoP directs NPPA to re-fix ceiling prices of clomiphene 100 mg and 50 mg tablets. PharmaBiz.com
Shankar, R. (2017i, August 31). DoP directs NPPA to re-fix the ceiling price of Furosemide injection. PharmaBiz.com
Shankar, R. (2017j, January 12). DoP directs NPPA to revise ceiling price of formulation methyldopa 500 mg tablet as per para 4(1) and para 6 of DPCO, 2013. PharmaBiz.com
Shankar, R. (2017k, November 11). DoP directs NPPA to take expert panel's opinion on separate ceiling prices based on pack sizes of methylprednisole injection. PharmaBiz.com
Shankar, R. (2017l, January 4). NPPA fails to fix ceiling prices of coronary stents due to insufficient data. PharmaBiz.com
Shankar, R. (2017m, April 17). No provision in DPCO 2013 to differentiate consumer pack and dispensing pack while calculating ceiling price: DoP. PharmaBiz.com
Shankar, R. (2017n, April 27). Sun Pharma gets favourable review on carboxymethylcellulose drops 1% as DoP asks NPPA to re-fix ceiling price. PharmaBiz.com
Vijay, N. (2015, February 27). NPPA to discuss identification marks for drugs under ceiling price with trade, BDCDA wants red color on packs. PharmaBiz.com
Yadav, L. (2016, July 20). DoP agrees to AIOCD's demand for allowing sale of drugs at pre-revised prices until their batch number expires. PharmaBiz.com

Part III
The Impact of the 2013 DPCO

Chapter 6
How Effective Are the 2013 DPCO Regulations?

6.1 Introduction

In this chapter, we examine whether the 2013 DPCO has been successful in making essential medicines more affordable. Before we do so, it is useful to recall historical assessments of previous versions of the DPCO. Historical accounts indicate that the implementation of DPCO regulations in India has been ineffective. In the 1970s, the implementation of the recommendations of the Hathi Committee were delayed by 4 years. Although the committee established the importance of focusing price regulation based on the 'essentiality' of drugs rather than their prices, the recommendation was forgotten by 2002, leading to a fresh debate on the issue. In 1979, the control of drug prices led to a troubling shortage of essential drugs, causing hardships for patients (Basak 2008). The drafting of the drug policy was delayed in the 1980s due to opposition from industry associations (EPW 1985). In 1986, the pharmaceutical policy was still unclear about what drugs needed to be brought under price regulation, allowing industry associations to influence regulators on behalf of the pharmaceutical firms (Bal 1986a, b). In 1990, the industry and trade associations warned about a possible nationwide strike unless the implementation of price control was postponed (EPW 1990). Similarly, after the implementation of the 1995 price control regime, prices of essential medicines rose, which benefited pharmaceutical producers (Malhotra 2010; Rane 1996). Before we examine the effectiveness of the 2013 DPCO, we discuss the assessment by the NPPA as well as an assessment by the pharmaceutical industry lobby in collaboration with IMS.

A. Bhaskarabhatla, *Regulating Pharmaceutical Prices in India*, India Studies in Business and Economics, https://doi.org/10.1007/978-3-319-93393-1_6

6.2 Revisiting an Evaluation of the Price Control Regulations Conducted by IMS Health

IMS evaluated the 2013 DPCO and released a report in July 2015. The study was sponsored by the Organization of Pharmaceutical Producers of India (OPPI), an industry association of foreign pharmaceutical firms operating in India, who were less enthusiastic about the imposition of drug price controls in India. The IMS study argued that price controls are neither an effective nor a sustainable strategy for improving access to medicines for Indian patients and that they are counterproductive (PharmaBiz.com 2015). Nitin Goel, general manager, IMS Health South Asia notes (PharmaBiz 2015):

> Price control has limited impact on improving patient access and, furthermore, is not aligned with the requirements of a vibrant economy like India. Government's priority should be on strengthening India's healthcare infrastructure and extending universal insurance coverage.

The IMS report contains four key findings, which we list below (IMS Health 2015). We also identify potential limitations associated with each of the findings.

> Finding 1. For low-income households that are reliant on the government system for healthcare, DPCO would not improve the patient's ability to purchase drugs. This is supported by the fact that no significant penetration of price-controlled molecules in rural markets is visible, with consumption in rural towns decreasing at ~7% over the last two years. The price controlled molecules has also witnessed muted growth in prescriptions outside metros (town class I) as compared to 5% Rx growth in non-DPCO molecules.

In theory, a decline in prices should make the medicines more affordable, particularly to low-income households in rural areas. Yet the study points to a decline in prescriptions for price-controlled medicines compared to others. The result is surprising, and the study does not elaborate on the potential underlying mechanisms causing such decline in prescriptions in rural areas. Nevertheless, the study concludes that the DPCO is ineffective. We identify the following limitations with this conclusion. First, a decline in prescriptions can result from a shift in production as well as the promotional effort by pharmaceutical firms away from regulated medicines and into unregulated medicine markets. We will examine this mechanism in greater detail in Chap. 7. Second, although the IMS study chooses to focus on low-income households, access to affordable medicines remains a problem for not only low-income families but also for the vast majority of the population in India. Hence, the focus of the 2013 DPCO is not merely to make medicines affordable to low-income families alone, but to control the inexplicably high profit margins for both manufacturers and retailers in the pharmaceutical industry, as discussed in Chap. 3.

> Finding 2. DPCO has an impact on the tail-end brands than the leading players thereby increasing market concentration and resulting in discontinuation of brands, with the average number of brands in DPCO molecules reducing from 36 in 2013 to 32 in 2015. These market forces can move towards strengthening of oligopolistic behavior, which will result in reduced set of choices for the doctors/patients.

The basis for the assertion by IMS that the DPCO has an impact on the tail-end brands alone is unclear. By contrast, as we discussed in Chap. 4, the DPCO takes into account SKUs with more than 1% market share in determining the ceiling price. As a result, in the market for 500 mg Paracetamol tablets, the 14 SKUs with more than 1% market share influence the ceiling price, but more than 100 tail-end brands have no such influence. Also, as we documented in Chap. 3, the leading players in the market usually also charge relatively higher prices. Consequently, the ceiling price is generally non-binding concerning the tail-end firms. One would expect that a well-executed DPCO sets ceiling prices that are binding for the leading brands. The market structure of the medicine markets with more than 30 SKUs indicates that there are a small number of dominant firms and a large number of relatively small firms, commonly referred to as the competitive fringe. It is unclear from the IMS finding whether SKUs produced by the dominant firms exited the market on those of the tail-end firms. Overall, if the 2013 DPCO is designed and implemented well, and pharmaceutical firms comply with price controls, and doctors and patients shop for better prices, then the intensity of competition should increase between the tail-end and the leading players.

> Finding 3. The decline in R&D resulting in fewer new introductions of generic products; Post DPCO 2013, the average number of new introductions in DPCO molecules has declined, which also indicates increasing concentration and reducing competitive intensity.

The medicines brought under the DPCO are generally older, out-of-patent medicines. Pharmaceutical firms in India focus on promoting these medicines rather than invest in R&D. It is unclear what IMS consider to be R&D in the context of DPCO medicines, and whether the study can come to such conclusions without examining medicine-specific and dosage-specific investments in R&D. To our knowledge, such data are not compiled by the Center for Monitoring the Indian Economy (CMIE). In addition, interpreting new SKU introductions of generic products as a measure of R&D is highly problematic for several reasons. First, as we will examine later in the book, the new introductions of generic products in the Indian pharmaceutical industry typically involve innovations in packaging, branding, and marketing that have *per se* no added therapeutic value. Second, as discussed in Chap. 3, a company like Cipla introduces three different varieties of the same medicine under different brand names and with different prices, and the brand with highest prices typically has the highest market share. The presence of multiple such SKUs does not indicate higher R&D expenses by Cipla. Third, there is anecdotal evidence to suggest that pharmaceutical firms introduced new SKUs to circumvent DPCO regulations. For example, GSK claimed that its new SKU of Paracetamol, introduced in August 2011, at a per-tablet price of Rs. 1.59 and a retail margin of 26%. GSK also discontinued all older Crocin brands. The consumer division of GSK argued that Crocin Advance is an innovative drug with an advanced technology compared to any other brand of Paracetamol (Nautiyal 2014a, b, c April 7). GSK went on to claim exemption from the DPCO regulations and refused to comply with the ceiling price (Nautiyal 2014a, b, c April 7):

> Crocin Advance has a superior pharmacokinetic profile to standard paracetamol tablets and has been approved as New Drug Formulation by CDSCO. GSK had applied to NPPA through Remedix Pharmaceuticals, the manufacturer of the drug, for grant of exemption from price control under the provisions of Para 32, in DPCO 2013.

Naturally, the NPPA rejected GSK's surprisingly generous interpretation of novelty and the added therapeutic value of its Crocin Advance SKU, resulting in recovery of Rs. 5399.37 lakhs by the NPPA by March 14, 2017 for overcharging consumers (NPPA 2017). Therefore, IMS's view that new SKU introductions of generic products is a measure of R&D is questionable.

> Finding 4. Macro-economic impact: Price control and the unstable regulatory environment have increased the margin pressures for companies, thereby impacting their sustainability especially small and mid-sized players. This further impacts the employment generation potential of the industry. These factors dampen the sentiments across the industry and potential domestic and international investors.

While the study speculates that at the macroeconomic level, price controls have a negative impact, there is little evidence gathered in the study to support the assertion. Nonetheless, at the macro level, price controls on commonly used pharmaceuticals can also have a positive impact on the health of the workers in the economy, which can lead to higher productivity, and it is problematic to draw such far-reaching conclusions without conducting a proper analysis.

The IMS study argues that drug price controls implemented in other countries have failed to benefit the poor. In the Philippines, the sales of regulated drugs have declined while unregulated drug sales increased. Some generic drug producers experienced a decline in revenues by 50% due to lower drug prices under the price control regime, which adversely impacted their ability to launch new drugs. Similarly, in China, drug price controls led to a near zero profitability of drug manufacturers and retailers. Since hospitals and stores did not want to give up their margins, they started prescribing and selling more expensive unregulated drugs to remain profitable, which hurt the availability and affordability of drugs for the poor.

The IMS study provides several recommendations. The study suggests that the government could: (i) strengthen healthcare financing by extending universal health coverage; (ii) invest in healthcare infrastructure; (iii) promote joint and bulk procurement by state governments; (iv) establish a tax on tobacco and liquor industry to fund the healthcare sector and subsidize essential medicines from taxes; and (v) setup dedicated generic medicine stores. The sweeping conclusions and recommendations of the study are surprisingly based on an examination of only 18 medicines under the 2013 DPCO and 18 comparable counterparts not under price control regulation. The IMS study claims that the list of medicines is "representative of the whole universe and with strong statistical significance" and validated by key stakeholders (IMS Health 2015, p. 3).

We deepen our examination of the manner of selection of 18 medicines employed in the IMS study. We find that these medicines collectively account for 7% of the Indian pharmaceutical industry between 2011 and 2012. Also, the medicines are partially regulated, that is, only some dosages of the 18 medicines are regulated and others not, and the regulated dosages account for 77% of the overall sales during 2011–2012, indicating that the overall share of the regulated doses of the 18 medicines is closer to 5% of the Indian pharmaceutical market. The 18 medicines represent 6.7% of the 269 medicines under the 2013 DPCO during 2013–2014, as contained in the Pharmatrac dataset. We present in Table 6.1 the list of 18 medicines under the 2013

Table 6.1 Selection of medicines in the IMS study evaluating the effectiveness of the 2013 DPCO

#	3-digit medicine code	Representative DPCO medicine selected by IMS for comparison	DPCO sales	Non-DPCO counterpart selected in IMS study	Non-DPCO sales	3-digit substitutes	2-digit substitutes	DPCO/Non-DPCO sales
1	A10B	Metformin|A10B6	5	Glimepiride|A10B4	4.95	46	59	1.01
2	J2A	Fluconazole|J2A4	2.18	Ketoconazole|D1A3	1.26	14	14	1.74
3	C8A	Amlodipine|C8A1	6.22	Cilnidipine|C8A24	0.28	12	32	22.14
4	C10A	Atorvastatin|C10A1	13.92	Rosuvastatin|C10A6	5.31	6	39	2.62
5	C9D	Losartan|C9D3	3.95	Telmisartan|C9D4	5.9	6	48	0.67
6	B1C	Aspirin|B1C1	0.64	Prasugrel|B1C23	0.28	12	34	2.32
7	C7A	Metoprolol|C7A29	6.4	Carvedilol|C7A19	1.21	12	42	5.3
8	A6B	Bisacodyl|A6B5	0.86	Lactulose|A6A4	2.63	5	25	0.33
9	A3F	Metoclopramide|A3F19	0.64	Prochlorperazine|A4B4	1.1	41	92	0.58
10	A4A	Ondansetron|A4A2	4.54	Granisetron|A4A1	0.19	8	23	23.72
11	N5D	Alprazolam|N5D1	2.96	Etizolam|N5C8	0.34	16	62	8.64
12	M2A	Diclofenac|M2A2	7.03	Aceclofenac|M1A1	1.22	12	17	5.74
13	N2B	Paracetamol|N2B1	9.48	Analgin|N2B7*	0.87	11	28	10.9
14	R6A	Cetirizine|R6A3	3.01	Levocetirizine|R6A13	2.34	47	47	1.29
15	P1B	Albendazole|P1B1	1.98	Mebendazole|P1B2	0.2	11	46	9.84
16	J1C	Amoxycillin|J1C1	5.7	Piperacillin|J1H5	0.0	25	153	>100
17	J1F	Azithromycin|J1F1	9.8	Lincomycin|J1F6	0.5	15	153	19.54
18	J1D	Ceftriaxone|J1D17	11.61	Cefoperazone|J1D22	0.31	58	153	37.73

Notes: The table shows the 18 medicines under the 2013 DPCO selected for study by IMS and 18 other medicines not under DPCO selected for comparison. The sales are based on Pharmatrac data between January 2011 and December 2012 and measures in billions of rupees. The 3-digit and 2-digit substitutes represent the number of other medicines under the same therapeutic category at the 3-digit or 2-digit medicine code of the medicine under price regulation. The ratio DPCO/Non-DPCO sales show the relative size of the regulated medicine compared to the unregulated medicine

Source: Author's calculations

*Metamizole (commonly known as Analgin) is briefly banned in India in 2013 (Bhaumik 2013; Business Standard 2014)

DPCO selected for study by IMS and the list of 18 other medicines not under DPCO selected for comparison. The sales of these medicines are reported in billions of rupees based on Pharmatrac data between January 2011 and December 2012. While IMS has chosen only one medicine for comparison for each medicine under DPCO, there are a large number of potentially comparable medicines within the 3-digit and 2-digit therapeutic categories of the DPCO medicines. We identify the "3-digit and 2-digit substitutes," which indicate the number of other medicines under the same therapeutic category at the 3-digit or 2-digit medicine code of the medicine under price regulation. The ratio DPCO/Non-DPCO Sales shows the relative size of the regulated medicine compared to the unregulated medicine. The ratio is significantly more than one in more than half the cases, indicating that the comparison medicines chosen for the study are significantly smaller relative to the medicines entering the 2013 DPCO.

Some medicines chosen for comparison are not the ideal choices. For example, the choice of Metamizole, a drug banned in India in 2013 (since 1974 in Sweden and 1977 in the US due to an increased risk of agranulocytosis) as a comparison for Paracetamol is surprising (Bhaumik 2013). Although the ban on Metamizole was lifted in 2014, the manufacturers were required to display on packaging and promotional materials the following: "The drug is indicated for severe pain or pain due to tumor and also for bringing down temperature in refractory cases when other antipyretics fail to do so" (Business Standard 2014). In addition, the market for Metamizole is more than ten times smaller compared to Paracetamol. We also found the choice of Piperacillin as a comparison to Amoxicillin surprising, because it is more than 100 times smaller than Amoxicillin in sales.

The choices of medicines for comparison are surprising particularly because the 3-digit and 2-digit therapeutic categories contain a large number of other potential substitutes. We compile the top-selling medicines in each of the 3-digit therapeutic categories containing the 18 medicines selected for study by the IMS. We list the top ten medicines including the medicine under the 2013 DPCO. For example, within the A10B 3-digit category, Metformin is the third largest medicine in sales. Although Glimepiride is comparable in sales to Metformin, two fixed-dose combinations of Metformin outsell both Metformin and Glimepiride. Similarly, in the case of Amoxicillin, its fixed-dose combination with Clavulanic Acid outsells the plain medicine. Overall, as shown in Table 6.2, in six of the 18 cases, the comparison is not present in the same 3-digit therapeutic category.[1]

Next, we limit the dataset to tablet and capsule formulations of the medicines chosen in the IMS study and examine their prices over time. We compare the normalized prices of 16 of the 18 DPCO medicines and their counterparts in the IMS study, which have data for tablets or capsules. We plot in Fig. 6.1, the normalized prices of both prices for each of the medicines, with solid line representing the price trend for the DPCO

[1]Table 6.2 also reveals a significant limitation of the 2013 DPCO. While it controls the price of plain medicines, its combinations are excluded from regulation. Also, several larger, often-prescribed medicines within the same 3-digit therapeutic category are excluded. Overall, the use of relatively smaller, and insignificant medicines for comparison cannot be described as a strength of the IMS study design.

Table 6.2 Top-selling medicines during 2011–2012 by 3-digit therapeutic categories containing the 18 medicines chosen for analysis in the IMS Health (2015)

#	Metformin	DPCO medicine	IMS control	Sales (Million Rs.)
1	Glimepiride + Metformin|A10B11			13730.1
2	Glimepiride + Metformin + Pioglitazone|A10B36			7742.23
3	Metformin|A10B6	Yes		5001.63
4	Glimepiride|A10B4		Yes	4947.46
5	Gliclazide + Metformin|A10B10			3311.11
6	Voglibose|A10B22			3236.64
7	Vildagliptin + Metformin|A10B69			2626.35
8	Sitagliptin|A10B66			2300.11
9	Sitagliptin + Metformin|A10B68			2206.07
10	Vildagliptin|A10B67			2129.55
Fluconazole				
1	Fluconazole|J2A4	Yes		2184.03
2	Terbinafine|J2A9			998.62
3	Caspofungin acetate|J2A23			728.167
4	Itraconazole|J2A7			488.84
5	Amphotericin B|J2A2			414.171
6	Voriconazole|J2A14			399.022
7	Griseofulvin|J2A8			322.486
8	Ketoconazole|J2A3		Yes	239.008
9	Anidulafungin|J2A19			88.449
10	Micafungin|J2A18			75.3856
Amlodipine				
1	Amlodipine|C8A1	Yes		6223.78
2	S-Amlodipine|C8A2			2369.28
3	Diltiazem|C8A6			1500.64
4	Nifedipine|C8A16			1046.18
5	Cilnidipine|C8A24		Yes	281.105
6	Verapamil|C8A23			193.037
7	Nimodipine|C8A18			125.313
8	Lercanidipine|C8A12			88.9306
9	Felodipine|C8A7			44.8254
10	Levosimendan|C8A26			13.2279
Atorvastatin				
1	Atorvastatin|C10A1	Yes		13917.5
2	Rosuvastatin|C10A6		Yes	5306.67
3	Simvastatin|C10A7			521.698
4	Pitavastatin|C10A8			29.1274
5	Fluvastatin|C10A3			12.0721
6	Lovastatin|C10A4			6.73759
7	Pravastatin|C10A5			0.197357

(continued)

Table 6.2 (continued)

#	Metformin	DPCO medicine	IMS control	Sales (Million Rs.)
Losartan				
1	Telmisartan|C9D4		Yes	5897.52
2	Losartan|C9D3	Yes		3948.55
3	Olmesartan|C9D7			2605.03
4	Valsartan|C9D5			402.809
5	Irbesartan|C9D2			130.687
6	Candesartan|C9D1			15.5745
7	Eprosartan|C9D8			0.288236
Aspirin				
1	Clopidogrel|B1C5			3366.53
2	Aspirin + Clopidogrel|B1C19			2201.65
3	Aspirin + Dipyridamole|B1C21			2011.84
4	Aspirin + Atorvastatin + Clopidogrel|B1C20			869.183
5	Tirofiban|B1C9			817.563
6	Aspirin|B1C1	Yes		643.544
7	Prasugrel|B1C23		Yes	277.624
8	Eptifibatide|B1C8			207.075
9	Abciximab|B1C7			131.896
10	Ozagrel|B1C18			54.9724
Metoprolol				
1	Metoprolol|C7A29	Yes		6396.76
2	Atenolol|C7A5			2751.57
3	Nebivolol|C7A43			1520.2
4	Propranolol|C7A37			1361.38
5	Carvedilol|C7A19		Yes	1207.23
6	S-Metoprolol|C7A44			843.372
7	Bisoprolol|C7A10			802.56
8	Labetalol|C7A25			223.907
9	S-Atenolol|C7A6			54.6204
10	Sotalol|C7A38			17.0823
Bisacodyl				
1	Bisacodyl|A6B5	Yes		860.362
2	Sodium Picosulphate|A6B7			455.014
3	Senna|A6B3			81.2178
4	Other contact Laxatives|A6B6			52.0171
5	Phenolpathalein|A6B4			2.2016
Metoclopramide				
1	Domperidone + Pantoprazole|A3F12			6949.89
2	Domperidone + Rabeprazole|A3F13			6767.27
3	Domperidone + Omeprazole|A3F9			3662.19
4	Domperidone + Esomeprazole|A3F10			1518.44
5	Levosulpiride + Rabeprazole|A3F47			1008.97

(continued)

Table 6.2 (continued)

#	Metformin	DPCO medicine	IMS control	Sales (Million Rs.)
6	Domperidone|A3F7			954.097
7	Pantoprazole + Itopride|A3F24			764.485
8	Rabeprazole + Itopride|A3F25			641.827
9	Metoclopramide|A3F19	Yes		637.557
10	Levosulpiride + Pantoprazole|A3F50			503.65
Ondansetron				
1	Ondansetron|A4A2	Yes		4535.36
2	Granisetron|A4A1		Yes	191.172
3	Ramosetron|A4A7			167.628
4	Ondansetron + Omeprazole|A4A9			153.625
5	Ondansetron + Ranitidine|A4A8			78.8965
6	Palonosetron|A4A4			76.451
7	Other Ondansetron Combinations|A4A6			9.94007
8	Ondansetron + Paracetamol|A4A3			2.17127
Alprazolam				
1	Alprazolam|N5D1	Yes		2963.39
2	Lorazepam|N5D11			1241.24
3	Diazepam|N5D9			711.968
4	Chlordiazepoxide|N5D7			470.713
5	Alprazolam + Propranolol|N5D4			282.26
6	Alprazolam + Sertraline|N5D5			179.576
7	Midazolam|N5D16			170.566
8	Alprazolam + Melatonin|N5D2			95.6862
9	Alprazolam + Fluoxetine|N5D15			66.1076
10	Diazepam + Propranolol|N5D10			60.6792
Diclofenac				
1	Diclofenac|M2A2	Yes		7029.45
2	Nimesulide|M2A8			199.392
3	Aceclofenac|M2A1			104.348
4	Flurbiprofen|M2A3			96.7099
5	Piroxicam|M2A9			73.6313
6	Dexketoprofen|M2A15			60.2535
7	Ketoprofen|M2A5			27.4077
8	Thiocolchicoside + Diclofenac|M2A16			17.1606
9	Etoricoxib|M2A14			9.51849
10	Ibuprofen|M2A4			4.56302
Paracetamol				
1	Paracetamol|N2B1	Yes		9476.23
2	Paracetamol + Tramadol|N2B3			2310.73
3	Tramadol|N2B5			1656.84
4	Analgin|N2B7		Yes	869.15
5	Pentazocine|N2B6			715.575

(continued)

Table 6.2 (continued)

#	Metformin	DPCO medicine	IMS control	Sales (Million Rs.)
6	Paracetamol + Dextropropoxyphene|N2B2			558.845
7	Tramadol + Paracetamol + Domperidone|N2B9			165.815
8	Paracetamol + Racemethionine|N2B4			115.509
9	Tramadol + Paracetamol + Serratiopeptidase|N2B11			27.0603
10	Other Non-Narcotics and Anti-Pyretics|N2B8			1.66055
Cetirizine				
1	Montelukast + Levocetirizine|R6A42			5241.17
2	Cetirizine|R6A3	Yes		3007.91
3	Levocetirizine|R6A13		Yes	2339.21
4	Fexofenadine|R6A11			1815.43
5	Pheniramine|R6A17			1040.18
6	Hydroxyzine|R6A12			757.601
7	Cetirizine + Ambroxol|R6A25			642.991
8	Methdilazine|R6A15			432.44
9	Montelukast + Fexofenadine|R6A36			425.255
10	Loratidine|R6A14			370.29
Albendazole				
1	Albendazole|P1B1	Yes		1981.72
2	Pyrantel Pamoate|P1B3			488.122
3	Albendazole + Ivermectin|P1B9			422.283
4	Mebendazole|P1B2		Yes	201.44
5	Levamisole|P1B4			133.195
6	Ivermectine|P1B5			97.6756
7	Piperazine|P1B6			89.5352
8	Fluconazole + Ivermectin|P1B13			14.9957
9	Other Anthelmintics, excluding Schistosomicides|P1B8			12.3113
10	Albendazole + Levamisole|P1B10			5.5549
Amoxycillin				
1	Amoxycillin + Clavulanic acid|J1C4			23738.8
2	Amoxycillin|J1C1	Yes		5703.74
3	Ampicillin + Cloxacillin|J1C8			2742.53
4	Ampicillin + Dicloxacillin|J1C27			942.002
5	Amoxycillin + Cloxacillin|J1C5			779.94
6	Ampicillin|J1C7			655.803
7	Amoxycillin + Dicloxacillin + Lactobacillus|J1C28			549.173
8	Amoxycillin + Clavulanic acid + Lactobacillus|J1C21			542.34

(continued)

Table 6.2 (continued)

#	Metformin	DPCO medicine	IMS control	Sales (Million Rs.)
9	Amoxycillin + Dicloxacillin|J1C26			398.006
10	Amoxycillin + Cloxacillin + Lactobacillus| J1C22			309.506
Azithromycin				
1	Azithromycin|J1F1	Yes		9801.6
2	Linezolid|J1F7			2519.28
3	Erythromycin|J1F4			2013.12
4	Clarithromycin|J1F2			1930.95
5	Clindamycin|J1F3			1388.96
6	Roxithromycin|J1F10			1336.39
7	Doripenem|J1F21			600.674
8	Clindamycin + Clotrimazole|J1F16			529.315
9	Lincomycin|J1F6		Yes	501.68
10	Spiramycin|J1F12			443.986
Ceftriaxone				
1	Cefixime|J1D26			15657.1
2	Ceftriaxone|J1D17	Yes		11607.9
3	Cefpodoxime|J1D16			10417.7
4	Cefuroxime|J1D12			9210.21
5	Cefoperazone + Sulbactum|J1D23			4819.05
6	Cefalexin|J1D1			4462.42
7	Cefpodoxime + Clavulanic acid|J1D37			4443.44
8	Ceftriaxone + Sulbactum|J1D18			4440.73
9	Cefotaxime|J1D13			4144.58
10	Cefixime + Ofloxacin|J1D45			4085.17

medicine. We obtain the normalized price by dividing the maximum retail price at the SKU-level by the number of tablets in the SKU as well as the strength of the tablet to obtain a per-milligram price. We then divide the price we observe for the medicine in the first month they appear in the dataset, which results in the initial price of one. In more than half of the graphs, the price trends for the DPCO and the non-DPCO molecule vary differently over time. Using a similar procedure, we plot in Fig. 6.2 the normalized sales of these 16 medicines in their tablet or capsule form over time. We find that the normalized sales of the DPCO and other medicines depart from each other significantly in as many as eight cases.

A significant limitation of the IMS study is that it compares medicines that are selected for price regulation with other medicines. As we discussed so far, any such comparisons, however well-conceived, remain open to criticism, as different medicines are only imperfect substitutes with fundamental differences in their prescription and usage patterns over time. One alternative is to examine different dosages of the same medicine that entered price control regulation. We will exploit this insight in our own evaluation of the efficacy of the 2013 DPCO subsequently.

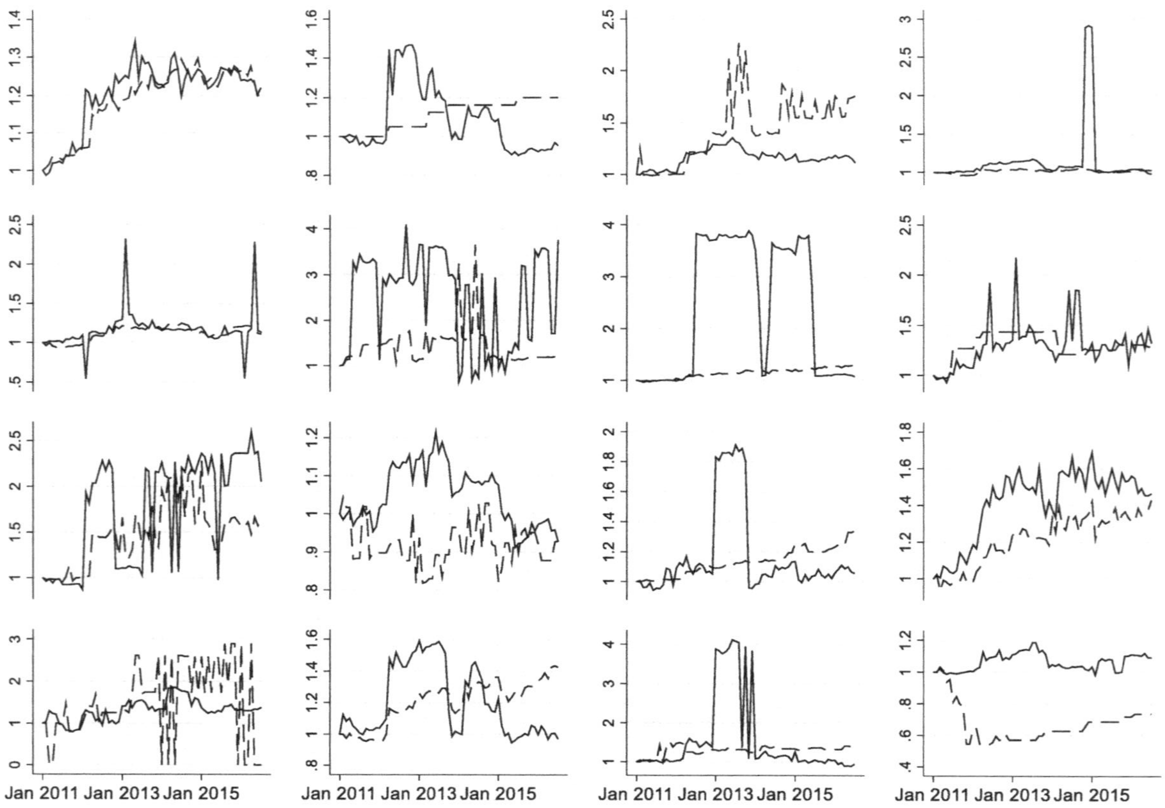

Fig. 6.1 Normalized price trends, plotted on y-axis, of 16 of the 18 DPCO medicines and their counterparts in the IMS study, the solid line represents DPCO medicine. Notes: The 16 DPCO medicines from left to right and then from top to bottom are Metformin, Fluconazole, Amlodipine, Atorvastatin, Losartan, Aspirin, Metoprolol, Bisacodyl, Metoclopramide, Ondansetron, Alprazolam, Diclofenac, Paracetamol, Cetirizine, Albendazole, and Azithromycin

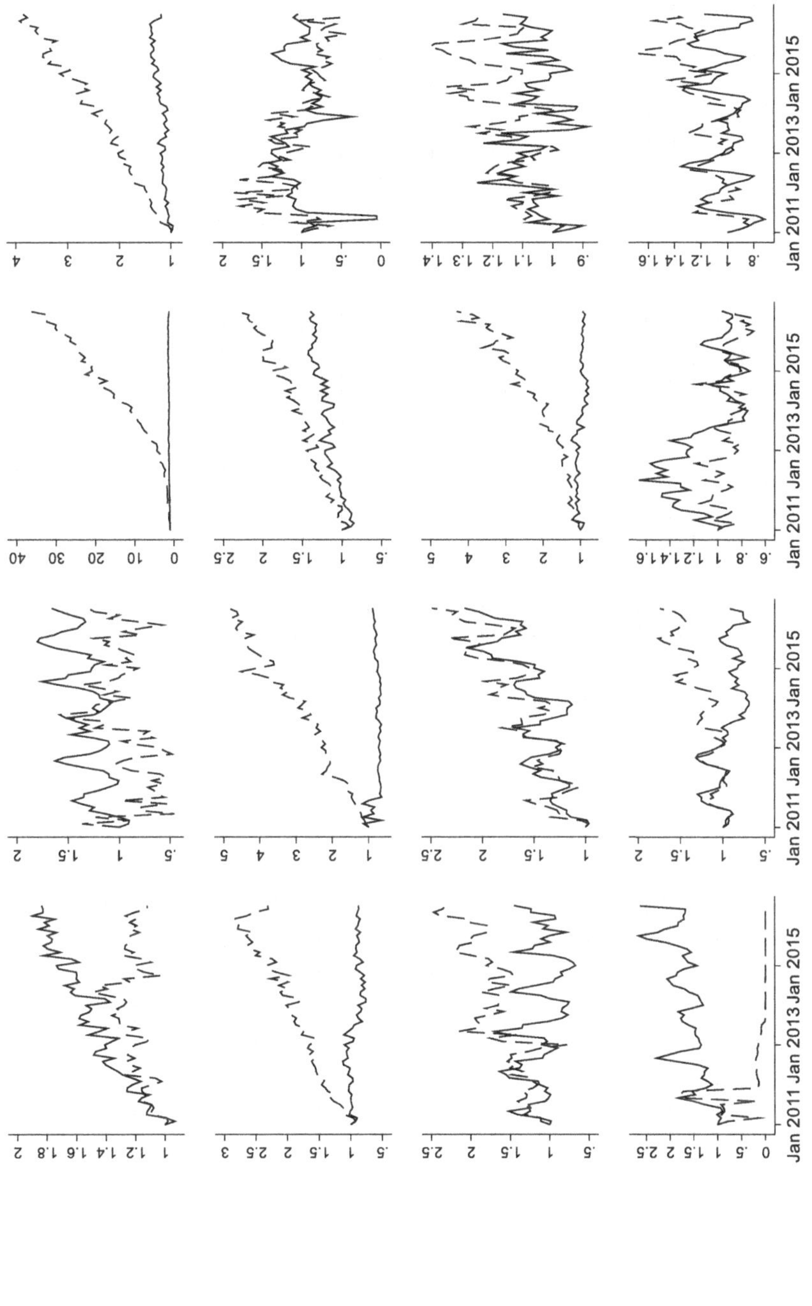

Fig. 6.2 Sales over time for 16 of the 18 DPCO medicines and their counterparts in the IMS study

We revisited the IMS study in this section primarily to highlight the difficulty in evaluating the effectiveness of the 2013 price control regulations. In light of the above shortcomings of the study, it is important to deepen the analysis and examine how firms responded to the regulations.

6.3 The 2013 DPCO Controls a Declining Share of the Indian Pharmaceutical Market

The 2013 DPCO regulated 348 medicines while more than 2900 medicines are sold in India. One way to gauge the effectiveness of the 2013 DPCO is by its scope. Recall that the scope of pharmaceutical regulation varied significantly since the 1970s. The 1979 DPCO controlled 347 bulk drugs covering nearly 80% of the market. However, the proposed (but never implemented) policy of 2004 reduced the number of medicines to 35, which covered only 20% of the market. By contrast, the 2013 DPCO has covered nearly 350 medicines. On the surface, it appears that a significant portion of the market must be affected by the expansion of the number of medicines under price controls in 2013.

To examine the scope of 2013 DPCO, we plot the sales of medicines under regulation and those excluded from regulation in Fig. 6.3. We find that the sales of regulated medicines remain constant at around 10 billion rupees while that of the unregulated market doubled from 40 billion in 2011 to 80 billion in 2016. The share of sales of regulated medicines decreased from 20% of the overall market in 2011 to 11% in 2016. Next, we plot the number of SKUs for the regulated and unregulated

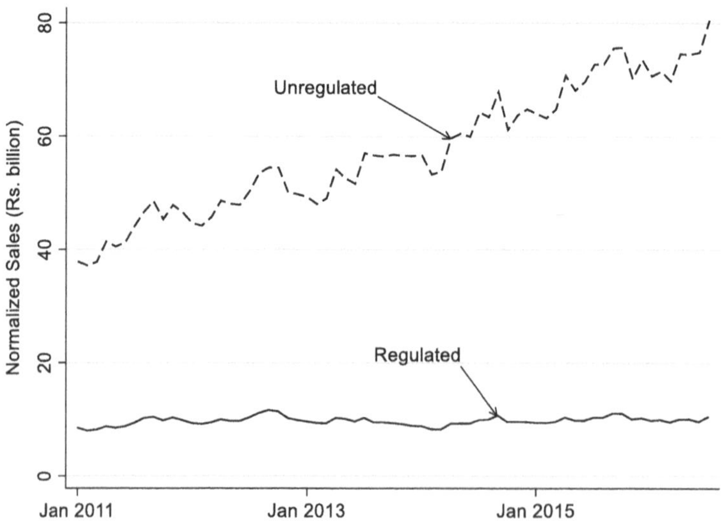

Fig. 6.3 The sales of medicines under 2013 DPCO over time in billion rupees

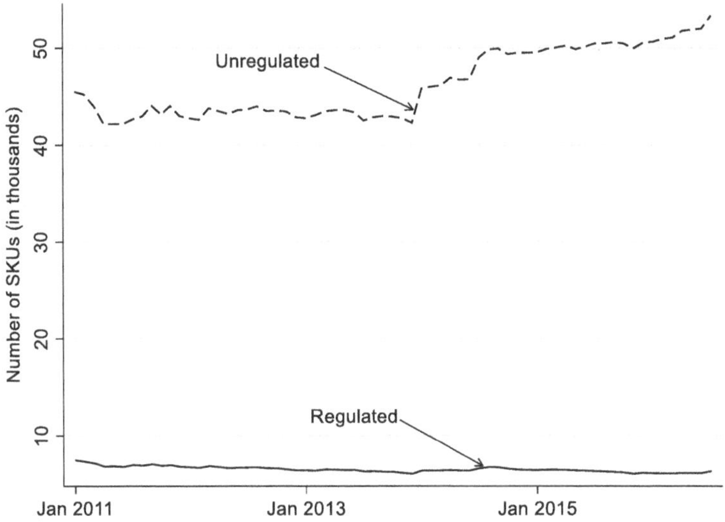

Fig. 6.4 The number of unique SKUs under 2013 DPCO over time in thousands

medicines in Fig. 6.4. We find that the number is declining for the regulated medicines from 7466 in January 2011 to 6323 in July 2016. By contrast, the number of SKUs for the unregulated medicines increased from 45,515 to 53,361 during the same period, indicating a potential adverse impact of regulation on the introduction of new varieties, as the IMS study concludes. While the IMS study interprets these numbers as reflective of investments in R&D, we hypothesize that the pharmaceutical firms strategically reduced the number of SKUs in regulated medicines and increased the number of SKUs in unregulated medicines to mitigate the adverse impact of regulation. A close examination of the trends indicates that the number of SKUs among the unregulated medicines remained constant until the end of 2013, and began to increase rapidly afterward.

Next, we report the share of sales attributed to regulated medicine SKUs by 3-digit therapeutic category. We do so for the partial list of 3-digit categories with a non-zero percent of the market that in 2011 is likely to enter regulation. In other words, we exclude from this list those 3-digit classes that were unaffected by the 2013 regulation, as they would have a zero percent share of sales attributed to the regulated medicines. Among the 127 categories in the list, there are 46 categories with less than 10% of the market under regulation and six categories with more than 90% of the market under regulation. Overall, for 101 3-digit category markets, the percentage of regulated medicines by sales is less than 50, indicating that the scope of the 2013 DPCO is limited.

As noted in our discussion of the IMS study, the presence of a large number of potential substitutes within the same 3-digit therapeutic category that are not regulated allows firms to mitigate the impact of regulation. The limitation of the 2013 DPCO goes further than the number of medicines it regulates, but the extent of the dosages within each medicine market that it regulates. Next, we examine the partial nature of the price regulation at the medicine level Table 6.3.

Table 6.3 The percentage share of sales by regulated medicines in 3-digit therapeutic category markets

#	3-digit category	Share in 2011	Share in 2012	Share in 2013	Share in 2014	Share in 2015
1	A10B	6.17	5.95	5.3	4.72	4.11
2	A10G	70.69	69.32	59.65	56.56	53.86
3	A10H	70.88	70.59	62.53	56.65	62.85
4	A11E	0.05	0.18	0.22	0.22	0.24
5	A11X	9.03	24.76	4.96	4.75	4.73
6	A12A	0	0.19	0.39	0.3	0.14
7	A12C	78.63	80.8	78.72	77.16	74.39
8	A2A	0.73	1.1	4.42	5.7	5.85
9	A2B	4.85	5.49	4.78	4.02	3.86
10	A2C	28.59	28.4	26.54	23.14	24.77
11	A2E	2.69	1.8	2.01	0.44	0.06
12	A3A	29.16	30.7	28.33	20.96	18.76
13	A3F	5.35	4.65	3.67	2.84	2.34
14	A4A	67.85	68.15	67.58	68.53	63.66
15	A4B	21.61	19.86	17.91	15.47	13.87
16	A6B	43.8	48.96	45.21	34.14	37.48
17	A6C	44.84	40.95	39.31	37.97	37.78
18	A7A	8.88	8.17	9.18	9.66	9.14
19	A7E	41.38	36.74	34.15	30.48	27.85
20	A7G	63.14	61.81	57.55	57.17	57.08
21	B1A	7.91	7.49	9.47	5	4.31
22	B1B	64.29	69	68.31	69.17	69.46
23	B1C	32.15	36.48	39.75	36.6	33.94
24	B1D	14.66	17.17	19.91	15.23	18.45
25	B1X	28.75	15.35	12.76	8.47	7.29
26	B2D	40.93	34.64	61.87	1.25	8.92
27	B3A	7.16	7.15	5.18	4.25	4.97
28	C10A	38.83	34.53	29.75	24.38	22.05
29	C1A	93.89	92.78	89.96	91.27	92.25
30	C1B	78.75	75.95	78.64	78.28	78.58
31	C1C	16.72	15.16	9.22	6.72	5.29
32	C1E	26.01	25.05	22.17	17.51	16.08
33	C2A	37.53	30.53	23.93	20.42	6.29
34	C2B	0.19	0.27	0.1	0.06	0.17
35	C3A	19.28	19.69	11.9	9.37	7.49
36	C3C	7.36	6.77	5.52	3.69	3.1
37	C3F	94.23	98.8	98.86	98.83	98.43
38	C7A	52.86	52.55	50.9	46.99	46.86
39	C8A	60.14	61.05	58.89	51.6	47.88
40	C9A	17.21	16.88	18.9	16.11	15.62
41	C9D	32.64	28.1	23.64	18.96	17.48

(continued)

Table 6.3 (continued)

#	3-digit category	Share in 2011	Share in 2012	Share in 2013	Share in 2014	Share in 2015
42	D1A	4.17	4.32	3.41	2.66	2.04
43	D2A	6.83	6.61	5.93	5.56	3.33
44	D6A	10.99	10.76	9.93	9.66	11.2
45	D6B	86.13	83	88.11	83.32	83.48
46	D7A	2.69	3.75	4.12	4.68	4.54
47	D8A	60.55	57.35	48.22	26.45	24.89
48	G2A	73.45	77.64	69.44	60.07	58.88
49	G2B	100	100	100	100	100
50	G3A	26.5	26.56	22.81	20.11	19.08
51	G3B	28.67	25.52	18.63	12.84	11.92
52	G3G	5.37	6.56	4.86	4.01	3.78
53	G3J	40.47	31.67	19.55	9.57	10.5
54	G3X	32.68	25.58	19.92	16.25	14.28
55	G4A	32.13	34.77	35.7	37.35	43.39
56	H2A	48.69	47.74	47.33	41.68	41.46
57	H3A	74.49	71.57	66.17	60.99	57.88
58	H3B	61.73	65.65	66.53	63.25	60.01
59	H4B	100	100	100	100	100
60	J1A	10.87	9.32	8.52	5.64	0.61
61	J1C	58.49	60	59.56	60.08	60.19
62	J1D	29	27.31	26	24.24	24.41
63	J1F	52.42	51.27	48.92	48.45	46.58
64	J1G	43.76	43.67	41.59	40.14	33.33
65	J1H	0.01	0	0	0	0
66	J1K	13.8	13.24	11.91	10.61	10.57
67	J1X	15.71	14.87	13.12	12.11	17.49
68	J2A	43.67	39.35	33.56	30.46	27.63
69	J3A	0.03	0.02	0.01	0	0
70	J4A	20.65	21.22	21.48	21.94	21.81
71	J4B	15.26	12.79	12.77	19.89	13.9
72	J5A	42.05	41.9	37.94	36.6	19.58
73	J5B	24.28	18.59	16.74	10.91	7.93
74	J6A	51.55	62.86	48.06	40.3	56.68
75	J6E	86.52	82.94	79.98	75.74	76.94
76	J7A	38.71	40.43	40.57	36.68	27.46
77	K1A	70.49	73.35	70.01	71.7	75.53
78	K1C	78.22	79.55	71.01	84.12	68.99
79	K2A	100	100	100	100	100
80	K5A	60.57	34.5	54.54	64.05	28.4
81	L1A	18.26	21.77	17.28	11	15.02
82	L1B	49.27	40.65	37.92	44.56	45.43
83	L1C	4.78	2.88	2.97	3.74	3.71

(continued)

Table 6.3 (continued)

#	3-digit category	Share in 2011	Share in 2012	Share in 2013	Share in 2014	Share in 2015
84	L1D	41.64	35.52	42.19	40.24	38.31
85	L1X	25.12	19.98	14.48	13.14	16.31
86	L2B	9.56	11.88	9.76	8.14	10.47
87	L3A	56.87	59.64	72.3	68.69	63.84
88	L3B	4	2.35	3.27	1.02	0.5
89	L4A	30.52	26.28	25.34	21.45	23.4
90	M1A	4.81	3.33	2.58	2.23	2.05
91	M1C	19.76	19.17	25.77	15.96	11.12
92	M3A	10.64	5.76	7.52	5.43	8.27
93	M4A	52.71	43.69	35.41	22.28	20.11
94	M5C	50.48	43.18	54.47	44.51	39.86
95	N1A	94.12	92.64	94.15	98.54	98.83
96	N1B	78.4	74.56	68.89	61.37	66.54
97	N1C	64.61	42.2	37.33	36.96	36.73
98	N2A	1.93	0.18	0.06	0.52	0.05
99	N2B	24.36	26.15	23.3	20.96	18.87
100	N3A	17.85	17.08	14.8	12.24	10.28
101	N4A	53.23	53.79	46.73	41.8	42.18
102	N5A	15.54	14.7	13.29	11.63	10.77
103	N5B	3.91	3.3	3.96	4.16	7.28
104	N5D	52.21	51.65	51	42.99	44.74
105	N6A	8.21	7.78	6.39	5.05	4.53
106	N7C	5.15	3.75	3.45	3.81	3.6
107	N7E	3.51	2.17	1.28	1.32	0.61
108	P1A	0.74	0.89	0.9	0.64	0.5
109	P1B	52	61.34	52.3	46.07	44.04
110	P1C	0	0	0	0	0
111	P1D	22.75	22.3	21.6	20.07	21.35
112	P1E	35.77	38.64	30.15	34.09	37.2
113	P2A	22.29	23.06	20.04	16.76	14.94
114	R3A	9.81	8.55	7.31	6.33	5.67
115	R5D	0.18	0.04	0.01	0	0.01
116	R5E	0.06	0.02	0.02	0.01	0
117	R5F	0.02	0.02	0.02	0.04	0.03
118	R6A	17.73	16.34	13.57	11	10.05
119	S1A	2.63	2.32	1.87	1.39	1.05
120	S1D	22.3	20.56	16.76	13.34	12.17
121	S1E	31.58	34.35	31.5	32.44	36.59
122	S1F	0.3	0.3	0.2	0.13	0.1
123	S3A	32.4	30.19	29.8	28.79	22.93
124	S3B	56.58	38.59	54.69	71.86	64.73
125	V3D	4.31	5.09	7.81	6.23	7.84

(continued)

Table 6.3 (continued)

#	3-digit category	Share in 2011	Share in 2012	Share in 2013	Share in 2014	Share in 2015
126	V3E	41.1	47.93	55.23	58.45	58.93
127	V3F	6.64	6.63	2.08	1.3	0.98

Notes: We report the percentage share of sales by regulated medicines by 3-digit therapeutic category during 2011–2015. The regulation comes into effect in mid-2013, but we report the share of sales for the SKUs that will enter 2013 DPCO in 2011 and 2012. Overall, there are several 3-digit categories with relatively small fraction of the market under regulation

6.4 The 2013 DPCO Controls Medicine Markets Only Partially

The 2013 DPCO only partially regulates the Indian pharmaceutical industry. Not only does the DPCO exclude a large number of medicines but it also excludes several dosage markets within many regulated medicines. To illustrate the nature of such incomplete regulation, we compile a list of 108 medicines in their tablet or capsule form that entered the 2013 DPCO but contained some regulated and other unregulated dosages. We present the list in Table 6.4. We calculate the market share of each of the dosage within the medicine market during 2011–2012 using the Pharmatrac dataset. Some dosages have a very small market share of less than 0.01, but we include them for completeness and report their market share approximated as 0.00. At the top of the table, Aciclovir tablets are sold in four dosage markets, 200 mg, 400 mg, 800 mg, and 1200 mg. The 200 mg and 400 mg dosage markets are regulated, and they account for 14 and 39% market shares respectively. The 800 mg and 1200 mg dosage markets are unregulated and account for nearly 46.5% market share. The effectiveness of the regulation is significantly affected by such partial regulation, as firms can adjust to price controls in the regulated dosage markets by shifting production to the unregulated dosage markets and increasing prices in those markets.

Although the DPCO regulated some dosages, for some medicines the market share of the regulated doses more than 90%. For example, 400 mg of Albendazole is regulated and accounts for nearly 99% of the market. However, as we discussed in Table 6.2, fixed-dose combinations of Albendazole, such as Albendazole + Ivermectin and Albendazole + Levamisole are not regulated. Also, other close plain medicine substitutes within the same 3-digit category, such as Mebendazole are not regulated, which undermines the effectiveness of the regulation.

We compile a similar list of partially regulated medicines in their injection or infusion form in Table 6.5 and for medicines administered as syrups in Table 6.6. Some injection SKUs contained in the Pharmatrac data do not report their dosage strength. Consequently, we do not take into account these SKUs in calculating the market shares during 2011–2012. Nonetheless, we find as many as 70 medicines with some injection doses regulated and other unregulated and 17 such syrups.

Table 6.4 The partial or incomplete nature of the 2013 price controls for 108 essential medicine in their tablet form

#	Medicine|4-digit category	Regulated tablet doses (market share)	Unregulated tablet doses (market share)	Paragraph-19 doses (market share)
1	Aciclovir|J5A4	400 mg (39.40), 200 mg (14.02)	1200 mg (.67), 800 mg (45.90)	
2	Albendazole|P1B1	400 mg (99.33)	200 mg (.66)	
3	Allopurinol|M4A4	100 mg (83.69)	250 mg (2.89), 300 mg (13.39), 20 mg (.01)	
4	Alprazolam|N5D1	0.5 mg (56.88), 0.50 mg (.49), 0.25 mg (36.25)	20 mg (.02), 100 mg (0.00), 12.5 mg (0.00), 1.5 mg (.36), 0.125 mg (.05), 6.25 mg (0.00), 2 mg (.18), 1 mg (5.71), 10 mg (.00), 5 mg (0.00), 15 mg (0.00)	
5	Amitriptyline|N6A1	25 mg (35.95)	5 mg (.12), 10 mg (52.75), 75 mg (4.82), 50 mg (6.34)	
6	Amlodipine|C8A1	5 mg (74.59), 2.5 mg (16.21)	7.5 mg (.01), 50 mg (0.00)	10 mg (9.15)
7	Amoxycillin|J1C1	250 mg (19.79), 500 mg (50.15)	500 mg (3.00), 100 mg (.00), 50 mg (0.00), 125 mg (5.86), 200 mg (.30), 400 mg (.28), 250 mg (20.40), 875 mg (.20), 228.5 mg (0.00)	
8	Ampicillin|J1C7	250 mg (29.84), 500 mg (57.66)	500 mg (.01), 125 mg (4.23), 2.5 mg (.02), 5 mg (.01), 250 mg (8.18)	
9	Aspirin|B1C1	75 mg (39.29), 325 mg (2.41), 100 mg (14.17)	162.5 mg (.25), 50 mg (3.95), 80 mg (.09), 650 mg (.02), 20 mg (0.00), 150 mg (38.72), 60 mg (0.00), 163 mg (1.05)	
10	Atenolol|C7A5	50 mg (60.38), 100 mg (2.91)	40 mg (0.00), 500 mg (.01), 750 mg (0.00), 75 mg (.02)	12.5 mg (.87), 25 mg (35.77)
11	Atorvastatin|C10A1	5 mg (3.83), 10 mg (48.11)	20 mg (.00), 1000 mg (0.00)	20 mg (28.84), 80 mg (3.00), 40 mg (16.19)
12	Azathioprine|L4A3	50 mg (98.70)	25 mg (1.28)	
13	Azithromycin|J1F1	250 mg (31.81), 100 mg (2.81), 500 mg (64.77)	20 mg (0.00), 250 mg (.17), 600 mg (0.00), 150 mg (.17), 500 mg (.09), 10 mg (0.00), 50 mg (.00), 1000 mg (.14), 200 mg (0.00)	

(continued)

Table 6.4 (continued)

#	Medicine|4-digit category	Regulated tablet doses (market share)	Unregulated tablet doses (market share)	Paragraph-19 doses (market share)
14	Bisacodyl|A6B5	5 mg (96.33)	10 mg (3.66)	
15	Bromocriptine|N4A2	2.5 mg (58.00), 1.25 mg (21.72)	1.6 mg (.27), 0.8 mg (19.72), 5 mg (.07), 10 mg (.20)	
16	Calcium|A12A1	500 mg (1.13)	225 mg (73.75), 740 mg (2.57), 200 mg (22.47), 500,500 mg (.05)	
17	Carbamazepine|N3A1	100 mg (6.15), 200 mg (60.68)	200 mg (.00), 150 mg (0.00), 400 mg (20.21), 300 mg (12.93)	
18	Carbimazole|H3B1	5 mg (36.13), 10 mg (46.75)	20 mg (17.12)	
19	Cefalexin|J1D1	250 mg (14.32), 500 mg (41.43)	250 mg (11.84), 125 mg (7.55), 500 mg (2.05), 625 mg (0.00), 333 mg (.00), 750 mg (11.88), 375 mg (10.89)	
20	Cefixime|J1D26	100 mg (15.38), 200 mg (79.29)	50 mg (3.93), 500 mg (.00), 100 mg (.03), 200 mg (.43), 400 mg (.88), 1000 mg (.02)	
21	Cetirizine|R6A3	10 mg (95.06)	250 mg (0.00), 10 mg (1.49), 5 mg (2.57), 180 mg (0.00), 20 mg (.86)	
22	Chlorambucil|L1A1	2 mg (40.38)	5 mg (59.61)	
23	Chlorpheniramine|R6A4	4 mg (99.23)	2 mg (.76)	
24	Chlorpromazine|N5B2	50 mg (32.02), 100 mg (61.09), 25 mg (4.57)	10 mg (2.19), 200 mg (.10)	
25	Ciprofloxacin|J1G1	250 mg (15.93), 500 mg (81.40)	500 mg (0.00), 250 mg (0.00), 750 mg (.75), 50 mg (0.00), 125 mg (.01), 100 mg (.23), 1000 mg (1.58), 25 mg (.00), 200 mg (.05), 75 mg (.00)	
26	Clindamycin|J1F3	300 mg (71.20)	300 mg (15.78), 150 mg (13.00)	
27	Clomifene|G3G2	100 mg (20.56), 50 mg (51.70)	50 mg (10.5.00), 150 mg (.01), 2.5 mg (.31), 25 mg (16.89)	
28	Clopidogrel|B1C5	75 mg (97.30)		300 mg (.18), 150 mg (2.51)

(continued)

Table 6.4 (continued)

#	Medicine|4-digit category	Regulated tablet doses (market share)	Unregulated tablet doses (market share)	Paragraph-19 doses (market share)
29	Cloxacillin|J1C23	250 mg (10.43), 500 mg (85.80)	250 mg (.97), 125 mg (.40), 625 mg (2.38)	
30	Cyclophosphamide|L1A3	50 mg (76.23)	500 mg (23.76)	
31	Cyclosporin|L4A4	25 mg (11.15), 100 mg (55.29), 50 mg (29.04)	10 mg (.07), 25 mg (.07), 50 mg (1.25), 100 mg (3.08)	
32	Danazol|G3B3	100 mg (35.15), 50 mg (14.93)	100 mg (.69), 200 mg (49.20)	
33	Dapsone|J4B3	50 mg (1.03), 100 mg (95.87)	25 mg (3.08)	
34	Dexamethasone|H2A5	0.5 mg (77.31)	8 mg (.30), 4 mg (1.80), 250 mg (0.00), 200 mg (.02), 2 mg (.46), 5 mg (20.04), 500 mg (.01)	
35	Dextromethorphan|R5F3	30 mg (11.97)	5 mg (.30), 10 mg (42.27), 20 mg (45.45)	
36	Diazepam|N5D9	5 mg (56.90), 2 mg (14.60)	10 mg (28.47)	
37	Diclofenac|M1A12	50 mg (27.45)	100 mg (53.86), 75 mg (8.90), 25 mg (.11), 50 mg (9.18), 200 mg (.02), 150 mg (.41)	
38	Didanosine|J5B4	400 mg (63.29), 250 mg (30.03)	250 mg (2.10), 400 mg (4.57)	
39	Diethylcarbamazine|P1E2	50 mg (50.31)	150 mg (2.80), 100 mg (46.86)	
40	Digoxin|C1A1	0.25 mg (.00)	250 mg (0.00)	
41	Diltiazem|C8A6	60 mg (11.02), 30 mg (20.87)	180 mg (2.93), 60 mg (0.00), 240 mg (.01), 20 mg (.02), 300 mg (0.00)	90 mg (48.84), 120 mg (16.28)
42	Domperidone|A3F7	10 mg (89.11)	5 mg (8.18), 8 mg (0.00), 40 mg (.05), 20 mg (1.96), 1 mg (.03), 6 mg (.56), 30 mg (.09), 4 mg (0.00)	
43	Doxycycline|J1A6	100 mg (61.93)	500 mg (.02), 50 mg (.18), 250 mg (.03), 100 mg (37.70), 200 mg (.10)	
44	Efavirenz|J5B6	200 mg (4.07), 600 mg (27.45)	200 mg (4.61), 100 mg (.02), 600 mg (63.79), 300 mg (.01)	
45	Enalapril|C9A6	2.5 mg (25.25), 5 mg (60.84)	20 mg (.01)	10 mg (13.89)

(continued)

Table 6.4 (continued)

#	Medicine|4-digit category	Regulated tablet doses (market share)	Unregulated tablet doses (market share)	Paragraph-19 doses (market share)
46	Erythromycin|J1F4	250 mg (51.65), 500 mg (44.08)	40 mg (0.00), 125 mg (4.19), 333 mg (.00), 100 mg (.05), 150 mg (0.00)	
47	Ethambutol|J4A3	600 mg (13.47), 200 mg (2.47), 800 mg (56.06), 400 mg (5.05)	825 mg (.20), 1000 mg (22.72)	
48	Ethinylestradiol|G3A18	0.01 mg (14.01), 0.05 mg (83.73)	1 mg (1.27), 0.02 mg (.97)	
49	Etoposide|L1C4	100 mg (23.05)	50 mg (76.94)	
50	Famotidine|A2B2	20 mg (28.34)	20 mg (0.00), 50 mg (0.00), 10 mg (.09), 40 mg (71.56)	
51	Fluconazole|J2A4	100 mg (.99), 200 mg (10.93), 50 mg (6.19), 150 mg (77.55)	25 mg (0.00), 400 mg (4.09), 10 mg (0.00), 20 mg (.05), 5 mg (0.00), 300 mg (.18)	
52	Fluoxetine|N6A8	20 mg (73.12)	25 mg (0.00), 90 mg (0.00), 10 mg (10.09), 40 mg (4.86), 60 mg (10.43), 20 mg (1.46), 75 mg (0.00)	
53	Folic acid|B3A4	1 mg (2.81), 5 mg (96.76)	10 mg (.18), 5 mg (.23)	
54	Glibenclamide|A10B1	5 mg (88.98), 2.5 mg (10.72)	1.25 mg (.27), 10 mg (.01)	
55	Glyceryl Trinitrate|C1E4	0.5 mg (1.25)	6.5 mg (3.84)	2.6 mg (66.75), 2.5 mg (12.64), 6.4 mg (15.48)
56	Griseofulvin|J2A8	250 mg (68.95)	375 mg (30.96), 150 mg (0.00), 500 mg (.07)	
57	Hydrochlorothiazide|C3C8	12.5 mg (66.48), 25 mg (33.40)	50 mg (.10)	
58	Hydroxychloroquine|P1D2	200 mg (86.80)	400 mg (13.18), 300 mg (0.00)	
59	Hyoscine|A3A32	10 mg (.00)	20 mg (0.00)	
60	Ibuprofen|M1A30	200 mg (9.17), 400 mg (61.25)	400 mg (.00), 600 mg (29.53), 300 mg (.03)	
61	Imatinib Mesylate|L1X16	100 mg (5.51), 400 mg (78.26)	100 mg (14.55), 400 mg (1.66)	
62	Imipramine|N6A10	25 mg (70.66), 75 mg (19.26)	75 mg (8.55), 50 mg (.87), 10 mg (.64)	
63	Isoniazide|J4A6	100 mg (17.92), 300 mg (82.08)		

(continued)

Table 6.4 (continued)

#	Medicine|4-digit category	Regulated tablet doses (market share)	Unregulated tablet doses (market share)	Paragraph-19 doses (market share)
64	Isosorbide Dinitrate|C1E3	20 mg (.03), 10 mg (57.24)	6.4 mg (0.00), 5 mg (42.59), 2.6 mg (.10), 20 mg (0.00)	
65	Isosorbide-5-Mononitrate|C1E1	10 mg (11.68), 20 mg (31.77)	20 mg (0.00), 25 mg (1.65), 50 mg (1.71)	60 mg (10.80), 30 mg (36.20), 40 mg (6.17)
66	Lamivudine|J5B1	150 mg (13.02)	30 mg (.01), 300 mg (.15), 100 mg (86.80)	
67	Leflunomide|M5C1	20 mg (64.27), 10 mg (35.52)	100 mg (.15), 5 mg (.03)	
68	Lithium|N6A11	300 mg (28.32)	400 mg (57.45), 450 mg (14.21), 250 mg (.00)	
69	Losartan|C9D3	25 mg (28.26), 50 mg (70.98)	100 mg (.75), 0.25 mg (0.00)	
70	Medroxyprogesterone|G3A19	10 mg (99.63)	100 mg (.07), 2.5 mg (.28)	
71	Mesalazine|A7E1	400 mg (41.29)	800 mg (21.69), 1200 mg (31.40), 10 mg (1.12), 500 mg (4.48)	
72	Metformin|A10B6	500 mg (62.59)		850 mg (7.05), 1000 mg (28.36), 250 mg (1.98)
73	Methotrexate|L1B1	5 mg (10.76), 2.5 mg (33.34), 7.5 mg (34.06), 10 mg (12.35)	15 mg (9.46), 20 mg (0.00), 50 mg (.00)	
74	Metoclopramide|A3F19	10 mg (81.97)	5 mg (2.43), 15 mg (15.60)	
75	Metoprolol|C7A29	50 mg (50.68), 25 mg (33.43)	25 mg (2.56), 50 mg (4.67), 100 mg (1.02), 0.50 mg (0.00), 0.25 mg (0.00), 12.5 mg (.37), 75 mg (.05)	12.5 mg (1.73), 100 mg (5.42)
76	Metronidazole|A7A1	400 mg (85.19), 200 mg (14.80)	500 mg (0.00), 1000 mg (0.00)	
77	Metylergometrine|G2A3	0.125 mg (99.91)	0.2 mg (.07)	
78	Mifepristone|G3X2	200 mg (99.29)	1.5 mg (.27), 250 mg (.43)	
79	Nifedipine|C8A16	10 mg (33.52), 20 mg (53.00), 5 mg (5.11)	20 mg (.55), 30 mg (7.11), 5 mg (.68)	
80	Nitrofurantoin|G4A3	100 mg (62.61)	150 mg (11.31), 100 mg (24.86), 50 mg (1.21)	

(continued)

Table 6.4 (continued)

#	Medicine|4-digit category	Regulated tablet doses (market share)	Unregulated tablet doses (market share)	Paragraph-19 doses (market share)
81	Norethisterone|G3A12	5 mg (99.62)	10 mg (.37), 50 mg (0.00), 25 mg (0.00)	
82	Ofloxacin|J1G9	100 mg (4.96), 200 mg (72.70)	5 mg (.07), 300 mg (1.55), 10 mg (.07), 2 mg (.14), 20 mg (.02), 600 mg (.14), 800 mg (.15), 250 mg (0.00), 500 mg (0.00), 400 mg (20.07), 50 mg (.07)	
83	Olanzapine|N5A5	5 mg (32.06), 10 mg (38.40)	20 mg (4.78), 15 mg (0.00), 2.5 mg (11.72), 7.5 mg (6.86), 15 mg (6.11)	
84	Omeprazole|A2C1	20 mg (86.20), 40 mg (.17), 10 mg (1.85)	200 mg (0.00), 150 mg (0.00), 100 mg (.00), 20 mg (8.39), 40 mg (3.13), 500 mg (.07), 10 mg (.11), 250 mg (.05)	
85	Ondansetron|A4A2	4 mg (88.52), 8 mg (10.60)	2 mg (.83), 1 mg (.00), 500 mg (.00)	
86	Paracetamol|N2B1	500 mg (53.24)	30 mg (0.00), 1000 mg (1.39), 240 mg (0.00), 300 mg (.74), 250 mg (1.55), 325 mg (.01), 750 mg (.40), 125 mg (.98), 100 mg (.01), 500 mg (0.00), 150 mg (0.00), 600 mg (0.00), 650 mg (41.63)	
87	Phenobarbitone|N3A10	60 mg (68.08), 30 mg (31.90)	15 mg (.00)	
88	Phenytoin|N3A12	50 mg (3.43), 100 mg (85.98)	150 mg (2.20), 25 mg (.23), 200 mg (.23), 300 mg (7.92)	
89	Plain Vitamin C|A11X31	100 mg (.21), 500 mg (99.30)	375 mg (.47), 350 mg (0.00)	
90	Prednisolone|H2A6	20 mg (12.69), 5 mg (41.52), 10 mg (42.22)	6 mg (.28), 2.5 mg (.15), 40 mg (2.29), 30 mg (.80), 15 mg (0.00)	
91	Primaquine|P1D6	7.5 mg (18.45), 2.5 mg (6.03)	45 mg (.66), 15 mg (74.83)	
92	Promethazine|A4B1	25 mg (88.36), 10 mg (11.59)	650 mg (.05), 50 mg (0.00)	
93	Propranolol|C7A37	10 mg (25.11), 40 mg (41.15)	60 mg (1.92), 8 mg (.01), 40 mg (21.43), 80 mg (4.05)	20 mg (6.30)

(continued)

Table 6.4 (continued)

#	Medicine|4-digit category	Regulated tablet doses (market share)	Unregulated tablet doses (market share)	Paragraph-19 doses (market share)
94	Pyrazinamide|J4A10	1500 mg (3.53), 750 mg (52.41), 1000 mg (20.96), 500 mg (20.70)	300 mg (0.00), 250 mg (0.00), 1200 mg (2.35)	
95	Pyridostigmine| N7C11	60 mg (92.80)	180 mg (7.19)	
96	Quinine|P1D8	300 mg (86.44)	600 mg (7.17), 100 mg (6.23), 150 mg (.11)	
97	Rifampicin|J4A12	300 mg (21.21), 450 mg (45.95), 150 mg (3.90)	100 mg (0.00), 600 mg (28.92)	
98	Salbutamol|R3A11	4 mg (67.15), 2 mg (22.45)	4 mg (5.32), 8 mg (5.05)	
99	Sodium Valproate| N3A14	500 mg (28.77), 200 mg (60.00)	1000 mg (.18), 300 mg (10.26), 750 mg (.79)	
100	Spironolactone|C3A3	25 mg (42.20)	50 mg (21.73), 100 mg (36.06)	
101	Sulfasalazine|A7E3	500 mg (49.13)	1000 mg (50.86)	
102	Terbutaline|R5D3	2.5 mg (33.11)	7.5 mg (8.55), 5 mg (58.33)	
103	Tramadol|N2B5	50 mg (38.59)	100 mg (40.45), 200 mg (.46), 120 mg (0.00), 60 mg (.00), 150 mg (.05), 50 mg (20.44), 37.5 mg (0.00)	
104	Trihexyphenidyl| N4A10	2 mg (99.55)	1 mg (.00), 5 mg (.44)	
105	Verapamil|C8A23	80 mg (12.18), 40 mg (48.79)	240 mg (6.36), 120 mg (32.65)	
106	Vitamin B1 plain| A11E13	100 mg (29.37)	75 mg (70.62)	
107	Warfarin|B1X9	5 mg (64.95)	1 mg (8.68), 2.5 mg (.23), 2 mg (20.56), 3 mg (5.55)	
108	Zidovudine|J5B2	300 mg (74.37)	100 mg (11.89), 250 mg (.09), 300 mg (13.47)	

One may argue that it is sufficient to regulate one of the doses of an essential medicine and that it would automatically lower prices in other dosage markets. For example, in the market for Aciclovir, if the 800 mg tablet is more expensive because it is unregulated, an informed consumer can potentially substitute it with two 400 mg tablets, which are price-controlled. However, as we discussed in Chap. 3, consumers are not aware of the choices they have, and physicians and pharmacies have an incentive to prescribe and sell the relatively more expensive medicine because they receive a higher profit margin in absolute terms.

Table 6.5 The partial or incomplete nature of the 2013 price controls for 70 essential medicine in their injection form

#	Medicine|4-digit category	Regulated dose (market share)	Unregulated dose (market share)	Paragraph-19 dose (market share)
1	Adenosine|C1B1	3 mg (25.52)	30 mg (3.42), 6 mg (71.05)	
2	Amikacin|J1 K4	250 mg (16.28)	100 mg (12.30), 500 mg (71.00), 50 mg (.00), 25 mg (.03), 1000 mg (.37)	
3	Amiodarone|C1B3	50 mg (1.78)	150 mg (98.20)	
4	Amphotericin B|J2A2	50 mg (77.97)	500 mg (0.00), 10 mg (12.46), 100 mg (8.27), 25 mg (1.29)	
5	Ampicillin|J1C7	500 mg (62.40)	250 mg (22.14), 100 mg (6.84), 1000 mg (8.60)	
6	Atracurium|M3A2	10 mg (14.32)	50 mg (24.02), 25 mg (53.72), 100 mg (3.38), 2.5 mg (4.55)	
7	Azithromycin|J1F1	500 mg (.00)	250 mg (0.00)	
8	Betamethasone|H2A9	4 mg (99.98)	5 mg (.00)	
9	Carboplatin|L1X2	150 mg (25.45), 450 mg (74.05)	600 mg (.5.00)	
10	Cefotaxime|J1D13	250 mg (16.47), 125 mg (4.34), 500 mg (26.70)	375 mg (.03), 750 mg (0.00), 1000 mg (52.43)	
11	Ceftazidime|J1D20	1000 mg (62.95), 250 mg (20.03)	500 mg (4.44), 125 mg (2.98), 2000 mg (9.57)	
12	Ceftriaxone|J1D17	1000 mg (67.69), 250 mg (11.85)	500 mg (13.85), 125 mg (2.02), 2000 mg (4.55)	
13	Chloroquine|P1D1	40 mg (96.52)	64.5 mg (3.47)	
14	Ciprofloxacin|J1G1	200 mg (68.19)	100 mg (.76), 125 mg (4.86), 400 mg (1.42), 2 mg (21.60), 250 mg (.44), 500 mg (2.42), 50 mg (.27)	
15	Cisplatin|L1X3	50 mg (87.51), 10 mg (12.30)	100 mg (.18)	
16	Cloxacillin|J1C23	250 mg (9.56)	500 mg (90.44)	
17	Cyclophosphamide|L1A3	500 mg (27.56)	200 mg (18.13), 1000 mg (54.29)	
18	Cyclosporin|L4A4	100 mg (53.88)	50 mg (46.11)	
19	Dacarbazine|L1A23	500 mg (49.75)	200 mg (49.95), 100 mg (.30)	
20	Dexamethasone|H2A5	4 mg (99.76)	20 mg (.20), 10 mg (.00), 0.5 mg (0.00)	
21	Diazepam|N5D9	5 mg (10.53)	10 mg (89.45)	
22	Diclofenac|M1A12	25 mg (18.79)	50 mg (.40), 12.5 mg (.00), 80 mg (0.00), 75 mg (80.70), 3 mg (0.00), 100 mg (.07)	

(continued)

Table 6.5 (continued)

#	Medicine|4-digit category	Regulated dose (market share)	Unregulated dose (market share)	Paragraph-19 dose (market share)
23	Dicyclomine|A3A1	10 mg (79.45)	20 mg (20.54)	
24	Digoxin|C1A1	0.25 mg (29.73)	0.5 mg (70.26)	
25	Dobutamine|C1C5	50 mg (20.22)		250 mg (79.76)
26	Dopamine|C1C7	40 mg (66.51)	200 mg (33.49)	
27	Doxorubicin (Liposomal)|L1D13	10 mg (1.42), 50 mg (6.78)	20 mg (22.26), 2 mg (69.51)	
28	Doxorubicin (Plain)|L1D5	50 mg (69.12), 10 mg (28.94)	20 mg (1.95)	
29	Enoxaparin|B1B3	60 mg (54.18), 40 mg (40.56)	30 mg (0.00), 80 mg (1.59), 300 mg (.01)	20 mg (3.65)
30	Esmolol|C7A23	10 mg (20.12)	100 mg (79.87)	
31	Fluorouracil|L1B5	250 mg (11.71)	50 mg (1.30), 500 mg (86.98)	
32	Gemcitabine|L1B10	200 mg (25.56), 1000 mg (68.18)	1400 mg (6.25)	
33	Gentamicin|J1 K1	10 mg (.02), 40 mg (8.31)	4 mg (0.00), 5 mg (0.00), 80 mg (87.69), 60 mg (1.13), 20 mg (2.79), 800 mg (.00)	
34	Glyceryl Trinitrate|C1E4	5 mg (45.93)	50 mg (16.35), 25 mg (37.70)	
35	Haloperidol|N5B9	5 mg (67.62)	50 mg (31.88), 0.25 mg (.46)	
36	Hydrocortisone|H2A7	400 mg (.83), 200 mg (14.65), 100 mg (82.26)	40 mg (.15), 250 mg (.07), 500 mg (.97), 25 mg (0.00), 1000 mg (.81), 125 mg (.20)	
37	Hyoscine|A3A32	20 mg (99.86)	250 mg (.14)	
38	Ifosfamide|L1A4	1000 mg (3.19)	500 mg (96.80)	
39	Ketamine|N1B2	10 mg (4.53), 50 mg (71.44)	100 mg (16.00), 500 mg (8.01)	
40	Lorazepam|N5D11	2 mg (99.98)	1 mg (.00)	
41	Mesna|V3D5	200 mg (26.15)	600 mg (73.66), 100 mg (.17)	
42	Methotrexate|L1B1	50 mg (49.52)	25 mg (.57), 1000 mg (2.56), 500 mg (16.23), 15 mg (30.37), 250 mg (.00), 20 mg (0.00), 7.5 mg (.69)	
43	Methyl Prednisolone|H2A8	40 mg (19.85)	1000 mg (30.59), 80 mg (17.37), 250 mg (0.00), 500 mg (16.68), 125 mg (15.47)	
44	Metoclopramide|A3F19	5 mg (96.91)	10 mg (3.07)	
45	Metoprolol|C7A29	1 mg (71.51)	5 mg (28.47)	
46	Metronidazole|A7A1	500 mg (99.72)	100 mg (.28)	
47	Metylergometrine|G2A3	0.20 mg (5.11), 0.2 mg (93.76)	1 mg (.00), 0.125 mg (1.11)	

(continued)

Table 6.5 (continued)

#	Medicine|4-digit category	Regulated dose (market share)	Unregulated dose (market share)	Paragraph-19 dose (market share)
48	Midazolam|N5D16	5 mg (17.80), 1 mg (79.58)	10 mg (1.88), 7.5 mg (.72)	
49	Mitomycin|L1D8	10 mg (44.79)	2 mg (30.53), 40 mg (24.67)	
50	Neostigmine|N7C10	0.5 mg (74.37)	15 mg (.77), 2.5 mg (24.84)	
51	Ondansetron|A4A2	2 mg (48.29)	50 mg (0.00), 4 mg (42.93), 8 mg (8.77)	
52	Oxaliplatin|L1X4	50 mg (31.22)	100 mg (68.76)	
53	Paclitaxel|L1C8	30 mg (3.06)	300 mg (22.13), 260 mg (27.20), 200 mg (.34), 100 mg (38.34), 110 mg (.05), 6 mg (.10), 250 mg (8.72)	
54	Pantoprazole|A2C4	40 mg (.00)	20 mg (0.00), 60 mg (0.00)	
55	Paracetamol|N2B1	150 mg (27.61)	500 mg (3.29), 125 mg (1.28), 40 mg (.00), 10 mg (7.78), 1000 mg (59.93), 650 mg (.01), 100 mg (.05)	
56	Pheniramine|R6A17	22.75 mg (99.62)	25 mg (.37)	
57	Phytomenadione|B1A5	10 mg (61.66)	1 mg (38.33)	
58	Prednisolone|H2A6	20 mg (7.65)	500 mg (5.03), 2.5 mg (75.51), 1000 mg (11.78)	
59	Promethazine|A4B1	25 mg (99.86)	40 mg (.14)	
60	Protamine|V3E4	10 mg (65.29)	50 mg (34.70)	
61	Quinine|P1D8	300 mg (92.44)	600 mg (2.18), 150 mg (5.36)	
62	Ranitidine|A2B4	25 mg (41.00)	50 mg (27.45), 20 mg (0.00), 75 mg (.11), 40 mg (.17), 150 mg (31.27)	
63	Streptomycin|J4A18	750 mg (81.40)	0.75 mg (18.60)	
64	Suxamethonium|M3A11	50 mg (86.16)	500 mg (6.13), 100 mg (7.69)	
65	Testosterone|G3B2		100 mg (10.23), 40 mg (.12), 250 mg (62.02), 200 mg (.00)	
66	Tramadol|N2B5	50 mg (21.56)	100 mg (78.27), 200 mg (.15)	
67	Vancomycin|J1X2	1000 mg (5.30), 500 mg (87.31)	250 mg (7.38)	
68	Verapamil|C8A23	2.5 mg (53.33)	5 mg (46.66)	
69	Vinblastine|L1C1	10 mg (99.02)	1 mg (.97)	
70	Vincristine|L1C2	1 mg (99.41)	2 mg (.57)	

Table 6.6 The partial or incomplete nature of the 2013 price controls for 70 essential medicine in their syrup form

#	Medicine|4-digit category	Regulated dose (market share)	Unregulated dose (market share)
1	Albendazole|P1B1	200 mg (87.18)	400 mg (12.81)
2	Amoxycillin|J1C1	125 mg (79.44)	400 mg (.40), 250 mg (19.81), 50 mg (.03), 100 mg (.02), 200 mg (.25)
3	Ampicillin|J1C7	125 mg (77.00)	250 mg (23.00)
4	Azithromycin|J1F1	100 mg (41.79)	2000 mg (.75), 250 mg (.56), 50 mg (.15), 500 mg (.02), 200 mg (55.88), 125 mg (.62), 20 mg (.10), 40 mg (.10)
5	Cefalexin|J1D1	125 mg (49.08)	150 mg (0.00), 250 mg (50.86), 500 mg (.03)
6	Cetirizine|R6A3	5 mg (96.05)	10 mg (.70), 1 mg (3.25)
7	Chloroquine|P1D1	50 mg (85.83)	80 mg (10.68), 125 mg (.28), 160 mg (0.00), 250 mg (2.88), 100 mg (.33)
8	Domperidone|A3F7	1 mg (93.30)	5 mg (1.74), 10 mg (4.96)
9	Erythromycin|J1F4	125 mg (64.33)	100 mg (35.61), 250 mg (.03), 50 mg (.00)
10	Ibuprofen|M1A30	100 mg (74.47)	200 mg (25.53)
11	Metronidazole|A7A1	100 mg (4.84)	125 mg (6.30), 200 mg (88.84)
12	Ofloxacin|J1G9	50 mg (64.94)	400 mg (.74), 100 mg (30.76), 200 mg (3.56)
13	Ondansetron|A4A2	2 mg (97.98)	4 mg (1.50), 12 mg (.50)
14	Paracetamol|N2B1	125 mg (26.06)	250 mg (48.24), 156.25 mg (.25), 60 mg (.00), 156 mg (.00), 240 mg (.00), 100 mg (.20), 150 mg (1.19), 500 mg (.15), 650 mg (.02), 120 mg (23.80)
15	Piperazine|P1B6	750 mg (98.81)	500 mg (1.17)
16	Promethazine|A4B1	5 mg (99.93)	250 mg (.05), 125 mg (.02)
17	Sodium Valproate|N3A14	200 mg (99.41)	100 mg (.57)

After the NPPA fixed prices of several medicines in 2013, it noticed that the prices of several anti-diabetic medicines that are not regulated but serve as close substitutes (such as Glimepiride for Metformin in the IMS study) were brought under price regulation by invoking the 19th Paragraph of the 2013 DPCO, which applies to the fixation of ceiling prices under special circumstances (DPCO 2013, p. 17):

> Notwithstanding anything contained in this order, the Government may, in case of extraordinary circumstances, if it considers necessary so to do in public interest, fix the ceiling price or retail price of any Drug for such period, as it may deem fit and where the ceiling price or retail price of the drug is already fixed and notified, the Government may allow an increase or decrease in the ceiling price or the retail price, as the case may be, irrespective of annual wholesale price index for that year.

Using paragraph-19, the NPPA fixed the prices of 108 medicines in mid-2014 although they were not initially regulated under the 2013 DPCO, and were not included in the National List of Essential Medicines in 2011. In some cases, new dosages of previously price-controlled medicines were added to the list. For example, 10 mg tablets of Amlodipine were added to the list of regulated medicines after

2.5 mg and 5 mg were initially included. Similarly, 12.5 mg and 25 mg tablets of Atenolol were added to the initial list of 50 mg and 100 mg doses under price regulation. The move indicates the potential weakness the NPPA identified in the 2013 DPCO. However, due to considerable opposition from the industry as well as noncompliance, the government ended up withdrawing the regulation of additional medicines and dosages under paragraph 19.

The NPPA's move to expand medicines by invoking paragraph 19 was met with resistance by the pharmaceutical industry. The Indian Pharmaceutical Alliance and the OPPI filed lawsuits on behalf of several pharmaceutical companies questioning the order (Nautiyal 2014b). The pharmaceutical firms and the pharmacists' trade association raised concerns that the move would result in significant losses (Nautiyal 2014c):

> Pharma companies feel that NPPA action may lead to a business loss of Rs. 600 crore which can impact the annual turnover to the tune of Rs. 6000 crore under the diabetes and cardiovascular segments. The drugs that will become cheaper would include atorvastatin, gliclazide, glimepiride, heparin, metolazone propranolol, ramipril, rosuvastatin, simvastatin, telmisartan, terazosin, torasemide, trimetazidine and valsartan among others. Retail trade associations inform that they have not received any revised price list of 108 nonscheduled formulations from the manufacturers, the state drug regulator says that it is awaiting an intimation from the government on its implementation.

In the interim, companies such as Pfizer, Cipla, and Sanofi lowered prices on some diabetic medicines previously not listed under 2013 DPCO and lobbied against the order directly with the union minister for chemicals and fertilizers (Nautiyal 2014c). In a surprise move, the Indian government rolled back the NPPA's invocation of paragraph 19 by directing its Department of Pharmaceuticals in the Ministry of Chemicals and Fertilizers to withdraw its guidelines with immediate effect (Nautiyal 2014c). The OPPI noted that they appreciated the government's decision to withdraw and that they look forward to working with the government toward a common goal (Nautiyal 2014c).

6.5 The 2013 DPCO Did Not Lower Prices of Regulated Medicines Overall

The extent of decline in prices is an important indicator of the effectiveness of design of the price cap regulation. The government chose to set as the ceiling price the simple average of the prices of SKUs with more than 1% market share. In this section, we examine the extent of price changes in the regulated SKUs of various medicines brought under price controls. We cannot easily compare the prices of a medicine across tablets, injections, and syrups. Therefore, we first restrict ourselves to the analysis of prices for tablets. We also cannot directly compare the prices of SKUs, as different SKUs contain different numbers of tablets and also different dosage strengths. We normalize the price of the regulated doses of medicines and plot the normalized price per milligram of a tablet. Since different SKUs are sold at different prices, we weigh the price of each SKU by the number of units it sells to obtain a weighted, normalized, per-milligram tablet price. We also exclude a small number of combination medicines such as Amoxicillin Clavulanic Acid, as it is difficult to normalize the price of a medicine that contains more than one ingredient in different dosages. We further normalize the prices of different medicines with their initial price at the beginning of the dataset. As a result, the price of the composite medicine composed of all the regulated tablet medicines is set at one in January 2011.

We plot the evolution over time of the weighted price in Fig. 6.5. The price starts at one due to normalization and increases by 30% in the year before the 2013 DPCO implementation begins. Recall that the NPPA selected prices for May 2012 to estimate the ceiling price as the simple average price of SKUs with more than 1% market share. The prices sharply increased in May 2012 from approximately 1.1–1.25, which inflated the ceiling price. We then see a sharp decline in prices once the implementation of DPCO began in August 2013 to 1.1, the level before May 2012, and then steadily rises to 1.3 by mid-2016. The figure indicates that there is no perceptible decline in the price index of regulated medicines overall. Also, a suspicious increase in price coinciding with May 2012 and decline coinciding with August 2013, suggests that the design and implementation of the 2013 DPCO are likely compromised by the coordinated action by firms in the market.

One concern with Fig. 6.5 is that it includes a large number of relatively small firms, whose actions can affect the overall trends. Therefore, we exclude from the price index, SKUs with more than 1% market share, calculated on a monthly basis from the beginning of the dataset, and plot the index over time in Fig. 6.6. The patterns we find in Fig. 6.6 are similar to those in Fig. 6.5, but the price index does not reach the high of 1.3 before the implementation of the DPCO. The trends in Fig. 6.6 confirm that the extraordinary period of high prices in the year before regulation is not driven by the small SKUs with less than 1% market share charging

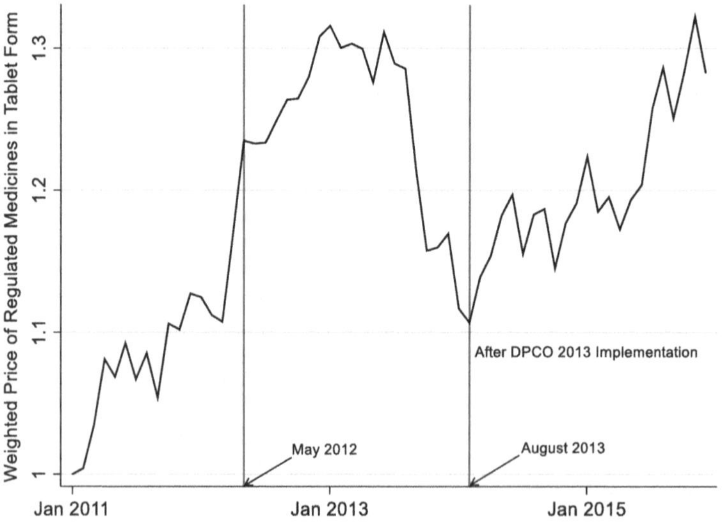

Fig. 6.5 Weighted price of regulated medicines in tablet form over time

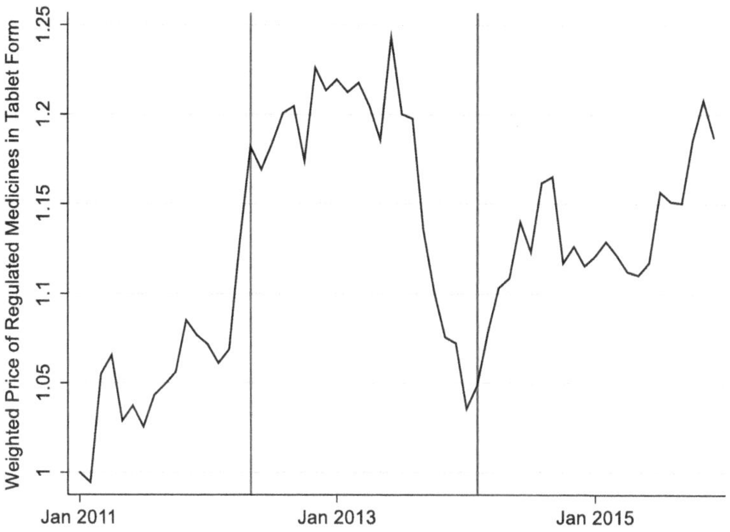

Fig. 6.6 Weighted price of regulated medicines in tablet form over time, excluding SKUs with 1% market share

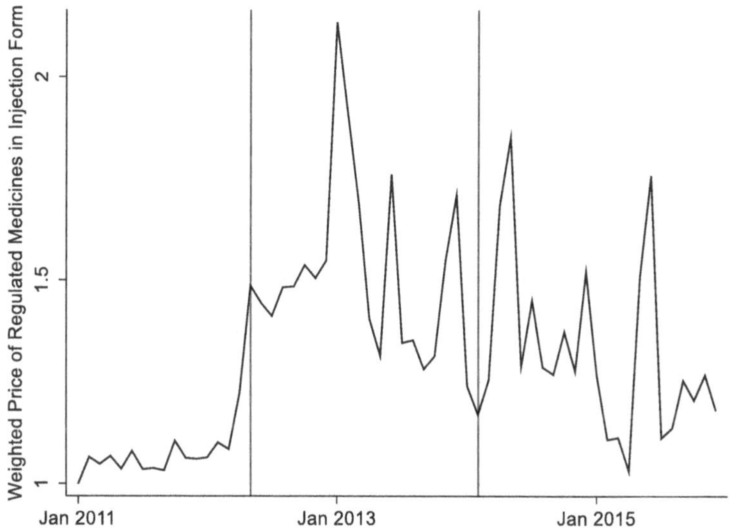

Fig. 6.7 Weighted price of regulated medicines in injection form over time

high prices, but due to the pricing choices of the large SKUs that contributed to the determination of the ceiling price eventually.

We repeat the analysis for drug types other than tablets and find similar results. In Fig. 6.7, we plot the price index for injections and find an increase much larger than that observed for Tablets. We find an increase of 50% in May 2012 compared to the initial level of one in January 2011. In Fig. 6.8, we plot the price index for syrup and

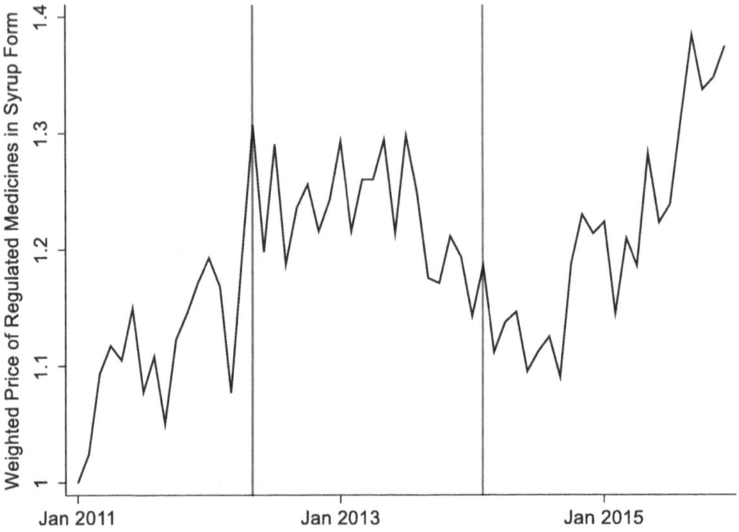

Fig. 6.8 Weighted price of regulated medicines in syrup form over time

Fig. 6.9 Weighted price of top 3 SKUs of regulated medicines in tablet form over time

suspension SKUs that entered the 2013 DPCO and find a similar increase in the price index to 1.3 in May 2012 and although the index declines to 1.1 in late 2013, it then steadily increases to 1.4. We also restrict the SKUs to top three by market share and repeat the analysis. We plot the price index as well as the aggregate market share of the top 3 SKUs in Fig. 6.9. The price index increases to approximately 1.15 in May 2012 and the aggregate market share of the top three SKUs increases by 2% from 87.5 to 89.5.

6.6 Some Regulated Medicines Experienced a Decline in Prices

We examine the changes in the price index for each medicine to identify medicines that experienced a decrease in prices. In Table 6.7, we compiled the list of medicines and prices at four points during the 5-year period starting January 2011. We show the price index in January 2011, which is by definition one. Next, we list the price index in May 2012, as the NPPA utilized the prices from this month to determine the ceiling price. We also list the price index for August 2013, when the implementation of DPCO began, and for December 2015, the end of the 5 year period. Among the 128 medicines in the list, the price index decreased for 40 medicines, even though only marginally in several cases. The price index decreased by more than half for only four of the 128 medicines during this period, although the DPCO aimed at lowering prices by half and tinkered with the appropriate the method to average market prices to achieve that objective. The price index increased significantly in the interim for some of these medicines. For example, the price index for Biscodyl increased to 1.46 in May 2012 and for Imatinib Mesylate to 1.21 in August 2013. The price index varied between 1 and 2 for the next 40 medicines on the list, indicating that the prices doubled despite the price cap regulation.

Table 6.7 The weighted price index for regulated medicines over time

#	Medicine|4-digit category	Jan 2011	May 2012	August 2013	December 2015
1	Clindamycin|J1F3	1	1.14	0.38	0.36
2	Ciprofloxacin|S3A2	1	1.04	0.05	0.38
3	Testosterone|G3B2	1	0.78	0.61	0.48
4	Procarbazine|L1X19	1	0.54	0.6	0.49
5	Warfarin|B1X9	1	1.13	0.74	0.54
6	Cyclophosphamide|L1A3	1	1.14	0.82	0.61
7	Amitriptyline|N6A1	1	1.19	0.61	0.61
8	Ritonavir|J5B9	1	1.87	1	0.63
9	Flutamide|L2B5	1	2.09	1.79	0.66
10	Zidovudine|J5B2	1	1.06	1.05	0.66
11	Vitamin B1 plain|A11E13	1	0.62	1.24	0.68
12	Leflunomide|M5C1	1	1.04	0.71	0.7
13	Trihexyphenidyl|N4A10	1	1.3	0.66	0.72
14	Metoclopramide|A3F19	1	0.81	0.7	0.72
15	Neostigmine|N7C10	1	1.14	0.67	0.75
16	Salbutamol|R3A11	1	0.88	1.15	0.76
17	Chlorpromazine|N5B2	1	0.53	0.58	0.77
18	Bisacodyl|A6B5	1	1.46	0.76	0.78
19	Metoprolol|C7A29	1	1.03	0.8	0.78
20	Clomifene|G3G2	1	0.92	0.61	0.81

(continued)

Table 6.7 (continued)

#	Medicine|4-digit category	Jan 2011	May 2012	August 2013	December 2015
21	Ethinylestradiol|G3A18	1	1.19	0.95	0.82
22	Olanzapine|N5A5	1	1.05	0.8	0.82
23	Chlorambucil|L1A1	1	0.91	0.91	0.82
24	Imatinib Mesylate|L1X16	1	1.05	1.21	0.83
25	Cyclosporin|L4A4	1	1.16	0.96	0.83
26	Acetazolamide systemic|S1D2	1	1	0.51	0.83
27	Dapsone|J4B3	1	1.05	0.88	0.84
28	Fluconazole|D1A17	1	1.18	0.31	0.85
29	Amiodarone|C1B3	1	1.1	0.87	0.85
30	Glyceryl Trinitrate|C1E4	1	1.1	0.96	0.87
31	Azathioprine|L4A3	1	0.79	0.79	0.88
32	Sodium Valproate|N3A14	1	1.34	0.92	0.88
33	Ampicillin|J1C7	1	1.31	1.08	0.89
34	Verapamil|C8A23	1	0.94	1.03	0.9
35	Cetirizine|R6A3	1	1.43	0.88	0.9
36	Promethazine|A4B1	1	0.93	0.89	0.9
37	Pyrimethamine|P1D3	1	0.99	0.99	0.94
38	Dexamethasone|H2A5	1	1.17	1.22	0.95
39	Lithium|N6A11	1	1.14	0.78	0.98
40	Colchicine|M4A2	1	0.78	0.9	0.98
41	Diloxanide|P1A4	1	1.15	1.27	1
42	Didanosine|J5B4	1	1.05	1.02	1
43	Famotidine|A2B2	1	0.89	1.29	1.01
44	Imipramine|N6A10	1	1.04	1.01	1.01
45	Methotrexate|L1B1	1	0.83	0.93	1.02
46	Penicillamine|M1C5	1	0.66	0.95	1.02
47	Norethisterone|G3A12	1	1.2	1.02	1.03
48	Atorvastatin|C10A1	1	1.17	0.88	1.04
49	Hyoscine|A3A32	1	1.7	0.56	1.04
50	Fluconazole|J2A4	1	1.23	1.12	1.04
51	Diazepam|N5D9	1	1.34	0.84	1.04
52	Paracetamol|N2B1	1	1.13	0.97	1.05
53	Isoniazide|J4A6	1	1.1	0.61	1.05
54	Hydroxychloroquine|P1D2	1	0.73	0.67	1.05
55	Metylergometrine|G2A3	1	1.08	0.77	1.06
56	Dextromethorphan|R5F3	1	1.04	1.06	1.06
57	Mefloquine|P1D18	1	1.06	1.1	1.06
58	Cefalexin|J1D1	1	1.52	0.95	1.07
59	Lamivudine|J5B1	1	0.77	1.04	1.08
60	Domperidone|A3F7	1	1.08	0.97	1.09
61	Clofazimine|J4B2	1	1.03	0.83	1.09
62	Losartan|C9D3	1	1.17	1.02	1.11

(continued)

Table 6.7 (continued)

#	Medicine|4-digit category	Jan 2011	May 2012	August 2013	December 2015
63	Cefixime|J1D26	1	1.2	1.01	1.12
64	Tamoxifen|L2B1	1	1.29	0.88	1.12
65	Folic acid|B3A4	1	1.41	0.9	1.13
66	Fluoxetine|N6A8	1	1.2	1.04	1.14
67	Primaquine|P1D6	1	1.28	1.27	1.14
68	Phenobarbitone|N3A10	1	1.92	0.76	1.14
69	Mercaptopurine|L1B8	1	1.04	1.04	1.15
70	Propranolol|C7A37	1	1.24	1.07	1.15
71	Nitrofurantoin|G4A3	1	1.07	1.01	1.15
72	Diclofenac|M1A12	1	1.39	0.99	1.15
73	Albendazole|P1B1	1	1.33	0.96	1.15
74	Spironolactone|C3A3	1	0.98	1.02	1.16
75	Sulfasalazine|A7E3	1	1.36	1.42	1.17
76	Ciprofloxacin|J1G1	1	1.43	1.86	1.17
77	Aspirin|B1C1	1	0.97	0.3	1.19
78	Amlodipine|C8A1	1	1.09	1.11	1.19
79	Carbamazepine|N3A1	1	1.21	1.48	1.2
80	Phenytoin|N3A12	1	1.17	0.9	1.21
81	Metformin|A10B6	1	1.17	1.13	1.22
82	Ondansetron|A4A2	1	1.22	1.06	1.22
83	Azithromycin|J1F1	1	1.25	1.09	1.22
84	Metronidazole|A7A1	1	1.22	1.22	1.24
85	Hydrochlorothiazide|C3C8	1	1.1	1.07	1.26
86	Plain Vitamin C|A11X31	1	4.14	1.33	1.29
87	Melphalan|L1A5	1	1.36	1.39	1.29
88	Allopurinol|M4A4	1	1.23	1.82	1.31
89	Stavudine|J5B3	1	1.52	1.52	1.32
90	Atenolol|C7A5	1	1.38	1.16	1.33
91	Nifedipine|C8A16	1	1.31	1.39	1.33
92	Bromocriptine|N4A2	1	1.25	1.38	1.36
93	Aciclovir|J5A4	1	1.09	1.07	1.38
94	Isosorbide Dinitrate|C1E3	1	1.04	0.37	1.4
95	Diltiazem|C8A6	1	1.11	1.02	1.41
96	Ibuprofen|M1A30	1	0.92	0.78	1.42
97	Digoxin|C1A1	1	1.41	0.86	1.43
98	Erythromycin|J1F4	1	1.59	1.89	1.43
99	Amoxycillin|J1C1	1	1.69	1.47	1.44
100	Enalapril|C9A6	1	1.26	1.3	1.5
101	Glibenclamide|A10B1	1	1.25	1.51	1.5
102	Clopidogrel|B1C5	1	1.16	1.19	1.51
103	Tramadol|N2B5	1	1.88	1.11	1.54
104	Danazol|G3B3	1	1.34	1.29	1.56

(continued)

Table 6.7 (continued)

#	Medicine|4-digit category	Jan 2011	May 2012	August 2013	December 2015
105	Terbutaline|R5D3	1	3.16	3.04	1.57
106	Carbimazole|H3B1	1	1.17	1.22	1.57
107	Isosorbide-5-Mononitrate|C1E1	1	1.32	1.17	1.59
108	Alprazolam|N5D1	1	1.37	1.15	1.61
109	Omeprazole|A2C1	1	1.48	1.5	1.62
110	Ofloxacin|J1G9	1	1.33	1.35	1.67
111	Rifampicin|J4A12	1	1.15	1.57	1.68
112	Efavirenz|J5B6	1	0.94	1.78	1.7
113	Medroxyprogesterone|G3A19	1	1.08	1.15	1.72
114	Mesalazine|A7E1	1	1.29	1.3	1.82
115	Mifepristone|G3X2	1	1.34	1.5	1.88
116	Pyridostigmine|N7C11	1	1.24	1.78	1.91
117	Ethambutol|J4A3	1	1.27	1.73	1.94
118	Pyrazinamide|J4A10	1	1.71	1.34	1.95
119	Diethylcarbamazine|P1E2	1	1.26	1.34	1.96
120	Quinine|P1D8	1	1.21	1.33	2
121	Indinavir|J5B8	1	1.2	1.02	2.17
122	Methyldopa|C2A7	1	1.02	1.1	2.45
123	Doxycycline|J1A6	1	1.97	2.41	2.64
124	Chlorpheniramine|R6A4	1	1.21	1.96	3.27
125	Prednisolone|H2A6	1	1.81	3.06	4.02
126	Raloxifene|G3 J2	1	1.81	1.87	4.07
127	Cloxacillin|J1C23	1	0.97	1.39	4.27
128	Griseofulvin|J2A8	1	2.21	2.67	7.2

Notwithstanding these price trends, it is difficult to assess the effectiveness of the regulation, as we do not know how the prices would have changed in the absence of the price cap regulation. One may argue that the regulation prevented further, significant increases in prices. As we noted earlier in discussing the IMS study, comparing the prices of different medicines can lead to unreliable conclusions. Similarly, limiting the focus to regulated formulations can also lead to inaccurate conclusions. However, the patterns are useful to argue that partial regulation has not managed to lower the prices of several regulated medicines formulations in absolute terms.

References

Bal, A. (1986a). Distortions in drug policy: Who is to be blamed? *Economic and Political Weekly, 21*(23), 1029–1032.

Bal, A. (1986b). Drug Policy. *Economic and Political Weekly, 21*, 2009–2014.

Basak, S. C. (2008). The genesis of drug price control. *PharmaBiz* [online]. Available from http://pharmabiz.com/ArticleDetails.aspx?aid=42905&sid=9

Bhaumik, S. (2013). India's health ministry bans pioglitazone, metamizole, and flupentixol-melitracen. *British Medical Journal, 347*, f4366.

Business Standard. (2014, March 19). *Govt lifts ban on painkiller Analgin*. Available online http://www.business-standard.com/article/companies/govt-lifts-ban-on-painkiller-analgin-114031900803_1.html

DPCO. (2013, May 15). Drug price control order 2013. The Gazette of India, Extraordinary, Part II, Section 3, Sub-section (ii). Ministry of Chemicals and Fertilizers, Government of India.

EPW. (1985). Drug policy in limbo. *Economic and Political Weekly, 20*, 772–774.

EPW. (1990). Towards a drug policy? *Economic and Political Weekly, 25*, 1919–1920.

IMS Health. (2015). Assessing the impact of price control measures on access to medicines in India. IMS Health India Report.

Malhotra, P. (2010). *The impact of TRIPS on India: An access to medicines perspective*. London: Palgrave Macmillan.

Nautiyal, S. (2014a, September 25). Pharma cos have to comply with NPPA's July 10 order although guidelines stands withdrawn. PharmaBiz.com

Nautiyal, S. (2014b, September 12). Cipla, Pfizer, Sanofi cut prices of diabetic, cardiac drugs as per NPPA order on July 10. PharmaBiz.com

Nautiyal, S. (2014c, July 24). Pharma cos refuse to cut prices of 108 products despite NPPA order on July 10. PharmaBiz.com

NPPA. (2017). *Compliance with DPCO 1995 and DPCO 2013*. Available online http://www.nppaindia.nic.in/order/stmt-14-03-2017.pdf

PharmaBiz. (2015). Price control unlikely to improve access to medicines in India: IMS study. *PharmaBiz* [online]. Available from http://pharmabiz.com/NewsDetails.aspx?aid=89417&sid=2

Rane, W. (1996, August 24–31). Analysis of drug prices, 1980–1995. *Economic and Political Weekly, 31*, 2331–2340.

Chapter 7
Firm Strategies to Mitigate the Impact of Price Control Regulation

7.1 Introduction

In the previous chapter, we examine the limitations in the design of the 2013 DPCO. It is reasonable to expect that pharmaceutical firms likely to be affected by the regulation undertook actions to mitigate their impact. Because of such strategic actions, regulations, despite being well-intentioned, can sometimes make matters worse (Noll 1989). Have the 2013 DPCO regulations made consumers worse-off than they were before? In this chapter, we examine some of the strategies firms used to mitigate the impact of price controls. We are aware of more strategies than we discuss below. Documenting the larger set of firm strategies is part of our ongoing research agenda.

7.2 Coordinated Price Increases Before Regulation

Glazer and McMillan (1992) note firms that are going to be subject to regulation are aware of them well before the actual passage of legislation. Therefore, firms under the threat of regulation can undertake actions, both independently and as a group, to reduce the probability of regulation as well as to mitigate the impact of regulation. Ellison and Wolfram (2006) show that those firms that are more vulnerable to regulation coordinated to lower prices to forestall the 1993 healthcare reform in the US. Similarly, in India, the pharmaceutical industry coordinated through its industry associations and lobby groups, as the demand for broader and more effective regulation of drug prices in India for more than a decade between 2002 and 2013. As noted in Chap. 2, the deliberations during this period involved the formation of several committees and drafting of many proposals and reports. We begin this chapter by documenting several instances of a coordinated response by pharmaceutical firms to forestall or influence in their favor the 2013 DPCO.

A. Bhaskarabhatla, *Regulating Pharmaceutical Prices in India*, India Studies in Business and Economics, https://doi.org/10.1007/978-3-319-93393-1_7

First, the pharmaceutical industry effectively coordinated to oppose cost-based regulated and the idea of controlling all essential medicines. After the Supreme Court of India stayed the implementation of the 2002 Pharmaceutical Policy, the government was reluctant to control the prices of all essential medicines and filed an appeal to implement the 2002 policy (The Financial Express 2005). Since the Supreme Court refused to reconsider its judgment, the government set up the Sen Committee to explore alternative options to price control. The Sen Committee held several meetings with drug industry associations and with other stakeholders such as the citizen groups. Several industry experts expressed their concerns about cost-based price regulation due to its hidden influence on quality and innovation (Ray 2013). The Committee, therefore, concluded that the government should regulate the prices of medicines in accordance with a ceiling price, as opposed to a uniform price (The Sen Committee 2005). At the same time, it highlighted the risk of effort diversion when imposing a ceiling price (i.e., the movement from controlled to non-controlled drugs, making controlled drugs fall out of the market). To avoid this, the committee recommended the coverage of all formulations of the same drug, as well as the price monitoring of all therapeutic substitutes. However, the government disapproved some of the recommendations (Deshpande 2006). It released a new draft policy based on the recommendations of the committee in December 2005, but did not disclose the section regarding price regulation (Balakrishnan 2006).

Second, the industry associations argued for partial regulation, counter to the recommendations of the Sen Committee. The pharmaceutical firms were willing to accept the control of prices of all drugs on the NLEM – but only the strengths that were included in the NLEM and no other formulations (Mathew 2006). In order to address the issue of price control, the government set up a new committee, highly represented by the industry – it concluded that the 354 drugs on the NLEM (2003) and their formulations did not need to be regulated since some of the prices were considered 'reasonable' by the industry. Despite this, the government wanted to keep the option of cost-based price regulation open for discussion and instituted a Pharma Advisory Forum, which, as industry representatives argued, was tilted in favor of the regulator and the ministry (Mukherjee 2006).

Third, the pharmaceutical firms also came together to preempt regulation by advocating voluntary self-regulation. Uncertain about the outcome of the discussions of the Advisory Forum, industry associations proposed that they would voluntarily lower the prices of several medicines. Malhotra (2010) notes that 11 companies agreed to reduce the prices of 886 SKUs by October 2006. These firms included Alembic, Alkem Laboratories, Cadila Healthcare, Cipla, Emcure Pharmaceuticals, Lupin, Medley Pharmaceuticals, Nicholas Piramal, Ranbaxy Laboratories, Unichem Laboratories, and Wockhardt. Malhotra (2010) finds that the drugs included in the voluntary agreement were not the essential medicines, and even included formulations of traditional medicine. Such a coordinated response was effective in delaying the regulation, as contemporaneous press statements highlight: "As a result of the pulling of various forces and interest groups it appears that the Cabinet may defer any decision of finalizing the policy and might refer it either to a Group of Ministers or a Committee of Secretaries to formulate a consensus that seems to be elusive till now" (The Hindu Business Line 2007). The Minister of

Chemicals and Fertilizers blamed the industry lobby for the delay in the implementation of the policy, "We have been trying hard to get the policy cleared for long. But it is still stuck with the Cabinet. You know, the private lobby is so strong, and they have been trying to stop it" (PharmaQuest 2009). The policy proposal remained with the GoM until 2012 when the 2012 NPPP was announced. Although the Supreme Court was leaning towards maintaining the cost-based method of pricing, the GoM finally decided on the market-based approach. Moreover, it overruled the Health Ministry's proposal to fix the price cap based on the average price of the three lowest priced brands and instead recommended that the ceiling price is calculated based on the three top-selling brands (Unnikrishnan 2012a).

Fourth, the industry argued for a market-based regulation and for the ceiling price to be based on the average of the MRP of top-three SKUs in the market by sales (Mathew 2005). After much criticism, the ceiling prices were calculated based on the simple average of all brands having 1% or more market share. Although this was more acceptable than the initial suggestion, it still determined the maximum price based on the top brands and ensured higher profits for pharmaceutical companies in comparison to the cost-based alternative. As such, the reduction in prices using the market-based formula were inferior to the reduction in prices using the cost-based formula, which was still being used under the 1995 DPCO (Gopakumar 2017). According to a statement by the managing trustee of LOCOST at the time, "Bulk drug prices left to the market can lead to cartelization on vital drugs. In some vital drugs (like anti-TB Rifampicin) only 2–3 major manufacturers are present. The government has no recourse if bulk drug prices shoot up without reason (or with reason). Smaller manufacturers for all drugs will have to rely on higher priced local manufacturers of bulk drugs. This will render smaller manufacturers of formulations uncompetitive" (Pradhan 2011). Although pharmaceutical companies maintained that the price control policy would affect their profitability, they pushed for the market-based approach, as it would allow them to set their profit margins, provided the prices of their products do not exceed the ceiling prices. An account by one of the industry lobbies stated, "Though the average profitability of the pharmaceutical industry will be impacted badly by about 25%, the Indian Pharmaceutical Alliance (IPA) is reconciled to the new policy as it moves away from the intrusive and opaque pricing regime to a more transparent system of pricing" (Unnikrishnan 2012b).

Finally, we argue that the pharmaceutical firms timed their coordinated price increases just before May 2012, likely indicating their knowledge of the policy process and their influence on its timing and content.

7.3 Evidence of Coordinated Price Increase in Regulated and Unregulated Dosage Markets

We begin by examining the price index developed in the previous chapter for regulated and unregulated doses of the partially regulated medicines. We computed separately the weighted, normalized, per-milligram prices for regulated and

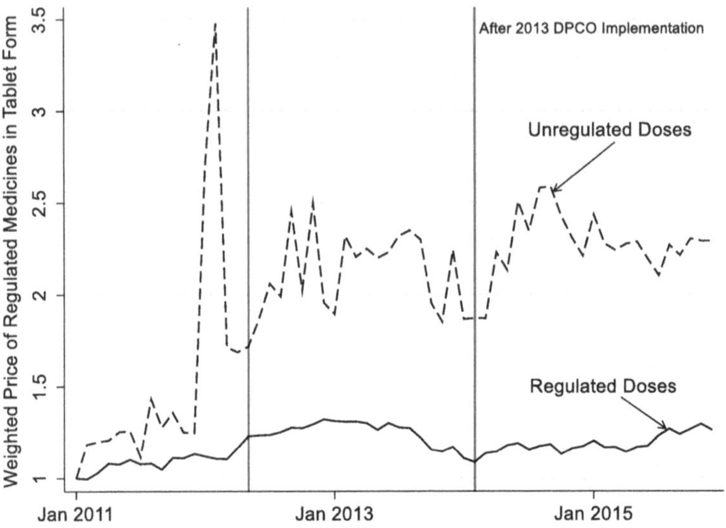

Fig. 7.1 Comparing the price index for regulated and unregulated doses of medicines in their tablet form

unregulated doses of partially regulated medicines and plotted the price indices in Fig. 7.1. We find that the price index increased much more for the unregulated doses of the medicines that entered the regulation. The price index for the unregulated doses, shown by the dashed line, is twice as high as that for the regulated doses at 2.25 in December 2015. The unregulated doses also experienced a much sharper increase in price in the months before May 2012, indicating that the pharmaceutical firms looked to compensate the price declines in the regulated markets with price increases in the unregulated markets. We argue, based on Fig. 7.1, that partial regulation has been a significant limitation of the 2013 DPCO, undermining its effectiveness in lowering prices overall. We plot in Figs. 7.2 and 7.3 the price indices for regulated and unregulated doses of medicines administered in an injection form. The price index for the unregulated doses, shown in dashed line, increased by more than 15 times in the months leading up to the implementation of the DPCO, and eventually declined to about five times the price index for the regulated doses. We observe a similar pattern for medicines administered as syrups or suspensions. The increase in prices in both the regulated and unregulated doses happens well before the regulation is implemented. Consistent with Glazer and McMillan (1992), pharmaceutical firms increased prices in the unregulated doses as early as in May 2012, which remained high after the implementation of the regulation. The prices in the unregulated dosage markets also increased in May 2012, more than a year before the regulation was to be implemented, and declined on the eve of implementation of regulation in August 2013. However, the prices of regulated doses increased subsequently.

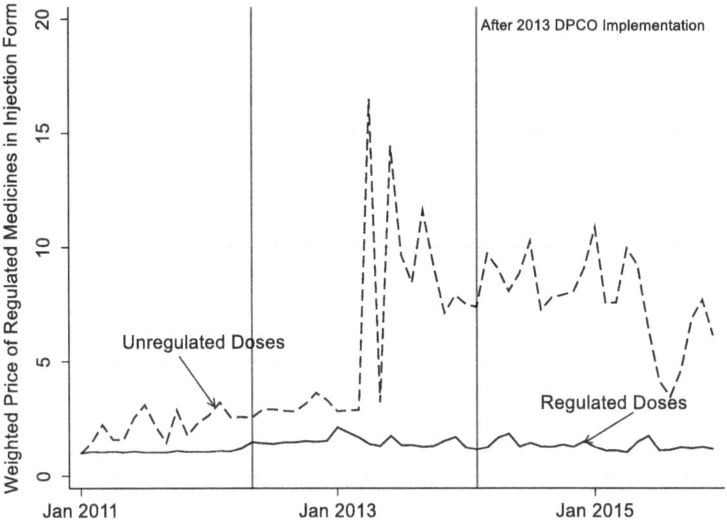

Fig. 7.2 Comparing the price index for regulated and unregulated doses of medicines in their injection form

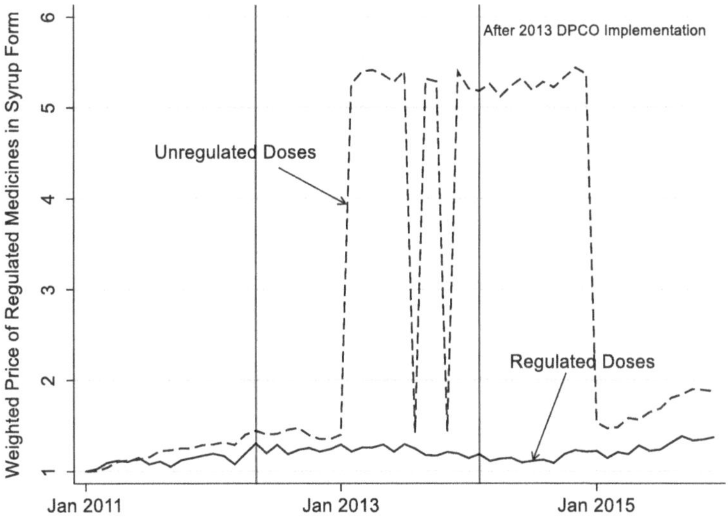

Fig. 7.3 Comparing the price index for regulated and unregulated doses of medicines in their syrup form

Next, we examine the overall impact of the regulation on prices of medicines by including both regulated and unregulated doses. To examine the overall effect of the price control regulation on the prices of partially regulated medicines, we average the separately normalized prices for regulated and unregulated doses and plot them in

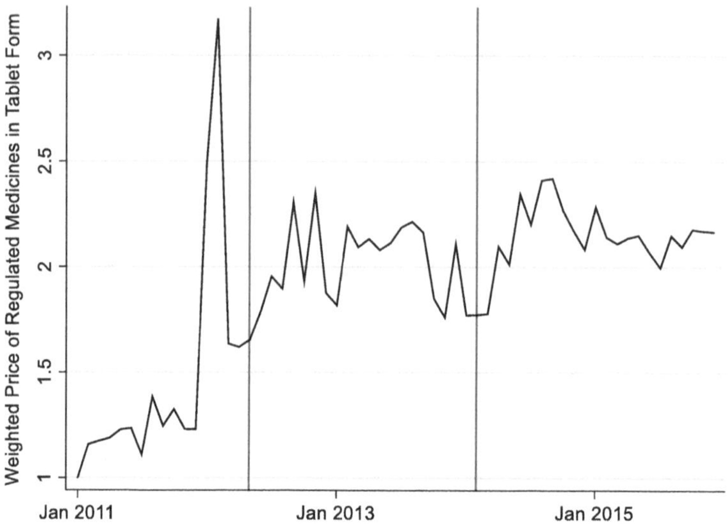

Fig. 7.4 Price index averaged across regulated and unregulated doses of medicines in their tablet form

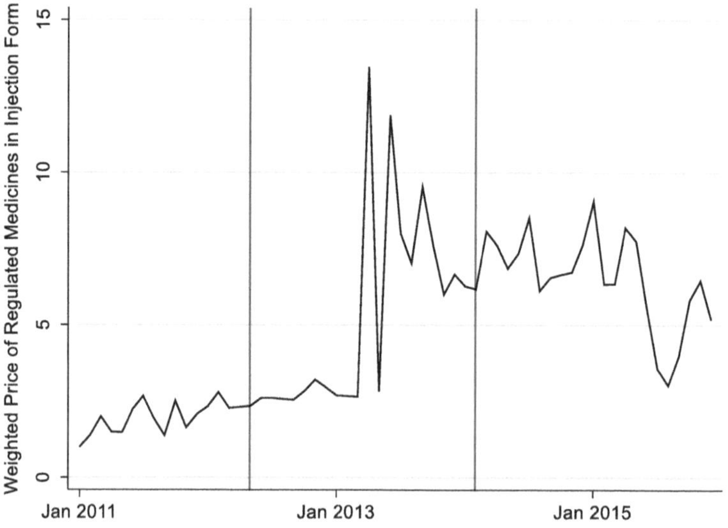

Fig. 7.5 Price index averaged across regulated and unregulated doses of medicines in their injection form

Figs. 7.4, 7.5 and 7.6 for tablets, injections, and syrups respectively. The trends show that the overall price at least doubled during 2011–2015, and in the case of injections and syrups price more than doubled.

To illustrate the extent to which firms coordinated on prices, Bhaskarabhatla et al. examine the case study of the Metformin medicine, which is used extensively to treat

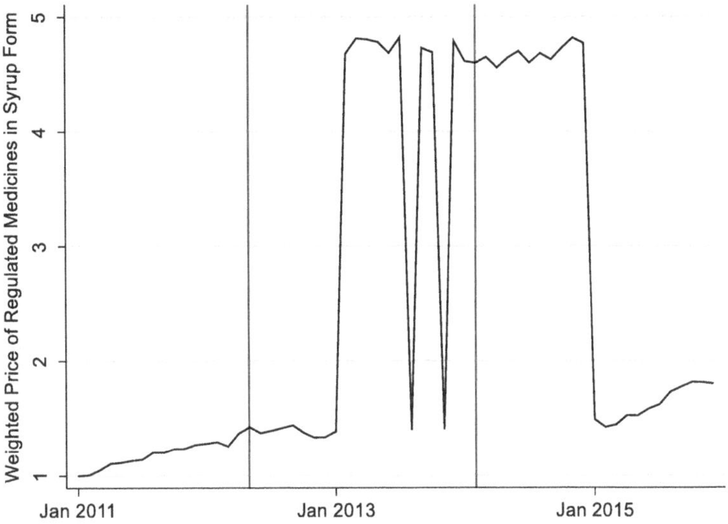

Fig. 7.6 Price index averaged across regulated and unregulated doses of medicines in their syrup form

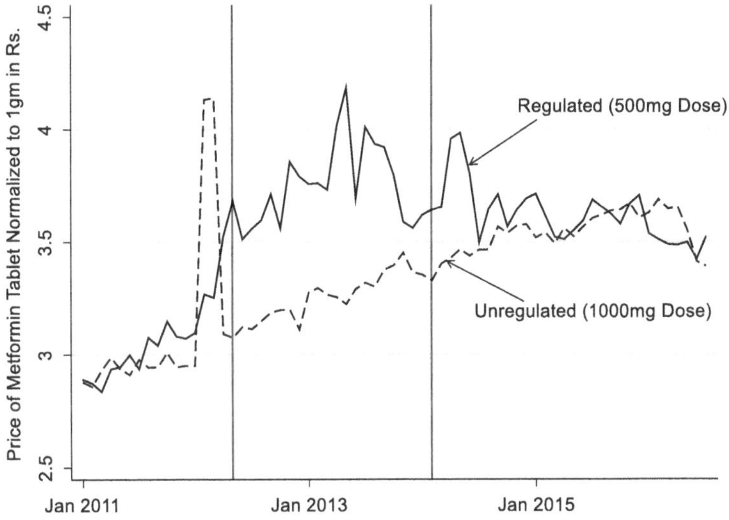

Fig. 7.7 Price of regulated and unregulated doses of metformin tablets

patients with diabetes mellitus in India. They show that firms coordinated to selectively increase the prices of SKUs containing the regulated dosage. We build on their example of Metformin medicine and plot in Fig. 7.7 the average MRP for 500 mg and 650 mg Metformin tablets for a longer time series after the implementation of the regulation. The figure shows that the average price of 500 mg

Metformin tablets, normalized per 1000 mg, remained identical to the average price of 100 mg Metformin tablets before the implementation of the regulation at around three rupees per tablet. The average price of 500 mg SKUs selectively increased in May 2012 and subsequently declined after August 2013. The average prices of both doses converged again at 3.5 rupees per tablet after the 2013 DPCO was implemented. Bhaskarabhatla et al. argued that such a coordinated, temporary increase was aimed at inflating the prospective ceiling price. The government, likely aware of such coordinated action, decided to use PTR as the basis for regulation (for further details see Chap. 4).

While the trends indicate that the consumers as a whole are worse off, if the most vulnerable segments of the society have enjoyed better access to lower-priced, regulated medicines, then the 2013 DPCO can be considerable as valuable for some segments of the consumers. However, there is little evidence based on prescriptions data that physicians prescribe price-regulated medicine dosages for lower-income households. Also, as the IMS study (2015) pointed out, the imposition of price controls may have crowded out producers from the production of regulated doses. Next, we examine such diversion of production resources.

7.4 Diverting Production from Regulated to Unregulated SKUs

Armstrong and Sappington (2007, pp. 1637–1639) describe the challenges in designing regulation when firms operate in both regulated as well as related but unregulated markets. We continue to examine the Metformin market and plot in Fig. 7.8 the share of the 500 mg tablet market as a percentage of the total market for Metformin tablets composed of 500 mg and 1000 mg doses. We find that the share increased temporarily before the regulation but subsequently declined. Although the extent of decline in Metformin is not significantly high (it ranges between 65 and 70% based on market share during the 5 year period), the shift in production can potentially be substantial for other medicines. To examine the trends overall, we expand the set of medicines to include all those affected by the 2013 DPCO. We plot in Figs. 7.9, 7.10 and 7.11 the quantity share of regulated doses as a percentage of the total quantity of the medicine for tablets, injections, and syrups. The patterns indicate that the quantity of regulated medicines as a share of the total sales of the medicine did not decline substantially overall. We present the quantity share of regulated SKUs by medicine in Table 7.1. Although one would expect a decline in prices to increase the share of sales for the regulated SKUs, overall, there is a decline in sales in the case of some medicines, albeit by a small percentage. Particularly, top-selling medicines such as Atorvastatin and Paracetamol have experienced a decline of more than 5% during 2011–2015. Bhaskarabhatla et al. (2018) examine the case of Paracetamol in greater detail. They define effort diversion as the redirection of production resources from regulated to unregulated market segments. They argue

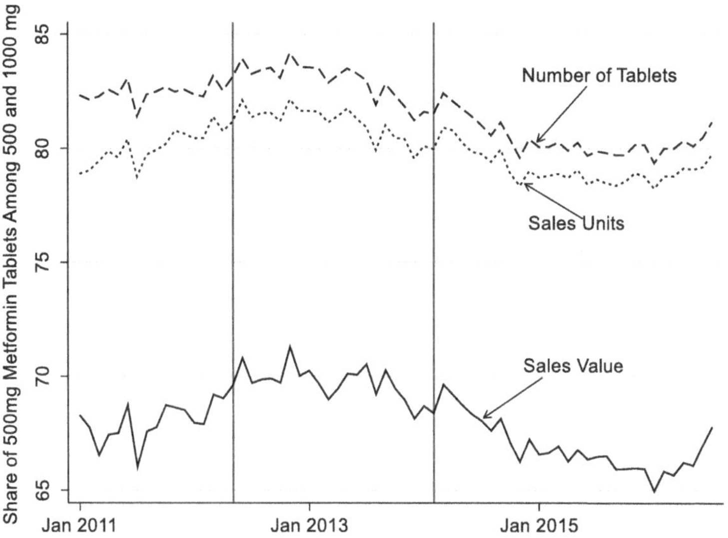

Fig. 7.8 Share of 500 mg metformin tablets as a percentage of 500 mg and 1000 mg metformin markets

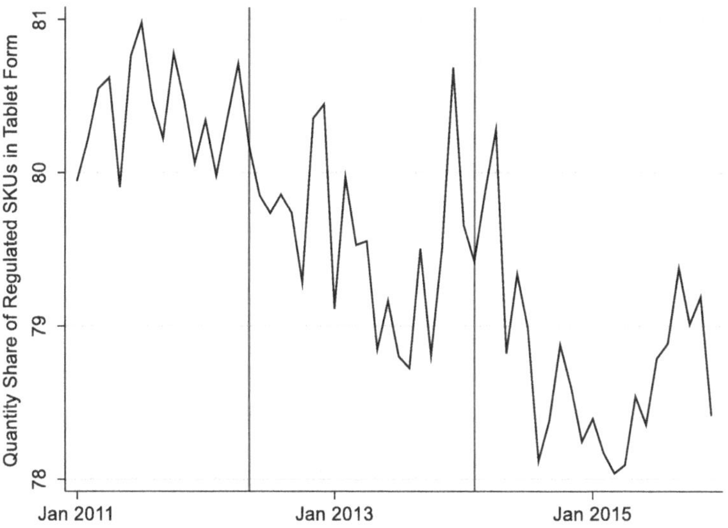

Fig. 7.9 Quantity share of regulated SKUs among all SKUs of regulated medicines in tablet form

that when the costs of production in the regulated and unregulated markets are similar—as is the case for different dosages markets of the same medicine—then even if the costs are not known, information asymmetries on the demand side can lead to inefficient effort diversion. Using Pharmatrac data on Paracetamol between

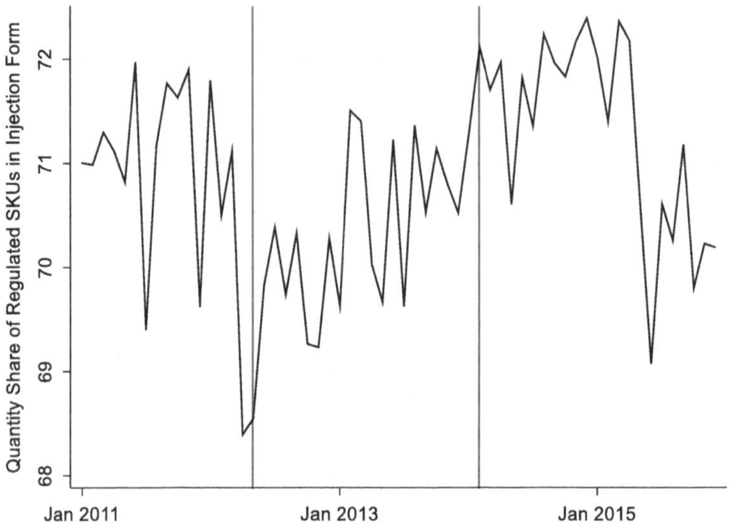

Fig. 7.10 Quantity share of regulated SKUs among all SKUs of regulated medicines in injection form

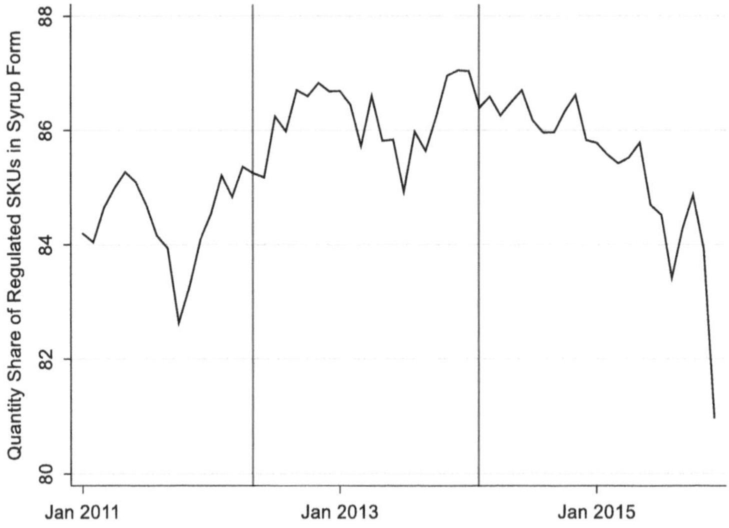

Fig. 7.11 Quantity share of regulated SKUs among all SKUs of regulated medicines in syrup form

March 2007 and June 2015, they document the nature and extent of effort diversion from 500 mg to 650 mg tablets. They also find that firms successfully increased the relative price in the unregulated market *and* diversified away from the regulated 500 mg segment into the unregulated 650 mg segment, thus limiting the overall effectiveness of regulation.

Table 7.1 The share of units of regulated SKUs among all SKUs of partially regulated medicines in tablet form

#	Medicine I 4-digit Category	Jan 2011	May 2012	August 2013	December 2015
1	Glyceryl Trinitrate I C1E4	3.12	2.44	1.98	1.32
2	Doxycycline I J1A6	66.54	55.32	50.92	5.9
3	Dextromethorphan I R5F3	7.27	8.38	9.61	9.24
4	Efavirenz I J5B6	58.64	41.9	10.22	10.87
5	Lamivudine I J5B1	9.36	12.64	19.37	11.62
6	Chlorambucil I L1A1	56.27	62.65	41.34	22.44
7	Famotidine I A2B2	35.11	36.68	29	27.31
8	Amitriptyline I N6A1	30.87	30.1	30.05	27.96
9	Primaquine I P1D6	27.61	28.64	35.41	32.26
10	Lithium I N6A11	35.78	35.57	34.73	33.53
11	Diclofenac I M1A12	48.58	33.43	35.92	34.95
12	Zidovudine I J5B2	58.92	64.02	67.07	35.75
13	Methyldopa I C2A7	100	100	100	36.34
14	Mesalazine I A7E1	70.04	60.37	46.58	39.28
15	Ritonavir I J5B9	61.26	30.88	14.22	39.79
16	Isosorbide Dinitrate I C1E3	46.54	46.58	43.4	41.02
17	Warfarin I B1X9	56.19	52.3	52.9	41.65
18	Vitamin B1 Plain I A11E13	7.3	32.28	46.44	41.85
19	Tramadol I N2B5	53.12	49.69	57.31	45.31
20	Paracetamol I N2B1	54.44	56.53	50.24	49.47
21	Diltiazem I C8A6	54.45	52.38	53.52	50.51
22	Rifampicin I J4A12	57.88	46.96	54.37	51.73
23	Clindamycin I J1F3	47.44	56.32	47.89	51.74
24	Isosorbide-5-Mononitrate I C1E1	60.34	61.31	56.38	55.5
25	Spironolactone I C3A3	62.95	75.25	57.94	56.53
26	Atenolol I C7A5	53.38	55.06	54.12	57.18
27	Cefalexin I J1D1	45.59	48.19	56.4	57.7
28	Diethylcarbamazine I P1E2	31.51	45.75	42.54	58.83
29	Sulfasalazine I A7E3	66.7	65.49	62.85	60.57
30	Aspirin I B1C1	56.37	57.09	61.31	61.05
31	Fluoxetine I N6A8	69.81	72.8	69.43	62.88
32	Atorvastatin I C10A1	73.6	69.97	67.47	63.4
33	Propranolol I C7A37	78.18	74.08	72.3	63.88
34	Aciclovir I J5A4	69.64	66.43	66.27	64.14
35	Olanzapine I N5A5	67.11	65.07	64.57	64.76
36	Nitrofurantoin I G4A3	68.35	70.6	66.91	66.47
37	Bromocriptine I N4A2	78.13	62.47	53.47	67.54
38	Metformin I A10B6	68.2	69.74	68.64	67.59
39	Amoxycillin I J1C1	63.62	65.36	61.08	69.17
40	Ibuprofen I M1A30	72.64	81.95	75.84	73.57
41	Clomifene I G3G2	70.64	79.11	72.73	73.68
42	Carbamazepine I N3A1	79.7	78.86	76.71	74.26

(continued)

Table 7.1 (continued)

#	Medicine ǀ 4-digit Category	Jan 2011	May 2012	August 2013	December 2015
43	Danazol ǀ G3B3	47.54	70.36	74.85	75.44
44	Cyclophosphamide ǀ L1A3	60.86	68.76	77.9	76.76
45	Verapamil ǀ C8A23	82.44	81.82	77.64	77.46
46	Chlorpheniramine ǀ R6A4	98.18	96.58	94.9	77.84
47	Metoclopramide ǀ A3F19	92.6	93.21	82.3	78.83
48	Imatinib Mesylate ǀ L1X16	80.97	76.05	81.48	79.05
49	Ethambutol ǀ J4A3	84.27	83.67	83.72	79.88
50	Diazepam ǀ N5D9	82.76	80.79	78.63	81.52
51	Cyclosporin ǀ L4A4	99.1	93.28	90.98	82.72
52	Metoprolol ǀ C7A29	83.37	83.77	83.71	82.87
53	Domperidone ǀ A3F7	82.98	83.39	82.69	83.66
54	Phenytoin ǀ N3A12	88.33	84.85	84.83	84.14
55	Dapsone ǀ J4B3	96.94	97.4	94.44	84.46
56	Methotrexate ǀ L1B1	97.75	93.36	92.57	86.26
57	Hydroxychloroquine ǀ P1D2	93.08	91.36	89.1	86.74
58	Allopurinol ǀ M4A4	90.5	91.12	88.69	87.48
59	Quinine ǀ P1D8	76.13	83.19	83.67	87.64
60	Sodium Valproate ǀ N3A14	89.86	88.28	88.28	88.84
61	Ofloxacin ǀ J1G9	87.42	87.05	88.76	89.39
62	Terbutaline ǀ R5D3	33.21	16.9	43.27	90.67
63	Acetazolamide Systemic ǀ S1D2	88.48	92.67	90.64	91.11
64	Enalapril ǀ C9A6	91.55	92.02	93.46	91.85
65	Cefixime ǀ J1D26	88.29	88.42	91.14	91.88
66	Carbimazole ǀ H3B1	90.69	91.12	92.42	91.91
67	Norethisterone ǀ G3A12	99.06	99.26	99.6	92.86
68	Erythromycin ǀ J1F4	88.76	93.01	93.23	93.41
69	Fluconazole ǀ J2A4	98.2	96.26	95.83	93.63
70	Omeprazole ǀ A2C1	89.37	88.33	91.42	94.31
71	Ampicillin ǀ J1C7	89.36	91.3	94.28	94.33
72	Nifedipine ǀ C8A16	94.95	95.4	95	95.08
73	Ethinylestradiol ǀ G3A18	90.84	94.39	95.35	95.5
74	Dexamethasone ǀ H2A5	90.11	92.78	88.73	95.65
75	Alprazolam ǀ N5D1	94.17	95.24	96.16	95.96
76	Imipramine ǀ N6A10	93.73	95.48	94.96	96.15
77	Pyridostigmine ǀ N7C11	96.63	96.65	96.98	96.45
79	Cetirizine ǀ R6A3	93.48	94.41	96.55	96.47
78	Amlodipine ǀ C8A1	94.75	95.01	95.09	96.47
80	Testosterone ǀ G3B2	97.08	98.5	98.66	97.33
81	Medroxyprogesterone ǀ G3A19	98.74	98.96	99	97.58
82	Clopidogrel ǀ B1C5	97.68	97.57	97.42	97.66
83	Tamoxifen ǀ L2B1	100	100	92.45	97.71
84	Ciprofloxacin ǀ J1G1	96.89	97.31	97.91	98.12
85	Salbutamol ǀ R3A11	95.27	87.79	96.97	98.24

(continued)

Table 7.1 (continued)

#	Medicine I 4-digit Category	Jan 2011	May 2012	August 2013	December 2015
86	Bisacodyl I A6B5	97.2	96.82	98.94	98.3
87	Prednisolone I H2A6	98.96	98.77	98.49	98.4
88	Azathioprine I L4A3	98.67	98.79	98.6	98.63
89	Ondansetron I A4A2	98.1	97.81	97.83	98.66
90	Hyoscine I A3A32	99.98	100	100	98.77
91	Griseofulvin I J2A8	84.53	90.49	99.84	98.84
92	Pyrazinamide I J4A10	97.81	97.89	97.61	98.86
93	Glibenclamide I A10B1	98.57	98.86	98.57	98.87
94	Azithromycin I J1F1	99.55	99.58	98.88	98.92
95	Folic Acid I B3A4	99.68	99.27	98.47	98.96
96	Plain Vitamin C I A11X31	98.83	99.4	96.82	99.49
97	Leflunomide I M5C1	98.24	99.79	99.14	99.62
98	Chlorpromazine I N5B2	99.45	97.87	99.51	99.65
99	Trihexyphenidyl I N4A10	99.69	99.72	99.6	99.68
100	Losartan I C9D3	99.67	99.64	99.64	99.7
101	Metylergometrine I G2A3	99.86	99.9	99.79	99.89
102	Mifepristone I G3X2	97.99	80.93	100	99.9
104	Albendazole I P1B1	99.01	99.2	99.94	99.95
103	Hydrochlorothiazide I C3C8	99.9	99.93	99.96	99.95
128	Phenobarbitone I N3A10	99.77	100	100	100
123	Flutamide I L2B5	100	100	100	100
118	Amiodarone I C1B3	100	100	100	100
107	Mefloquine I P1D18	100	100	100	100
106	Fluconazole I D1A17	100	100	100	100
105	Metronidazole I A7A1	100	100	100	100
116	Cloxacillin I J1C23	98.48	96.04	100	100
115	Indinavir I J5B8	100	100	100	100
125	Neostigmine I N7C10	100	100	100	100
114	Isoniazide I J4A6	100	100	100	100
119	Mercaptopurine I L1B8	100	100	100	100
112	Promethazine I A4B1	100	99.83	99.84	100
126	Ciprofloxacin I S3A2	100	100	100	100
121	Clofazimine I J4B2	100	100	100	100
120	Digoxin I C1A1	100	100	100	100
127	Pyrimethamine I P1D3	100	100	100	100
122	Raloxifene I G3 J2	100	100	100	100
109	Penicillamine I M1C5	100	100	100	100
110	Didanosine I J5B4	95.57	94.12	93	100
108	Stavudine I J5B3	100	100	100	100
117	Diloxanide I P1A4	100	100	100	100
111	Melphalan I L1A5	100	100	100	100
113	Colchicine I M4A2	100	100	100	100
124	Procarbazine I L1X19	38.08	100	41.93	100

7.5 Introduction of Product Varieties of Regulated and Unregulated SKUs

7.5.1 Exemptions for New Products Under the 2013 DPCO

Pharmaceutical firms can, in theory, introduce new product varieties of the same medicine to attempt to mitigate the impact of the 2013 DPCO. For example, the pharmaceutical firms can over-invest in innovation in the unregulated market segments of a medicine, thus softening price-competition and generating greater demand in those segments. As discussed in Chap. 3, using the same active ingredient(s), companies can develop several product varieties with little to no cost. For example, Cipla sells three different brands of 400 mg Alebndazole tablets, Bendex, Tiobend, and X Worm. Similarly, Klar Sehen sells the same brand of 400 mg Albendazole tablets, but in three different package sizes, containing one, two, or 20 tablets. It is rational for pharmaceutical companies to develop and sell SKUs that cater to different segments of the population conveniently. Also, launching new product varieties under different brand names or package sizes can lower the risk of failure by allowing the firm to learn and discover the brands and package sizes that succeed in the market. From a consumer's point of view, having many distinct brands and variety should also, in theory, increase welfare by providing them with the product characteristics they prefer. For regulators, however, dealing with product varieties remains a challenging issue, as the regulation should exempt newer varieties that are not merely packaging and marketing innovations, but enhance the efficacy of a drug. A regulation that is too strict can potentially hinder incremental innovations. To that effect, the NPPA decided to create a subsection in the DCPO regulation (section 32):

Non–application of the provisions of this order in certain cases:

i. A manufacturer producing a new drug patented under the Indian Patent Act, 1970 (39 of 1970) (product patent) and not produced elsewhere, if developed through indigenous Research and Development, for five years from the date of commencement of its commercial production in the country.
ii. A manufacturer producing a new drug in the country by a new process developed by indigenous Research and Development and patented under the Indian Patent Act, 1970 (39 of 1970) (process patent) for five years from the date of the commencement of its commercial production in the country.
iii. A manufacturer producing a new drug involving a new delivery system developed through indigenous Research and Development for a period of five years from the date of its market approval in India: Provided that the provision of this paragraph shall apply only when a document showing approval of such new drugs from Drugs Controller General (India) is produced before the Government.

In other words, the NPPA allowed for a 5-year exemption for any new drug or novel delivery system. This exemption is a way for the NPPA to promote research and development in the newly regulated market, as innovators could still finance their research by increasing their price and gain from their newly acquired competitive advantage. But despite its advantages, this system also has an important drawback, namely that it can create an important loophole in the ceiling price mechanism. As Abbott (1995) notes,

> The critical question is how to define the product for purposes of the price cap. Is a bottle of 50 400 mg tablets the same product as a bottle of 25 800 mg tablets? What if additional active ingredients are added to one but not the other? Or, what if one product is in solid form and the other in liquid? Clearly, there are many ways in which the same basic active ingredient could be incorporated into a "new product," and the pharmaceutical industry is noted for its ingenuity in developing alternative presentations. Introducing one and phasing out the other might enable the pharmaceutical firm to avoid the price cap and could be very difficult to detect -- was the product changed in order to get around the price cap or is the "new" product really better for consumers?

Regulators must be able to answer such questions case by case and weigh the advantages and disadvantages each time. Is the innovation substantial? What are the advantages for the Indian population? Is it worth the price? Regulating and assessing the quality of an innovation is extremely hard, especially in a market where the stakes are this high. The NPPA thus has to weigh each decision assessing the public's interest while keeping an eye on the pharmaceutical companies' interest, which is a challenging trade-off to balance.

Historically, however, pharmaceutical firms have introduced new product varieties of existing medicines to avoid price controls. For example, Pfizer changed the composition of its cough syrup, Corex to dodge the 1995 drug price controls (Ghangurde 1998). Similarly, Burroughs Wellcome, a subsidiary of Glaxo, replaced pseudo-ephidrine with phenyl propalomina in its brand of anti-cold medicine brand, Actifed (Ghangurde 1998). Gulhati (2004) elaborated on the economics behind the choice:

> Actifed, a cough and cold remedy of Glaxo is an international brand. All over the world it contains pseudoephedrine while in India it contains phenylpropanolamine. Last year PPA was found to be causing strokes. Coldarin [Johnson & Johnson] issued front page ads to inform readers that its product was free from PPA. Yet recently they themselves have changed their own formula by using the discredited, dangerous PPA. Why? Because PPA is cheaper while psuedoephedrine is not only expensive but under price control. Since both are decongestants, they should be subjected to similar price controls or remain out of price control.

7.5.2 *Pharmaceutical Firms' Reaction to the DCPO Legislation*

Next, we examine how pharmaceutical firms responded to the DPCO by introducing new product varieties. First, pharmaceutical firms applied for exemptions from the 2013 DPCO by changing the route of administration. As noted in Chap. 5, the case of Crocin Advance is one of the significant cases of unsuccessful attempts to gain exemption from the 2013 DCPO. Crocin is a brand of Paracetamol produced by GlaxoSmithKline, and it is widely used in India. The 2013 DPCO regulated the

500 mg Crocin tablets. In response, GSK decided to launch a new product called Crocin Advance, which contained the same dosage of Paracetamol but had a new and innovative delivery system discovered through research and development to be exempted from the price cap. GSK thus decided to launch Crocin Advance at Rs. 30 for a 15 tablet and discontinue the old Crocin that was priced at Rs. 12.70 (Nautiyal 2014). According to GSK, Crocin Advance has substantial benefit compared to the regular slow release version, as "Crocin Advance is India's first paracetamol tablet with Optizorb technology. It starts releasing its medicine in as little as 5 min. It gets absorbed 25% faster than standard paracetamol."[1] In other words, GSK justified a 130% increase in price because patients would be able to feel the effect of Paracetamol approximately 1 min and 30 sec earlier. GSK hoped that the NPPA would agree to keep Crocin Advance out of the ambit of 2013 DPCO for 5 years to cover GSK's research and development expenses, as specified under paragraph III of section 32. The NPPA did not agree with GSK's arguments because they considered that Paracetamol was not a new drug. A special technical committee of the NPPA ruled that a different way of manufacturing a new drug or a faster delivery system does qualify as an innovation for the NPPA. The section of DCPO 2013 thus did not apply to this case. An injunction on the sale of Crocin Advance was then released, and GSK had to recall the entire stock of Crocin Advance, and relabel it to comply with the ceiling price. By March 2017, GSK paid Rs. 53.99 crores to the NPPA as reimbursement for overcharging the consumers and violating the 2013 DPCO. Depending on the importance of the innovation on the delivery system, the NPPA has however allowed for exemptions. Drugs with innovative delivery systems can be sold at a higher price by setting a different ceiling price for these. For example, "Glycerol Trinitrate" has a different price ceiling for its sustained release tablet or capsule (Shankar 2014a). But overall, the Department of Pharmaceutical stated that "no drug can fall out of price control merely because it involves a New Drug Delivery System. Hence, merely because a capsule is conventional or non-conventional does not make it cease to be capsule" (Shankar 2017).

Second, pharmaceutical firms tweaked the dosages of their brands to mitigate the impact of the DPCO. For example, GSK argued that its Crocin suspension was not subject to 2013 DCPO as 120 mg/ml was not mentioned in the 2011 edition of the National List of Essential Medicines. GSK continued to sell the medicine at Rs. 37.77, even though the NPPA fixed the price of Crocin suspension at Rs.19.20. The 2011 National List of Essential Medicine includes 125 mg/ml but not 120 mg/ml. By exploiting this loophole, GSK tried to push other medicines of the Crocin brand like Crocin drops. According to the Maharashtra Food and Drug Administration, other Crocin products like Crocin drops were available at Rs.32 even though the ceiling price was set at Rs. 4.80 (Nautiyal 2014). All these maneuvers were met with skepticism by the Maharashtra Food and Drug Administration, and the NPPA decided to rule against GSK, which had to reimburse the overcharged amount. The practice of tweaking dosages was widespread before the implementation of DCPO

[1] http://www.crocin.com/products/crocin-advance.html

2013, and the Department of Pharmaceutical has demanded to the NPPA "to vigorously pursue the issue with the Ministry of Health to its logical conclusion" (Alexander 2013).

Third, pharmaceutical firms have developed combinations to avoid price controls. This manipulation can have two different goals. First, adding an active ingredient in a drug creates a gray area where regulators have to decide whether or not it is subject to DCPO 2013. For example, a company can add caffeine to paracetamol arguing it is not the same medication anymore, or that the added product brings an improvement worthy of an exemption to the price ceiling. An analysis of the petitions submitted to the Department of Pharmaceutical gives us a good overview of how companies try to circumvent the regulation. Medications are composed of two things: the active ingredient, like paracetamol, the molecule that is supposed to "solve the problem," and the excipient, the vehicle of the active ingredient. Cipla tried to persuade the NPPA to consider their medication differently by arguing that excipients are also active ingredients. The review was finally rejected by the DoP "the ground that DPCO does not distinguish between prices based on different excipients" (Alexander 2014). Finally, adding other components to the drug such as vitamins can also create an opportunity to change the legal classification of the product. The practice has been used by the Indian pharmaceutical firms for a long time and was even present before the implementation of DCPO 2013. Indeed, adding nutritional supplements can make active substances to be considered as a dietary supplement under the Prevention of Food Adulteration Act of 1954 which is not under the responsibility of the NPPA and not subject to the DCPO 2013 price ceiling (Alexander 2013). Overall, since the Crocin Advance scandal, both the NPPA and the pharmaceutical companies have been more careful in their product introductions. Any variant of a drug has to be first submitted to the NPPA, which decides if the medication should be subject to the DCPO 2013 or not (Nagappa et al. 2015). As PharmaBiz.com (2017) notes:

> Some pharmaceutical companies have launched formulations by altering a scheduled formulation, with strength other than as specified in DPCO 2013 and/or in combination with other non-scheduled medicines without even applying for price approval from NPPA as required.

We described how pharmaceutical firms attempted to use new product varieties to circumvent the 2013 DPCO by relying on publicly reported cases. However, it is likely that we missed several other strategies firms employed to avoid regulation.

7.6 Evidence of Temporary Increases in Product Margins

7.6.1 Introduction

Price controls and trade margins are twin issues that must be addressed together. However, the 2013 DPCO remains silent on the issue of trade margins. Although the ceiling prices were initially designed to be based on MRP in 2005, when the DPCO

2013 was publicly notified, the government based it on PTR and allowed for a 16% margin for retailers (see for more details, Chap. 4). The move led to a considerable disagreement between pharmaceutical firms and the AIOCD, the union of pharmaceutical traders in India. According to Vijay pharmacies in Karnataka refused to stock medicines that newly entered price control regulation because the trade margins on such medicines became lower:

> The only way to come out of this situation would be to see that manufacturers comprehend our situation and call to restore the margins as this is only going to hamper not just our sales but revenues of the pharma companies too following the reluctance to sell these drugs by pharmacy outlets.

Our subsequent analysis focuses on trade margins on pharmaceutical firms and how they evolved historically and changed in response to the imposition of price controls. As noted in Chap. 3, trade margins account for a significant share of the prices consumers pay. Moreover, margins provide incentives along the vertical value chain that contradict cost-efficiencies for consumers, since absolute returns from margins are higher for products that are sold at higher prices and margins. As we discussed in Chap. 5, such incentives increase the sales of more expensive drugs, adversely affecting the affordability of medicines. Although the problem relates to products sold across several industries in India in general, it is more pronounced in the pharmaceutical industry, because of the relationships between pharmacists, physicians and pharmaceutical firms in generating demand for prescriptions. Trade margins also play an important role in undermining the overall competitiveness of the regulated markets. For example, in the presence of price controls, physicians and pharmacists have an incentive to promote the medicines with prices closer to the ceiling price, as those medicines likely involve greater margins. Accordingly, trade margins have been a long-deliberated issue in the Indian pharmaceutical industry.

7.6.2 The Role of All India Organization of Chemists and Druggists

Pharmacies in India played a significant role in increasing trade margins on medicines. The pharmacies are represented by the trade association, All India Organization of Chemists and Druggists (AIOCD). The AIOCD fought for higher trade margins following the 1979 DPCO. The AIOCD argued that the government allocated generous profit margins on regulated medicines for pharmaceutical manufacturers, but considerably lower margins for retailers. Indeed, the 1979 DPCO provided margins as high as 100% on some regulated medicines and even higher margins for unregulated medicines. The AIOCD organized boycotts of pharmaceutical firms to coerce them into increasing trade margins. Singh (1984) notes:

> The drug industry finally buckled last year, and representative associations of the manufacturers agreed to allow an 8 per cent wholesale margin and 18 per cent retail margin on all drugs classified under the Government's non-essential category IV.

Monopolies and Restrictive Trade Practices Commission (MRTPC) judged AIOCD's use of boycotts to extract higher trade margins illegal, but their use continued unabated (Dubashi 1985). The AIOCD agreed with the trade associations of pharmaceutical manufacturers IDMA and OPPI, which fixed the trade margins for unregulated medicines at 30% and for the regulated medicines at 24%. Whenever medicines enter or exit the DPCO, the AIOCD and pharmaceutical firms renegotiate the trade margins, leading to a period of threats of boycotts. The case of the 2013 DPCO was no different. The 2013 DPCO did not resolve the long-standing dispute between the pharmaceutical firms and the retail trade associations. The IDMA and AIOCD continued to lobby for higher margins for their membership respectively (Shankar 2014b). Bhaskarabhatla et al. document evidence that the AIOCD boycotted firms such as GSK that refused to increase margins on their best-selling medicines (e.g., Augmentin) entering the 2013 DPCO. Following the boycotts, several firms pledged not to lower margins on newly regulated medicines from 30 to 24%. We will examine how the margins changed during this period of bargaining momentarily.

In 2015, the AIOCD criticized that the 2013 DPCO neglects the important role of wholesalers in the pharmacy trade chain (Vijay 2015a). The criticism focuses on two aspects: first, the AIOCD general secretary, Suresh Gupta, criticized that the DPCO capped the retail margins at 16%, despite the recommendation to use 20% as a benchmark for the retail margin; second, Gupta criticized that the DPCO did not mention any wholesaler margin. In line with this criticism, the president of the AIOCD Shinde declared his organization's disagreement with the cap on margins as regulated in the DPCO 2013 and announced that the AIOCD would accept "nothing less" than margins of 20% to retailers and 10% to wholesalers and "strongly oppose" any related action by the government (Vijay 2015b). Similar to the criticism by Gupta, Shinde complained that the DPCO regulation did not mention wholesaler margins. The IDMA also formulated a harsh criticism of the DPCO-regulation, urging the government "not to initiate the capping of trade margin on generic drugs as this would force the retailers to close their business resulting in non-availability of medicines in rural areas" (Rana 2015).

In response to reports of excessive trade margins on pharmaceuticals, on behalf of the Prime Minister's office (PMO), a committee was formed to prevent the "unethical practice of pharmaceutical companies". In particular, the PMO criticized that margins for essential drugs were "running up to 4000%," clearly violating the DPCO 2013. The committee was headed by Sudhansh Pant, joint secretary in the Department of Pharmaceuticals. Moreover, the committee was joined by representatives from the NPPA, the Competition Commission of India and participants from the industry.

7.6.3 Report by the Committee on High Trade Margins

In the Indian pharmaceutical industry, trade margins were first capped as part of the 1970 DPCO. Interestingly, regulations on trade margins were significantly stricter at that time compared to the most recent DPCO in 2013. For instance, under the 1970 and 1979 DPCOs, the trade margin for wholesalers is fixed at 2%, and for retailers, the margin varied from 10 to 12% based on whether the medicine was ethical or non-ethical category. The retailer margin was fixed at 16% under the 1987 and 1995 DPCOs, but the ceiling price was computed based on manufacturing costs rather than market-based prices. By contrast, the DPCO 2013 includes a notional retail margin of 16%, which applies only to price-controlled drugs. The stipulated margin is considered notional because, as we will elaborate momentarily, there is nothing preventing firms from providing margins greater than 16%. It is useful to recall that the DPCO 1970 originally introduced "a combined trade margin for all intermediary levels between manufacturer and retailer including retailer" (Pant et al. 2016). However, an amendment introduced on 11th January 1971 separately fixed the trade margins for wholesalers and retailers. Pant et al. (2016) note:

> Initially, wholesaler and retailer margin was fixed but subsequently Government tried to lift control on upstream margins and wholesaler margin was not specified in the later DPCOs. Under DPCO, 2013 except for adding margin to price to retailer while fixing ceiling/retail prices, DPCO, 2013 does not specify any other trade margins to be paid by the manufacturer or trader.

Moreover, the Pant report acknowledges that the discussion on trade margins has become a heated issue related to the 2013 DPCO due to the large number of complaints the NPPA received identifying the cases of exorbitant margins. In particular, the NPPA received several complaints through its Centralized Public Grievance Redress and Monitoring System and through the Ministry of Chemicals and Fertilizers, which indicated that the trade margins were 300–5000% (Pant et al. 2016, p. 13). The report notes that there is a considerable difference between "the sale price of the company to the distributor/wholesaler and the MRP printed on it." Such discrepancy between prices throughout the value chain critically affects the equilibrating process in the market. The Pant report mentions the case of M/s Ranbaxy Laboratories Ltd. v/s State of Haryana, in which the drug is sold to dealers at Rs. 2, but the MRP printed on the strip is Rs. 26. The report cites the judgment of the Punjab and Haryana High Court (Pant et al. 2016):

> Before parting with the judgement, it has to be noticed that although the petitioner is allegedly selling the drug in question to the consumer at about 900% of the reasonable price of the drug, but there appears to be no legal provision in force to save the consumers from such naked fleecing of the consumers by the petitioner or other drug manufacturers by over-pricing the drug to such an extent. It is surprising that no remedial or ameliorating step has been taken either by State or by the Union of India in this regard. The court hopes that now at least the concerned authorities shall wake up and shall take some remedial step to save the consumers from such fleecing.

Although India tried to cap trade margins of unregulated medicines in 2000, its law ministry at the time opined that doing so can potentially be challenged under article 14 of the Indian constitution guaranteeing the right to equality. However, in 2007, the ministry modified its opinion and stated that controlling unfair trade margins by putting a ceiling is in consonance with article 14. The Sandhu Committee also opined on the matter in 2004, suggesting a trade margin of 8–10% for wholesalers and 16–20% for retailers on branded generics and 15 and 35% for generic medicines.

In its meetings with the NPPA in July 2015, the industry representatives argued that high trade margins facilitate the distribution and sale medicines in remote areas, thus increasing the availability of medicines in India. The NPPA, however, argued for debranding plain generics containing only one ingredient on the basis that the Drug Controller General of India (DCGI) issues licenses in generic names. Also, the NPPA suggested that paragraph 7(2) of the 2013 DPCO should be amended, which would restrict the notional margin of 16% to the actual trade margin that can be enforced by the law. The Competition Commission of India surprisingly stated that capping trade margins is considered anti-competitive, unless there is a "strong justification on the grounds of public policy" (Pant et al. 2016).

In consultation meetings with several stakeholders and lobbyists from the industry as well as trade associations in 2015, traders pointed out that they agree on capping trade margins and that by doing so the availability of drugs will not be affected. However, traders also underlined their demand to raise the cap on margins. Moreover, traders required distinguishing generic-generic medicines from others allowing for higher margins in that segment. Concerning generic medicines, traders argued that higher margins were necessary for generic drugs as "marketing expenses are passed on to the retailers" and "no return from retail on account of expiry and breakage is accepted" (Pant et al. 2016).

In general, the analysis of the committee concluded that "instead of controlling MRP, the Government should only cap the trade margins" (Pant et al. 2016). Moreover, the report recommended capping the overall trade margin which would leave companies the freedom to adjust margins for different trade channels. In contrast to the DPCO 2013 regulation, the committee suggested: "that the cap on trade margin should be calculated backward with reference to the retail price (MRP)" (Pant et al. 2016). Furthermore, the committee pointed out that "[h]igh Trade margins are not specific to a particular type of drug. It is generally prevalent in non-scheduled drugs due to historical reasons, but abnormally high margins have also been observed in scheduled drugs" (Pant et al. 2016). Moreover, the report concluded that capping trade margins does not conflict with existing legislations and, in particular, does not violate the Competition Act, 2002.

After long deliberations, the committee came up with the proposal of a gradual system to cap the margins. The committee opined that capping the trade margin on lower-priced medicines will push traders to shift to higher-priced medicines. To mitigate such effects, they suggested to cap margins of medicines with an MRP of Rs 50 and above at 35%, while margins of medicines with an MRP between 20 and 50 were suggested at 40%. For medicines with an MRP between Rs 2 and Rs 20, the trade margin is suggested to be capped at 50%. Further, the committee recommended avoiding capping margins of medicines below Rs 2. Finally, the committee proposed to cap trade margins of "all drugs including generics, branded, scheduled, and non-scheduled drugs". The Pant Committee made additional, but related recommendations, which we list below (Pant et al. 2016, p. 33–34):

- Recommended a cap on the trade margins, including medical devices such as stents and orthopedic implants
- Recommended capping trade margins concerning price to the trader rather than maximum retail price.
- Recommended an amendment to Form V submitted by manufacturers to the NPPA under the 2013 DPCO to include price to the trade so that it can be monitored.
- Recommended adjusting the trade margins appropriately when manufacturers offer promotional offers.
- Recommended amending paragraph 7(2) of the 2013 DPCO as stated below: "No manufacturer shall sell a drug to the Trade, unless otherwise permitted under the provisions of this order or any order made thereunder, the MRP of which exceeds the margins notified by the Government from time to time with reference to the price to trade."

The Pant Committee also clarified that the practice of providing high trade margins is unethical, defined as not consistent with the rules or standards for right conduct or practice especially the standards of a profession. Also, the NPPA clarified that the consumers of generic medicines are often adversely affected due to higher prices compared to branded generic equivalents. As an example, the Committee noted that Alken sold the generic version of 50 mg Nandrolone injection at an MRP of Rs. 185. However, PCI Pharma sold the same medicine under the brand name Decapic at an MRP of Rs. 14.25 and Jaksonpal Pharma sold the medicine under the brand name of Metadec at an MRP of Rs. 260. Similarly, the generic version of a pack of ten 20 mg Piroxicam tablets is sold by Alkem at an MRP of Rs. 43. By contrast, Indswift sold the same medicine at an MRP of Rs. 3.75 for ten tablets under the brand name Doloswift and Akumentis sold at Rs. 85 under the brand name Pirover.

The Pant Committee also refuted the claim that capping trade margins is inherently anticompetitive. The committee noted that capping trade margins will neither create entry barriers nor push existing manufacturers out of the market. The committee argued that placing an upper limit on the trade margin allows pharmaceutical firms the freedom to choose their margins, but protects consumers against exorbitant margins. Therefore, the committee argued that capping trade margins are not in violation of the Competition Act of 2002.

7.6.4 Representations to the Pant Committee and Deliberations After the Committee's Recommendations

The pharmaceutical firms and their industry associations provided a coordinated opposition to the idea of limiting trade margins. The extent of coordination is visible in their representations to the Pant Committee. For example, the three pharmaceutical manufacturers, Alken Laboratories, Micro Labs, and Cipla, submitted letters to the Pant Committee. A cursory examination of the letters reveals that the letters are substantively identical, each containing the same 11 points. We document the responses by the IDMA, the IPA, pharmaceutical firms, AICDF, and the Competition Commission of India in Table 7.2. In general, the industry associations and their members argued that capping trade margins would compel them to legally challenge the NPPA. In a letter to the DoP, the Indian Drug Manufacturers Association stated: "that any move to cap trade margins would seriously impact micro, small and medium scale drug companies engaged in manufacturing such medicines". The IDMA's criticism (or a veiled threat) went as far as to argue that medicines in rural areas may become partly unavailable as a consequence. Although the committee's recommendations on trade margins were far more generous compared to the initial regulations of the DPCO 2013, different industry and trade bodies proceeded to oppose their implementation. Once more, in their criticism, they argued with the availability of drugs in rural areas and the affordability for small manufacturers. Only a few days later, in another statement the AIOCD threatened the government again, warning that any reduction of the trade margins below the requested level of 10% to retailers and 20% to retailers would come at the cost that "the supply of medicines to the patients will be severely affected" (Rana 2016). The continued opposition by the AIOCD and the IDMA drew criticism from industry observers (Francis 2016):

> Such a stand and threats issued by the associations representing pharma industry and trade on the availability of medicines in the event of capping margins are not fair. Retail margins of 1000 per cent and more on any product are unethical and when it is on a lifesaving product it is totally unjustified. Therefore, DoP has to come out with the notification capping margins without any further delay.

Two months after the announcement of the recommendations by the committee, the AIOCD again pushed their claims, now demanding to increase the cap on trade margins to 50%, including a retailer margin of 35% as well as a wholesaler margin of 15%, valid for "all generics, scheduled and non-scheduled drugs, ethical, non-ethical medicines, surgical equipment viz. stents, orthopedic implants" (Yadav 2016). With respect to the introduction of margin caps, Kaustav Ganguli, Healthcare Lead and Senior Director at Alvarez & Marsal argued that "there has to be a mechanism to ensure that the impact of lower prices is borne in a fair manner by all stakeholders across the value chain covering hospitals and distributors instead of only by manufacturers" (Vijay 2016). The controversy persisted in 2017, as the AIOCD opposed

Table 7.2 Stakeholder responses to the proposal to limit trade margins on the sale of medicines

Stakeholders	Response to the proposal to cap trade margin in the sale of medicines
Indian Drug Manufacturers Association	Capping trade margins will disrupt sales in rural areas and adversely affect small and medium-sized pharmaceutical firms
Organization of Pharmaceutical Producers of India	Trade margins are a matter between the manufacturer and the trade. So long as the availability of drugs at mandated ceiling price is maintained, there is no reason for additional regulatory guidance
	Capping trade margins will adversely affect the availability of medicines in remote villages.
	Fixing and maintaining a "Stokist Price" (that is, price to the trader) could be deemed anti-competitive as the manufacturer should be free to sell the product at any price as negotiated between manufacturers and stockists as long as the same conforms with the DPCO.
	Amending Form V to include price to the trader is burdensome as the IPDMS website is not user-friendly.
Indian Pharmaceutical Alliance	Trade margins are not regulated for any commodity or product, however essential.
	Regulating trade margin can violate competition laws and adversely affect competition.
	Regulated trade margin will compromise access to medicines in remote areas.
	Capping the trade margin will embolden the traders to seek the minimum stipulated amount and settle for nothing less.
Confederation of Indian Pharmaceutical Industry	Manufacturers are compelled to give margins higher than 16% because otherwise, retailer's associations boycott their products
Alkem, Cipla, and Micro Labs	Capping trade margins will be in violation Article 14 of the Indian constitution.
	Capping trade margins will lead to severe shortages.
	The trade margins are not capped in any other country.
	Prices of price-controlled and non-controlled medicines are already among the cheapest in India as compared to other developing countries and the increase in prices have always been below or at par with inflation.
	Capping trade margins will not lower MRP. Instead, the MRPs will rise because the PTR will rise. As a result, the ceiling prices, currently calculated by PTR, will rise.
	The calculation of mark-ups is incorrect.
	Higher trade margins allow for distribution to rural areas
All India Chemists & Distributors Federation	Support capping trade margins
	Argued for strengthening rules around disclosing PTR through Form V, which would not allow manufacturers to hide actual trade margins and restrict the practice of allowing extraordinary discount or margin or incentive or bonus to any dealer
	Capping
Competition Commission of India	Generally, any kind of fixation of trade margin and the price is considered anti-competitive, unless there is strong justification on the grounds of public policy.

(continued)

Table 7.2 (continued)

Stakeholders	Response to the proposal to cap trade margin in the sale of medicines
National Pharmaceutical Pricing Authority	Supported limiting trade margins by amending the 2013 DPCO to include paragraph 7(2): "No manufacturer is allowed to give margin to retailer exceeding the margin specified in sub para (1) of this paragraph"

Source: Pant et al. (2016).

the government's evolving policy on online pharmacies and proposed changes to the DPCO. The AIOCD general secretary noted (Yadav 2017a):

> At present wholesalers get 10 per cent margin on non-scheduled drugs and 8 per cent margin on scheduled drugs from drug manufacturers. On the other hand, retailers receive 20 per cent margin on non-scheduled drugs and 16 per cent margin on scheduled drugs from drug manufacturers. Given the existing margin cap, it's impossible for chemists to offer 25-30 per cent discount to customers. We have appealed to the government to prevent e-pharmacies from offering heavy discount or remove existing margin cap for wholesalers, retailers, he said.

Recently, the AIOCD demanded changes in the DPCO 2013 (Yadav 2017b), their criticism addressed the calculation of the price ceiling for scheduled formulations. The AIOCD proposed the following formula (Yadav 2017b):

> 1) retail price (RP) minus percentage (DPCO 1995 formula) then the retailers margin is equal to RP minus 20 per cent; 2) if the margin is to be calculated on PTS then the formula should be as follows: Price to stockiest (PTS) plus 39 per cent as to maintain 20% margin to retailer and 10 per cent margin to distributor.

As can be concluded from these intense deliberations, the definition of maximum margins is a controversial topic in the Indian pharmaceutical industry. In the following subsection, we use Pharmatrac data to descriptively analyze the size of trade margins as well as highlight how trade margins changed in the period surrounding the implementation of the 2013 DPCO.

7.6.5 Analysis of Trade Margins Using the Pharmatrac Data

Using Pharmatrac data, we examine the extent of trade margins before and after the 2013 DPCO. The pharmaceutical industry claims that the high trade margins are prevalent among generics. However, our analysis of price-controlled medicines, most of which are branded, out-of-patent medicines, indicates relatively high trade margins. We limit the analysis to all SKUs that entered price cap regulation in 2013. We plot in Fig. 7.12, the percentage of trade margins, calculated as 100* (MRP-PTR)/PTR. The trade margin increased from an average of 29% in January 2011 to 33% in March 2012. However, the average trade margin increased suddenly in the next month to 73% and reached a high of 105% in January 2013. The margin decreased briefly after the 2013 DPCO was implemented but soon increased to a high of 74% in January 2015. The trade margins declined subsequently and hovers at

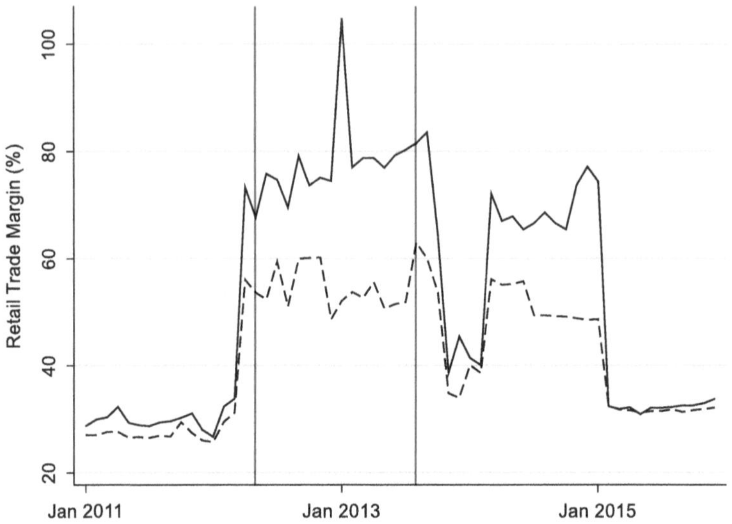

Fig. 7.12 Retail trade margin for regulated SKUs before and after the 2013 DPCO implementation

around 40% at the end of our dataset in July 2016. The Figure shows how pharmaceutical firms strategically doubled or tripled margins, even though the 2013 DPCO assumes a margin of 16% in determining the ceiling price.

We examine the extent to which margins changed for the top 16 price-regulated medicines in our dataset with more Rs. 10 billion in sales during January 2011 and July 2016. We plot the evolution of margins before and after the 2013 DPCO in Fig. 7.13. Although the margins did not increase substantially in the case of four medicines, in the remaining cases, they increased multiple times the initial margin. For example, in the case of Paracetamol, the margins increased to more than 250% during August 2013.

Next, we report in Table 7.3 the average trade margin for all the price-controlled medicines during 2011–2015. We find that in 2015, none of the medicines had an average trade margin of less than 16%, the lowest being 16.7 for Deferoxamine. For many of the medicines, the trade margins in 2012, 2013, and 2014 remained considerably higher compared to 2011 and 2015, indicating the manner in which pharmaceutical firms collectively manipulated the margins during the implementation of the 2013 DPCO. Therefore, one can conclude that the DPCO 2013 did not succeed in lowering trade margins in the Indian pharmaceutical industry. Additionally, the lines for scheduled and non-scheduled drugs deviate towards the end of the observed period, with the line for scheduled drugs increasing more rapidly. Overall, these analyses suggest that pharmaceutical firms strategically changed their margins to mitigate the impact of the 2013 DPCO. Since we observed similar patterns of changes to trade margins for both scheduled and non-scheduled tablets, there is strong evidence that the DPCO 2013 failed to contain trade margins.

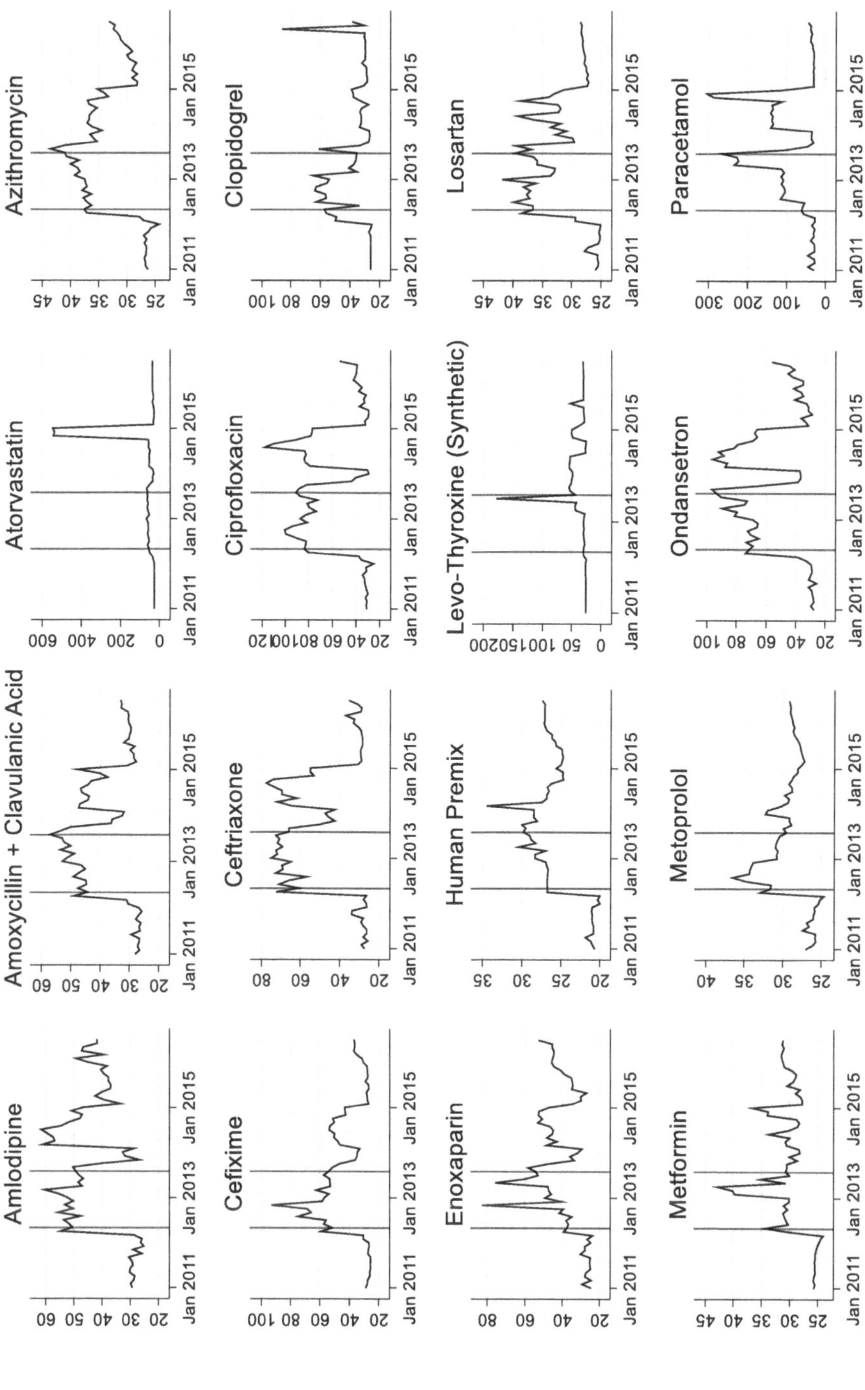

Fig. 7.13 The evolution of retail trade margins for the top 16 medicines with more than Rs. 10 billion in sales during Jan 2011–Jul 2016

Table 7.3 Average trade margin, as a percentage, by year for price-controlled medicines

Medicine I 4-digit category	2011	2012	2013	2014	2015
Water For Injection I K5A1	84.02	2656.28	2288.04	1507.79	330.29
Metylergometrine I G2A3	35.23	215.71	196.09	184	109.66
Cetirizine I R6A3	54.51	223.46	238.7	190.57	88.47
Atorvastatin I C10A1	25.5	49.03	54.74	128.93	74.14
Tramadol I N2B5	36.55	131.57	176.2	177.69	73.72
Enalapril I C9A6	25.41	73.2	211.2	79.03	66.92
Mifepristone I G3X2	40.93	121.47	87.18	119.85	66.41
Omeprazole I A2C1	54.88	148.51	182.33	176.17	66.08
Suxamethonium I M3A11	25	65.33	71.82	64.95	65.07
1/1 Electrolyte Solutions I K1A1	26.23	77.27	99.29	91.04	62.85
Diclofenac I M1A12	34.21	82.16	89.08	102.38	59.46
Propofol I N1B5	24.93	62.51	77.39	79.39	57.47
Vancomycin I J1X2	26.86	65	77.75	67.24	57.11
Albendazole I P1B1	32.07	115.11	124.7	101.53	54.55
Streptokinase I B1D2	22.85	54.84	68.43	53.07	50.66
Hepatitis B I J7A3	105.38	118.87	110.46	145.88	48.1
Ofloxacin I J1G9	31.21	72.83	82.17	81.83	47.34
All Oral Electrolytes - Ors I A7G2	27.67	68.15	88.42	81.16	43.1
Sodium Bicarbonate I A2A20	24.98	49.47	49.78	40.05	42.78
Folic Acid I B3A4	28.09	81.18	107.78	125.49	41.91
Domperidone I A3F7	32.14	125.39	144.04	147.54	41.29
Amikacin I J1 K4	32.45	89.4	100.89	92.46	41
Snake-Bite Sera I J6A1	25	25.54	49.96	73.46	40.33
Fluconazole I J2A4	33.75	108.36	108.11	89.87	40.05
Ringers And Ringers Lactate Solutions I K1A7	29.33	120.66	116.26	142.37	39.4
Amlodipine I C8A1	28.81	45.75	46.87	51	39.23
Paracetamol I N2B1	32.42	72.82	135.29	144.19	37.35
Ondansetron I A4A2	28.91	60.63	74.05	73.98	37.09
Pantoprazole I A2C4	28.28	57.47	75.69	55.32	36.87
Norethisterone I G3A12	25.87	34.68	36.99	36.59	36.86
Ciprofloxacin I J1G1	31.52	73.89	75.71	79.39	36.52
Amoxycillin I J1C1	27.77	93.93	106.01	80.08	36.36
Alprazolam I N5D1	40.26	66.96	198.61	94.62	36.26
Cefalexin I J1D1	28.53	115.54	97.43	105.41	36.14
Enoxaparin I B1B3	26.57	38.67	50.82	45.51	35.94
Povidone Iodine I D8A2	35.53	77.38	103.5	83.71	35.81
Lidocaine I N1C10	24.97	78.45	63.72	51.6	35.58
Tetanus I J7A2	25.81	38.88	44.99	46.87	35.45
Allopurinol I M4A4	32.39	55.14	64.12	72.49	35.37
Bisacodyl I A6B5	26.53	40.02	51.83	84.89	35.25
Thiopental Sodium I N1B6	25.42	70.93	82.5	35.93	34.4
Iuds Containing Hormones I G3A9	35.2	44.25	33.6	42.93	34.26

(continued)

Table 7.3 (continued)

Medicine | 4-digit category	2011	2012	2013	2014	2015
Atenolol | C7A5	25.47	42.48	55.72	44.25	34.18
Ampicillin | J1C7	26.84	71.28	88.26	69.8	34.15
Leflunomide | M5C1	26.85	28.45	30.49	34.34	34.1
Isoflurane | N1A4	24.57	83.94	296.86	351.57	33.86
Levo-Thyroxine (Synthetic) | H3A2	25.61	28.04	53.45	41.88	33.61
Mesna | V3D5	38.23	27	55.81	91.39	33.28
Calamine | D2A12	26.51	30.34	31.88	34.26	33.01
Hydrocortisone | H2A7	30.19	78.68	91.76	62.41	32.37
Oxytocin | G2A4	31.68	82.59	61.15	96.53	31.77
Phenobarbitone | N3A10	24.14	27.98	32.24	30.17	31.65
Isosorbide-5-Mononitrate | C1E1	25.99	29.67	35.57	33.52	31.52
Metoclopramide | A3F19	28.36	39.25	39.84	41.74	31.49
Ceftriaxone | J1D17	28.37	56.63	64.72	63.35	31.41
Indinavir | J5B8	25	40.89	30.46	29.58	31.25
Ipratropium | R3A7	25	28.82	31.25	36.58	31.25
Mercaptopurine | L1B8	29.59	29.67	30.35	26.04	31.25
Gentamicin | S3A4	27.36	52.37	58.37	61.68	31.11
Amoxycillin + Clavulanic Acid | J1C4	26.95	42.16	49.69	42.09	31.1
Clotrimazole | D1A1	34	29.29	35.71	50.56	31.01
Digoxin | C1A1	20.98	26.7	60.83	91.41	31
Ceftazidime | J1D20	24.91	61.84	44.22	45.6	30.61
Promethazine | A4B1	27.08	41.92	56.7	45.59	30.39
Dexamethasone | H2A5	27.26	70.4	61.65	65.26	30.24
Diazepam | N5D9	44.08	45.62	45.18	58.35	30.22
Clopidogrel | B1C5	26.03	52.33	40.66	32.05	30.15
Glibenclamide | A10B1	25.09	299.78	60.66	40.43	30.14
Permethrin | P2A4	25.29	54.24	34.61	35.62	30.06
Zinc | A12C3	25.51	27.02	29.73	29.06	30.04
Esmolol | C7A23	25	33.59	42.84	30.82	30.03
Clindamycin | J1F3	25	29.69	31.25	63.89	30
Dextromethorphan | R5F3	24.99	29.04	29.99	29.99	29.99
Tropicamide Eye Drops/Ointment | S1E5	25.05	26.51	25.86	28.16	29.94
Framycetin | D6A5	24.97	24.31	25.49	28.93	29.93
Asparaginase | L1X32	30.18	15.59	21.07	52.54	29.91
Isosorbide Dinitrate | C1E3	24.87	28.53	28.5	26.48	29.9
Diloxanide | P1A4	24.95	27.71	29.81	34.23	29.88
Spironolactone | C3A3	24.97	24.15	25.47	28.43	29.87
Ciprofloxacin | S3A2	27.57	36.83	40.81	36.53	29.85
Hydrochlorothiazide | C3C8	24.95	27.1	31.86	28.44	29.84
Vitamin B1 Plain (With Additives) | A11E13	24.99	28.62	30.85	31.23	29.76
Miconazole | D1A4	29.53	117.45	61.43	47.93	29.66
Metformin | A10B6	25.5	29.33	33.35	30.43	29.65
Methyl Prednisolone | H2A8	25.12	42.62	46.27	39.46	29.65

(continued)

Table 7.3 (continued)

Medicine I 4-digit category	2011	2012	2013	2014	2015
Danazol I G3B3	25.02	31.05	29.68	27.57	29.58
Isoniazide I J4A6	19.01	28.12	31.55	29.29	29.57
Efavirenz I J5B6	35.5	35.36	31.41	38.57	29.41
Azithromycin I J1F1	26.54	34.37	39.13	35.81	29.4
Amiodarone I C1B3	26.02	30.02	30.81	27.87	29.33
Hydroxychloroquine I P1D2	25.92	29.81	28.91	28.05	29.26
Haloperidol I N5B9	23.73	27.27	26.74	25.6	29.21
Methotrexate I L1B1	25.87	33.42	32.67	30.88	29.19
Prednisolone I S3B7	24.99	41.46	51.27	24.43	29.1
Hyoscine I A3A32	25.39	36.07	27.71	40.59	29.03
Levodopa + Carbidopa I N4A6	35.38	26.21	23.27	23.07	28.99
Dactinomycin I L1D3	19.05	16.39	22.81	24.8	28.89
Cefixime I J1D26	26.56	55.74	51.04	46.37	28.88
Carbimazole I H3B1	25	39.18	36.18	25.6	28.83
Cisplatin I L1X3	20.14	33.71	36.45	32.01	28.8
Nitrofurantoin I G4A3	25.31	29.83	29.4	31.05	28.79
Timolol Eye Drops/Ointment I S1D24	30.28	29.32	28.83	35.96	28.76
Glyceryl Trinitrate I C1E4	24.99	28.73	33.38	30.33	28.66
Propranolol I C7A37	25.01	29.17	28.51	31.32	28.65
Midazolam I N5D16	26.91	46.92	59.13	32.08	28.64
Dicyclomine I A3A1	23.76	79.64	35.84	27.41	28.61
Lamivudine + Zidovudine I J5B18	33.98	28.6	52.92	32.39	28.54
Sodium Valproate I N3A14	25.87	28.26	30.67	29.66	28.51
Imipramine I N6A10	27.78	27.29	28.21	41.69	28.4
Nevirapine I J5B7	24.99	29.91	33.26	41.33	28.4
Aciclovir I D6B1	25.61	27.76	46.52	33.98	28.38
Ispaghula I A6C1	25.4	45.99	36.98	33.47	28.38
Homatropine Eye Drops/Ointment I S1E3	25.21	27.21	34.05	32.12	28.25
Glucose I K1C4	24.94	67.6	102.13	124.55	28.22
Nifedipine I C8A16	25.72	49	54.17	31.99	28.22
Mannitol I C3F5	27.49	75.5	105.94	73.64	28.21
Lorazepam I N5D11	27.1	28.17	28.53	27.44	28.2
Lamivudine + Stavudine I J5B19	26.91	29.01	31.78	30.8	28.2
Mesalazine I A7E1	25.2	26.83	24.59	25.59	28.17
Lamivudine I J5B1	25.04	50.91	113.52	27.01	28.11
Pyrimethamine I P1D3	24.94	29.68	31.26	31.26	28.1
Diltiazem I C8A6	26.04	29.39	28.94	28.12	28.1
Aciclovir I J5A4	25.83	37.23	35.9	36.43	28.07
Acetazolamide Systemic I S1D2	25.06	27.89	28.22	26.92	28.07
Ketamine I N1B2	24.98	34.13	49.18	74	28.02
Metoprolol I C7A29	26.26	31.75	30.18	29.62	27.97
Mefloquine I P1D18	25.07	28.68	28.98	24.06	27.97
Warfarin I B1X9	24.99	29.72	32.13	28.92	27.94

(continued)

Table 7.3 (continued)

Medicine	4-digit category	2011	2012	2013	2014	2015
Misoprostol	A2E1	24.99	29.64	31.18	31.62	27.92
Lamivudine + Stavudine + Nevirapine	J5B30	27.83	28.93	52.88	28.01	27.92
Losartan	C9D3	25.77	35.17	35.46	33.92	27.89
Atropine	A3A10	28.53	63.44	67.7	74.24	27.85
Ibuprofen	M1A30	25.24	48.78	47.19	54.64	27.83
Amitriptyline	N6A1	26.3	28.07	33.66	29.54	27.81
Clomifene	G3G2	25.8	27.76	36.2	35.26	27.72
Azathioprine	L4A3	25.92	61.02	53.55	36.23	27.67
Flutamide	L2B5	24.84	29.28	33.69	30.98	27.67
Betamethasone	D7A2	25.36	24.66	23.01	26.02	27.65
Zidovudine	J5B2	25	29.02	29.48	29.27	27.58
Unfractionated Heparins—Systemic	B1B1	28.3	54.16	43.36	56.36	27.56
Terbutaline	R5D3	25.88	54.97	37.3	31.96	27.52
Lithium	N6A11	25.09	25.5	30.16	30.81	27.52
Verapamil	C8A23	24.8	22.72	21.64	20.84	27.48
Aluminium + Magnesium	A2A15	25.13	27.28	28.23	99.89	27.46
Lamivudine + Zidavudine + Nevirapine	J5B22	27.5	60.4	35.49	31.59	27.46
Raloxifene	G3 J2	24.91	28.77	28.52	28.33	27.45
Ranitidine	A2B4	27.63	43.54	56.65	41.8	27.44
Ritonavir	J5B9	25	29.86	31.25	28.91	27.39
Povidone Eye Drops/Ointment	S1F25	29.69	29.69	28.12	28.37	27.24
Diethylcarbamazine	P1E2	25.06	152.76	163.54	46.5	27.24
Phenytoin	N3A12	25.2	27.66	30.12	28.13	27.21
Fluorouracil	L1B5	25.54	41.33	2405.19	32.33	27.15
Famotidine	A2B2	37.88	320.82	69.06	153.44	27.07
Olanzapine	N5A5	32.89	30.98	31.31	29.42	27.05
Albumin	J6A8	33.9	34.19	43.69	30.47	27.04
Dopamine	C1C7	24.75	37.68	78.98	40.69	27.03
Sulfasalazine	A7E3	24.98	52.84	30.8	23.79	27.02
Colchicine	M4A2	24.98	28	28.15	24.67	26.96
Bupivacaine	N1C4	24.99	37.78	31.23	32.54	26.94
Bcg	J7A11	27.47	28.51	29.42	28.27	26.86
Trihexyphenidyl	N4A10	24.87	28.7	49.38	28.75	26.85
Artesunate + Sulfadoxine + Pyrimethamine	P1D20	25	33.77	31.42	28.11	26.81
Medroxyprogesterone	G3A19	23.51	24.32	25.7	25.59	26.8
Cetrimide	D8A8	30.96	31.78	41.12	36.41	26.78
Neostigmine	N7C10	25.68	55.46	150.3	160.03	26.76
Quinine	P1D8	25.06	65.25	33.75	34.51	26.69
Salbutamol	R3A11	38.24	99.42	126.49	42.23	26.69
Pilocarpine Eye Drops/Ointment	S1D23	25.66	25.65	28.46	33.72	26.63

(continued)

Table 7.3 (continued)

Medicine I 4-digit category	2011	2012	2013	2014	2015
Fluoxetine I N6A8	25.09	45.2	62.01	41.17	26.57
Adenosine I C1B1	25	39.54	50.47	59.61	26.54
Testosterone I G3B2	25	26.78	29.51	26.1	26.53
Pyrazinamide I J4A10	20.63	85.75	40.43	37.05	26.52
Prednisolone I H2A6	24.94	24.79	24.09	26.76	26.51
Atropine Eye Drops/Ointment I S1E1	25.09	27.83	27.74	39.59	26.41
Gemcitabine I L1B10	26.26	46.93	114.78	93.14	26.39
Amphotericin B I J2A2	25	28.37	32.89	62.04	26.32
Ethambutol I J4A3	19.03	26.82	30.02	26.95	26.3
Tamoxifen I L2B1	25.29	38.66	45.95	28.78	26.29
Imatinib Mesylate I L1X16	28.87	61.13	69.2	95.01	26.28
Metronidazole I A7A1	25.57	44.31	35.48	26.99	26.26
Methyldopa I C2A7	25.35	23.22	24.25	22.44	26.21
Pyridostigmine I N7C11	24.99	25.9	27.64	24.51	26.15
Doxycycline I J1A6	25.47	104.81	91.51	56.74	26.09
Atracurium I M3A2	24.72	41.62	30.22	57.39	26.05
Gentamicin I J1 K1	58.95	38.07	33.91	29.06	26.01
Beclomethasone I R3A2	25	22.9	25	27.37	25.99
Carbamazepine I N3A1	21.66	26.71	25.39	29.59	25.98
Melphalan I L1A5	17.57	27.41	64.51	50.56	25.8
Filgrastim I L3A2	35.8	82.06	69.03	44.77	25.79
Cefotaxime I J1D13	24.87	35.56	37.26	33.94	25.77
Chlorpromazine I N5B2	26.8	25.5	58.56	24.35	25.76
Erythromycin I J1F4	25.43	36.55	41.31	25.14	25.64
Primaquine I P1D6	25.3	30.6	31.2	35.37	25.64
Nitroprusside I C2B21	26.68	30.61	26.38	32.9	25.63
Betaxol Eye Drops/Ointment I S1D5	24.99	24.54	23.88	25.41	25.62
Human Premix I A10G1	20.99	25.09	28.85	27.18	25.59
Codeine I R5E3	24.99	33.41	33.1	30.58	25.49
Pyrimethamine + Sulphadoxine I P1D4	24.92	24.85	24.44	25.54	25.49
Dobutamine I C1C5	25	61.75	56.84	26.84	25.48
Ethinylestradiol I G3A18	24.99	29.57	36.84	24.97	25.34
Dapsone I J4B3	25	30.87	39.47	25.88	25.32
Naloxone I N7E3	24.62	29	30.73	22.53	25.32
Regular Human Insulin I A10H1	24.19	23.49	25.66	25.8	25.19
Bromocriptine I N4A2	25.88	30.61	31.39	30.33	25.14
Cyclophosphamide I L1A3	25.02	33.38	27.74	29.95	25.13
Anti Rabies Vaccine - Arv I J7A16	23.72	28.66	30.31	29.38	25.07
Cyclosporin I L4A4	25.87	30.19	32.35	28.48	25.01
Phytomenadione I B1A5	24.78	29.69	30.49	30.92	25.01
Interferon Alpha 2B I L3B10	26.04	25.53	20.44	31.82	25
Adrenaline I C1C3	25	637.79	251.17	305	25

(continued)

Table 7.3 (continued)

Medicine | 4-digit category	2011	2012	2013	2014	2015
Stavudine | J5B3	24.99	136.04	255.4	29.32	25
Factor Viii | B2D1	79.08	48.05	57.94	39.8	25
Polio | J7A9	80.96	25	122.65	70.77	25
Hydrocortisone | D7A8	25	30.58	77.19	30.3	25
Topical Contraceptives | G2B1	25	25.09	24.31	19.67	25
Fentanyl | N2A4	24.99	23.15	11.62	24.33	25
Measles | J7A6	23.26	25	25	25	25
Cloxacillin | J1C23	23.52	27.5	408.64	382.99	24.99
Fluconazole | D1A17	23.77	27.87	25	39.02	24.96
Clofazimine | J4B2	24.98	40.17	24.36	19.47	24.94
Streptomycin | J4A18	18.99	22.43	22.48	20.63	24.76
Chloramphenicol | S1A2	24.99	26.36	26.16	29.71	24.68
Anti Rh-D Immunoglobulin | J6E2	25	25.34	25.72	24.55	24.68
Plain Vitamin C | A11X31	463.06	515.82	605.87	27.21	24.64
Sulfacetamide | S1A55	24.56	31.65	32.22	32.96	24.61
Chloroquine | P1D1	25.61	23.72	28.37	25.67	24.56
Ethinyl Estradiol + Levonorgestrel | G3A11	25.57	25.22	23.1	30.32	24.52
Chlorpheniramine | R6A4	24.99	26.96	35.84	28.08	24.5
Aspirin | B1C1	25.03	80.68	461.41	26.8	24.38
Low Dextrans (< = 50,000 Daltons) | K2A1	25	27.71	30.3	26.93	24.05
Urokinase | B1D1	19.29	55.45	63.42	18.58	23.89
Piperazine | P1B6	24.98	27.77	44.46	74.17	23.75
Betamethasone | H2A9	25.06	32.56	27.11	24.71	23.75
Protamine | V3E4	19.05	28.18	30.9	27.01	23.69
Vincristine | L1C2	21.77	33.36	33.33	27.78	23.61
Penicillamine | M1C5	27.22	26.24	31.33	23.3	23.39
Paclitaxel | L1C8	20.63	47.72	340.3	208.84	23.25
Dexchlorpheniramine | R6A27	24.98	28.82	29.32	34.11	22.28
Rifampicin | J4A12	19.22	21.27	23.65	23.58	22.16
Procarbazine | L1X19	19.05	26.93	172.99	45.86	21.95
Vitamin A | A11X25	26.08	24.24	22.99	19.26	21.89
Ifosfamide | L1A4	25.49	42.76	25.46	37.94	21.81
Griseofulvin | J2A8	24.98	82.08	150.26	34.25	21.78
Pheniramine | R6A17	24.93	24.22	23.81	22.59	21.65
Carboplatin | L1X2	23.04	53.19	52.43	35.08	21.44
Dacarbazine | L1A23	27.69	34.57	36.47	36.22	21.26
Etoposide | L1C4	20.34	55.99	49.89	43.82	21.08
Doxorubicin (Plain) | L1D5	26.71	56.32	34.01	31.76	21.04
Oxaliplatin | L1X4	45.95	72.59	65.88	49.71	20.73
Doxorubicin (Liposomal) | L1D13	19.05	89.73	80.14	46.05	20.25
Daunorubicin | L1D4	19.05	29.51	25.04	42.19	19.6
Vinblastine | L1C1	19.05	23.51	24.99	25.34	19.54

(continued)

Table 7.3 (continued)

Medicine I 4-digit category	2011	2012	2013	2014	2015
Bleomycin I L1D2	22.36	48.92	46.14	34.87	19.49
Mitomycin I L1D8	29.25	27.36	78.15	57.69	19.29
Glucagon I H4B1	18.53	27.78	29.19	32.26	19.21
Chlorambucil I L1A1	21.76	27.22	28.94	28.79	18.47
Deferoxamine I V3F2	19.05	13.4	60.91	78.93	16.7

References

Abbott, T. A. (1995). Price regulation in the pharmaceutical industry: Prescription or placebo? *Journal of Health Economics, 14*(5), 551–565.

Alexander, J. (2013). Panel asks DoP to identify pharma cos changing compositions to dodge price control provisions. *PharmaBiz* [online]. Available from http://pharmabiz.com/NewsDetails.aspx?aid=77362&sid=1

Alexander, J. (2014). DoP rejects review petitions by Cipla and two other firms against price revision of scheduled drugs. *PharmaBiz* [online]. Available from http://pharmabiz.com/NewsDetails.aspx?aid=80890&sid=1

Armstrong, M., & Sappington, D. (2007). Recent developments in the theory of regulation. In M. Armstrong & R. Porter (Eds.), *Handbook of industrial organization* (Vol. 3, pp. 1557–2440). New York: North Holland.

Balakrishnan, R. (2006). Drug price gimmicks may land govt in soup. *DNAIndia* [online]. Available from http://www.dnaindia.com/money/report-drug-price-gimmicks-may-land-govt-in-soup-1062506

Bhaskarabhatla, A., Anurag, P., Chatterjee, C., & Pennings, E. (2018). *Effort diversion as a firm strategy to respond to partial price cap regulation*. Erasmus School of Economics Working Paper.

Deshpande, R. (2006). Govt may oppose price control for essential drugs. *Times of India*. Available from http://m.timesofindia.com/india/Govt-may-oppose-price-control-for-essential-drugs/amp_articleshow/1682614.cms.

Dubashi, J. (1985, October 31). Opposition to druggists' doyen from within trade ranks grows. *India Today*.

Ellison, S.-F., & Wolfram, C. (2006). Coordinating on lower prices: Pharmaceutical pricing under political pressure. *RAND Journal of Economics, 37*(2), 324–340.

Ghangurde, A. (1998, July 27). Burroughs wellcome changes actifed content; gets it off DPCO. *Indian Express*. Available from http://expressindia.indianexpress.com/fe/daily/19980728/20955804p.html

Glazer, A., & McMillan, H. (1992). Pricing by the firm under regulatory threat. *Quarterly Journal of Economics, 107*(August), 1089–1099.

Gopakumar, K. (2017, May 19). Drug price control: For cheaper medicines, we need a cost-based formula for caps. Financial Express.

Gulhati, C. M. (2004). Why drug price regulation. *PharmaBiz* [online]. Available from http://pharmabiz.com/ArticleDetails.aspx?aid=24980&sid=21

Malhotra, P. (2010). *The Impact of TRIPS on India: An access to medicines perspective*. UK: Palgrave Macmillan.

Mathew, J. C. (2005). Industry unhappy over reference price plans. *PharmaBiz* [online]. Available from http://pharmabiz.com/NewsDetails.aspx?aid=28314&sid=2

Mathew, J. C. (2006). Technical approach to NLEM in new pharma policy may benefit drug industry. *PharmaBiz* [online]. Available from http://www.pharmabiz.com/NewsDetails.aspx?aid=33202&sid=2

Mukherjee, R. (2006). Pharma players to meet Paswan on pricing. *Times of India* [online]. Available from http://timesofindia.indiatimes.com/business/india-business/Pharma-players-to-meet-Paswan-on-pricing/articleshow/1398672.cms

Nagappa, A. N., Sharma, R., and Bokolia, R. (2015). Drug pricing reforms in changing times. *PharmaBiz* [online]. Available from http://pharmabiz.com/NewsDetails.aspx?aid=89310&sid=9

Nautiyal, S. (2014). State FDA to approach NPPA for overcharging Crocin drops. *PharmaBiz* [online]. Available from http://www.pharmabiz.com/NewsDetails.aspx?aid=81485&sid=1

Noll, R. G. (1989). The politics of regulation. In R. Schmalensee & R. Willig (Eds.), *Handbook of industrial organization*. New York: North Holland.

Pant, S., Sah, A. K., & Khurana, A. K. (2016). *Report of the committee on high trade margins in sale of drugs*. Department of Pharmaceuticals, Government of India. Available from https://ideas.repec.org/p/ess/wpaper/id10219.html

PharmaBiz.com. (2017, May 18). Drug regulator serves notices to pharma cos for violating pricing norms for combination drugs. PharmaBiz.com. Available from http://www.pharmabiz.com/NewsDetails.aspx?aid=102018&sid=2

PharmaQuest (2009). Paswan blames powerful industry lobby for thwarting national pharma policy. *PharmaQuest* [online]. Available from http://www.pharmaquest.biz/paswan-blames-powerful-industry-lobby-for-thwarting-national-pharma-policy/

Pradhan, R. (2011, November 25). New drug pricing policy may increase prices of essential medicines. *Moneylife.in* [online] Available from https://www.moneylife.in/article/new-drug-pricing-policy-may-increase-prices-of-essential-medicines/21707.html

Ray, T. J. (2013). New drug price control order of India: Is it directionally right improving access to medicines? [online]. Available from http://www.tapanray.in/new-drug-price-control-order-of-india-is-it-directionally-right-improving-access-to-medicines/

Rana, S. (2015). IDMA urges govt not to cap trade margin as it may affect availability of generic drugs in rural areas. *PharmaBiz* [online]. Available from http://www.pharmabiz.com/NewsDetails.aspx?aid=91838&sid=1

Rana, S. (2016). AIOCD vehemently opposes govt move to cap trade margin of retailers & wholesalers. *PharmaBiz* [online]. Available from http://pharmabiz.com/NewsDetails.aspx?aid=92776&sid=1

Shankar, R. (2014a). NPPA rejects demand to keep differentiated/modified dosage forms out of DPCO 2013. *PharmaBiz* [online]. Available from http://www.pharmabiz.com/NewsDetails.aspx?aid=85885&sid=1

Shankar, R. (2014b). FICCI seeks health minister's intervention to sort out issues arising out of implementation of DPCO 2013. *PharmaBiz* [online]. Available from http://www.pharmabiz.com/NewsDetails.aspx?aid=82467&sid=1

Shankar, R. (2017). Sun Pharma gets positive verdict from DoP on revision of ceiling price of nitrofurantoin capsule. *PharmaBiz* [online]. Available from http://pharmabiz.com/PrintArticle.aspx?aid=100994&sid=1

The Sen Committee. (2005). Report: Task force to explore options other than price control for achieving the objective of making available life-saving drugs at reasonable prices. New Delhi: Department of Chemicals and Petrochemicals, Government of India.

Unnikrishnan, C. H. (2012a). Market-based drug pricing formula gets GoM nod. *Live Mint* [online]. Available from http://www.livemint.com/Politics/9VC3FPESRKUFRyxHXMvgOJ/GoM-pitches-for-marketbased-system-for-drug-price-control.html

Unnikrishnan, C. H. (2012b). New drug pricing policy may hit profitability of firms. *Live Mint* [online]. Available from http://www.livemint.com/Industry/thYjee2K9jiIVshL6zQZ0O/New-drug-pricing-policy-may-hit-profitability-of-firms.html

Singh, C. U. (1984, January 15). Bombay retailers demand raise in margins by manufacturers, threaten series of boycotts. *India Today*. Available from https://www.indiatoday.in/magazine/economy/story/19840115-bombay-retailers-demand-raise-in-margins-by-manufacturers-threaten-series-of-boycotts-803574-1984-01-15

The Financial Express. (2005). Hows & whys of drug price control. *The Financial Express* [online]. Available from http://www.financialexpress.com/archive/hows-whys-of-drug-price-control/147672/

The Hindu Business Line (2007). Pharma industry opposes price control mechanism. *The Hindu Business Line* [online]. Available from http://www.thehindubusinessline.com/todays-paper/pharma-industry-opposes-price-control-mechanism/article1646222.ece

Vijay, N. (2015a). Govt should define role of wholesalers in DPCO 2013, frame norms for drug substitution: AIOCD. *PharmaBiz* [online]. Available from http://pharmabiz.com/NewsDetails.aspx?aid=89480&sid=1

Vijay, N. (2015b). BDCDA urges DoP to facilitate regulations to raise trade margins of wholesalers & retailers to 10% & 20% respectively. *PharmaBiz* [online]. Available from http://pharmabiz.com/NewsDetails.aspx?aid=90178&sid=1

Vijay, N. (2016). Price control on coronary stents necessitates margin regulations across value chain: Kaustav Ganguli. *PharmaBiz* [online]. Available from http://pharmabiz.com/NewsDetails.aspx?aid=96773&sid=1

Yadav, L. (2016). AIOCD demands capping trade margin on drugs at 50%. *PharmaBiz* [online]. Available from http://www.pharmabiz.com/NewsDetails.aspx?aid=94038&sid=1

Yadav, L. (2017a). AIOCD to go on day-long nationwide token strike in April. *PharmaBiz* [online]. Available from http://www.pharmabiz.com/NewsDetails.aspx?aid=100565&sid=1

Yadav, L. (2017b). AIOCD demands changes in DPCO provisions to ensure availability, affordability of drugs. *PharmaBiz* [online]. Available from http://www.pharmabiz.com/NewsDetails.aspx?aid=101734&sid=1

Part IV
Enforcement and Compliance

Chapter 8
Enforcement and Compliance with Price Ceilings on Essential Medicines

8.1 Introduction

The effectiveness of price control regulations depends as much on the design of the policy as on implementation. Yet rarely if ever studies examine the enforcement and compliance aspects of such price control regulations. In this chapter, we address this gap in the literature by examining the extent of compliance with price ceilings imposed on essential medicines in India in 2013 and how it has changed in response to enforcement efforts. We estimate the extent of noncompliance with the 2013 DPCO and the total overcharged amount. We identify firms and markets with significant levels of noncompliance. We also reflect on whether the regulator has followed a targeted approach to enforcement to induce compliance and whether such targeting has had any impact on overall compliance. We examine efforts by the regulator to ask firms to self-report their prices and whether that has had any impact on inducing compliance.

8.2 The Literature on Regulatory Compliance

The enactment of laws and regulations does not by itself ensure compliance. Some firms obey, others evade, and yet others defy them. Compliance depends on the regulator's ability to set and communicate standards, to design and implement mechanisms to monitor evasion and noncompliance and to enforce regulations by punishing—swiftly, demonstrably, and impartially—those that flout the standards. Regulations are pervasive, but compliance remains a global challenge for environmental protection, public finance and tax collection, consumer protection, and health and safety. A large body of work focuses on compliance issues in tax collection and environmental protection, but very little exists on compliance in the area of pharmaceutical price regulation. Heyes (2000) surveys the theoretical literature on

A. Bhaskarabhatla, *Regulating Pharmaceutical Prices in India*, India Studies in Business and Economics, https://doi.org/10.1007/978-3-319-93393-1_8

enforcement and compliance with a focus on environmental protection, but these theories are useful in our context as well.

Following Becker (1968), one would expect compliance to increase with fines and inspections. While in theory full compliance may be achieved by sufficiently increasing fines and inspections, in practice regulatory authorities have limited resources and ability to monitor, and there are practical, legal, and political constraints on the extent to which penalties can be imposed. For example, fines cannot exceed the total wealth of a violating firm. Also, large fines for small violations lead to poor marginal deterrence for large violations, that is, there is little incentive for firms to commit small violations instead of large ones if even small violations invite large fines (Stigler 1970). Besides fines and inspections, a third lever at the regulator's disposal is the regulatory standard itself. A regulator, for example, can decide how high or low should the price ceiling be on a given essential medicine. If the regulator believes it cannot achieve full compliance with a given standard using monitoring and punishment alone, then it can set a sufficiently strict *statutory* standard in an attempt to achieve the more lenient *informal* standard. However, Kambhu (1989) suggests that imposing stricter standards can, contrary to our intuition, lower compliance, as firms invest in defensive measures such as litigation or deception. Shaffer (1990) finds that stricter standards can increase compliance if nonlinear penalties can be implemented but such schemes may not be practical where inspectability and recovery of fines remain a challenge. In addition, when a regulator imposes a fine, firms invest in challenging the enforcement power of the regulator (Nowell and Shogren 1994), switching to production and operational procedures that are less transparent (Heyes 1994), and lobbying to weaken regulation and enforcement (Cheng and Lai 2012), all of which lower compliance when enforcement is strengthened.

Given the limits on the effectiveness of fines, inspections, and strict standards in achieving full compliance, some studies suggest innovative strategies to leverage limited enforcement resources to induce greater compliance. For example, a targeted enforcement strategy that divides firms into two (or more) groups based prior history of compliance and focuses on firms with a prior record of noncompliance is shown to be advantageous compared to random inspections (Greenberg 1984; Harrington 1988). Raymond (1999) shows that such targeting requires that the regulator know each firm's compliance costs, which may not be possible in many contexts. Malik (1990) suggests enforcement leverage based on screening for firms that gain more from potential violations, monitoring and imposing fines on them if they are found to violate while not enforcing the standard on the remaining firms can induce greater overall compliance. Kaplow and Shavell (1994) suggest enforcement leverage can be built by asking firms to self-report, as it can lead to savings because those who self-report violations do not require detection and they bear sanctions with certainty. Livernois and McKenna (1999) suggest that such self-reporting can increase compliance even under a regime of low fines if the regulator has the power to order any self-reporting, noncompliant firm to return to compliance. Heyes and Rickman (1998) suggest that when the regulator meets a regulated firm in more than one regulated market, the regulator tolerates violations in some markets to induce greater compliance in others, which they term regulatory dealing. Overall, the above theoretical literature suggests ways to induce greater compliance while recognizing that the regulatory resources and powers are limited and that fines are not costless transfers from noncompliant firms to the regulator.

Separate from these economic models, scholars have developed regulatory enforcement models that recognize economic, social, and normative motivations underlying compliance and noncompliance and the role of legitimacy and fairness of the regulation and enforcement procedure in achieving compliance. As Garvie and Keeler (1994) note, the non-economic literature distinguishes enforcement by deterrence and compliance regimes. Whereas a deterrence regime looks at each episode of violation independently and unforgivingly, a compliance regime promotes compliance through frequent contact between the regulator and the firm and through tolerance for intermittent violations as long as the firm is on a trajectory of compliance. Among the non-economic theories promoting such a compliance regime is the idea of responsive regulation, which suggests that compliance increases as the regulated firm has an increasingly positive assessment of and attitude towards the regulator (Ayres and Braithwaite 1992). These scholars suggest an incremental approach to the severity of punishments for violations starting with persuading the violating firm to change its behavior without imposing any fines. They also suggest that regulators can collaborate with NGOs to build social pressure and induce compliance, particularly in developing countries (Braithwaite 2006).

The empirical literature largely examines compliance with taxes and environmental standards in the US. Early empirical work finds that resources for enforcement play a significant role in compliance (Epple and Visscher 1984). Regens et al. (1997) find that firms invest in compliance-specific tools and personnel when the regulator's budget increases. Laplante and Rilstone (1996) find that inspections and the threat of inspections induce compliance. Gray and Deily (1996) find that regulators focus enforcement resources on identifying large violations and that greater enforcement leads to greater compliance. Magat and Viscusi (1990) and Nadeau (1997) find that rigorous enforcement has led to better compliance and shorter durations of noncompliance in the US pulp and paper industry. Harrison (1995) compares the US pulp and paper industry with the same industry in Canada and finds that the relatively less adversarial and cooperative approach of the Canadian regulator contributed to a relatively lower level of compliance in Canada. Helland (1998) finds that self-reporting by firms indicates their willingness to cooperate with the regulator and self-reporting increases after targeted inspections that detect violations. Yee et al. (2016) provide evidence to suggest that a clearer understanding of the enforced regulation and the fear being targeted arbitrarily play a role in increasing compliance in developing countries.

The literature on enforcement and compliance with pharmaceutical price controls is surprisingly limited given the number of countries experimenting with such regulations. In an exception, Menon (2001) suggests that the Canadian experience in controlling prices for patented medicines through annual reviews by a review board has been positive. The board does not set prices but highlights cases of excessive prices, asks firms to voluntarily lower prices, and if necessary, conducts public hearings. The board also has the option to take legal action if compliance is not reached. However, we are unaware of a quantitative analysis of the effectiveness of such an enforcement strategy. A separate stream of literature focuses on the impact of price controls on incentives for innovation and launch of patented medicines in developing countries (Cockburn et al. 2016; Berndt and Cockburn 2014; Kyle 2007; Danzon et al. 2003) and strategies for pricing such medicines in developing countries (Cockburn et al. 2016; Danzon et al. 2015).

Another stream of literature looks at the impact of pharmaceutical price controls on prices in developing countries (Yang et al. 2010; Yang et al.2013; Meng et al. 2005). Closely related to our context, Bhaskarabhatla et al. (2016) examine the impact of partial market-based price regulation of essential medicines implemented in India in 2013 on prices for Metformin, a widely-used antidiabetic medicine. They find that firms increased their prices in a coordinated manner before the implementation of the regulation to inflate the ceiling price. However, they do not examine issues surrounding enforcement and compliance. Chu et al. (2011) examine the impact of reforms in Taiwan found that average cost per prescription and the duration of prescriptions increased in Taiwan when price reduction policies were implemented as physicians found ways to circumvent the controls, reflecting challenges with compliance. The Philippines introduced pharmaceutical price controls in 2009, but anecdotal evidence suggests that it has led to the shortage of inexpensive generic medicines.[1] Overall, we are unaware of studies that examine enforcement strategies and compliance with price controls on essential medicines in developing countries. We address this gap by exploiting the recent revision of price controls on essential medicines in India.

8.3 Price Controls in India: Enforcement and Compliance

8.3.1 Historical Background for Pharmaceutical Price Controls in India

Price controls have been commonplace in India since its independence in 1947. Many controls on commodities instituted by the British before independence continued to exist even after. Price controls were made permanent through the Essential Commodities Act of 1955, which regulated the prices of a wide variety of products such as petroleum and related derivatives, food grains and seeds, textiles, fertilizers, and medicines. Noncompliance with these price controls was treated as a criminal offense. Activities such as hoarding, black-marketeering, tax evasion, food adulteration, and illegal trading in licenses and permits and such offenses invited imprisonment up to 3 years or fine or both as documented by De (2014: p. 289):

[1]Philippines President Arroyo Orders Drug Price Controls, Wall Street Journal July 28, 2009. Philippine Price Controls Hamper Rise of Generics, Wall Street Journal June 18, 2010.

> The controls system was undergirded by an exceptional regime of criminal law. These arose from the belief that these 'socio-economic' criminals needed stronger deterrence than fines and public shaming. Indeed, a socio-economic offence was characterised as one that was not challenged by the 'organised moral sentiments' of the community, because the crimes were often complex, and public agencies like the press were themselves controlled by businesses involved in violating these laws.... In recognition of the fact that companies were likely to try and contravene such orders, the controls regime made all directors, managers, and officers of a corporate body liable for a contravention unless they could prove that this took place without their knowledge or negligence. In cases of violation, deviating from the Indian Evidence Act, the burden of proof was shifted to the accused. Perhaps most ominously, those charged for violating control orders would be subject to a summary trial under the Criminal Procedure Code.

It is difficult to imagine noncompliance under such a stringent legal framework. Nonetheless, over the years the pendulum has swung in the opposite direction regarding enforcement of price controls in India although laws remain in place. For example, although tax evasion is considered a serious economic offense even today, only a small percent of the population in India pay taxes, indicating poor enforcement and compliance. It is in this new regulatory context that the pharmaceutical price controls operate in India. Price controls have been imposed on medicines in India through the Drug Price Control Order (DPCO) in 1970. Subsequently, several DPCOs have been issued in 1979, 1987, and 1995, each, according to a study by the regulator, with a progressively 'more liberalized and industry-oriented view' (NPPA 2002). Prior studies by the All India Drug Action Network (AIDAN), an NGO, identified cases of flagrant violations under the 1995 DPCO. We report in Table 8.1, a sample of medicine brands that violated the 1995 DPCO. The extent of violations was significant, often more than 100% of the ceiling price. We plot in Fig. 8.1 the overcharged amount recovered and not recovered under the DPCO 1995. We find that the recovered amount has remained constant, but the overcharged amount has sharply increased over time.

8.3.2 *The Enforcement Agency: National Pharmaceutical Pricing Authority*

It was not until 1995 that an enforcement agency was set up to determine the level of noncompliance and undertake remedial action, although price controls existed since 1970. The National Pharmaceutical Pricing Authority (hereafter, NPPA) is responsible for fixing and revising the prices of selected medicines and enforcing price ceilings and ensuring availability of medicines in the country. The NPPA currently has a pricing division that determines ceiling prices, a monitoring and enforcement division that collects data and identifies cases of overcharging, two divisions dedicated to recovering the overcharged amount from the pharmaceutical firms, and a legal division to prosecute noncompliant firms.

The NPPA operates by identifying instances of overcharging and sending notices demanding the return of the overcharged amount with interest. However, firms that

Table 8.1 Flagrant violations of DPCO 1995

Over pricing violating ceiling price				
Brand	Pack	Existing price	Approved price	Difference %
Astra Zeneca				
Theobric tabs	10's	7.45	2.88	158.68
Theobric SR tabs	10's	13	5.98	117.39
Glaxo Smith Kline				
Zevit syrup	30 ml	27	7.78	247.04
Salbutamol Resp	10 ml	12.69	7.78	63.11
Vent plus ease	30's	16.5	13.28	24.25
USV Limited				
Visyneral	15 ml	18.61	11.2	66.16
Covita plus	10's	34	5.24	548.85
MVI injection	10 ml	12.97	5.56	133.27
CPV Forte caps	10's	110	44.83	145.37
Glynase XL tabs	10's	19	9.53	99.37
Doxy-1 caps	8's	26.8	7.02	281.77
Visyneral Zink	15 ml	28.58	8.7	228.51
Wockhardt				
Dexvita drops	15 ml	27	10.35	160.87
Dexvita syrup	120 ml	39	14.28	173.11

Source: All India drug action network

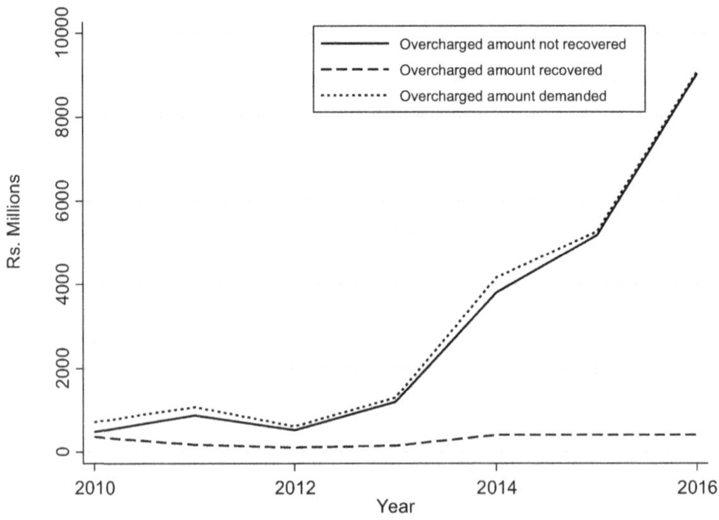

Fig. 8.1 Overcharging by pharmaceutical firms and recovery of fines by the NPPA under DPCO 1995

violate price ceilings do not pay any additional fines beyond the interest rate on the overcharged amount. The NPPA has a nearly two-decade-long record of enforcement of price ceilings on bulk drugs under the DPCO 1995 regime. During this period, the NPPA has sent more than 1280 notices, but it has a poor record of recovering the overcharged amount. Using data from the NPPA, we plot in Fig. 8.1 the amount the NPPA identified as overcharged and the amount that was recovered so far under the 1995 DPCO. The recovered amount has not increased while the extent of overcharging has been rapidly rising, reflecting the NPPA's inability to enforce price controls on medicines in the DPCO 1995 list itself. Responding to a question in the Indian parliament, a minister in the government noted that the NPPA had recovered only 7.8% of the nearly Rs. 49.28 billion it identified since August 1997 through March 31, 2016.[2] All India Drug Action Network (AIDAN), an NGO pursuing affordable access to essential medicines has identified several flagrant violations of the 1995 DPCO and argued that the process of recovering overpriced amount has been abandoned for years (see Table 8.1).

The increase in the number of medicines from 74 to 348 in the 2013 DPCO and the additional qualifications on dosages and delivery forms of a regulated medicine, makes the job of monitoring all the more challenging for the NPPA given its history of enforcement. For example, the NPPA now sets different prices for tablets and capsules of the same dosage strength of medicine in *some* cases, which the NPPA must also monitor. What is further troubling is the weakening of enforcement powers. For example, the 2013 DPCO provides NPPA "power of entry, search and seizure," but penalties under the Essential Commodities Act of 1955 do not apply. That is, the regime of criminal law that undergirded price controls in the post-independence era does not appear to apply to violations of the 2013 DPCO. The NPPA has sought to amend it so that a tougher law would discourage noncompliance (Dey 2016). Also, the 2013 DPCO elaborated on the procedure for the recovery of the overcharged amount under 1987 and 1995 DPCOs without mentioning the 2013 DPCO, leading to confusion among some experts (Vijay 2013).

Newspapers have documented violations of DPCO 2013 and editorials have called for an extensive price monitoring network that covers all state-level drug control offices (Francis 2013, 2014). A Parliamentary panel has also asked the NPPA to vigorously pursue defaulting firms and recover fines (Alexander 2013). In its response, the NPPA noted that recovery has not happened because several cases are pending in the courts, including in several High Courts and the Supreme Court. The NPPA responded to calls for effective action by approving a plan to set up monitoring cells across the country, but the implementation challenges remain (Francis 2016a):

> Recovery notices are sent by NPPA only when the violations of price fixing orders are detected. NPPA has been finding it difficult to ensure ground-level compliance of its orders on ceiling prices for both essential and non-essential medicines ever since it was set

[2]Government recovers just 7.8% of Rs 4928 crore drug overcharging fine, Economic Times, May 10, 2016.

> up. Being a Central body with no effective network of inspectors in States and Union Territories to monitor price violations, drug companies have been flouting DPCO until violations are noticed. NPPA has been trying hard to detect cases of major violations by seeking support from drug control administrations. Last year, the Authority made an attempt to involve the state governments in curbing price violations and requested the state drug control administrations to set up their own price monitoring cells. This did not work out with no cooperation from most of the state governments. Last June, NPPA announced that it was planning to set up Price Monitoring Units in seven states for better compliance of price fixing orders.

The NPPA has struggled to fix the prices of several medicines for more than 2 years after the government decided to control prices because of lack of data on prices of several medicines. It relied on IMS Health database, which did not contain data on some medicines manufactured by domestic firms. The NPPA in 2015 asked firms to self-report prices and began compiling a database of prices called Integrated Pharmaceutical Database Management System (IPDMS). Recently the NPPA clarified its procedures to recover the overcharged amount, partly leveraging the IPDMS (Shankar 2016a, b):

> The M&E division shall first examine all such cases based on the consolidated price list in Form I, Form II and Form V furnished by the manufacturers or available on IPDMS as per Para 15, 16, 24 and 25 of the DPCO, 2013 and verify the fact of overcharging. The manufacturer and dealers both will be responsible for overcharging on jointly or separate basis. If the manufacturer has not already furnished the information in Form 1, Form II and Form V or the information is not enough to draw a conclusion, the Monitoring division will send the prescribed time-bound preliminary notice (PN) to the company and seek requisite information on the prescribed format within 21 days from the date of receipt of the PN or 30 days from the date of issue of PN.

The NPPA has also launched a hotline for citizens to call in and report cases of overcharging and an online portal for registering such complaints. Yet it must be noted that pharmaceutical prices are in some ways challenging to monitor, as they can be changed from one production batch to the other. While the NPPA can use the data reported by IMS or Pharmatrac to set ceiling prices, these datasets have not been used widely for establishing noncompliance in a court of law, as pharmaceutical firms will argue that such databases are unreliable. As noted earlier in the book, if the IMS and Pharmatrac datasets are appropriate to determine the ceiling price, then they must also be valid for enforcement. As Shankar (2014) notes,

> One of the biggest challenges being faced by the NPPA today is to monitor ceiling/retail price compliance in respect of scheduled drugs/"new drugs." With over 600 scheduled formulations, which translate into more than 6000 packs (different brands) sold at over 6 lakh retail outlets spread across the length and breadth of the country the task of ensuring comprehensive oversight on price compliance by manufacturers, importers, marketers, distributors, retailers of pharmaceutical products is a very challenging task to accomplish in the absence widespread consumer awareness regarding ceiling/retail prices of scheduled drugs/"new drugs" notified by the NPPA as well as a greater degree of self-regulation and accountability among the pharmaceutical industry & trade.

8.4 Estimating the Overcharged Amount Under 2013 DPCO

We use the AIOCD's *PharmaTrac* data for our analysis. The data are widely used by the financial analysts, pharmaceutical firms, NGOs, retailers and wholesalers, policy makers in India and researchers around the world (Bhaskarabhatla et al. 2016; Evans and Pollock 2015). Since the data are compiled by the trade association of retailers, these data more accurately record prices and sales than other sources such as the IMS Health. We link data on ceiling prices, obtained from the Compendiums of Ceiling Prices for 2013, 2014, 2015, and 2016 as compiled by the NPPA. Overall, we find 2028 instances of price setting and revisions over the last 4 years under the 2013 DPCO. We match 783 medicines of a specific dosage and delivery form with entries in the PharmaTrac database for each month. That is, for Paracetamol, we match Rs. 0.83 as the ceiling price for the 500 mg tablet, Rs. 1.71 as the ceiling price for the 650 mg tablet. Therefore, we can measure for each Stock Keeping Unit (SKU), whether there is compliance in a given month or not. We can then estimate the amount of overcharging for each noncompliant SKU and finally the total amount of overcharging under DPCO 2013. We begin by illustrating how we calculate overcharging with the example of Paracetamol tablets for 1 month and highlighting the challenges in doing such an arithmetic. We then repeat the process to estimate the overall level of noncompliance.

8.4.1 Estimation of Overcharging Illustrated Using 500 Milligram Paracetamol Tablet SKUs

Our data on Paracetamol contains 835 SKUs for tablets, injections, suspensions, and oral drops. We focus on 163 SKUs related to 500 mg tablets, which have come under price regulation since June 2013. We exclude 22 SKUs with more than 30 tablets in the pack and exclude observations where the maximum retail price is more than ten times the price to the retailer. These choices reflect our conservative approach to estimating a lower bound for the overcharged amount and to avoid any suggestion that such an estimate is due to outliers in the data. We use the following formulae to convert the ceiling price specified by the 2013 DPCO per tablet into the SKU-specific ceiling price by multiplying with the number of tablets in the SKU, as shown in eq. (1).

$$SKU\ Ceiling\ Price = DPCO\ Ceiling\ Price * Number\ of\ Tablets\ in\ Pack \quad (8.1)$$

$$\begin{aligned} Overcharge = {} & (PharmaTrac\ Maximum\ Retail\ Price - SKU\ Ceiling\ Price) \\ & * Sales\ Units \end{aligned} \quad (8.2)$$

We then quantify the overcharged amount, as shown in eq. (2), by subtracting the SKU-specific ceiling price from the actual price as it appears in the *PharmaTrac* data for the SKU in a given month and multiplying the difference with the number of units of the SKU sold in India in that month. The ceiling price of 500 mg Paracetamol tablet was set at Rs. 0.94 in June 2013, and an SKU with ten tablets in the pack would have a ceiling price of Rs. 9.4. If the pharmaceutical firm sells for more than Rs. 9.4, then the firm is determined to be overcharging. Note that our estimate uses the appropriate ceiling price for any given month during this period as it has been revised over time.

Table 8.2 lists the pharmaceutical firm, the particular SKU of the firm in violation, and the overcharged amount for the top 50 SKUs with at least Rs. 100 million overcharged amount between June 2013 and July 2016. Not surprisingly, at the top

Table 8.2 Overcharging under the 2013 DPCO in Paracetamol 500 mg Tablet SKUs above Rs. 1 million during June 2013 and July 2016

Pharmaceutical firm	Stock keeping unit (SKU)	Overcharge (Rs. Millions)
Glaxosmithkline Pharmaceuticals Ltd.	Crocin advance 500 mg tablet 15	130.54
Glaxosmithkline Pharmaceuticals Ltd.	Calpol 500 mg tablet 15	114.05
Dew Drops Lab	Denim P 500 mg tablet 10	16.45
East India Pharmaceutical Works Ltd.	Pyrigesic 500 mg tablet 10	12.47
Ipca Laboratories Pvt. Ltd.	Pacimol Xp 500 mg tablet 10	10.95
Micro Labs Ltd.	Dolo 500 mg tablet 15	9.6
Ronak Labs	Cetcold 500 mg tablet 10	7.04
Themis Medicare Ltd.	Metacin 500 mg tablet 8	6.18
Apex Laboratories Ltd.	P 500 mg tablet 10	5.91
Abbott Healthcare Pvt. Ltd.	Malidens 500 mg tablet 10	4.62
Themis Medicare Ltd.	Metacin 500 mg tablet 15	4.5
Glaxosmithkline Pharmaceuticals Ltd.	Crocin 500 mg tablet 15	4.32
Mankind Pharmaceuticals Ltd.	T98 500 mg tablet 10	3.65
Indoco Remedies Ltd.	Febrex 500 mg tablet 10	3.16
Troikaa Pharmaceuticals Ltd.	Xykaa rapid 500 mg tablet 10	3.15
Medo Pharma	Medomol 500 mg tablet 10	2.96
Ipca Laboratories Pvt. Ltd.	Pacimol 500 mg tablet 10	2.95
Rekvina Pharmaceuticals	Dispar kid 500 mg tablet 10	2.83
Macleods Pharmaceuticals Pvt. Ltd.	Macfast 500 mg tablet 10	2.83
Veritaz Healthcare Ltd.	Fepanil 500 mg tablet 10	2.76
Exotic Laboratories Pvt. Ltd.	Eboo 500 mg tablet 10	2.2
Cipla Ltd.	Paracip 500 mg tablet 10	1.5
Apex Laboratories Ltd.	P 500 mg tablet 15	1.46
Ipca Laboratories Pvt. Ltd.	Pacimol 500 mg tablet 15	1.25
Indoco Remedies Ltd.	Febrex 500 mg tablet 15	1.18
Vanguard Therapeutics Pvt. Ltd.	Tyfy 500 mg tablet 10	1.14
Jagsonpal Pharmaceuticals Ltd.	Paracetamol-Jag 500 mg tablet	1.08
Total		360.73

of the list is the well-publicized case of GSK's Crocin Advance, which violated the DPCO and unilaterally claimed an exemption from price ceiling for 5 years on its Paracetamol tablet because it had a fast-release feature. Naturally, the claim was rejected, and GSK was asked to comply with the price regulation. According to the *PharmaTrac* data, GSK charged Rs. 30 for Crocin Advance SKU with 15 tablets between June 2013 and June 2014, when it should have charged a maximum of Rs. 14.1 or lower. GSK reduced the price from Rs. 30 to Rs. 29.76 during July and August 2014. In September 2014 GSK reduced the price to Rs. 15.72 while the actual ceiling price should have been Rs. 15. News reports in April 2014 suggested that it would price at Rs. 14.84 (Nautiyal 2014). GSK later increased the price to Rs. 16.36 in October 2015 and lowered it to Rs. 15.91 in June 2016. We estimate the total overcharged amount by GSK for "Crocin advance 500 mg tablet 15" SKU to be Rs. 130.54 million. Similarly, the overcharged amount for "Calpol 500 mg tablet 15" SKU, also manufactured by GSK, is estimated to be Rs. 114.05 million. There are 25 other SKUs with more than Rs. 1 million in illegal overcharging. Overall, the overcharged amount for Paracetamol 500 mg Tablet SKUs alone is estimated to be Rs. 369.53 million.

According to the NPPA's detailed statement of overcharging up to February 2017, GSK overcharged Rs. 5399.37 lakhs or Rs. 53.99 million on Crocin Advance tablets. Yet our estimates show that the overcharged amount until July 2016 is more than twice the amount recovered by the NPPA. Also, the NPPA has not identified any overcharged amount for GSK's other significant SKU of Paracetamol, Calpol, although our estimates show that the overcharged amount is as high as Rs. 114 million.

8.4.2 Estimation of Overcharging for all Medicines in the 2013 DPCO

We follow a similar approach to estimate the overcharged amount and find that there are 200 firms with at least Rs. 1 million and 104 firms with at least Rs. 10 million in overcharges. The list of 51 firms with at least Rs. 100 million is presented in Table 8.3. Sanofi tops the list with an overcharged amount of Rs. 3.5987 billion. It is not surprising to find Sanofi at the top of the list as prior market research and newspaper reports suggested that Sanofi would be hit the hardest due to price controls (Gokhale 2014):

> Paris-based Sanofi's Indian business is worst hit based on maximum retail prices and would have lost 1.39 billion rupees ($23.1 million) of sales in the past year under the curbs, market researcher AIOCD AWACS estimates.

It is clear from our estimates that, over the past 3 years, Sanofi did not fully comply with the 2013 DPCO and continued to charge prices above the ceiling price. It does not surprise us that Cipla is the second on the list with Rs. 3.471 billion in an illegal collection as Cipla already has outstanding notices for Rs. 1.768 billion under

Table 8.3 Overcharging above Rs. 100 million by pharmaceutical firms under the 2013 DPCO, during Jan 2011–Jul 2016

Pharmaceutical firm	Overcharging (Rs. Million)
Sanofi India Ltd.	3598.7
Cipla Ltd.	3471.55
Glaxosmithkline Pharmaceuticals Ltd.	2919.93
Zydus Cadila	2378.99
Pfizer Ltd.	2145.71
Ranbaxy Laboratories Ltd.	2083.35
Dr. Reddys Laboratories Ltd.	1364.54
Bharat Serums & Vaccines Ltd.	1333.5
Abbott Healthcare Pvt. Ltd.	1286.72
Micro Labs Ltd.	1277.18
Novartis India Ltd.	1245.69
Alkem Laboratories Ltd.	1010.07
Lupin Ltd.	903.29
Sun Pharma Laboratories Ltd.	895.99
Intas Pharmaceuticals Ltd.	868.13
Emcure Pharmaceuticals Ltd.	744.96
Jb Chemicals	661.05
Panacea Biotec Ltd.	644.07
Torrent Pharmaceuticals Ltd.	610.7
Ipca Laboratories Pvt. Ltd.	516.37
Wockhardt Ltd.	460.76
Alembic Ltd.	392.7
Cadila Pharmaceuticals Ltd.	390.98
Macleods Pharmaceuticals Pvt. Ltd.	326.45
Usv Ltd.	319.36
Unichem Laboratories Ltd.	306.59
Zuventus Healthcare Ltd.	300.48
Troikaa Pharmaceuticals Ltd.	275.93
Abbott India Ltd.	261.27
Rpg Life Sciences Ltd.	228.91
Hegde & Hegde	226.46
Franco Indian Pharmaceuticals Pvt. Ltd.	225.31
Glenmark Pharmaceuticals Ltd.	220.43
Apex Laboratories Ltd.	215.67
Allergan India Ltd.	190.2
Serum Institute of India Ltd.	184.67
Win-Medicare Pvt. Ltd.	181.88
Biocon Ltd.	181.13
Fdc Ltd.	176.05
Mankind Pharmaceuticals Ltd.	159.45
Indoco Remedies Ltd.	156.4
Natco Pharma Ltd.	136.12

(continued)

Table 8.3 (continued)

Pharmaceutical firm	Overcharging (Rs. Million)
Corona	129.97
Blue Cross Laboratories Ltd.	128.67
Samarth Life Sciences Pvt. Ltd.	122.91
Akumentis Healthcare Ltd.	122.11
Shield Pharmaceuticals	118.63
Biochem Pharmaceutical Inds	110.53
Janssen	108.99
Tablets India Ltd.	104.41
Astrazeneca Pharma India Ltd.	100.38
Total	36,524.29

the 1995 DPCO, or nearly 3.5% of the total fines imposed under the 1995 DPCO (Business Line 2016). The total amount of overcharging among all firms in our dataset is estimated to be Rs. 39.619 billion after excluding SKUs with large packs and SKUs where the maximum retail price is not more than ten times the price to the retailer. The estimate is slightly larger at Rs. 43.938 billion without these exclusions. Some critics of the procedure point to the presence of local taxes, which we have not incorporated in our estimates. While it is true that some local bodies impose one or 2% local taxes on medicines, the medicine packs state that the maximum retail price is *inclusive of all taxes*. Nonetheless, if we allow for a generous 5% on local taxes, we find that the estimate for the overcharged amount is Rs. 31.451 billion with the exclusion of large packs and cases where maximum retail price is more than ten times the price to the retailer and Rs. 34.639 billion without such exclusions.

8.5 Enforcement Activity by the NPPA for 1995 and 2013 DPCO

The NPPA has begun enforcement activities under the 2013 DPCO and sent two notices in 2013, 39 in 2014, 104 in 2015, and 21 until the end of June 2016. We examine NPPA's enforcement strategy based on these activities. We found that among the pharmaceutical firms that were sent notices under 2013 DPCO, 40 firms were not matched to any of the 919 firms in the Pharmatrac dataset, indicating that these are relatively small firms. We present the list of these firms in Table 8.4. While a targeted approach to enforcement would call for focusing on large firms with a prior history of violations, the limited resources of NPPA seem to be directed toward small firms, considered too small even to be included in the Pharmatrac dataset. We also examine the 47 SKUs, shown in Table 8.4, which matched those in the Pharmatrac data. We find that the total overcharging in these SKUs to be Rs. 0.735 billion during June 2013 and July 2016, slightly higher than the NPPA's estimate of Rs. 0.627 billion. However, we found that 30 of the 47 SKUs

Table 8.4 The market shares of selected SKUs facing enforcement under the 2013 DPCO

SKU reported as subject of enforcement	Market share	Overcharge (Rs. Million)
Ambistryn S 0.75 gm injection 1	3.53	17.77
Ambistryn S 1 gm injection 1	0.33	0.14
Andial 2 mg tablet 10	5.86	3.09
Atocor 10 mg tablet 10	0.13	43.68
Atocor 20 mg tablet 10	0.95	7.24
Atocor 5 mg tablet 10	0.15	3.81
Atorsave 10 mg tablet 10	0.06	13.03
Auxime 200 mg tablet 10	0	0.5
Aziclass 250 mg tablet 6	0.01	0.65
Calaptin 80 mg tablet 10	4.35	7.7
Cetfast 10 mg tablet 10	0	0.01
Cetfast 5 mg syrup 30 ml	0	0.01
Chlorocol eye 0.1% ointment 3 gm	2.69	1.18
Ciprolet ds 500 mg tablet 10	0.03	4.05
Crocin advance 500 mg tablet 15	0.4	130.54
Diapill D3 60,000 Iu tablet 4	0.01	0.02
Domperi 1 mg suspension 30 ml	0.06	0.34
Enoxsave 40 mg injection 0.4 ml	0.01	9.2
Eradiclav 500/125 mg tablet 6	0	0.09
Eradiclav duo 500/125 mg tablet 6	0	0.01
Fever X 500 mg tablet 10	0	0.07
Floxip 250 mg tablet 10	0.01	1.18
Floxip 500 mg tablet 10	0.01	3.65
Gardenal 60 mg tablet 20	1.33	36.55
Gardenal 60 mg tablet 30	2.63	36.96
Genticyn 0.3% eye drops 10 ml	5.56	1.99
Glyciphage 500 mg tablet Sr 10	0.45	193.73
Hcqs 200 mg tablet 10	1.76	85.92
Heksi 2 mg tablet 10	0.02	1
Homide 2% eye drops 5 ml	2.68	10.49
Inderal 10 mg tablet 10	1.6	19.09
Mazetol 100 mg tablet 10	0.68	0.42
Mixtard human 30/70 40 Iu injection 10 ml	17.81	46.87
Moxipil 250 mg tablet Dt 10	0	0.07
Neorof 1% injection 10 ml	0.58	8.67
Neorof 1% injection 20 ml	0.87	14.99
Oflavid 200 mg tablet 10	0	0.15
Pedimite 5% cream 30 gm	0.02	0.08
Perinorm 10 mg tablet 10	2.04	17.15
Perinorm 10 mg tablet md 10	3.23	1.61
Perinorm 5 mg drops 30 ml	2.35	4.9
Perinorm 5 mg syrup 30 ml	2.11	4.68

(continued)

Table 8.4 (continued)

SKU reported as subject of enforcement	Market share	Overcharge (Rs. Million)
R Mox cv 500/125 mg tablet 6	0	0.01
Sarotena 25 mg tablet 10	0.11	1.9
Triben 1% cream 20 gm	0.73	0.08
Vpl 2.5 mg injection 2 ml	4.55	0.07

have a market share of less than 1% and the average market share to be 1.5%, indicating that the NPPA is likely targeting small violations. We find that the absolute amount of overcharges is more than 44 times larger than what is identified by the regulator. Collecting overcharges is challenging because of considerable delays in the judicial process. However, if collected, the fines can be used to provide free medicine to much of India's population—if not all—given the budget for providing free medicines for a large state like Karnataka is Rs. 0.3 billion per year.

One may argue that weak enforcement by the NPPA must be understood in the context of a strict statutory standard the NPPA imposed. That is, the pharmaceutical firms violating the ceiling price may argue that the ceiling price is set at levels impossible for them to comply with profitably. The flaw with this argument is that prior work shows that pharmaceutical firms, particularly those with more than 1% market share, coordinated to inflate the ceiling price just before the implementation of the 2013 DPCO, resulting in a weak statutory standard at the beginning of the 2013 DPCO.

Overall, the enforcement activity has been characterized not only by the NPPA's low estimates of overcharging by the pharmaceutical firms but also the limited recovery of these overcharged amounts. We report in Table 8.5 the number and status of cases of overcharging under the 1995 DPCO since its inception until the end of February 2017. The percentage of the overcharged amount recovered is 15 between August 1997 and March 2009. We report the number and status of cases of overcharging under the 2013 DPCO in Table 8.6. According to the NPPA, the total amount recovered from the pharmaceutical companies is only 13.34% of the claims made by the NPPA. As we discussed in the previous section, the NPPA appears to have substantially underestimated the overcharged amount in the first place. Next, we report in Table 8.7 the outstanding amount various pharmaceutical companies owe to the NPPA under the 1995 DPCO. We also reported in Table 8.8 both the overcharged and the outstanding amounts owed to the NPPA under the 2013 DPCO.

The All India Chemists and Druggists Federation (AICDF), a competing and relatively small union of retailers compared to the AIOCD, has recently sent letters to the NPPA alleging that the pharmaceutical companies are continuing to violating

Table 8.5 The status of cases of overcharging under DPCO 1995 since inception until 28.02.2017

Particulars	Aug 1997–Mar 2009	2009–2010	2010–2011	2011–2012	2012–2013	2013–2014	2014–2015	2015–2016	2016–2017
DPCO	1995	1995	1995	1995	1995	1995	1995	1995	1995
Number of cases	653	87	42	40	103	88	90	160	24
Overcharged demanded amount including interest	2645.87	71.23	107.11	60.81	129.22	415.9	526.06	907.49	93.17
Total amount realized during the year	156.04	35.91	17.26	10.69	14.97	40.06	34.37	7.59	220.36
Total amount realized against the demands for the year	401.71	23.8	20.35	8.88	10.36	55.3	11.92	4.89	0.04
Percentage of the amount realized against the demand for the year (%)	15.18	33.41	19.00	14.60	8.02	13.30	2.27	0.54	0.04
Amount outstanding	2244.16	47.43	86.76	51.93	118.86	360.6	514.14	902.6	93.13

Source: NPPA (http://www.nppaindia.nic.in/order/stmt-14-03-2017.pdf)

Table 8.6 The status of cases of overcharging under DPCO 2013 since inception until 28.02.2017

Particulars	2013–2014	2014–2015	2015–2016	2016–2017	Cumulative total
DPCO	2013	2013	2013	2013	1995 & 2013
Number of cases	2	39	103	96	1527
Overcharged demanded amount including interest	0	53.99	20.47	7.43	5038.72
Total amount realized during the year	0.02	55.8	4.73	74.48	672.28
Total amount realized against the demands for the year	0.04	55.96	8.14	70.89	672.28
Percentage of the amount realized against the demand for the year (%)	0.00	103.70	39.77	954.10	13.34
Amount outstanding	−0.04	−1.97	12.33	−63.46	4366.44

Source: NPPA (http://www.nppaindia.nic.in/order/stmt-14-03-2017.pdf)

the ceiling prices imposed under the 2013 DPCO, and that the state drug regulators in West Bengal are ignoring such violations (Kunnathoor 2017):

> In a letter sent to the office of the national price regulator, Joydeep Sarkar, general secretary of AICDF has said that the law violating companies are not concerned about the regulatory body in the state. Despite so many complaints made against them by the law abiding wholesale traders, the manufacturers are continuing their unlawful activities. They are denying supplying life-saving medicines to the legitimate wholesalers.

One of the main challenges in enforcing the ceiling prices under 2013 DPCO lies in establishing the violations in a court of law. Yet the government has faced considerable difficulty in collecting data to determine the ceiling price. As we discussed in Chap. 5, the IMS and Pharmatrac data often provide different estimates of market shares and prices. As a result, relying on them for enforcement can lead to legal disputes. The NPPA has attempted to collect data directly from pharmaceutical companies. However, only 90 companies complied with the request for data and several companies failed to register and self-report data on prices and sales to the NPPA's Integrated Pharmaceutical Database Management System (Shankar 2014a). The effort to compile the database remains unfinished 2 years later despite repeated requests and extended deadlines since September 2014, when it was first announced (Shankar 2014b; Shankar 2016a, b).

As Francis (2016a, b) notes, the NPPA decided to set up Price Monitoring and Resource Units in seven states, Gujarat, Maharashtra, Odisha, Haryana, Kerala, Assam, and Manipur, to improve compliance with the DPCO. However, the proposed investment per state is Rs. 4–5 lakh, indicating the lack of resources and commitment to enforcement. Francis (2016a, b) notes that the NPPA does not have an effective network of inspectors in states to monitor price violations and the NPPA has not received cooperation from the state drug control administrations. Francis (2016a, b) summarizes the difficult facing the NPPA:

Table 8.7 Noncompliance with the 1995 DPCO

Company name	Outstanding amount in Rs. hundred thousands	N of cases	Medicine formulations where violations occurred
Cipla Ltd.	246,991	26	Ciprofloxacin; D-Fylin tab; Mebex plus tabs; Doxycycline; Duolin Rotacaps; Norflox based formulations; Asthalin 4 mg tabs; Duolin Rotacaps; Ciplox 500 mg tab; Asthalin SA 8 mg tab; salbutamol.; Ciprofloxacin based formulation; Aerocort Forte Rotacaps; Ciplox-TZ; Norfloxacin based formulation; Tetracycline 500 and 250; Salbutamol based formulation; Cloxacillin based formulation; Furazole-M tab; Norfloxacin based formulation; Ciplox E/E Drops; Erycin 500 tabs; Burnheal Cream; Ciplox 100 ml vial/Bottle; Duolin Inhaler; Maxirich caps
Johnson & Johnson Pvt. Ltd.	65799.56	6	Benadryl cough syrup 450 ml; Benadryl cough syrup 50 ml; Raricap tablets; Pedia 3 liquid; Raricap tablets; Benadryl cough syrup 150 ml
Okasa Pharma Ltd.	28735.38	13	Norfloxacin based addl demand; Ciplox D eye ointment; Cefadur; Betasalic ointment; Fourderm cream; Predone Forte; Ibugesic plus tab; Cloxacillin based formulations; Nutrolin B syrup; Cefadroxyl based formulations; Norflox TZ tabs; theophylline based formulations; Dytor plus 20 tab
Claris Life Science Ltd	10407.1	1	I V Fluid
Ranbaxy Labs Ltd	7734.84	8	Suprimox-P tabs; Cloxacillin based formulations; Norfloxacin based formulations; Ciprofloxacin; Cefazoline Sodium; Norfloxacin based formulations; Suprimox caps; Cloxacillin based formulations
Rexcin Pharmaceuticals Ltd.	7045.41	10	Diprovate-N 17 gm Creram; Diprovate plus Lotion 50 ml; Diprovate G plus 15 gm; Diprovate-S plus cream 15 gm; Diprovate S plus 20 gm; Diprovate plus cream 15 gm; Diprovate Lotion 50 ml; Diprovate plus 20 gm; Diprovate G plus 20 gm; Statum plus cream
Macleods Ltd.	6518.43	1	Doxoril 400 tab

Cheminova Pharmaceuticals/Cipla Ltd.	6045.5	1	Powergyl suspension 30 ml
Mars Therapheuticas	5276.23	3	Synsama tabs 15's pack; Bicil P; Synsama syrup
Swiss Garnier/Lupin	3619.91	1	Doxiflon
Baxter India Pvt. Ltd.	3551.72	3	Metrodazole; Dns/NS 500 ml; IV Fluid
Astalife/Usv Ltd.	3423.32	2	Doxy 1 LDR Forte; Ecosprin gold 20 forte caps
Tridoss Labs Pvt. Ltd.	2844.16	3	Aceten 25 mg; Captopril/Acetan; Phylobid tab SR
Franco Indian	2767.06	4	Benalgis; Surfaz-SN cream 7 gm * 1; native C 200; Native C 400
Cipla/Alchon	2437.9	1	Ciprofloxacin Inj.
Ipca Labs Ltd. Mumbai	2365.41	2	Ciprofloxacin based formulations; Lariago DS tablet
Dr Reddy'S	2307.96	6	Gris OD 375; Bio-E; Becozinc caps; Norfloxacin; Ciprofloxacin based formulation; Cloxacillin based formulation
Cadila Healthcare Ltd.	2256.91	17	Ofrex-M plus; Gertac; Gexofen; Deriphylline OD 300 & 450; Zydril Expectorant; Zygenta 20 ml Inj.; Deriphylin 300; Ciprofloxcin ciprobid 500; Cefadroxil; Gilpimet; Deriphyllin 450; Rimpazid kid tabs.; Megalox; Quadridus 5 gm; Citimed; Nortee 400 LB; Ciprobid 250 mg
Best Lab Pvt. Ltd.	2041.86	3	Riconia film coated tabs; Riconia film; Caserra
Mmc Healthcare	1931.07	1	Medineuron tabs
Indswift Ltd./Alliance Biotech	1922.95	1	Amibex TZ tabs
Star drugs	1874.14	1	Nervijan Inj.
Glenmark Pharmaceuticals	1862.27	2	E Cap-400 (Vitamin E Acetate 400 mg caps.); Doxovent tabs
Modi Mundi/T C Healthcare	1720.46	2	Unicortin CR-400; Unicortin CR-600
Universal Pharmaceuticals Ltd	1699.22	3	LCF cough formula; Analgin tabs. 10's; Emvit cap
Mars Therapheuticas/Dr. Reddy	1641.81	1	Doxobid tab
Usv Ltd.	1624.7	4	Glynase XL-5; Doxy-I (DPCO'87); Ecosprin AV 75; Pioz
Kopran Ltd.	1307.43	5	Cloxacillin based formulations; Norfloxacin based formulations; Salbutamol based formulations; Vent syrup; Cefadroxyl based formulations

(continued)

Table 8.7 (continued)

Company name	Outstanding amount in Rs. hundred thousands	N of cases	Medicine formulations where violations occurred
Pharmed Ltd./Mmc Healthcare	1205.92	1	Cartigen forte tab
Manish Pharmaceuticals	1182.71	3	Benadryl cough syrup 100 ml; Salbutamol Sulphate; Ceradrish 500
Laborate Pharmaceticals India Ltd.	1160.5	46	festive-D; Doxylab caps; MP-4 tab; Clear & Clean Cream; Doxy tab; Memory plus syrup 200 ml; Ceflox CF cream; Elthrocin-250 mg tab; Deco E/E Drops; LB Drox 250; Festive-M Suspension; Valerate-N; Ibuflam tablets; MP-16 tab; Cipdec E/E Drops; Lantac Inj.; Gentacord-D E/E Drops; Gentacort-MF cream; Cefadroxyl dry syrup 30 ml bottle; Dexalab Inj.; Norbin Oral susp.; Ceflox suspension,; Maligo-250 mg tabs; Doxylab capsule; Povirex plus ointment; Labizone; Nflox-TZ tab; N-TZ tabs; Betamox plus capsules; Ceflox D E/E Drops; Ceflox E/E drop; Ceflox E/E drop; LB Drox 500 tabs; Mediclox plus cap; Valerate 'C' skin cream 20 gm; Ceflox TZ tab; Nflox-B 400; Lantac Inj. and Betamox plus caps.; Gentalab Inj.; Sivez cream 20 gm; Gentalab E/E Drops; Quard cream 15 gm; Nflox E/E Drops; Quard cream; Norlab-TZ tab; Silvez plus cream
Lyka Labs Ltd.	1151.38	2	Cloxacillin based formulations; Lydin tabs.
Tristar Formulation P Ltd.	1020.09	2	Ecospin AV; Ecosprin gold
Rexin Pharmaceutical	891.95	1	Silverex cream 24 gm
Cipla/golden cross	862.43	1	Ibugesic plus suspension
Meridan enterprises	858.02	1	Tedral SA
Fdc Ltd.	835.73	3	ZoxanTZ tab; Doxiba syrup; Doxiba tabs
Pfizer Ltd.	745.5	10	Becosules Z caps.; Oxytetracycline; Zipron 500 tab.; Depo Medrol; Solu-Medrol 1000 mg AOV 8 ml; Becosules caps; Medrol 4 mg tab/Solumedrol 500 mg 4 ml aov/Solumedrol 1000 mg 8 ml AO > V; Benadryl syrup; Caladryl lotion; Becosules caps

Oscar Labs	695.16	1	Gramogyl/Gramoneg
Bdh Industries	648.12	1	Keralgo tab
Cadila Healthcare Ltd./German Remedies	559.87	1	Doxolin tab
Torque Pharmaceuticals	526.47	11	Glycort E/E Drops; Gencin B E/E Drops; Ticin suspension 60 ml; Gencin E/E Drops; Cipromac E/E Drops; Norgyl suspension; Bedex Forte; Doxymac caps; Cold go suspension; Cipromac caps; Cipromac D E/E Drops
Innova Cap Tab/Manish Pharma	464.12	1	Duoflam kid tab
Maneesh Pharmaceuticals Pvt. Ltd.	442.11	6	Elferri tonic; SCC-JR tabs; Sigma CT tabs; SCC-2 LW tabs; Sigma CTH tabs; SCC-2 tabs
Wyeth Ltd.	438.42	2	Prednisolone; Wymesone Inj. 2 ml Vial
Bestochem Formulaiton (I) Ltd.	432.32	2	Betawin-S and Betawin forte tab. 10's each; Doran-O tab, Doran-O Inj
Cadila Pharmaceuticals Ltd.	429.3	5	Ciprofloxacin based formulations; Envas 5; Cloxacillin based formulations; Ciprofloxacin; Envas 2.5
Saichem Pharma/Pharmed Ltd.	417.34	1	Citravite-Z
Sol Pharma	404.13	2	Ciprofloxacin based formulation; Theophylline based formulations (Theolong)
Gland Pharma	400.41	1	Huminsulin 30/70 Inj.
Vapi Care Pharma P Ltd./Bombay Tablet Mfg Company	397.08	1	LAA tab.
Martin & Harris Ltd.	393	1	Venusmin
Noel Pharma	357.52	9	Iclox Welfen & Welfen M; Vitatop tabs; Megadine-M Oint; Zenfer caps; Betaphil-T tab; Megadine-M Oint; Megatac tab;; Inor—400
Indswift Ltd.	314.18	7	Neurobex-SG; Cetin plus suspension; Provita, neurovit; Doxycycline; Swiflox; a) Stemin tab 0.5 mg.; Swiflox E/E Drops
Allergan India Pvt. Ltd.	307.91	2	Acetate; V-Ret plus
Ipca Labs	296.74	2	Norfloxacin based formulations; Normax-TZ

(continued)

Table 8.7 (continued)

Company name	Outstanding amount in Rs. hundred thousands	N of cases	Medicine formulations where violations occurred
Espi Chemicals	280.54	1	Rediplox
Biochem Pharmaceuticals Ind Ltd.	278.24	2	Amplox 250 mg Caps & Amplox LB cap; Mplox-C Vial 500 mg
Tuton Pharma	258.88	1	Tresmox LB
Saar Biotech/Biochem Pharmaceuticals	253.63	1	Clobet GM cream
Shimal Investment and Trading Company (Ranbaxy)	247.84	1	Gramoneg/Gramogyl formulations
Kemwell Pvt. Ltd.	241.8	2	Ventrorlin Exp./Sry.; Ventorlin expect.
Avis Life Sciences/Morepen	239.51	1	Norpen-TZ
Lark Labs (I) Ltd.	235.39	3	Infa-V; Livogard 60 ml; Ciprolar -FC 15 gm cream
Softesule Pvt. Ltd. & Alembac Ltd.	223.47	1	Farisis cap
Concept Pharmaceuticals Ltd.	198.27	6	Synabron tab; Anabest; Coprime DS; Ibucon plus suspension; Ibucon 400 plus; Synabron expectorant 100 ml
Cipla Ltd./Curetech Skincare	196.22	1	Burnheal cream 15 gm
Wanbury/Creative Healthcare	190.58	1	SET Cal Mom
Gmbell Healthcare/Universal Lifesciences	175.56	1	Clobed GM cream
Ak Labs	159.92	1	Doxicip 100 mg tab
Nicholas Piramal (I) Ltd.	159	3	Tetracycline 500 mg tabs; Quinobact eye drop & tabs; Norfloxacin based formulation
Sresan Pharmaceuticals	158.09	2	Respolite S syrup; Respolite ST syrup
Arvind Remedies Ltd.	152.92	4	Vitoxid AO; Racy 500 tabs; Cetafen; Crolox tabs
Shreya Lifesciences	145.51	2	Monto 4 tabs; Aspisol tabs
Somatico Labs Ltd	144.62	1	Somadox DT caps
Softech Pharma Pvt. Ltd./Dr. Reddy	140.65	1	Ovista caps.
Ajanta Pharma	134.49	1	Gate-PD E/E Drops

Lupin Ltd.	131.59	2	Tonact ASP 75; Odoxil 250 DT tabs
Palson Derma Pvt. Ltd.	116.61	1	Kensol-B 10 gm
Vapi Care Pharma Ltd./Tridoss Laboratories Pvt. Ltd.	115.54	1	Phylobid-300 CR
Ankur Drugs & Pharmaceuticals	106.2	1	Cipract TZ tabs
Themis Medicare Ltd.	104.49	1	Tetra Cox tabs

Source: NPPA (http://www.nppaindia.nic.in/order/stmt-30-6-2016.html)
Partial list of companies with an outstanding balance of more than 10 million rupees with the NPPA

Table 8.8 Noncompliance under the 2013 DPCO

Company	Overcharged amount in Rs. hundred thousand	Outstanding amount in Rs. hundred thousand	N of cases	Medicine formulation
Biological E Ltd.	3328.03	2496.03	1	Bett Tetanus Vaccine
Franco Indian Pharmaceuticals Pvt. Ltd.	896.41	896.41	1	Glyciphage SR 500 mg
Reliance Life Science	410.35	410.35	1	Albural-LS
Akumentis Healthcare	372.32	372.32	1	Bonheal 500 mg, Clomipure 50 mg, Goodova 50 mg & Clomipure 100 mg caps
Abbott Healthcare Ltd.	474.03	364.19	17	Phenergan 100 ml syrup; Floxip 500 mg; Bactrim syrup 50 ml; Becomex Forte BZ caps; Bactrim DS; Mazetol 100 mg tabs; Neo Mercazole tab; Autrima-DS tabs; Supradyn tabs; Floxip 250 mg; Inderal-10 tab; Gardenal 60 tabs; Ambistryn S 0.75 gm; Calaptin 80 mg tabs; Becozim C Forte; Genticyn 80 mg 2 ml Inj.; Genticyn 10 mg/ml & Pediatrics Inj.
Ipca Labs Ltd.	285.03	285.03	3	Domperi 1 mg/ml suspension 30 ml bottle; HCQS 200 mg tab; Perinorm syrup 30 ml
Neon Laboratories Ltd.	289.09	281.59	1	Neorof Inj.
Encube Ethicals/Golderma India	201.75	201.75	1	Pernite cream
Tidal Labs Pvt. Ltd.	100.82	100.82	1	Enzox plus tabs
Cambridge Healthcare Ltd./Oxeganon India Pvt. Ltd.	97.71	97.71	1	Ispaghula Granules & Naturolox powder
Allergan India Pvt. Ltd.	74.12	74.12	1	Albucid 20% eye drops
Cosmo Farma Laboratories Ltd.	63.75	63.75	1	Reglan tabs
Kivi Labs Ltd	58.14	58.14	3	Kimtrip tab; Kipnel 40 mg, Epigold 300 mg & Tracogold 100 mg; Hekri 2 & Vetodepder
Indoco Remedies	54.69	54.69	1	Homide eye drop
Torrent Pharmaceuticals	53.77	53.77	1	Azalin 4 tabs

Hll Lifecare	36.55	36.55	3	Novex DS tabs; Moods Choco; Moods Xtary
Panacea Biotech	30.15	30.15	1	Glizid 40 tabs
Scott Edil Pharmacia	31.71	26.27	6	Dexadran; Dulax tabs; Methiphar; Novamention Inj.; Aziphar suspension; Cifbax 250 tabs
Gracure Pharmaceuticals/ Pharma Concepts	24.38	24.27	2	Zolbend tabs; Memopen tabs
Seagull Laboratories Pvt. Ltd.	28.41	19.41	1	Capex expectorant
Dr Reddy'S Labs Ltd.	27.99	19.36	4	Atocor 5 mg; Atocor 10 mg; Ciprolet DS tabs; Aticore 20 mg
Allergan India/Piramal Healthcare	14.59	14.59	1	Albucid 20% eye drops
Shiva Pharmaceuticals	13.56	13.56	1	TLM-H tabs
Amanta Healthcare Ltd.	13.29	13.29	1	Sodium Choloride (0.9% w/v) Inj.
Jawa Pharmaceuticals (India) Pvt. Ltd.	11.06	10.3	1	Chlorocol ointment
Nivca Life Care/Relef Biotech Pvt. Ltd.	8.71	8.71	2	Nivox 250 caps; Omzec-D caps
Synchem Laboratories Ltd.	7.63	7.63	1	Tussin DMR tabs
Sizin Flora Pharma/Eris	23.7	6.61	1	Atorsave 10 tabs
Aishwarya Healthcare	6.09	6.09	1	Sodium Choloride infusion 100 ml
Reliance Formulation (P) Ltd.	5.35	5.35	1	R-mox CV 500/125 mg tab
Nulife Pharmaceuticals	4.85	4.85	1	Gamascab & Nulox lotion
Dales Laborarotíes Pvt. Ltd.	30.08	4.7	1	Sinus 77 tabs
Simson & Brown	4.23	4.23	1	Spasmol tabs
Veritaz Healthcare	8.889999	2.7	2	Andial 2 mg; RXMEF Susp. & Zondal tab
Laborate Pharmaceuticals India Ltd.	2.46	2.46	1	Labmox-250
Selab India	9.58	2.37	1	Glycerine 60 mg
Saket City Hospital	2.29	2.23	1	Evatocin, Phenergan, Reokay & Certofix Trio Inj.

(continued)

Table 8.8 (continued)

Company	Overcharged amount in Rs. hundred thousand	Outstanding amount in Rs. hundred thousand	N of cases	Medicine formulation
Scott Edil Pharmacia/Interphar	1.59	1.59	1	Patrova 40 mg
Sky Map /Elder Pharmaceuticals	1.49	1.49	1	Cetfast
Sterrkem Pharma	1.08	1.08	1	Genster Inj.
Votary Laboratories	0.91	0.91	1	Softner Susp. 200 ml
Vanugard Therapeuticals	3.29	0.64	1	Neurogard tabs
Psychotropics India Ltd.	0.54	0.54	1	Moxipil 250 mg tab
Msn Laboratories	38.26	0.18	2	Floxsafe 100 ml; Cefight CV 325 mg tabs, Vitasafe tabs & PAH 20 mg tabs
Lupin Ltd.	2.11	0.16	1	Timoblu 0.5 eye drop
Prexair India Pvt. Ltd.	63.64	0.16	1	Mox Nitrous Oxcide
Combiotic Global Caplet Pvt. Ltd.	1.42	0.16	2	Grisonex tabs; Grisonex tabs
Morepen Laboratories Ltd.	4.32	0.12	3	Metopen 10 tabs; Fever-X tabs; Eradiclav 500 & 125 mg tab
Palmer Labs/Talent Healthcare	0.3	0.08	1	Povicream ointment
Apex Laboratories	25.91	0.02	6	Zincoderm; Lozee cream; Ark spray 100; Aziclass 250 tabs; Lozee-M cream; P-125 Susp. 60 ml
Baxter India Pvt. Ltd.	2.58	0.01	1	Dextrose Inj.
Crescent Formulations Pvt. Ltd.	1.42	0.01	2	Olatin plus tabs; Ambidex 20 mg tabs, Alpaz 2 tab, Divalex OD 125 tab & Pregacent 75 tab
Icpa Health Products Ltd.	0.85	0	1	Xicaine Inj.
Vasco Drugs Labs	1.75	0	1	Glycrin 25 gm
Shankus Acme Pharma Pvt. Ltd.	0.37	0	1	Zylid 500 tabs
Menarini India Pvt. Ltd.	83.16	0	1	Cetrilate Adult Soap & Etan-GM cream
Fulford (India) Ltd.	1.07	0	1	Polaramine Syr.

An Pharmacia	0.47	0	1	Nortrip 25 mg tabs
Axa Parentrals Ltd.	19.97	0	5	NS 100 ml; DNS Inj. 500 ml; 5D Inj. 500 ml; NS Inj. 500 ml; Axagyl Inj. 500 mg
Elite Pharma Pvt. Ltd.	0.14	0	1	Magrelite tabs
Jenburkt Pharmaceuticals	12.79	0	1	Triben skin cream
Tas Med (India)	1.18	0	2	Anglit 2.6 mg; Lotus 50 mg
Glasston Pharmaceuticals/Leo	0.08	0	1	Azelio suspension
Lesanto Laboratories	0.11	0	1	Lacitron syrup 100 ml
Biovitamins Pvt. Ltd.	1.17	0	1	Fanty XT tabs
Kinesis Pharmaceuticals	0.77	0	1	Abdifer caps
Entod Pharmaceuticals	7.04	0	1	Waxonil & Otobiotic ear drops
Gerrysum Pharmaceuticals/ Brooks Labs Ltd.	0.2	0	1	Geripen Inj.
Ridley Lifescience Ltd.	0.07	0	1	Paluhit 400 tabs
Saipliss Drugs & Pharma/Max Lifesciences	0.36	0	1	Agifit 500 tabs
Morepan Labs/Pharma Concepts	0.75	0	2	Foly-ACT; Cetipen-LO tabs
Beekay Pharmaceuticals	0.05	0	1	Belenz-5 tab
Quasar Labs/Unistar Biotech	0.43	0	1	Zyopin MD 10 tabs
Profic Organic Ltd.	0.14	0	1	NP Com 500 tab
Eris Lifesciences	6.45	0	2	Enoxsare 40 mg Inj.; Superclop 75 tabs
Kayvee Aeropham Pvt. Ltd.	0.06	0	1	Povin solution
Nitin Life Sciences Ltd./ Abbott Healthcare	28.28	0	2	Ambistryn-S 1 gm Inj.; Gentcyn 80 mg 2 ml Inj.
Novo Nordisk India Pvt. Ltd.	97.93	0	1	Mixtard 30 Flexpen, Insulatard Flexpen, Novorapid Penfill, Novomix Penfill and Novofine Niddles

(continued)

Table 8.8 (continued)

Company	Overcharged amount in Rs. hundred thousand	Outstanding amount in Rs. hundred thousand	N of cases	Medicine formulation
Obsurge Biotech Ltd.	9.32	0	3	Venosuf caps; Ultracid suspension 100 ml; Kulfi 20 mg syrup 100 ml
Tosmed India Pvt. Ltd.	8.83	0	1	UDA 300 mg & Clotas 0.5 mg tabs
Samarth Lifesciences	0.02	0	1	VPL Inj.
Mega Healthcare	0.31	0	1	Itrataze caps
Serdia Pharmaceuticals India Pvt. Ltd.	20.01	0	1	Daflon 500
Curatio Healthcare	0.34	0	1	Triodloc cream 25 gm & 20 gm and Atogla cream 100 gm
Satven & Mer	0.01	0	1	Alopm 100 mg tabs
Aurz Pharmaceuticals	0.27	0	1	Auxime-200
Ordain Healthcare Global Pvt. Ltd.	8.22	0	2	Diapill tabs, Misonac SR Tabs & Complete TD tabs; Tribose M & MS tabs
Creative Healthcare/Sapat & Company	0.3	0	1	Ome Saplus caps
Indchemie Health Spec Pvt. Ltd.	4.33	0	1	DVeOK caps
Gag Pharmaceuticals	0.57	0	1	Atease 10 tabs
Leeford Healthcare Ltd.	2.13	0	1	Oflarid-200
Percos India Pvt. Ltd.	3.51	0	1	Protar K 100 ml

Source: NPPA (http://www.nppaindia.nic.in/order/stmt-30-6-2016.html)

> NPPA has to collect a total sum of Rs.4551 crores from various pharmaceutical companies up to February 2016 for overcharging of drugs from 1995 onwards when the earlier DPCO was notified. In 2015-16 alone, NPPA issued demand notices to 263 companies for recovery of Rs. 928.32 crores but could collect only Rs. 12 crores. There are no indications when the NPPA will be able to recover such a huge sum of money. As the NPPA price violation cases are fought in different courts and are in various stages of hearing, it looks difficult to recover such a huge amount by the government from the drug companies even with the price monitoring units in the states. After the notification of the new DPCO in 2013 covering 348 drugs, health ministry revised the National List of Essential Medicines in last December raising the total number of drugs under DPCO to 384. With this, NPPA has a bigger task in fixing and monitoring the additional number of drug prices. Now, the circumvention and violation of the DPCO provisions have to be expected on a much bigger scale looking at the track record of the pharmaceutical companies. Considering the fact that the litigations have been going on with several companies for more than 20 years, it is futile to expect the recovery of this amount will be possible under the existing judicial process. The Central government needs to find some extra judicial option to recover these amounts.

Gujarat has enforced the DPCO regulations better than many other states, indicating that the quality of state drug control administration plays an important role in enforcement. In 2014 alone Gujarat's regulator referred 629 cases of DPCO violations to the NPPA, as Shirodkar (2015) notes:

> We have been training our inspectors on a regular basis as an ongoing effort on all the basics of how to effectively calculate the prices of the medicines available in the market, compare and check it with the notified prices and how to efficiently and timely report or refer all the cases to the NPPA. All our efforts are targeted to ensure full compliance with the existing laws such as Drugs & Cosmetics Act, the DPCO and others.

Overall, the extent of overpricing is substantial in some of the SKUs during the 2013–2016 period. We compiled in Appendix A1 the annual revisions to the ceiling prices of various medicines and in Appendix A2, the MRP, PTR, the ceiling prices of some of the SKUs with an MRP at least double the ceiling price. Targeting such instances of significant violations of the ceiling price can prove to be an effective enforcement strategy.

References

Alexander, J. (2013, August 28). Parliamentary panel asks NPPA to adopt arbitration to cut cases of overcharging. PharmaBiz.com

Ayres, I., & Braithwaite, J. (1992). *Responsive Regulation: Transcending the Deregulation Debate*. Oxford: Oxford University Press.

Becker, G. S. (1968). Crime and punishment: An economic approach. *Journal of Political Economy, 76*(2), 169–217.

Berndt, E., & Cockburn, I. (2014). The hidden cost of low prices: Limited access to new drugs in India. *Health Affairs, 33*(9), 1567–1575.

Bhaskarabhatla, A. S., Chatterjee, C., Anurag, P., & Pennings, H. P. G. (2016). Mitigating regulatory impact: The case of partial price controls on Metformin in India. *Health Policy and Planning, 32*(2), 194–204.

Braithwaite, J. (2006). Responsive regulation and developing economies. *World Development, 34* (5), 884–898.

Business Line. (2016, October 21). Supreme Court rules against Cipla in drug price overcharging case. *The Hindu Business Line* [online]. Available from https://www.thehindubusinessline.com/companies/supreme-court-rules-against-cipla-in-drug-price-overcharging-case/article9252368.ece

Cheng, C.-C., & Lai, Y.-B. (2012). Does a stricter enforcement policy protect the environment? A political economy perspective. *Resource and Energy Economics, 34*(4), 431–441.

Chu, H.-L., Liu, S.-Z., & Romeis, J. C. (2011). Assessing the effects of drug price reduction policies on older people in Taiwan. *Health Services Management Research, 24*, 1–7.

Cockburn, I., Lanjouw, J., & Schankerman, M. (2016). Patents and the global diffusion of new drugs. *American Economic Review, 106*(1), 136–164.

Danzon, P. M., Richard Wang, Y., & Wang, L. (2003). The impact of price regulation on the launch delay of new drugs – Evidence from twenty-five major markets in the 1990s. *Health Economics, 14*(3), 269–292.

Danzon, P. M., Mulcahy, A. W., & Towse, A. K. (2015). Pharmaceutical pricing in emerging markets: Effects of income, competition, and procurement. *Health Economics, 24*(2), 238–252.

De, R. (2014). 'Commodities must be controlled': Economic crimes and market discipline in India (1939–1955). *International Journal of Law in Context, 10*(3), 277–294.

Dey, S. (2016, March 13). Govt mulls hefty fines to curb drug overpricing. *Times of India*. [online] Available from https://timesofindia.indiatimes.com/india/Govt-mulls-hefty-fines-to-curb-drug-overpricing/articleshow/51376854.cms

Epple, D., & Visscher, M. (1984). Environmental pollution: Modeling occurrence, detection, and deterrence. *Journal of Law & Economics, 27*(1), 29–60.

Evans, V., & Pollock, A. (2015). The proliferation of irrational metformin fixed dose combinations in India. *The Lancet Diabetes and Endocrinology, 3*, 98–100.

Francis, P. (2013, January 3). Price monitoring and new policy. PharmaBiz.com

Francis, P. (2014, May 14). Violation of DPCO 2013. PharmaBiz.com

Francis, P. (2016a, June 22). NPPA fight for 20 years. PharmaBiz.com

Francis, P. (2016b, September 7). NPPA guidelines for recovery. PharmaBiz.com

Garvie, D., & Keeler, A. (1994). Incomplete enforcement with endogenous regulatory choice. *Journal of Public Economics, 55*(1), 141–162.

Gokhale, K. (2014, July 19). Price caps on drugs hurt Indian units of global pharma firms. *Live Mint* [online]. Available from https://www.livemint.com/Companies/LEMUIazD96HeWnq9QkALpM/Price-caps-on-drugs-hurt-Indian-units-of-global-pharma-compa.html

Gray, W., & Deily, M. (1996). Compliance and enforcement: Air pollution regulation in the U.S. steel industry. *Journal of Environmental Economics and Management, 31*(1), 96–111.

Greenberg, J. (1984). Avoiding tax avoidance: A (repeated) game-theoretic approach. *Journal of Economic Theory, 32*, 1–13.

Harrington, W. (1988). Enforcement leverage when penalties are restricted. *Journal of Public Economics, 37*(1), 29–53.

Harrison, K. (1995). Is cooperation the answer? Canadian environmental enforcement in comparative context. *Journal of Policy Analysis and Management, 14*(2), 221–244.

Helland, E. (1998). The enforcement of pollution control laws: Inspections, violations, and self-reporting. *Review of Economics and Statistics, 80*(1), 141–153.

Heyes, A. (1994). Environmental Enforcement when 'Inspectability' is Endogenous: A model with overshooting properties. *Environmental & Resource Economics, 4*(5), 479–494.

Heyes, A. (2000). Implementing environmental regulation: Enforcement and compliance. *Journal of Regulatory Economics, 17*(2), 107–129.

Heyes, A., & Rickman, N. (1998). A theory of regulatory dealing—Revisiting the Harrington paradox. *Journal of Public Economics, 72*(1), 361–378.

Kambhu, J. (1989). Regulatory standards, noncompliance, and enforcement. *Journal of Regulatory Economics, 1*, 103–114.

Kaplow, L., & Shavell, S. (1994). Optimal law enforcement with self-reporting of behavior. *Journal of Political Economy, 102*(3), 583–606.

Kunnathoor, P. (2017, April 29). AICDF wants NPPA to take action against violation of DPCO 2013 by manufacturers, alleges inaction on side of West Bengal DCA. PharmaBiz.com

Kyle, M. (2007). Pharmaceutical price controls and entry strategies. *Review of Economics and Statistics, 89*(1), 88–99.
Laplante, B., & Rilstone, P. (1996). Environmental inspections and emissions of the pulp and paper industry in Quebec. *Journal of Environmental Economics and Management, 31*(1), 19–36.
Livernois, J., & McKenna, C. (1999). Truth or consequences: enforcing pollution standards with self-reporting. *Journal of Public Economics, 71*(1999), 415–440.
Magat, W., & Viscusi, W. (1990). Effectiveness of the EPA's regulatory enforcement: The case of industrial effluent standards. *Journal of Law and Economics, 33*(2), 331–360.
Malik, A. (1990). Avoidance, screening and optimum enforcement. *Rand Journal of Economics, 21* (1990), 341–353.
Meng, Q., Cheng, G., Silver, L., Sun, X., Rehnberg, C., & Tomson, G. (2005). The impact of China's retail drug price control policy on hospital expenditures: A case study in two Shandong hospitals. *Health Policy and Planning, 20*(3), 185–196.
Menon, D. (2001). Pharmaceutical cost control in Canada: Does it work? *Health Affairs, 20*(3), 92–103.
Nadeau, L. (1997). EPA effectiveness at reducing the duration of plant-level noncompliance. *Journal of Environmental Economics and Management, 34*, 54–78.
Nautiyal, S. (2014, April 7). GSK starts nationwide recall of Crocin advance following state FDA's stop sale order. *PharmaBiz.com* [online]. Available from http://www.pharmabiz.com/NewsDetails.aspx?aid=81260&sid=1
Nowell, C., & Shogren, J. F. (1994). Challenging the enforcement of environmental regulation. *Journal of Regulatory Economics, 6*, 265–282.
NPPA. (2002). *A study on availability and prices of medicines in India*. National Pharmaceutical Pricing Authority. Available online http://www.nppaindia.nic.in/report/voicerep.html
Raymond, M. (1999). Enforcement leverage when penalties are restricted: A reconsideration under asymmetric information. *Journal of Public Economics, 73*(2), 289–295.
Regens, J., Seldon, B., & Elliott, E. (1997). Modeling compliance to environmental regulation: Evidence from manufacturing industries. *Journal of Policy Modeling, 19*(6), 683–696.
Shaffer, S. (1990). Regulatory compliance with nonlinear penalties. *Journal of Regulatory Economics, 2*(1), 99–103.
Shankar, R. (2014, November 18). NPPA issues draft proposal for display of distinguishing mark & ceiling price of scheduled drugs on label. PharmaBiz.com
Shankar, R. (2014a, October 20). NPPA's directive to register under IPDMS evokes poor response from manufacturers. PharmaBiz.com
Shankar, R. (2014b, December 5). NPPA further extends last date to register under IPDMS for companies by one month. PharmaBiz.com
Shankar, R. (2016a, June 14). NPPA to start action against many cos for not registering under IPDMS. PharmaBiz.com
Shankar, R. (2016b, August 29). NPPA issues guidelines to expedite monitoring & recovery in overcharging cases. PharmaBiz.com
Shirodkar, S. (2015, March 17). NPPA moots to replicate Gujarat FDCA model of efficient reporting of DPCO violation cases across India. PharmaBiz.com
Stigler, G. (1970). The optimum enforcement of Laws. *Journal of Political Economy, 78*, 526–536.
Vijay, N. (2013, August 6). DPCO 2013 skips penalty clause for violators in drug manufacturing, pharmacy outlets: Experts. PharmaBiz.com
Yang, H., Dib, H. H., Zhu, M., Qi, G., & Zhang, X. (2010). Prices, availability and affordability of essential medicines in rural areas of Hubei Province, China. *Health policy and planning, 25*(3), 219–229.
Yang, L., Liu, C., Ferrier, J. A., Zhou, W., & Zhang, X. (2013). The impact of the national essential medicines policy on prescribing behaviours in primary care facilities in Hubei province of China. *Health policy and planning, 28*(7), 750–760.
Yee, W.-H., Tang, S.-Y., & Lo, C. W.-H. (2016). Regulatory compliance when the rule of law is weak: Evidence from China's environmental reform. *Journal of Public Administration Research and Theory, 26*(1), 95–112.

Chapter 9
Conclusion

In this book, we attempted to examine the effectiveness of the design, implementation, and compliance with partial price control regulations on pharmaceuticals in India. We presented anecdotal evidence to suggest the history of cost-based regulation in this sector leading up to the 2013 DPCO had been ineffective. The government spent nearly a decade from 2002 until 2012 to decide on the design of the regulation. The new design deviated from the earlier design by relying on a market-based mechanism for determining price ceilings and using the prices of firms with a relatively larger market share. We find that the design of the regulation is ineffective. In particular, the partial nature of the regulation and the exclusion of other dosages of the same medicines as well as fixed-dose combinations of important substitute medicines led to compensatory shifts in the demand and prices in unregulated markets. We also find evidence to suggest that the implementation of the regulation has been suboptimal. In particular, the regulator had limited access to reliable data on the prices, which led to delays in fixing ceiling prices and disputes with the pharmaceutical firms, which challenged the ceiling price orders in several cases. The regulator has also compounded the problem by following at times what appears to be inexplicable interpretations of simple formulae to determine the ceiling price. The regulator's efforts over the last 3–4 years to develop a database of prices and market shares by requiring firms to submit such information received low levels of cooperation from the industry. The enforcement of price control regulations in India has been historically weak with the absence of built-in penalties to dissuade pharmaceutical firms from for charging prices above the ceiling price, the regulator identifying a small fraction of the potential ceiling price violations, and then recovering only a small fraction of the overcharged amount successfully after years of legal proceedings. We find that the pharmaceutical firms responded by increasing prices before the implementation of the regulation, shifting the demand away from the regulated to unregulated medicines, introducing more product varieties of unregulated medicines, and increasing retailer incentives to push products with higher margins. While in the short term the impending regulation increased the prices of both regulated and unregulated medicines, in the medium term, the

A. Bhaskarabhatla, *Regulating Pharmaceutical Prices in India*, India Studies in Business and Economics, https://doi.org/10.1007/978-3-319-93393-1_9

weighted average prices of partially regulated medicines have not declined in absolute terms. A major limitation of the current regulation is its inability to limit exorbitant retail margins resulting from consumer prices that are several times higher than the wholesale prices. While we find evidence to suggest that pharmaceutical firms coordinated to undermine the effectiveness of the regulation, their trade associations have also supported studies questioning the economic rationale for pharmaceutical price regulations in India. It is also concerning that IMS has taken up the task to evaluate the effectiveness of price control regulations despite its key role in providing data for determining the ceiling price as well as the many questions raised about the quality of its data.

One may be tempted to conclude from the sobering description of the deficiencies of the current pharmaceutical price control regime in India that such regulations must be eliminated altogether. We, however, argue that such a conclusion is problematic for several reasons. First, regulation in this sector is an ongoing process, and it can be improved based on the lessons learned over the last 4 years of implementation. There is evidence to suggest that the regulator has been relatively more proactive in identifying cases of overcharging as well as addressing issues arising from the partial nature of regulation by expanding the scope and setting up monitoring of prices for both regulated and unregulated medicines. The design of the regulation can be improved by updating the National List of Essential Medicines once every 2 years as does the WHO and by expanding the ambit of regulation to include all dosages of a medicine and their fixed dose combinations. Second, with each revision of the price ceilings, the regulator can significantly improve the implementation and enforcement activities. The regulator's ability to extract cooperation from the state administrators in monitoring and enforcement can also positively influence the effectiveness of the regulation. Third, one can learn about the potential impacts of eliminating regulations altogether by examining the pricing patterns in pharmaceutical markets with little or no regulations. Until recently, medical devices represented such pharmaceutical markets in India, as they were excluded from the 2013 price cap regulation.

The efforts to bring stents, medical devices used to prevent heart attacks, provides an excellent case for why price regulations become necessary. In July 2014, the Maharashtra Food and Drug Administration informed the Drug Controller General of India and the National Pharmaceutical Pricing Authority about the inexplicably high consumer prices of stents relative to their wholesale prices (Nautiyal 2014a, 2015c). Stents, like other medical devices, were considered as drugs under the Drugs and Cosmetics Act of 1940 but they were not regulated under the 2013 DPCO. The Maharashtra FDA found that the manufacturers of stents were coordinating with the importers, distributors, and hospitals to set arbitrarily high maximum resale prices (MRP). For example, drug-eluting stents manufactured by Medtronic and imported by India Medtronic, at Rs. 30,848 has an MRP of Rs. 162,000 printed on its package, sold to a distributor named Bhalani Biomedicals at a price of Rs. 67,000, which the distributor sold to Jaslok hospital at Rs. 106,050 (Nautiyal 2014a). The absence of regulation led to a trade margin of 425% in drug-eluting stents. Nautiyal (2014a) notes that in another case, stents manufactured by Abbott's subsidiary in the Netherlands and imported by the subsidiary in India at Rs. 40,710 had an MRP of Rs. 150,000, resulting in a trade margin of 72%. The stents were sold to a distributor named Sinocare at a price of Rs. 73,440, which sold it to P D Hinduja hospital at a price of Rs. 113,400 and the patient paid a price of Rs. 119,070. Similarly, stents manufactured by Cordis were imported by Johnson & Johnson at Rs. 45,115 with an MRP of Rs. 135,000.

In response to the letter written by the Maharashtra FDA, the NPPA notified device manufacturers that medical devices are classified under non-scheduled drug category, that their prices are subject to monitoring and cannot be increased more than 10% of MRP annually, and that pricing information must be supplied to the NPPA using Form V (Nautiyal 2015a). The Maharashtra FDA suggested that five categories of devices such as Neuro Coils, Cochlear Implants, Cardiac Stents, Ortho Implants and Bone Cement can be brought under the NLEM and DPCO (Nautiyal 2015b, 2014c). The NPPA sent letters reminding the manufacturers to share their pricing information once in 2015 and four times in 2016 and mandated the sharing of information in 2017 after including stents under NLEM in 2016 (Shankar 2016, 2017a). The state of Karnataka joined monitoring of stent prices in 2017 (Vijay 2017), and the NPPA mandated the printing of MRP (Shankar 2017b). The NPPA imposed a price ceiling on drug-eluting stents at Rs. 29,000 and on bare metal stents at Rs. 7260 in February 2017. Francis (2017) summarizes the timeline of events involving the pricing of stents:

> Stents were included in the National List of Essential Medicines in July last year and were added to the Schedule I of the DPCO 2013, in December, bringing these devices under price control. Prior to that Union health ministry had accepted the recommendations of an expert panel, set up to examine the issue of essentiality of coronary stents, and decided to include this life saving product in the NLEM. The health ministry's decision is subsequent to a Delhi High Court direction to the government in February 2015 in response to a public interest litigation seeking relief to lakhs of heart patients in the country. It was after the Court order, the expert committee headed by Prof Y K Gupta was appointed to examine the essentiality and excessive profiteering in coronary stents. The NPPA order is certainly going to be opposed by the hospital managements and stent suppliers as this is the first step from the government to regulate stent prices and bring down the profiteering in these life saving products. Monitoring violation and circumvention of price fixing order by hospitals and stent suppliers are going to be a big task for NPPA as it has no officials in most of the states. Enforcement of ceiling prices may, therefore, have to be undertaken by the state drug control administrations as the NPPA is a Central body. In Maharashtra, the state FDA has already started acting on its own and is trying to enforce compliance of the NPPA order.

The NPPA enforced the price ceilings by expediting 300 cases of price ceiling violations (Nautiyal 2017). The NPPA also revised the DPCO to include importers and distributors under the definition of manufacturers (Shankar 2017c). Some reports suggested that hospitals responded to the capping of stent prices by charging exorbitant prices for consumables such as cardiac catheters, balloon catheters and guide wire (Sreenivasan 2018). However, such compensatory prices increases cannot be a reason for not limiting the prices of stents in the first place. Instead, the NPPA has responded to these reports by requiring hospitals to provide detailed invoices to their patients undergoing procedures involving stents (Sreenivasan 2018):

> Since cardiac catheters are necessarily used during angioplasties and are an integral part of the package, healthcare institutions which are performing angioplasty and billing the patients shall also mention cost of cardiac catheters, balloon catheter and guide wire separately along with their respective brand name, if any, name of the company, batch number and specifications in order to bring in greater transparency in the billing and monitoring of compliance with the MRPs by the NPPA under para 20 of DPCO, 2013.

Although there is growing evidence to indicate that stents do not prevent heart attacks and that they are unnecessary and expensive procedures involving adverse events such as heart attacks and renal failure (Carroll 2018; Al-Lamee et al. 2017; Brown and Redberg 2018), the Indian medical community is far from limiting their use. Consequently, the NPPA's role in limiting excessive profiteering from the sale of stents must be counted as a success of the 2013 DPCO regulation. While the government has addressed the pricing of stents, Nautiyal (2014b) provides examples of the partial or incomplete nature of this regulation and suggests that the lack of regulation has led to arbitrarily high prices for similar medical devices used in different medical procedures:

> Products are often being labeled with a high price due to lack of any regulation in pricing as most of the medical devices have not been notified by the government. A case in point being that drug eluting stent (DES) meant for cardiac disorder is notified but Cerebral shunt meant for neurological disorders is not notified. Endotracheal tube used in anaesthesia devices which falls under the catheter category is notified by the government while Laryngeal Mask Airway is not notified. All the anaesthesia intubation devices therefore need to be regulated and not only endotracheal tube. It has also been observed that notified medical device like endotracheal tube is imported and sold in the name of "tube" to evade local rules and import duty.

Overall, despite the many deficiencies in the design, implementation, and enforcement of the 2013 DPCO, we expect that over time it will become more binding and limit excessive increases in prices and margins. To achieve this objective, the NPPA must continually analyze and interpret disaggregated data compiled by organizations such as the AIOCD and IMS Health and by itself through the IPDMS, which runs into tens of thousands of SKU-level observations each month.

According to the budget estimates published on the NPPA's website for the 2015–2016, the largest amount of expenses is allocated for consumer awareness programs (see Table 9.1). In early 2017, the NPPA launched its mobile app *Pharma Sahi Daam* in its efforts to spread awareness among consumers about the ceiling prices of price-controlled medicines (Datta 2017). Given the extent of price-ceiling violations that have been documented over the past several years and the limited resources at the NPPA's disposal, it can benefit from collaborating with academic researchers to improve the design as well as to lower the cost of monitoring and enforcement. Instead, the NPPA's efforts to outsourcing the burden of enforcement and compliance to consumers through its public grievance redressals mechanisms such as *Pharma Jan Samadhan* can only contribute to an erosion of its regulatory authority.

Table 9.1 Budgetary allocation for the National Pharmaceutical Pricing Authority, 2015–2016

Non-planned and planned spending	Budget estimates in rupees
Period	(2015–2016)
Salaries	38,000,000
Wages	7,000,000
OTA	100,000
Medical treatment	1,000,000
Travelling allowance (D)	2,500,000
Travelling allowance (F)	500,000
Office expenses	10,000,000
Rent, rate and taxes	30,500,000
Other administrative expenses	500,000
Professional services	12,000,000
Consumer awareness scheme	50,000,000

Source: NPPA website's right to information act tab
URL: http://www.nppaindia.nic.in/last accessed on March 25, 2018

References

Al-Lamee, R., Thompson, D., Dehbi, H.-M., et al. (2017, November 2). Percutaneous coronary intervention in stable angina (ORBITA): A double-blind, randomized controlled trial. Lancet. https://doi.org/10.1016/S0140-6736(17)32714-9.

Brown, D. L., & Redberg, R. F. (2018). Last nail in the coffin for PCI in stable angina. *Lancet, 391* (10115), 6–12. https://doi.org/10.1016/S0140-6736(17)32757-5.

Carroll, A. E. (2018, February 12). Heart stents are useless for most stable patients. They're still widely used. *New York Times.*

Datta, J. (2017, January 2). NPPA's mobile app: When consumers can get the price right on medicines. *The Hindu BusinessLine.*

Francis, P. (2017, February 23). Stent pricing order. PharmaBiz.com

Nautiyal, S. (2014a, July 22). Maha FDA writes to NPPA to bring medical devices under DPCO to curb profiteering. PharmaBiz.com

Nautiyal, S. (2014b, July 03). Hospitals making huge profit on simple disposables in collusion with stockists. PharmaBiz.com

Nautiyal, S. (2014c, October 9). Maha FDA recommends NPPA to bring five categories of medical devices under DPCO. PharmaBiz.com

Nautiyal, S. (2015a, January 7). State FDA writes to NPPA to regulate price of cardiac stents. PharmaBiz.com

Nautiyal, S. (2015b, May 26). Maha FDA recommends NPPA to bring cardiac stents under NLEM. PharmaBiz.com

Nautiyal, S. (2015c, May 29). Maharashtra FDA detects 5 distributors involved in overpricing of cardiac stents. PharmaBiz.com

Nautiyal, S. (2017, April 29). NPPA fast tracks 300 overcharging cases of stents in hospitals based on anomalies in medical bills. PharmaBiz.com

Shankar, R. (2016, October 14). NPPA asks medical devices cos again to provide data of notified devices to monitor prices. PharmaBiz.com

Shankar, R. (2017a, January 19). NPPA makes registration on IPDMS mandatory for coronary stent manufacturers, importers and marketers. PharmaBiz.com

Shankar, R. (2017b, March 15). NPPA warns of action against cos selling notified medical devices without MRP. PharmaBiz.com

Shankar, R. (2017c, August 7). NPPA issues addendum on its order on ceiling price fixation of coronary stents to redefine 'manufacturer.' PharmaBiz.com

Sreenivasan, A. (2018, February 14). NPPA's directive to hospitals to mention cost of consumables to help check prices of consumables used in angioplasty.

Vijay, N. (2017, February 24). Karnataka drugs control dept. all set for monitoring stent prices across hospitals in state. PharmaBiz.com

Appendix

Table A.1 Ceiling prices per tablet for tablet formulations of medicines under the 2013 DPCO

Medicine	Strength	Date	Revised price ceiling
Aciclovir	200 mg	Jun-13	7.3
Aciclovir	200 mg	Apr-14	7.76
Aciclovir	200 mg	Feb-15	8.06
Aciclovir	200 mg	Jun-16	6.29
Aciclovir	400 mg	Jun-13	11.64
Aciclovir	400 mg	Apr-14	12.38
Aciclovir	400 mg	Feb-15	12.86
Aciclovir	400 mg	Jun-16	11.42
Albendazole	400 mg	Jun-13	9.12
Albendazole	400 mg	Apr-14	9.7
Albendazole	400 mg	Jul-14	9.92
Albendazole	400 mg	Feb-15	10.3
Albendazole	400 mg	Jun-16	7.15
Albendazole	400 mg	Jul-16	10.3
Allopurinol	100 mg	Sep-13	2.09
Allopurinol	100 mg	Apr-14	2.22
Allopurinol	100 mg	Feb-15	2.31
Allopurinol	100 mg	Jun-16	1.76
Alprazolam	0.25 mg	Jun-13	0.96
Alprazolam	0.25 mg	Apr-14	1.02
Alprazolam	0.25 mg	Feb-15	1.06
Alprazolam	0.5 mg	Jun-13	2.01
Alprazolam	0.5 mg	Apr-14	2.14
Alprazolam	0.5 mg	Feb-15	2.22
Aluminium + Magnesium	50/250 mg	Sep-14	0.49
Aluminium + Magnesium	50/250 mg	Feb-15	0.51
Amiodarone	100 mg	Jun-13	6.52

(continued)

A. Bhaskarabhatla, *Regulating Pharmaceutical Prices in India*, India Studies in Business and Economics, https://doi.org/10.1007/978-3-319-93393-1

Table A.1 (continued)

Medicine	Strength	Date	Revised price ceiling
Amiodarone	100 mg	Apr-14	6.93
Amiodarone	100 mg	Feb-15	7.2
Amiodarone	100 mg	Jun-16	5.3
Amiodarone	200 mg	Jun-13	11.67
Amiodarone	200 mg	Apr-14	12.41
Amiodarone	200 mg	Feb-15	12.89
Amiodarone	200 mg	May-16	10.51
Amitriptyline	25 mg	Jun-13	2.12
Amitriptyline	25 mg	Apr-14	2.25
Amitriptyline	25 mg	Feb-15	2.34
Amitriptyline	25 mg	Jun-16	2.1
Amlodipine	2.5 mg	Jun-13	2.03
Amlodipine	2.5 mg	Dec-13	1.79
Amlodipine	2.5 mg	Jan-14	2.03
Amlodipine	2.5 mg	Apr-14	1.9
Amlodipine	2.5 mg	Jun-14	2.03
Amlodipine	2.5 mg	Jul-14	1.9
Amlodipine	2.5 mg	Aug-14	2.03
Amlodipine	2.5 mg	Sep-14	1.9
Amlodipine	2.5 mg	Feb-15	1.97
Amlodipine	2.5 mg	May-15	2.03
Amlodipine	2.5 mg	Jun-16	1.53
Amlodipine	2.5 mg	Jul-16	1.9
Amlodipine	5 mg	Jun-13	3.06
Amlodipine	5 mg	Dec-13	2.83
Amlodipine	5 mg	Jan-14	3.06
Amlodipine	5 mg	Apr-14	3.01
Amlodipine	5 mg	Nov-14	3.06
Amlodipine	5 mg	Dec-14	3.01
Amlodipine	5 mg	Jan-15	3.06
Amlodipine	5 mg	Feb-15	3.13
Amlodipine	5 mg	May-16	2.33
Amlodipine	5 mg	Jun-16	3.13
Amoxycillin + Clavulanic Acid	500/125 mg	Jun-13	22.46
Amoxycillin + Clavulanic Acid	500/125 mg	Apr-14	23.88
Amoxycillin + Clavulanic Acid	500/125 mg	Feb-15	24.8
Amoxycillin + Clavulanic Acid	500/125 mg	May-16	16.14
Amoxycillin + Clavulanic Acid	500/125 mg	Jun-16	24.8
Amoxycillin + Clavulanic Acid	625 mg	Feb-15	24.8
Amoxycillin + Clavulanic Acid	625 mg	May-16	16.14
Aspirin	100 mg	Sep-14	0.14
Aspirin	100 mg	Feb-15	0.15

(continued)

Table A.1 (continued)

Medicine	Strength	Date	Revised price ceiling
Aspirin	100 mg	May-16	0.15
Aspirin	325 mg	Sep-14	0.44
Aspirin	325 mg	Feb-15	0.46
Aspirin	75 mg	Mar-14	0.26
Aspirin	75 mg	Aug-14	0.28
Aspirin	75 mg	Feb-15	0.29
Atenolol	100 mg	Jun-13	3.72
Atenolol	100 mg	Apr-14	3.96
Atenolol	100 mg	Feb-15	4.11
Atenolol	100 mg	Jul-16	3.24
Atenolol	50 mg	Jun-13	2.07
Atenolol	50 mg	Apr-14	2.2
Atenolol	50 mg	Feb-15	2.28
Atenolol	50 mg	Jun-16	1.66
Atenolol	50 mg	Jul-16	2.2
Atorvastatin	10 mg	Jun-13	5.91
Atorvastatin	10 mg	Apr-14	6.28
Atorvastatin	10 mg	Jul-14	6.49
Atorvastatin	10 mg	Feb-15	6.74
Atorvastatin	10 mg	Mar-16	5.09
Atorvastatin	10 mg	Apr-16	6.74
Atorvastatin	5 mg	Jun-13	3.82
Atorvastatin	5 mg	Apr-14	4.06
Atorvastatin	5 mg	Feb-15	4.22
Azathioprine	50 mg	Jun-13	9.89
Azathioprine	50 mg	Apr-14	10.52
Azathioprine	50 mg	Feb-15	10.92
Azathioprine	50 mg	Jun-16	9.02
Azathioprine	50 mg	Jul-16	10.92
Azithromycin	100 mg	Jul-13	5.13
Azithromycin	100 mg	Apr-14	5.45
Azithromycin	100 mg	Feb-15	5.66
Azithromycin	250 mg	Jul-13	10.26
Azithromycin	250 mg	Apr-14	10.91
Azithromycin	250 mg	Feb-15	11.33
Azithromycin	250 mg	May-16	9.06
Azithromycin	250 mg	Jun-16	11.33
Azithromycin	500 mg	Jun-13	19.86
Azithromycin	500 mg	Nov-13	20.51
Azithromycin	500 mg	Apr-14	21.81
Azithromycin	500 mg	Feb-15	22.65
Azithromycin	500 mg	May-16	17.83

(continued)

Table A.1 (continued)

Medicine	Strength	Date	Revised price ceiling
Azithromycin	500 mg	Jun-16	22.65
Bisacodyl	5 mg	Jul-13	0.97
Bisacodyl	5 mg	Apr-14	1.03
Bisacodyl	5 mg	Feb-15	1.07
Bisacodyl	5 mg	Jun-16	0.93
Bisacodyl	5 mg	Jul-16	1.07
Bromocriptine	1.25 mg	Jun-13	7.58
Bromocriptine	1.25 mg	Apr-14	8.06
Bromocriptine	1.25 mg	Feb-15	8.37
Bromocriptine	2.5 mg	Jun-13	13.6
Bromocriptine	2.5 mg	Apr-14	14.46
Bromocriptine	2.5 mg	Feb-15	15.02
Busulfan	2 mg	Apr-14	3.63
Busulfan	2 mg	Oct-15	3.63
Calcium	500 mg	Jul-13	1.67
Calcium	500 mg	Apr-14	1.78
Calcium	500 mg	Feb-15	1.85
Carbamazepine	100 mg	Apr-14	0.7
Carbamazepine	100 mg	Aug-14	0.74
Carbamazepine	100 mg	Feb-15	0.77
Carbamazepine	200 mg	Apr-14	1.37
Carbamazepine	200 mg	Aug-14	1.46
Carbamazepine	200 mg	Feb-15	1.52
Carbamazepine	200 mg	Mar-16	1.44
Carbamazepine	200 mg	Apr-16	1.52
Carbamazepine	200 mg	Jun-16	1.28
Carbamazepine	200 mg	Jul-16	1.44
Carbimazole	10 mg	Jun-13	3.43
Carbimazole	10 mg	Apr-14	3.65
Carbimazole	10 mg	Feb-15	3.79
Carbimazole	10 mg	May-16	3.42
Carbimazole	5 mg	Jun-13	1.77
Carbimazole	5 mg	Apr-14	1.88
Carbimazole	5 mg	Feb-15	1.95
Carbimazole	5 mg	Jun-16	1.76
Cefixime	100 mg	Jun-13	7.69
Cefixime	100 mg	Apr-14	8.18
Cefixime	100 mg	Feb-15	8.49
Cefixime	200 mg	Jul-13	11.25
Cefixime	200 mg	Apr-14	11.96
Cefixime	200 mg	Feb-15	12.42
Cefixime	200 mg	May-16	8.48

(continued)

Table A.1 (continued)

Medicine	Strength	Date	Revised price ceiling
Cefixime	200 mg	Jun-16	12.42
Cetirizine	10 mg	Jun-13	1.81
Cetirizine	10 mg	Apr-14	1.92
Cetirizine	10 mg	Feb-15	1.99
Cetirizine	10 mg	Jun-16	1.53
Cetirizine	10 mg	Jul-16	1.99
Chlorambucil	2 mg	Nov-13	45.22
Chlorambucil	2 mg	Apr-14	48.08
Chlorambucil	2 mg	Feb-15	49.93
Chlorambucil	2 mg	Dec-15	49.93
Chlorambucil	2 mg	Jul-16	32.84
Chlorpheniramine	4 mg	Jul-13	0.1
Chlorpheniramine	4 mg	Apr-14	0.11
Chlorpheniramine	4 mg	Feb-15	0.11423
Chlorpheniramine	4 mg	Jul-16	0.08514
Chlorpromazine	100 mg	Sep-14	0.68
Chlorpromazine	100 mg	Feb-15	0.71
Chlorpromazine	25 mg	Aug-14	0.29
Chlorpromazine	25 mg	Feb-15	0.3
Chlorpromazine	50 mg	Sep-14	0.41
Chlorpromazine	50 mg	Feb-15	0.43
Ciprofloxacin	250 mg	Sep-14	2.02
Ciprofloxacin	250 mg	Feb-15	2.1
Ciprofloxacin	250 mg	May-16	1.62
Ciprofloxacin	250 mg	Jun-16	2.1
Ciprofloxacin	500 mg	Sep-14	3.86
Ciprofloxacin	500 mg	Feb-15	4.01
Ciprofloxacin	500 mg	May-16	3.3
Ciprofloxacin	500 mg	Jun-16	4.01
Ciprofloxacin	250 mg	Sep-14	2.02
Ciprofloxacin	250 mg	Feb-15	2.1
Ciprofloxacin	250 mg	May-16	1.62
Ciprofloxacin	500 mg	Sep-14	3.86
Ciprofloxacin	500 mg	Feb-15	4.01
Ciprofloxacin	500 mg	Jul-15	4.01
Ciprofloxacin	500 mg	Dec-15	4.01
Ciprofloxacin	500 mg	May-16	3.3
Clindamycin	300 mg	Nov-13	13.09
Clindamycin	300 mg	Apr-14	13.92
Clindamycin	300 mg	Feb-15	14.46
Clindamycin	300 mg	May-16	13.56
Clindamycin	300 mg	Jul-16	14.46

(continued)

Table A.1 (continued)

Medicine	Strength	Date	Revised price ceiling
Clomifene	100 mg	Jun-13	12.18
Clomifene	100 mg	Apr-14	12.95
Clomifene	100 mg	Feb-15	13.45
Clomifene	50 mg	Jun-13	7.93
Clomifene	50 mg	Apr-14	8.43
Clomifene	50 mg	Feb-15	8.75
Clopidogrel	75 mg	Jul-13	10.03
Clopidogrel	75 mg	Apr-14	10.66
Clopidogrel	75 mg	Feb-15	11.07
Clopidogrel	75 mg	May-16	6.44
Clopidogrel	75 mg	Jun-16	11.07
Colchicine	0.5 mg	Jun-13	2.88
Colchicine	0.5 mg	Apr-14	3.06
Colchicine	0.5 mg	Feb-15	3.18
Colchicine	0.5 mg	Jul-16	2.88
Cyclophosphamide	50 mg	Jun-13	3.75
Cyclophosphamide	50 mg	Apr-14	3.99
Cyclophosphamide	50 mg	Feb-15	4.14
Cyclophosphamide	50 mg	Jul-16	3.61
Dapsone	100 mg	Sep-13	0.22
Dapsone	100 mg	Apr-14	0.23
Dapsone	100 mg	Feb-15	0.24
Dapsone	50 mg	Sep-13	0.2
Dapsone	50 mg	Apr-14	0.21
Dapsone	50 mg	Feb-15	0.22
Dexamethasone	0.5 mg	Apr-14	0.19
Dexamethasone	0.5 mg	Aug-14	0.2
Dexamethasone	0.5 mg	Feb-15	0.21
Dexamethasone	0.5 mg	May-16	0.18
Dextromethorphan	30 mg	Sep-14	5.77
Dextromethorphan	30 mg	Feb-15	5.99
Diazepam	2 mg	Aug-13	1.44
Diazepam	2 mg	Apr-14	1.53
Diazepam	2 mg	Feb-15	1.59
Diazepam	2 mg	Jul-16	1.39
Diazepam	5 mg	Jun-13	1.32
Diazepam	5 mg	Apr-14	1.4
Diazepam	5 mg	Feb-15	1.45
Diazepam	5 mg	Jul-16	1.32
Diclofenac	50 mg	Jun-13	1.95
Diclofenac	50 mg	Apr-14	2.07
Diclofenac	50 mg	Feb-15	2.15

(continued)

Table A.1 (continued)

Medicine	Strength	Date	Revised price ceiling
Diclofenac	50 mg	Jun-16	1.77
Diclofenac	50 mg	Jul-16	2.07
Didanosine	250 mg	Sep-13	23.93
Didanosine	250 mg	Apr-14	25.44
Didanosine	250 mg	Feb-15	26.42
Didanosine	250 mg	Dec-15	26.42
Didanosine	400 mg	Sep-14	32.83
Didanosine	400 mg	Feb-15	34.09
Didanosine	400 mg	Nov-15	34.09
Diethylcarbamazine	50 mg	Jun-13	0.47
Diethylcarbamazine	50 mg	Apr-14	0.5
Diethylcarbamazine	50 mg	Feb-15	0.52
Diethylcarbamazine	50 mg	Jun-16	0.5
Digoxin	0.25 mg	Jun-13	1.26
Digoxin	0.25 mg	Apr-14	1.34
Digoxin	0.25 mg	Feb-15	1.39
Digoxin	0.25 mg	May-16	1.11
Diloxanide	500 mg	Nov-13	1.61
Diloxanide	500 mg	Apr-14	1.71
Diloxanide	500 mg	Feb-15	1.78
Diltiazem	30 mg	Jun-13	2.27
Diltiazem	30 mg	Apr-14	2.41
Diltiazem	30 mg	Feb-15	2.5
Diltiazem	30 mg	Jun-16	2.23
Diltiazem	60 mg	Jun-13	4.79
Diltiazem	60 mg	Apr-14	5.09
Diltiazem	60 mg	Feb-15	5.29
Diltiazem	60 mg	Jun-16	4.53
Domperidone	10 mg	Jul-13	2.26
Domperidone	10 mg	Apr-14	2.4
Domperidone	10 mg	Feb-15	2.49
Domperidone	10 mg	Jun-16	2.24
Domperidone	10 mg	Jul-16	2.49
Doxycycline	100 mg	Apr-14	0.94
Doxycycline	100 mg	Aug-14	1
Doxycycline	100 mg	Feb-15	1.04
Enalapril	2.5 mg	Jun-13	1.78
Enalapril	2.5 mg	Apr-14	1.89
Enalapril	2.5 mg	Feb-15	1.96
Enalapril	2.5 mg	Jun-16	1.78
Enalapril	5 mg	Jun-13	2.96
Enalapril	5 mg	Apr-14	3.15

(continued)

Table A.1 (continued)

Medicine	Strength	Date	Revised price ceiling
Enalapril	5 mg	Feb-15	3.27
Enalapril	5 mg	Jun-16	2.97
Enalapril	5 mg	Jul-16	3.27
Ethambutol	200 mg	Sep-13	0.97
Ethambutol	200 mg	Apr-14	1.03
Ethambutol	200 mg	Feb-15	1.07
Ethambutol	200 mg	Jul-16	0.94
Ethambutol	400 mg	Jun-13	2.17
Ethambutol	400 mg	Apr-14	2.31
Ethambutol	400 mg	Feb-15	2.4
Ethambutol	400 mg	Jul-16	2.14
Ethambutol	600 mg	Jun-13	3.15
Ethambutol	600 mg	Apr-14	3.35
Ethambutol	600 mg	Feb-15	3.48
Ethambutol	600 mg	Jul-16	3.15
Ethambutol	800 mg	Jun-13	3.74
Ethambutol	800 mg	Apr-14	3.98
Ethambutol	800 mg	Feb-15	4.13
Ethambutol	800 mg	Jun-16	3.77
Ethambutol	800 mg	Jul-16	4.13
Ethinyl Estradiol + Levonorgestrel	0.03/0.15 mg	Jul-13	3.05
Ethinyl Estradiol + Levonorgestrel	0.03/0.15 mg	Apr-14	3.24
Ethinyl Estradiol + Levonorgestrel	0.03/0.15 mg	Feb-15	3.36
Ethinyl Estradiol + Levonorgestrel	0.03/0.15 mg	Jun-16	3.07
Ethinylestradiol	0.01 mg	Jun-13	2.12
Ethinylestradiol	0.01 mg	Apr-14	2.25
Ethinylestradiol	0.01 mg	Feb-15	2.34
Ethinylestradiol	0.01 mg	Jul-16	2.1
Ethinylestradiol	0.05 mg	Nov-13	3.53
Ethinylestradiol	0.05 mg	Apr-14	3.75
Ethinylestradiol	0.05 mg	Feb-15	3.89
Famotidine	20 mg	Apr-14	0.21
Famotidine	20 mg	Aug-14	0.22
Famotidine	20 mg	Sep-14	0.29
Famotidine	20 mg	Feb-15	0.3
Fluconazole	150 mg	Jul-13	14.45
Fluconazole	150 mg	Apr-14	15.36
Fluconazole	150 mg	Feb-15	15.95
Fluconazole	150 mg	Jun-16	10.99
Fluconazole	100 mg	Jun-13	14.16
Fluconazole	100 mg	Apr-14	15.05
Fluconazole	100 mg	Feb-15	15.63

(continued)

Table A.1 (continued)

Medicine	Strength	Date	Revised price ceiling
Fluconazole	100 mg	Jul-16	7.4
Fluconazole	150 mg	Jul-13	14.45
Fluconazole	150 mg	Apr-14	15.36
Fluconazole	150 mg	Feb-15	15.95
Fluconazole	150 mg	Jun-16	10.99
Fluconazole	150 mg	Jul-16	15.95
Fluconazole	200 mg	Jun-13	25.86
Fluconazole	200 mg	Apr-14	27.49
Fluconazole	200 mg	Feb-15	28.55
Fluconazole	200 mg	Jun-16	17.43
Fluconazole	50 mg	Jun-13	7.83
Fluconazole	50 mg	Apr-14	8.32
Fluconazole	50 mg	Feb-15	8.64
Flutamide	250 mg	Apr-14	9.16
Flutamide	250 mg	Feb-15	9.51
Flutamide	250 mg	Jun-16	8.62
Folic Acid	1 mg	Nov-13	0.25
Folic Acid	1 mg	Apr-14	0.27
Folic Acid	1 mg	Feb-15	0.28
Folic Acid	5 mg	Jun-13	1.15
Folic Acid	5 mg	Dec-13	1.37
Folic Acid	5 mg	Apr-14	1.46
Folic Acid	5 mg	Feb-15	1.52
Glibenclamide	2.5 mg	Jun-13	0.48
Glibenclamide	2.5 mg	Apr-14	0.51
Glibenclamide	2.5 mg	Feb-15	0.53
Glibenclamide	5 mg	Jun-13	0.96
Glibenclamide	5 mg	Apr-14	1.02
Glibenclamide	5 mg	Feb-15	1.06
Glyceryl Trinitrate	0.5 mg	Jun-13	1.85
Glyceryl Trinitrate	0.5 mg	Apr-14	1.97
Glyceryl Trinitrate	0.5 mg	Feb-15	2.05
Glyceryl Trinitrate	0.5 mg	Jul-16	1.68
Griseofulvin	250 mg	Apr-14	1.45
Griseofulvin	250 mg	Feb-15	1.6
Griseofulvin	250 mg	Jun-16	1.48
Hydrochlorothiazide	12.5 mg	Jun-13	0.97
Hydrochlorothiazide	12.5 mg	Apr-14	1.03
Hydrochlorothiazide	12.5 mg	Feb-15	1.07
Hydrochlorothiazide	25 mg	Jun-13	1.66
Hydrochlorothiazide	25 mg	Apr-14	1.76
Hydrochlorothiazide	25 mg	Feb-15	1.83

(continued)

Table A.1 (continued)

Medicine	Strength	Date	Revised price ceiling
Hydroxychloroquine	200 mg	Jun-13	5.64
Hydroxychloroquine	200 mg	Apr-14	6
Hydroxychloroquine	200 mg	Feb-15	6.23
Hydroxychloroquine	200 mg	May-16	5.5
Hyoscine	10 mg	Nov-13	2.83
Hyoscine	10 mg	Apr-14	3.01
Hyoscine	10 mg	Feb-15	3.13
Hyoscine	10 mg	Jun-16	2.77
Imatinib Mesylate	100 mg	Jun-13	87.59
Imatinib Mesylate	100 mg	Apr-14	93.13
Imatinib Mesylate	100 mg	Feb-15	96.71
Imatinib Mesylate	100 mg	Mar-16	96.71
Imatinib Mesylate	100 mg	May-16	96.71
Imatinib Mesylate	100 mg	Jul-16	96.71
Imatinib Mesylate	400 mg	Jun-13	268.33
Imatinib Mesylate	400 mg	Apr-14	285.29
Imatinib Mesylate	400 mg	Feb-15	296.27
Imatinib Mesylate	400 mg	Jun-16	213.32
Imipramine	25 mg	Jun-13	0.75
Imipramine	25 mg	Apr-14	0.8
Imipramine	25 mg	Feb-15	0.83
Imipramine	75 mg	Jun-13	2
Imipramine	75 mg	Apr-14	2.13
Imipramine	75 mg	Feb-15	2.21
Isoniazide	100 mg	Sep-13	0.72
Isoniazide	100 mg	Apr-14	0.77
Isoniazide	100 mg	Feb-15	0.8
Isoniazide	300 mg	Jul-13	1.27
Isoniazide	300 mg	Apr-14	1.35
Isoniazide	300 mg	Feb-15	1.4
Isoniazide	300 mg	Mar-16	1.86
Isoniazide	300 mg	Apr-16	9999
Isosorbide Dinitrate	10 mg	Jul-13	0.69
Isosorbide Dinitrate	10 mg	Apr-14	0.73
Isosorbide Dinitrate	10 mg	Feb-15	0.76
Isosorbide Dinitrate	10 mg	Mar-16	0.69
Isosorbide Dinitrate	20 mg	Dec-14	2
Isosorbide Dinitrate	20 mg	Feb-15	2.08
Isosorbide-5-Mononitrate	10 mg	Jun-13	1.92
Isosorbide-5-Mononitrate	10 mg	Apr-14	2.04
Isosorbide-5-Mononitrate	10 mg	Feb-15	2.12
Isosorbide-5-Mononitrate	20 mg	Jun-13	3.29

(continued)

Table A.1 (continued)

Medicine	Strength	Date	Revised price ceiling
Isosorbide-5-Mononitrate	20 mg	Apr-14	3.5
Isosorbide-5-Mononitrate	20 mg	Feb-15	3.63
Lamivudine	150 mg	Jun-13	9.4
Lamivudine	150 mg	Apr-14	9.99
Lamivudine	150 mg	Feb-15	10.37
Lamivudine + Stavudine	150/30 mg	Jun-13	9.2
Lamivudine + Stavudine	150/30 mg	Apr-14	9.78
Lamivudine + Stavudine	150/30 mg	Feb-15	10.16
Lamivudine + Stavudine	150/30 mg	Jul-16	8.86
Lamivudine + Stavudine + Nevirapine	150/30/200 mg	Jun-13	17.29
Lamivudine + Stavudine + Nevirapine	150/30/200 mg	Apr-14	18.38
Lamivudine + Stavudine + Nevirapine	150/30/200 mg	Feb-15	19.09
Lamivudine + Zidavudine + Nevirapine	150/300/200 mg	Jun-13	19.05
Lamivudine + Zidavudine + Nevirapine	150/300/200 mg	Apr-14	20.25
Lamivudine + Zidavudine + Nevirapine	150/300/200 mg	Feb-15	21.03
Lamivudine + Zidovudine	150/300 mg	Jun-13	19.63
Lamivudine + Zidovudine	150/300 mg	Apr-14	20.87
Lamivudine + Zidovudine	150/300 mg	Feb-15	21.67
Lamivudine + Zidovudine	150/300 mg	Jul-16	18.61
Leflunomide	10 mg	Jun-13	15.1
Leflunomide	10 mg	Apr-14	16.05
Leflunomide	10 mg	Feb-15	16.67
Leflunomide	10 mg	Jun-16	9.3
Leflunomide	20 mg	Jun-13	28.63
Leflunomide	20 mg	Apr-14	30.44
Leflunomide	20 mg	Feb-15	31.61
Leflunomide	20 mg	Jun-16	18.13
Levo-Thyroxine (Synthetic)	100 mcg	Jun-13	1.11
Levo-Thyroxine (Synthetic)	100 mcg	Apr-14	1.18
Levo-Thyroxine (Synthetic)	100 mcg	Feb-15	1.23
Levo-Thyroxine (Synthetic)	100 mcg	Mar-16	1.11
Levo-Thyroxine (Synthetic)	100 mcg	Jun-16	1.23
Levo-Thyroxine (Synthetic)	100 mcg	Jul-16	1.11
Levo-Thyroxine (Synthetic)	50 mcg	Jul-13	1.01
Levo-Thyroxine (Synthetic)	50 mcg	Apr-14	1.07
Levo-Thyroxine (Synthetic)	50 mcg	Feb-15	1.11
Levo-Thyroxine (Synthetic)	50 mcg	Mar-16	0.91
Levodopa + Carbidopa	100/10 mg	Mar-14	1.44
Levodopa + Carbidopa	100/10 mg	Aug-14	1.61
Levodopa + Carbidopa	100/10 mg	Feb-15	1.67
Levodopa + Carbidopa	100/10 mg	May-16	1.44
Levodopa + Carbidopa	100/25 mg	Apr-14	2

(continued)

Table A.1 (continued)

Medicine	Strength	Date	Revised price ceiling
Levodopa + Carbidopa	100/25 mg	Aug-14	2.26
Levodopa + Carbidopa	100/25 mg	Feb-15	2.35
Levodopa + Carbidopa	100/25 mg	Mar-16	3.1
Levodopa + Carbidopa	100/25 mg	May-16	2.1
Levodopa + Carbidopa	250/25 mg	Mar-14	3.46
Levodopa + Carbidopa	250/25 mg	Aug-14	3.85
Levodopa + Carbidopa	250/25 mg	Feb-15	4
Lithium	300 mg	Jun-13	1.41
Lithium	300 mg	Apr-14	1.5
Lithium	300 mg	Feb-15	1.56
Losartan	25 mg	Jun-13	2.5
Losartan	25 mg	Apr-14	2.66
Losartan	25 mg	Feb-15	2.76
Losartan	50 mg	Jun-13	4.3
Losartan	50 mg	Apr-14	4.57
Losartan	50 mg	Feb-15	4.75
Medroxyprogesterone	10 mg	Jun-13	5.24
Medroxyprogesterone	10 mg	Apr-14	5.57
Medroxyprogesterone	10 mg	Feb-15	5.78
Medroxyprogesterone	10 mg	Jun-16	4.99
Mefloquine	250 mg	Jun-13	50.06
Mefloquine	250 mg	Apr-14	53.22
Mefloquine	250 mg	Feb-15	55.27
Mefloquine	250 mg	Jun-16	47.31
Melphalan	2 mg	Nov-13	108.53
Melphalan	2 mg	Apr-14	115.39
Melphalan	2 mg	Feb-15	119.83
Melphalan	2 mg	Dec-15	119.83
Melphalan	2 mg	Apr-16	119.83
Melphalan	2 mg	Jul-16	87.3
Melphalan	5 mg	Nov-13	182.06
Melphalan	5 mg	Apr-14	193.57
Melphalan	5 mg	Feb-15	201.02
Melphalan	5 mg	Jul-15	193.57
Melphalan	5 mg	Aug-15	201.02
Melphalan	5 mg	Nov-15	193.57
Melphalan	5 mg	Apr-16	201.02
Melphalan	5 mg	Jul-16	149.73
Mercaptopurine	50 mg	Nov-13	8.93
Mercaptopurine	50 mg	Apr-14	9.49
Mercaptopurine	50 mg	Feb-15	9.86
Metformin	500 mg	Jun-13	1.56

(continued)

Table A.1 (continued)

Medicine	Strength	Date	Revised price ceiling
Metformin	500 mg	Apr-14	1.66
Metformin	500 mg	Feb-15	1.72
Metformin	500 mg	Mar-16	1.77
Metformin	500 mg	Jun-16	1.39
Metformin	500 mg	Jul-16	1.77
Methotrexate	10 mg	Jun-13	13.95
Methotrexate	10 mg	Apr-14	14.83
Methotrexate	10 mg	Feb-15	15.4
Methotrexate	10 mg	Jun-16	10.81
Methotrexate	2.5 mg	Jun-13	4.72
Methotrexate	2.5 mg	Apr-14	5.02
Methotrexate	2.5 mg	Feb-15	5.21
Methotrexate	2.5 mg	Jun-16	4.26
Methotrexate	2.5 mg	Jul-16	5.21
Methotrexate	5 mg	Jun-13	7.6
Methotrexate	5 mg	Apr-14	8.08
Methotrexate	5 mg	Feb-15	8.39
Methotrexate	7.5 mg	Jun-13	11.27
Methotrexate	7.5 mg	Apr-14	11.98
Methotrexate	7.5 mg	Feb-15	12.44
Methotrexate	7.5 mg	Jun-16	10.32
Methyldopa	250 mg	Dec-14	1.69
Methyldopa	250 mg	Feb-15	1.76
Metoclopramide	10 mg	Jun-13	1.04
Metoclopramide	10 mg	Apr-14	1.11
Metoclopramide	10 mg	Feb-15	1.15
Metoclopramide	10 mg	Jul-16	1.08
Metoprolol	25 mg	Jul-13	3.73
Metoprolol	25 mg	Dec-13	3.38
Metoprolol	25 mg	Feb-14	3.73
Metoprolol	25 mg	Mar-14	3.38
Metoprolol	25 mg	Apr-14	3.59
Metoprolol	25 mg	Feb-15	3.73
Metoprolol	25 mg	Jun-16	2.88
Metoprolol	50 mg	Jul-13	5.3
Metoprolol	50 mg	Dec-13	5.01
Metoprolol	50 mg	Apr-14	5.33
Metoprolol	50 mg	Feb-15	5.54
Metoprolol	50 mg	Jun-16	4.36
Metronidazole	200 mg	Jun-16	0.4
Metronidazole	400 mg	May-16	0.75
Mifepristone	200 mg	Jul-13	357.13

(continued)

Table A.1 (continued)

Medicine	Strength	Date	Revised price ceiling
Mifepristone	200 mg	Apr-14	379.7
Mifepristone	200 mg	Feb-15	394.31
Mifepristone	200 mg	May-16	298.49
Mifepristone	200 mg	Jul-16	394.31
Misoprostol	100 mcg	Jun-13	9.43
Misoprostol	100 mcg	Apr-14	10.03
Misoprostol	100 mcg	Feb-15	10.42
Morphine	10 mg	Apr-14	5.36
Morphine	10 mg	Mar-15	5.36
Neostigmine	15 mg	Nov-13	4.63
Neostigmine	15 mg	Apr-14	4.92
Neostigmine	15 mg	Feb-15	5.11
Nifedipine	10 mg	Jun-13	1.13
Nifedipine	10 mg	Apr-14	1.2
Nifedipine	10 mg	Feb-15	1.25
Nifedipine	10 mg	Jun-16	1.15
Nifedipine	10 mg	Jul-16	1.25
Nifedipine	20 mg	Dec-13	0.32
Nifedipine	20 mg	Apr-14	0.34
Nifedipine	20 mg	Feb-15	0.35
Nitrofurantoin	100 mg	Jun-13	6.88
Nitrofurantoin	100 mg	Apr-14	7.31
Nitrofurantoin	100 mg	Feb-15	7.59
Norethisterone	5 mg	Jun-13	5.07
Norethisterone	5 mg	Apr-14	5.39
Norethisterone	5 mg	Feb-15	5.6
Norethisterone	5 mg	Jun-16	4.75
Ofloxacin	100 mg	Jul-13	3.3
Ofloxacin	100 mg	Apr-14	3.51
Ofloxacin	100 mg	Feb-15	3.65
Ofloxacin	200 mg	Jul-13	4.9
Ofloxacin	200 mg	Apr-14	5.21
Ofloxacin	200 mg	Feb-15	5.41
Olanzapine	10 mg	Jun-13	5.32
Olanzapine	10 mg	Apr-14	5.66
Olanzapine	10 mg	Feb-15	5.88
Olanzapine	5 mg	Jun-13	2.9
Olanzapine	5 mg	Apr-14	3.08
Olanzapine	5 mg	Feb-15	3.2
Ondansetron	4 mg	Jul-13	4.76
Ondansetron	4 mg	Apr-14	5.06
Ondansetron	4 mg	Feb-15	5.25

(continued)

Table A.1 (continued)

Medicine	Strength	Date	Revised price ceiling
Ondansetron	4 mg	Jun-16	4.35
Ondansetron	4 mg	Jul-16	5.25
Ondansetron	8 mg	Jun-13	11.07
Ondansetron	8 mg	Apr-14	11.77
Ondansetron	8 mg	Feb-15	12.22
Ondansetron	8 mg	Jun-16	9.06
Ondansetron	8 mg	Jul-16	12.22
Paracetamol	500 mg	Jun-13	0.94
Paracetamol	500 mg	Apr-14	1
Paracetamol	500 mg	Feb-15	1.04
Paracetamol	500 mg	Jun-16	0.83
Paracetamol	500 mg	Jul-16	1.04
Phenobarbitone	30 mg	Jun-13	0.93
Phenobarbitone	30 mg	Apr-14	0.99
Phenobarbitone	30 mg	Jul-14	1.48
Phenobarbitone	30 mg	Feb-15	1.54
Phenobarbitone	30 mg	Jun-16	1.12
Phenobarbitone	60 mg	Jun-13	1.69
Phenobarbitone	60 mg	Apr-14	1.8
Phenobarbitone	60 mg	May-14	2.53
Phenobarbitone	60 mg	Feb-15	2.63
Phenobarbitone	60 mg	Jun-16	1.64
Phenytoin	100 mg	Jun-13	1.42
Phenytoin	100 mg	Apr-14	1.51
Phenytoin	100 mg	Feb-15	1.57
Phenytoin	100 mg	May-16	1.27
Phenytoin	50 mg	Jun-13	0.77
Phenytoin	50 mg	Apr-14	0.82
Phenytoin	50 mg	Feb-15	0.85
Phenytoin	50 mg	May-16	0.7
Phenytoin	50 mg	Jun-16	0.85
Prednisolone	10 mg	Apr-14	0.92
Prednisolone	10 mg	Aug-14	0.98
Prednisolone	10 mg	Feb-15	1.02
Prednisolone	10 mg	May-16	0.9
Prednisolone	20 mg	Mar-14	1.72
Prednisolone	20 mg	Apr-14	1.83
Prednisolone	20 mg	Feb-15	1.9
Prednisolone	20 mg	Jun-16	1.81
Prednisolone	5 mg	Apr-14	0.55
Prednisolone	5 mg	Aug-14	0.58
Prednisolone	5 mg	Feb-15	0.6

(continued)

Table A.1 (continued)

Medicine	Strength	Date	Revised price ceiling
Prednisolone	5 mg	May-16	0.52
Primaquine	2.5 mg	Jun-13	1.55
Primaquine	2.5 mg	Apr-14	1.65
Primaquine	2.5 mg	Feb-15	1.71
Primaquine	7.5 mg	Jun-13	1.98
Primaquine	7.5 mg	Apr-14	2.11
Primaquine	7.5 mg	Feb-15	2.19
Promethazine	10 mg	Sep-13	0.93
Promethazine	10 mg	Apr-14	0.99
Promethazine	10 mg	Feb-15	1.03
Promethazine	25 mg	Jun-13	2.49
Promethazine	25 mg	Apr-14	2.65
Promethazine	25 mg	Feb-15	2.75
Propranolol	10 mg	Jul-13	1.09
Propranolol	10 mg	Apr-14	1.16
Propranolol	10 mg	Feb-15	1.2
Propranolol	10 mg	Jun-16	1.07
Propranolol	10 mg	Jul-16	1.2
Propranolol	40 mg	Aug-13	2.56
Propranolol	40 mg	Apr-14	2.72
Propranolol	40 mg	Feb-15	2.82
Propranolol	40 mg	Jun-16	2.59
Propranolol	40 mg	Jul-16	2.82
Pyrazinamide	1000 mg	Jun-13	8.3
Pyrazinamide	1000 mg	Apr-14	8.82
Pyrazinamide	1000 mg	Feb-15	9.16
Pyrazinamide	1000 mg	Jun-16	8.39
Pyrazinamide	1500 mg	Aug-13	9.78
Pyrazinamide	1500 mg	Apr-14	10.4
Pyrazinamide	1500 mg	Feb-15	10.8
Pyrazinamide	1500 mg	Jul-16	9.29
Pyrazinamide	500 mg	Jun-13	3.77
Pyrazinamide	500 mg	Apr-14	4.01
Pyrazinamide	500 mg	Feb-15	4.16
Pyrazinamide	500 mg	Jun-16	3.77
Pyrazinamide	750 mg	Jun-13	6.91
Pyrazinamide	750 mg	Apr-14	7.35
Pyrazinamide	750 mg	Feb-15	7.63
Pyrazinamide	750 mg	Jun-16	5.73
Pyridostigmine	60 mg	Jun-13	12.69
Pyridostigmine	60 mg	Apr-14	13.49
Pyridostigmine	60 mg	Feb-15	14.01

(continued)

Table A.1 (continued)

Medicine	Strength	Date	Revised price ceiling
Pyrimethamine	25 mg	Jul-14	0.89
Pyrimethamine	25 mg	Feb-15	0.92
Quinine	300 mg	Jun-13	5.1
Quinine	300 mg	Apr-14	5.42
Quinine	300 mg	Feb-15	5.63
Quinine	300 mg	Jun-16	5.09
Quinine	300 mg	Jul-16	5.63
Raloxifene	60 mg	Jun-13	9.89
Raloxifene	60 mg	Apr-14	10.52
Raloxifene	60 mg	Feb-15	10.92
Rifampicin	150 mg	Sep-14	1.22
Rifampicin	150 mg	Feb-15	1.27
Rifampicin	300 mg	Sep-14	2.76
Rifampicin	300 mg	Feb-15	2.87
Rifampicin	450 mg	Feb-15	4.22
Salbutamol	2 mg	Apr-14	0.14
Salbutamol	2 mg	Aug-14	0.15
Salbutamol	2 mg	Feb-15	0.16
Salbutamol	4 mg	Apr-14	0.17
Salbutamol	4 mg	Aug-14	0.18
Salbutamol	4 mg	Feb-15	0.19
Salbutamol	4 mg	Jun-16	0.17
Salbutamol	4 mg	Jul-16	0.18
Sodium Valproate	200 mg	Jun-13	3.07
Sodium Valproate	200 mg	Apr-14	3.26
Sodium Valproate	200 mg	Feb-15	3.39
Sodium Valproate	200 mg	Jun-16	2.75
Sodium Valproate	500 mg	Jun-13	7.18
Sodium Valproate	500 mg	Apr-14	7.63
Sodium Valproate	500 mg	Feb-15	7.92
Sodium Valproate	500 mg	Jun-16	6.43
Spironolactone	25 mg	Sep-14	1.22
Spironolactone	25 mg	Feb-15	1.27
Sulfasalazine	500 mg	Apr-14	3.65
Sulfasalazine	500 mg	Aug-14	3.88
Sulfasalazine	500 mg	Feb-15	4.03
Sulfasalazine	500 mg	May-16	3.7
Tamoxifen	10 mg	Jun-13	4.35
Tamoxifen	10 mg	Apr-14	4.62
Tamoxifen	10 mg	Feb-15	4.8
Tamoxifen	20 mg	Jun-13	2.77
Tamoxifen	20 mg	Apr-14	2.95

(continued)

Table A.1 (continued)

Medicine	Strength	Date	Revised price ceiling
Tamoxifen	20 mg	Feb-15	3.06
Terbutaline	2.5 mg	Jun-13	0.98
Terbutaline	2.5 mg	May-14	0.98
Terbutaline	2.5 mg	Feb-15	1.08
Trihexyphenidyl	2 mg	Jun-13	1.36
Trihexyphenidyl	2 mg	Apr-14	1.45
Trihexyphenidyl	2 mg	Feb-15	1.51
Trihexyphenidyl	2 mg	Jun-16	1.13
Verapamil	40 mg	Sep-14	0.47
Verapamil	40 mg	Feb-15	0.49
Verapamil	80 mg	Sep-14	0.9
Verapamil	80 mg	Feb-15	0.93
Vitamin B1 Plain (With additives)	100 mg	Sep-14	4.16
Vitamin B1 Plain (With additives)	100 mg	Feb-15	4.32
Warfarin	5 mg	Jun-13	2.24
Warfarin	5 mg	Apr-14	2.38
Warfarin	5 mg	Feb-15	2.47
Warfarin	5 mg	Jun-16	2.2
Zidovudine	300 mg	Jun-13	14.97
Zidovudine	300 mg	Apr-14	15.92
Zidovudine	300 mg	Feb-15	16.53
Zidovudine	300 mg	Jul-16	12.69

Source: NPPA

Table A.2 A partial list of top-1157 SKUs violating the 2013 DPCO during 2013-2016 by charging MRP at least double the DPCO ceiling price

Medicine	Company	SKU	MRP	Ceiling	PTR
Aciclovir	Eli Lilly And Company (India) Pvt. Ltd.	Lovir (Eli Lilly) 200 mg tablet 5	365	36.5	58.48
Aciclovir	Eli Lilly And Company (India) Pvt. Ltd.	Lovir (Eli Lilly) 400 mg tablet 5	365	58.2	99.65
Aciclovir	Eli Lilly And Company (India) Pvt. Ltd.	Lovir (Eli Lilly) 400 mg tablet 5	124.56	58.2	99.65
Albendazole	Zydus Cadila	Zelbend (Zydus Cadila) 400 mg tablet 1	125	9.12	1.75
Albendazole	Alde Medi Impex	Aldezole 400 mg tablet 1	125	9.92	11.95
Albendazole	Alde Medi Impex	Aldezole 400 mg tablet 1	118	9.7	11.95

(continued)

Table A.2 (continued)

Medicine	Company	SKU	MRP	Ceiling	PTR
Albendazole	Maan Pharmaceuticals Ltd.	Velocid 400 mg tablet 1	60	9.12	45.71
Albendazole	Maan Pharmaceuticals Ltd.	Velocid 400 mg tablet 1	65	10.3	49.52
Albendazole	Maan Pharmaceuticals Ltd.	Velocid 400 mg tablet 1	60	9.7	45.71
Albendazole	Ipca Laboratories Pvt Ltd.	Nemozole 400 mg tablet 1	55.57	9.12	44.46
Albendazole	Maan Pharmaceuticals Ltd.	Velocid 400 mg tablet 1	60	9.92	45.71
Albendazole	Maan Pharmaceuticals Ltd.	Velocid 400 mg tablet 1	55	9.12	41.9
Albendazole	Maan Pharmaceuticals Ltd.	Velocid 400 mg tablet 1	52.37	9.12	45.71
Albendazole	Maan Pharmaceuticals Ltd.	Velocid 400 mg tablet 1	52.37	9.12	41.9
Albendazole	Glaxosmithkline Pharmaceuticals Ltd.	Zentel 400 mg tablet 5	184	45.6	140.2
Albendazole	Glaxosmithkline Pharmaceuticals Ltd.	Zentel 400 mg tablet 5	184	45.6	78.6
Albendazole	Ravian Pharmaceuticals Pvt Ltd	Exporm 400 mg tablet 1	27	9.12	6.92
Albendazole	Glaxosmithkline Pharmaceuticals Ltd.	Zentel 400 mg tablet 5	102.7	35.75	78.2
Albendazole	Maneesh Pharmaceuticals Ltd	Goworm 400 mg tablet 1	19.05	7.15	15.24
Albendazole	Morepen Laboratories Limited	Zolbend 400 mg tablet 1	22	9.12	2
Albendazole	Indchemie Health Specialities Pvt. Ltd.	Dispel 400 mg tablet 1	21.5	9.12	16.56
Albendazole	Glaxosmithkline Pharmaceuticals Ltd.	Zentel 400 mg tablet 2	33.32	14.3	26.66
Albendazole	Morepen Laboratories Limited	Zolbend 400 mg tablet 1	22	9.7	1.35
Albendazole	Nestor Pharmaceuticals	Albest 400 mg tablet 1	20.56	9.12	16.45
Albendazole	Shrinivas Gujarat Laboratories Pvt Ltd	Helminex 400 mg tablet 1	16.1	7.15	12.88
Albendazole	Morepen Laboratories Limited	Zolbend 400 mg tablet 1	22	9.92	1.35

(continued)

Table A.2 (continued)

Medicine	Company	SKU	MRP	Ceiling	PTR
Albendazole	Kare Health Specialities Pvt Ltd	Abz (Kare Health) 400 mg tablet 1	19.8	9.12	7.87
Albendazole	Kare Health Specialities Pvt Ltd	Abz (Kare Health) 400 mg tablet 1	19.8	9.12	14.86
Albendazole	Indoco Remedies Ltd	Abz 400 mg tablet 2	39.6	18.24	30.18
Albendazole	Indoco Remedies Ltd	Abz 400 mg tablet 2	39.6	18.24	30.02
Albendazole	Shrinivas Gujarat Laboratories Pvt Ltd	Alvela 400 mg tablet 1	20.95	9.7	16.76
Albendazole	Glaxosmithkline Pharmaceuticals Ltd.	Zentel 400 mg tablet 5	98.25	45.6	78.6
Albendazole	Indchemie Health Specialities Pvt. Ltd.	Dispel 400 mg tablet 1	19.6	9.12	7.86
Albendazole	Indchemie Health Specialities Pvt. Ltd.	Dispel 400 mg tablet 1	19.6	9.12	16.56
Albendazole	Pfizer Ltd	Combantrin A 400 mg tablet 1	15.18	7.15	12.15
Albendazole	Alkem Laboratories Ltd.	Noworm 400 mg tablet 1	19.3	9.12	14.86
Albendazole	Shrinivas Gujarat Laboratories Pvt Ltd	Alvela 400 mg tablet 1	20.95	9.92	16.76
Albendazole	Glaxosmithkline Pharmaceuticals Ltd.	Zentel 400 mg tablet 5	95.8	45.6	78.6
Albendazole	Glaxosmithkline Pharmaceuticals Ltd.	Zentel 400 mg tablet 5	75.1	35.75	57.2
Albendazole	Shrinivas Gujarat Laboratories Pvt Ltd	Albela 400 mg tablet 1	19.15	9.12	14.4
Albendazole	Cipla Ltd.	Tiobend 400 mg tablet 1	15	7.15	2
Albendazole	Glaxosmithkline Pharmaceuticals Ltd.	Zentel 400 mg tablet 5	101.7	48.5	83.5
Albendazole	Alde Medi Impex	Aldezole 400 mg tablet 1	14.93	7.15	11.95
Albendazole	Maneesh Pharmaceuticals Ltd	Goworm 400 mg tablet 1	19.03	9.12	15.23

(continued)

Table A.2 (continued)

Medicine	Company	SKU	MRP	Ceiling	PTR
Albendazole	Almet Corporation Ltd.	Vermanth 400 mg tablet 1	19	9.12	14.63
Albendazole	Shrinivas Gujarat Laboratories Pvt Ltd	Alvela 400 mg tablet 1	18.9	9.12	16.76
Albendazole	Magnum Laboratories Pvt. Ltd.	Allbend 400 mg tablet 1	18.9	9.12	10.6
Albendazole	Shrinivas Gujarat Laboratories Pvt Ltd	Alvela 400 mg tablet 1	18.9	9.12	14.4
Albendazole	Indoco Remedies Ltd	Abz 400 mg tablet 2	37.72	18.24	30.18
Albendazole	Glaxosmithkline Pharmaceuticals Ltd.	Zentel 400 mg tablet 5	105.6	51.5	83.8
Albendazole	Glaxosmithkline Pharmaceuticals Ltd.	Zentel 400 mg tablet 5	101.7	49.6	80.8
Albendazole	Shrinivas Gujarat Laboratories Pvt Ltd	Albela 400 mg tablet 1	18.6	9.12	15.63
Albendazole	Shrinivas Gujarat Laboratories Pvt Ltd	Albela 400 mg tablet 1	18.6	9.12	14.4
Albendazole	Shrinivas Gujarat Laboratories Pvt Ltd	Albela 400 mg tablet 1	18.6	9.12	12.88
Albendazole	Almet Corporation Ltd.	Vermanth 400 mg tablet 1	21	10.3	16.16
Albendazole	Moxy Lab	Thelmin 400 mg tablet 1	18.45	9.12	14.76
Albendazole	Glaxosmithkline Pharmaceuticals Ltd.	Zentel 400 mg tablet 1	18.4	9.12	14.02
Albendazole	Shrinivas Gujarat Laboratories Pvt Ltd	Alvela 400 mg tablet 3	62.32	30.9	49.86
Albendazole	Indoco Remedies Ltd	Olban 400 mg tablet 1	18.3	9.12	7.87
Albendazole	Indoco Remedies Ltd	Olban 400 mg tablet 1	18.3	9.12	14.79
Albendazole	Indoco Remedies Ltd	Olban 400 mg tablet 1	18.3	9.12	14.09
Albendazole	Indoco Remedies Ltd	Olban 400 mg tablet 1	18.3	9.12	7.38
Albendazole	Shrinivas Gujarat Laboratories Pvt Ltd	Albela 400 mg tablet 1	19.44	9.7	14.4

(continued)

Table A.2 (continued)

Medicine	Company	SKU	MRP	Ceiling	PTR
Amitriptyline	Shine Pharmaceuticals Ltd	Shine 25 mg tablet 10	58	21.2	44.19
Amitriptyline	Shine Pharmaceuticals Ltd	Shine 25 mg tablet 10	58	21.2	44.63
Amitriptyline	Shine Pharmaceuticals Ltd	Shine 25 mg tablet 10	58	21.2	33.9
Amitriptyline	Shine Pharmaceuticals Ltd	Shine 25 mg tablet 10	58	22.5	33.9
Amitriptyline	Shine Pharmaceuticals Ltd	Shine 25 mg tablet 10	47.85	21	36.46
Amitriptyline	Shine Pharmaceuticals Ltd	Shine 25 mg tablet 10	46.76	21	37.41
Amlodipine	Ozone Pharmaceuticals	Amlozone 2.5 mg tablet 10	97.32	20.3	77.86
Amlodipine	Serve Pharmaceuticals	Bpc 5 mg tablet 10	100	28.3	8.23
Amlodipine	Emcure Pharmaceuticals Ltd	Numlo 5 mg tablet 10	78.65	23.3	60.55
Amlodipine	Emcure Pharmaceuticals Ltd	Numlo 5 mg tablet 10	78.55	23.3	60.46
Amlodipine	Serve Pharmaceuticals	Bpc 5 mg tablet 10	100	30.1	8.23
Amlodipine	Pfizer Ltd	Amlogard 2.5 mg tablet 10	66	20.3	50.82
Amlodipine	Alkem Laboratories Ltd.	Amlokem 5 mg tablet 10	71.9	23.3	57.52
Amlodipine	Wockhardt Ltd	Myodura 2.5 mg tablet 7	35.42	12.53	28.34
Amlodipine	Wockhardt Ltd	Myodura 5 mg tablet 7	60.46	21.42	48.37
Amlodipine	Pfizer Ltd	Amlogard 5 mg tablet 10	86	30.6	66.21
Amlodipine	Alkem Laboratories Ltd.	Amlogen 5 mg tablet 10	82.76	30.6	66.21
Amlodipine	Pfizer Ltd	Amlogard 5 mg tablet 10	82.76	30.6	26.35
Amlodipine	Wockhardt Ltd	Myodura 2.5 mg tablet 7	35.42	14.21	28.34
Amlodipine	Alkem Laboratories Ltd.	Amlokem 5 mg tablet 10	71.9	31.3	57.52
Amlodipine	Pfizer Ltd	Amlogard 2.5 mg tablet 15	66	30.45	50.82
Amlodipine	Alkem Laboratories Ltd.	Amlokem 5 mg tablet 10	60	28.3	48
Amlodipine	Micro Labs Ltd	Amlong 2.5 mg tablet 10	43	20.3	32.76

(continued)

Table A.2 (continued)

Medicine	Company	SKU	MRP	Ceiling	PTR
Amlodipine	Cipla Ltd.	Amlopres 5 mg tablet 10	49.1	23.3	37.79
Amlodipine	Alkem Laboratories Ltd.	Amlokem 5 mg tablet 10	63	30.1	48
Amlodipine	Pfizer Ltd	Amlogard 2.5 mg tablet 15	63.52	30.45	25.77
Amlodipine	Zydus Cadila	Amlodepin (Zydus) 5 mg tablet 10	58.9	28.3	45.35
Amlodipine	Cipla Ltd.	Amlopres 5 mg tablet 10	47.77	23.3	36.77
Amlodipine	Zydus Cadila	Amlodepin (Zydus) 5 mg tablet 10	56.68	28.3	45.35
Amoxycillin + Clavulanic Acid	Organic Laboratories	Clavoseal 500/125 mg tablet 3	246.1	48.42	196.88
Amoxycillin + Clavulanic Acid	Organic Laboratories	Clavoseal 500/125 mg tablet 3	246.1	74.39999	196.88
Amoxycillin + Clavulanic Acid	United Biotech (P) Ltd	Clavotec 500/125 mg tablet 3	219.5	67.38	135
Amoxycillin + Clavulanic Acid	United Biotech (P) Ltd	Clavotec 500/125 mg tablet 3	219.5	67.38	167.24
Amoxycillin + Clavulanic Acid	Organic Laboratories	Clavoseal 500/125 mg tablet 3	230.18	74.39999	184.15
Amoxycillin + Clavulanic Acid	United Biotech (P) Ltd	Clavotec 500/125 mg tablet 3	219.5	71.64	167.24
Amoxycillin + Clavulanic Acid	Ranbaxy Laboratories Ltd	Moxclav 500/125 mg tablet 6	402.99	134.76	307.05
Amoxycillin + Clavulanic Acid	Cadila Pharmaceuticals Ltd	Symbiotik Xl 500/125 mg tablet Xl 6	260.4	96.84	198.4
Amoxycillin + Clavulanic Acid	Grandcure Healthcare Pvt. Ltd.	Grandmox 500/125 mg tablet 6	260	96.84	198.1
Amoxycillin + Clavulanic Acid	Abbott Healthcare Pvt. Ltd	Amoxyclav 500/125 mg tablet 6	260	96.84	45
Amoxycillin + Clavulanic Acid	Dr. Johns Laboratories Pvt Ltd	Roclav 500/125 mg tablet 6	250.7	96.84	190.48

(continued)

Table A.2 (continued)

Medicine	Company	SKU	MRP	Ceiling	PTR
Amoxycillin + Clavulanic Acid	Marc Pharma	Amoclave 500/125 mg tablet Dt 6	248	96.84	198.4
Amoxycillin + Clavulanic Acid	Wallace Pharmaceuticals Ltd.	Nable A 500/125 mg tablet 6	238.3	96.84	181.56
Amoxycillin + Clavulanic Acid	Dr. Johns Laboratories Pvt Ltd	Roclav 500/125 mg tablet 6	238.1	96.84	190.48
Amoxycillin + Clavulanic Acid	Dr. Johns Laboratories Pvt Ltd	Roclav 500/125 mg tablet 6	237.63	96.84	190.11
Amoxycillin + Clavulanic Acid	United Biotech (P) Ltd	Clavox (United) 500/125 mg tablet 4	219.5	89.84	167.24
Amoxycillin + Clavulanic Acid	Algen Healthcare Pvt Ltd	Fmclav 500/125 mg tablet 6	235	96.84	179.05
Amoxycillin + Clavulanic Acid	United Biotech (P) Ltd	Clavox (United) 500/125 mg tablet 4	209.05	89.84	167.24
Amoxycillin + Clavulanic Acid	United Biotech (P) Ltd	Clavox (United) 500/125 mg tablet 4	149.9	64.56	120
Amoxycillin + Clavulanic Acid	Algen Healthcare Pvt Ltd	Fmclav 500/125 mg tablet 6	223.81	96.84	179.05
Amoxycillin + Clavulanic Acid	Dr. Johns Laboratories Pvt Ltd	Jonclav 500/125 mg tablet 6	223.81	96.84	179.05
Amoxycillin + Clavulanic Acid	Dr. Johns Laboratories Pvt Ltd	Jonclav 500/125 mg tablet 6	222.75	96.84	178.2
Amoxycillin + Clavulanic Acid	United Biotech (P) Ltd	Clavox (United) 500/125 mg tablet 4	219.5	95.52	167.24
Amoxycillin + Clavulanic Acid	Unichem Laboratories Ltd	Myclav 500/125 mg tablet 6	220.49	96.84	181.03
Amoxycillin + Clavulanic Acid	Micro Labs Ltd	Hexamentin 500/125 mg tablet 6	325	143.28	260
Amoxycillin + Clavulanic Acid	Healall Pharma India Pvt. Ltd.	Hiclav 500/125 mg tablet 10	355.1	161.4	284.08
Amoxycillin + Clavulanic Acid	United Biotech (P) Ltd	Clavox (United) 500/125 mg tablet 4	209.05	95.52	167.24

(continued)

Table A.2 (continued)

Medicine	Company	SKU	MRP	Ceiling	PTR
Amoxycillin + Clavulanic Acid	Indswift Laboratories Ltd.	Topclav 500/125 mg tablet 4	193.8	89.84	148.39
Amoxycillin + Clavulanic Acid	Ritz Pharma	Moxiz Cv 500/125 mg tablet 10	347.5	161.4	278
Amoxycillin + Clavulanic Acid	United Biotech (P) Ltd	Clavox (United) 500/125 mg tablet 4	209.05	99.2	167.24
Amoxycillin + Clavulanic Acid	Nitin Pharmaceuticals	N Clav 500/125 mg tablet 6	203.93	96.84	163.15
Amoxycillin + Clavulanic Acid	Zydus Cadila	Augmed 500/125 mg tablet 6	307.68	148.8	246.15
Amoxycillin + Clavulanic Acid	Indswift Laboratories Ltd.	Topclav 500/125 mg tablet 4	185.48	89.84	148.33
Amoxycillin + Clavulanic Acid	Indswift Laboratories Ltd.	Topclav 500/125 mg tablet 4	185.48	89.84	148.39
Amoxycillin + Clavulanic Acid	Indswift Laboratories Ltd.	Topclav 500/125 mg tablet 4	185.41	89.84	148.33
Amoxycillin + Clavulanic Acid	Dr. Johns Laboratories Pvt Ltd	Roclav 500/125 mg tablet 6	274.9	134.76	178.88
Amoxycillin + Clavulanic Acid	Dr. Johns Laboratories Pvt Ltd	Roclav 500/125 mg tablet 6	274.9	134.76	209.45
Amoxycillin + Clavulanic Acid	Dr. Johns Laboratories Pvt Ltd	Roclav 500/125 mg tablet 6	274.9	134.76	178.2
Amoxycillin + Clavulanic Acid	Dr. Johns Laboratories Pvt Ltd	Jonclav 500/125 mg tablet 6	274.83	134.76	208.4
Amoxycillin + Clavulanic Acid	Dr. Johns Laboratories Pvt Ltd	Jonclav 500/125 mg tablet 6	274.83	134.76	219.86
Amoxycillin + Clavulanic Acid	Dr. Johns Laboratories Pvt Ltd	Jonclav 500/125 mg tablet 6	274.82	134.76	219.86
Amoxycillin + Clavulanic Acid	Sh Pharmaceuticals Ltd	Kokkos Clav 500/125 mg tablet 6	195	96.84	148.57
Amoxycillin + Clavulanic Acid	Lark Laboratories Ltd	Clavimox 500/125 mg tablet 6	271	134.76	100.04

(continued)

Table A.2 (continued)

Medicine	Company	SKU	MRP	Ceiling	PTR
Atenolol	Torrent Pharmaceuticals Ltd.	Betacard 50 mg tablet Xl 10	46	20.7	35.05
Atenolol	Torrent Pharmaceuticals Ltd.	Betacard 50 mg tablet Xl 10	46	20.7	24.98
Atenolol	Ipca Laboratories Pvt Ltd.	Teno 50 mg tablet 10	44.15	20.7	33.64
Atenolol	Ipca Laboratories Pvt Ltd.	Teno 50 mg tablet 10	44.15	20.7	25.06
Atenolol	Zydus Cadila	Catenol 50 mg tablet 10	43.9	20.7	33.8
Atenolol	Zydus Cadila	Catenol 50 mg tablet 10	43.9	20.7	33.47
Atenolol	Psychotropics India Ltd	Etopress 50 mg tablet 14	47.2	23.24	37.76
Atenolol	Ipca Laboratories Pvt Ltd.	Teno 50 mg tablet 10	33.55	16.6	26.62
Atenolol	Abbott Healthcare Pvt. Ltd	Tenormin 50 mg tablet 14	58.25	28.98	44.38
Atorvastatin	Orchid Chemicals & Pharmaceuticals Ltd	Avastin 10 mg tablet 10	28022	64.89999	39.98
Atorvastatin	Premier Nutraceuticals Pvt Ltd	Atorsyn 10 mg tablet 10	199	64.89999	42.51
Atorvastatin	Alembic Ltd	Eternex 10 mg tablet 10	147.5	50.9	118
Atorvastatin	Cadila Pharmaceuticals Ltd	Caditor 10 mg tablet 10	129.52	50.9	104.45
Atorvastatin	Indoco Remedies Ltd	Atherochek 10 mg tablet 10	126.3	50.9	96.76
Atorvastatin	Ordain Healthcare Pvt. Ltd	Nustat 10 mg tablet 10	145	59.1	47.67
Atorvastatin	Ordain Healthcare Pvt. Ltd	Nustat 10 mg tablet 10	145	59.1	60.74
Atorvastatin	Ordain Healthcare Pvt. Ltd	Nustat 10 mg tablet 10	145	62.8	47.67
Atorvastatin	Indoco Remedies Ltd	Atherochek 10 mg tablet 10	114.87	50.9	88.42
Atorvastatin	Ordain Healthcare Pvt. Ltd	Nustat 10 mg tablet 10	145	64.89999	47.67
Atorvastatin	Cure Quick Pharmaceuticals	Cholat 10 mg tablet 10	130	59.1	104
Atorvastatin	Cure Quick Pharmaceuticals	Cholat 10 mg tablet 10	130	59.1	94.35
Atorvastatin	Cadila Pharmaceuticals Ltd	Caditor 10 mg tablet 10	122.82	59.1	98.26

(continued)

Table A.2 (continued)

Medicine	Company	SKU	MRP	Ceiling	PTR
Atorvastatin	Cadila Pharma-ceuticals Ltd	Caditor 10 mg tablet 10	122.82	59.1	93.82
Atorvastatin	Cure Quick Pharmaceuticals	Cholat 10 mg tablet 10	130	62.8	94.35
Atorvastatin	Cure Quick Pharmaceuticals	Cholat 10 mg tablet 10	130	64.89999	94.35
Azathioprine	Zydus Cadila	Zymurine 50 mg tablet 4	93.48	36.08	74.79
Azathioprine	Zydus Cadila	Zymurine 50 mg tablet 4	93.48	43.68	74.79
Azathioprine	Zydus Cadila	Zymurine 50 mg tablet 4	90.97	43.68	72.78
Azithromycin	Seagull Labs (I) Ltd	Azimacro 500 mg tablet 3	240	59.58	45.44
Azithromycin	Seagull Labs (I) Ltd	Azimacro 500 mg tablet 3	240	61.53	45.44
Azithromycin	Cadila Pharma-ceuticals Ltd	Zycin(Cadila) 500 mg tablet 1	68.71	17.83	54.97
Azithromycin	Cadila Pharma-ceuticals Ltd	Zycin(Cadila) 500 mg tablet 1	68.56	17.83	54.85
Azithromycin	Salud Care (I) Pvt Ltd	Azito 500 mg tablet 3	220	59.58	167.62
Azithromycin	Salud Care (I) Pvt Ltd	Azito 500 mg tablet 3	210.51	59.58	168.41
Azithromycin	Salud Care (I) Pvt Ltd	Azito 500 mg tablet 3	209.52	59.58	167.62
Azithromycin	Salud Care (I) Pvt Ltd	Azito 500 mg tablet 3	208.53	59.58	167.64
Azithromycin	Salud Care (I) Pvt Ltd	Azito 500 mg tablet 3	209.55	61.53	166.82
Azithromycin	Salud Care (I) Pvt Ltd	Azito 500 mg tablet 3	209.55	61.53	167.64
Azithromycin	Salud Care (I) Pvt Ltd	Azito 500 mg tablet 3	208.53	61.53	166.82
Azithromycin	Salud Care (I) Pvt Ltd	Azito 500 mg tablet 3	208.52	61.53	166.82
Azithromycin	Cadila Pharma-ceuticals Ltd	Zycin(Cadila) 500 mg tablet 1	71.83	22.65	57.47
Azithromycin	Cadila Pharma-ceuticals Ltd	Zycin(Cadila) 500 mg tablet 1	71.81	22.65	57.45
Azithromycin	Cadila Pharma-ceuticals Ltd	Zycin(Cadila) 500 mg tablet 1	69.27	22.65	55.39
Azithromycin	Graf Laboratories Pvt Ltd	Zicin 500 mg tablet 3	200	65.43	46.48
Azithromycin	Cadila Pharma-ceuticals Ltd	Zycin(Cadila) 500 mg tablet 1	69.23	22.65	55.39

(continued)

Table A.2 (continued)

Medicine	Company	SKU	MRP	Ceiling	PTR
Azithromycin	Ipca Laboratories Pvt Ltd.	Azifast 250 mg tablet 3	71.47	27.18	57.18
Azithromycin	Zuventus Healthcare Ltd	Azitus 250 mg tablet 3	71	27.18	54.65
Azithromycin	Cadila Pharma-ceuticals Ltd	Zycin(Cdl) 250 mg tablet 3	84.1	32.73	63.71
Azithromycin	Ipca Laboratories Pvt Ltd.	Azifast 250 mg tablet 3	78.6	30.78	59.89
Azithromycin	Ipca Laboratories Pvt Ltd.	Azifast 250 mg tablet 3	78	30.78	59.89
Azithromycin	Cadila Pharma-ceuticals Ltd	Zycin(Cdl) 250 mg tablet 3	82.75	32.73	63.71
Azithromycin	Cadila Pharma-ceuticals Ltd	Zycin(Cdl) 250 mg tablet 3	68.6	27.18	54.88
Azithromycin	Zuventus Healthcare Ltd	Azitus 250 mg tablet 3	77	30.78	49.74
Azithromycin	Zuventus Healthcare Ltd	Azitus 250 mg tablet 3	77	30.78	59.71
Azithromycin	Zuventus Healthcare Ltd	Azitus 250 mg tablet 3	77	30.78	53.03
Azithromycin	Cadila Pharma-ceuticals Ltd	Zycin(Cdl) 250 mg tablet 3	79.63	32.73	63.71
Azithromycin	Ipca Laboratories Pvt Ltd.	Azifast 250 mg tablet 3	74.86	30.78	59.89
Azithromycin	Ipca Laboratories Pvt Ltd.	Azifast 250 mg tablet 3	78	32.73	59.89
Azithromycin	Zuventus Healthcare Ltd	Azitus 250 mg tablet 3	77	32.73	52.74
Azithromycin	Jb Chemicals	Azicyte 250 mg tablet 3	62.56	27.18	50.05
Azithromycin	Rkm Health Care	Azisym 250 mg tablet 10	230	102.6	181.7
Azithromycin	Rkm Health Care	Azisym 250 mg tablet 10	230	102.6	184
Azithromycin	Wockhardt Ltd	Aziwok 500 mg tablet 3	118.91	53.49	91.52
Azithromycin	Zuventus Healthcare Ltd	Azitus 250 mg tablet 3	66.63	30.78	53.31
Azithromycin	Alembic Ltd	Azithral 500 mg tablet 3	115.7	53.49	89.05
Azithromycin	Ipca Laboratories Pvt Ltd.	Azifast 250 mg tablet 3	72.38	33.99	57.91
Azithromycin	Rowan Bioteuticals (P) Ltd	Avitla 250 mg tablet 6	138.86	65.46	102.86
Azithromycin	Rkm Health Care	Azisym 250 mg tablet 10	230	109.1	184

(continued)

Table A.2 (continued)

Medicine	Company	SKU	MRP	Ceiling	PTR
Azithromycin	Ipca Laboratories Pvt Ltd.	Azifast 250 mg tablet 3	68.87	32.73	51.44
Azithromycin	Ipca Laboratories Pvt Ltd.	Azifast 250 mg tablet 3	71.47	33.99	57.18
Azithromycin	Ipca Laboratories Pvt Ltd.	Azifast 250 mg tablet 3	71.45	33.99	57.16
Azithromycin	Zuventus Healthcare Ltd	Azitus 250 mg tablet 3	57.05	27.18	43.91
Azithromycin	Zuventus Healthcare Ltd	Azitus 250 mg tablet 3	57.05	27.18	43.92
Azithromycin	Zuventus Healthcare Ltd	Azitus 250 mg tablet 3	64.6	30.78	49.74
Azithromycin	Cadila Pharmaceuticals Ltd	Zycin(Cdl) 250 mg tablet 3	68.6	32.73	54.88
Azithromycin	Zuventus Healthcare Ltd	Azitus 250 mg tablet 3	68.5	32.73	52.74
Azithromycin	Zuventus Healthcare Ltd	Azitus 250 mg tablet 3	71	33.99	54.65
Azithromycin	Rowan Bioteuticals (P) Ltd	Avitla 250 mg tablet 6	135	65.46	77.71
Azithromycin	Rowan Bioteuticals (P) Ltd	Avitla 250 mg tablet 6	135	65.46	77.53
Azithromycin	Salud Care (I) Pvt Ltd	Azito 250 mg tablet 6	125	61.56	95.24
Azithromycin	Zuventus Healthcare Ltd	Azitus 250 mg tablet 3	68.5	33.99	52.75
Azithromycin	Zuventus Healthcare Ltd	Azitus 250 mg tablet 3	68.5	33.99	52.74
Bisacodyl	Psychotropics India Ltd	Bisomer 5 mg tablet 10	60	10.3	3.46
Bisacodyl	Shreya Life Sciences Pvt. Ltd	Julax 5 mg tablet 10	31.05	9.3	23.66
Bisacodyl	Shreya Life Sciences Pvt. Ltd	Julax 5 mg tablet 10	31.05	10.7	23.66
Bisacodyl	Shreya Life Sciences Pvt. Ltd	Julax 5 mg tablet 10	28.36	10.3	21.61
Bisacodyl	Shreya Life Sciences Pvt. Ltd	Julax 5 mg tablet 10	25.9	9.700001	19.73
Bisacodyl	Shreya Life Sciences Pvt. Ltd	Julax 5 mg tablet 10	28.36	10.7	21.61
Bisacodyl	Shreya Life Sciences Pvt. Ltd	Julax 5 mg tablet 10	25.9	10.3	21.61
Bisacodyl	Shreya Life Sciences Pvt. Ltd	Julax 5 mg tablet 10	25.9	10.3	19.73

(continued)

Table A.2 (continued)

Medicine	Company	SKU	MRP	Ceiling	PTR
Bisacodyl	Shreya Life Sciences Pvt. Ltd	Julax 5 mg tablet 10	23.58	9.700001	17.97
Bisacodyl	Shreya Life Sciences Pvt. Ltd	Julax 5 mg tablet 10	23.58	9.700001	19.73
Carbamazepine	Crescent Formulations Pvt. Ltd.	Zigma 100 mg tablet 10	45	7.4	5.91
Carbamazepine	Talent Healthcare	Epilent 200 mg tablet 10	79.5	14.6	34.88
Carbamazepine	Talent Healthcare	Epilent 200 mg tablet 10	49.5	14.6	34.88
Carbamazepine	Talent Healthcare	Epilent 200 mg tablet 10	41.52	14.6	34.88
Carbamazepine	Talent Healthcare	Epilent 200 mg tablet 10	41.52	15.2	34.88
Carbamazepine	Intas Pharmaceuticals Ltd	Zen Retard 100 mg tablet 10	20.4	7.7	17.14
Carbamazepine	Intas Pharmaceuticals Ltd	Zen Retard 100 mg tablet 10	18.63	7.4	15.65
Carbamazepine	Tas Med (India) Private Ltd.	Epilep 200 mg tablet 10	31.51	12.8	26.47
Carbamazepine	Talent Healthcare	Epilent 200 mg tablet 10	31.34	12.8	26.33
Carbamazepine	Intas Pharmaceuticals Ltd	Zen Retard 100 mg tablet 10	18.63	7.7	15.65
Carbamazepine	Tas Med (India) Private Ltd.	Epilep 200 mg tablet 10	31.51	13.7	26.47
Carbamazepine	Talent Healthcare	Epilent 200 mg tablet 10	32.23	14.4	27.08
Carbamazepine	Tas Med (India) Private Ltd.	Epilep 200 mg tablet 10	31.51	14.4	26.47
Carbamazepine	Talent Healthcare	Epilent 200 mg tablet 10	31.34	14.4	26.33
Carbamazepine	Tas Med (India) Private Ltd.	Epilep 200 mg tablet 10	31.51	14.6	26.47
Carbamazepine	Talent Healthcare	Epilent 200 mg tablet 10	32.23	15.2	27.08
Carbamazepine	Tas Med (India) Private Ltd.	Epilep 200 mg tablet 10	31.51	15.2	26.47
Carbamazepine	Novartis India Ltd	Tegrital Cr 200 mg tablet 10	25.81	12.8	19.87
Carbimazole	Abbott India Ltd.	Thyrocab 10 mg tablet 60	428	205.8	326.1
Cefixime	Troikaa Pharmaceuticals Ltd	Zim 200 mg tablet 10	1126.73	84.8	901.39
Cefixime	Unicure India Pvt Ltd	Fiximo 200 mg tablet 4	284.7	47.84	66.6

(continued)

Table A.2 (continued)

Medicine	Company	SKU	MRP	Ceiling	PTR
Cefixime	Unicure India Pvt Ltd	Fiximo 200 mg tablet 4	260	45	65
Cefixime	Unicure India Pvt Ltd	Fiximo 200 mg tablet 4	260	45	64.4
Cefixime	Unicure India Pvt Ltd	Fiximo 200 mg tablet 4	260	47.84	66.6
Cefixime	Unicure India Pvt Ltd	Fiximo 200 mg tablet 4	260	47.84	65
Cefixime	Indoco Remedies Ltd	Vexim 200 mg tablet 4	196	45	112.9
Cefixime	Indoco Remedies Ltd	Vexim 200 mg tablet 4	196	45	160.79
Cefixime	Cipla Ltd.	Cefix 200 mg tablet 4	192.5	45	39
Cefixime	Indoco Remedies Ltd	Vexim 200 mg tablet 4	196	47.84	160.79
Cefixime	Trident Pharmaceuticals	Cixi 200 mg tab-let 4	132.75	33.92	106.2
Cefixime	Cipla Ltd.	Cefix 200 mg tablet 4	130.33	33.92	45
Cefixime	Reliance Formula-tion Pvt Ltd	Efoxim 200 mg tablet 4	172.07	45	137.66
Cefixime	Reliance Formula-tion Pvt Ltd	Efoxim 200 mg tablet 4	172.07	45	71.31
Cefixime	Kee Pharma	Axim-O 200 mg tablet 4	180	47.84	88
Cefixime	Micro Labs Ltd	Rite O Cef 200 mg tablet 4	122.15	33.92	97.72
Cefixime	Reliance Formula-tion Pvt Ltd	Efoxim 200 mg tablet 4	172.07	47.84	137.66
Cefixime	Leo Pharmaceuticals	Cefilife 200 mg tablet 4	115.21	33.92	92.17
Cefixime	Divine Lifecare Pvt Ltd	Oxim 200 mg tablet 4	112.37	33.92	89.9
Cefixime	Cachet Pharma-ceuticals Pvt Ltd	Traxol O 200 mg tablet 4	111.33	33.92	89.07
Cefixime	Cachet Pharma-ceuticals Pvt Ltd	Traxol O 200 mg tablet 4	108.33	33.92	86.67
Cefixime	Trident Pharmaceuticals	Cixi 200 mg tab-let 4	141.25	45	106.2
Cefixime	Rkm Health Care	R Cefi 200 mg tablet 10	264	84.8	160
Cefixime	Indica Laborato-ries Pvt. Ltd.	Cf Xim 200 mg tablet 4	105	33.92	84
Cefixime	Trident Pharmaceuticals	Cixi 200 mg tab-let 4	134.87	45	106.2

(continued)

Table A.2 (continued)

Medicine	Company	SKU	MRP	Ceiling	PTR
Cefixime	Trident Pharmaceuticals	Cixi 200 mg tablet 4	143.37	47.84	106.2
Cefixime	Trident Pharmaceuticals	Cixi 200 mg tablet 4	132.75	45	106.2
Cefixime	Trident Pharmaceuticals	Cixi 200 mg tablet 4	140.18	47.84	106.2
Cefixime	Trident Pharmaceuticals	Cixi 200 mg tablet 4	130.63	45	106.2
Cefixime	Indswift Laboratories Ltd.	Agicef 200 mg tablet 10	245	84.8	32.4
Cefixime	Divine Lifecare Pvt Ltd	Oxim 200 mg tablet 4	130	45	89.9
Cefixime	Divine Lifecare Pvt Ltd	Oxim 200 mg tablet 4	130	45	99.05
Cefixime	Calibar Pharmaceuticals	Safix 200 mg tablet Dt 4	130	45	100.1
Cefixime	Calibar Pharmaceuticals	Safix 200 mg tablet Dt 4	125.12	45	90.86
Cefixime	Calibar Pharmaceuticals	Safix 200 mg tablet Dt 4	125.12	45	100.1
Cefixime	Trident Pharmaceuticals	Cixi 200 mg tablet 4	132.75	47.84	106.2
Cefixime	Trident Pharmaceuticals	Cixi 200 mg tablet 4	132.75	49.68	106.2
Cefixime	Dial Pharmaceuticals Pvt. Ltd.	Maxi D 200 mg tablet 4	120	45	69.63
Cefixime	Dial Pharmaceuticals Pvt. Ltd.	Maxi D 200 mg tablet 4	120	45	93.71
Cefixime	Cipla Ltd.	Cefix 200 mg tablet 4	118.13	45	39
Cefixime	Cipla Ltd.	Cefix 200 mg tablet 4	118.13	45	37.94
Cefixime	Cipla Ltd.	Cefix 200 mg tablet 4	89.04	33.92	45
Cefixime	Medley Pharmaceuticals	Cefo (Medley) 200 mg tablet 4	89	33.92	68.52
Cefixime	Cipla Ltd.	Cefix 200 mg tablet 4	125.51	47.84	39
Cefixime	Cipla Ltd.	Cefix 200 mg tablet 4	125.51	47.84	40
Cefixime	Cipla Ltd.	Cefix 200 mg tablet 4	125.51	47.84	38.5
Cefixime	Cipla Ltd.	Cefix 200 mg tablet 4	130.33	49.68	42
Cefixime	Dial Pharmaceuticals Pvt. Ltd.	Maxi D 200 mg tablet 4	118	45	91.71

(continued)

Table A.2 (continued)

Medicine	Company	SKU	MRP	Ceiling	PTR
Cefixime	Dial Pharmaceuticals Pvt. Ltd.	Maxi D 200 mg tablet 4	117.13	45	93.71
Cefixime	Dial Pharmaceuticals Pvt. Ltd.	Maxi D 200 mg tablet 4	117.13	45	91.71
Cefixime	Dial Pharmaceuticals Pvt. Ltd.	Maxi D 200 mg tablet 4	123.81	47.84	91.71
Cefixime	Micro Labs Ltd	Rite O Cef 200 mg tablet 4	122.25	47.84	94.13
Cefixime	Cipla Ltd.	Cefix 200 mg tablet 4	125.51	49.68	40
Cefixime	Cipla Ltd.	Cefix 200 mg tablet 4	125.51	49.68	42
Cefixime	Cipla Ltd.	Cefix 200 mg tablet 4	125.51	49.68	41.63
Cefixime	Abbott Healthcare Pvt. Ltd	Cefi Od (Npil) 200 mg tablet 5	104.8	42.4	83.84
Cefixime	Cipla Ltd.	Cefix 200 mg tablet 4	118.13	47.84	39
Cefixime	Cipla Ltd.	Cefix 200 mg tablet 4	118.13	47.84	40
Cefixime	Cipla Ltd.	Cefix 200 mg tablet 4	118.13	47.84	37.94
Cefixime	Cipla Ltd.	Cefix 200 mg tablet 4	118.13	47.84	31.67
Cefixime	Alembic Ltd	Cifadin 200 mg tablet 4	118.1	47.84	45
Cefixime	Divine Lifecare Pvt Ltd	Oxim 200 mg tablet 4	118	47.84	89.9
Cefixime	Dial Pharmaceuticals Pvt. Ltd.	Maxi D 200 mg tablet 4	118	47.84	91.71
Cefixime	Micro Labs Ltd	Rite O Cef 200 mg tablet 4	117.66	47.84	94.13
Cefixime	Micro Labs Ltd	Rite O Cef 200 mg tablet 4	122.18	49.68	97.75
Cefixime	Micro Labs Ltd	Rite O Cef 200 mg tablet 4	110.67	45	88.54
Cefixime	Micro Labs Ltd	Rite O Cef 200 mg tablet 4	122.15	49.68	97.72
Cefixime	Trident Pharmaceuticals	Cixi 200 mg tablet 4	108.25	45	106.2
Cefixime	Unicure India Pvt Ltd	Fiximo 200 mg tablet 4	81.25	33.92	65
Cefixime	Vhb Life Sciences Inc	Focimel 200 mg tablet 10	200.9	84.8	160.72
Cefixime	Micro Labs Ltd	Rite O Cef 200 mg tablet 4	117.67	49.68	94.14

(continued)

Table A.2 (continued)

Medicine	Company	SKU	MRP	Ceiling	PTR
Cefixime	Micro Labs Ltd	Rite O Cef 200 mg tablet 4	117.66	49.68	94.13
Cefixime	Cachet Pharmaceuticals Pvt Ltd	Traxol O 200 mg tablet 4	105.9	45	81.39
Cefixime	Cachet Pharmaceuticals Pvt Ltd	Traxol O 200 mg tablet 4	105.9	45	73.35
Cefixime	Divine Lifecare Pvt Ltd	Oxim 200 mg tablet 4	112.37	47.84	89.9
Cefixime	Rkm Health Care	R Cefi 200 mg tablet 10	264	112.5	160
Cefixime	Indica Laboratories Pvt. Ltd.	Cf Xim 200 mg tablet 4	105	45	67.81
Cefixime	Indica Laboratories Pvt. Ltd.	Cf Xim 200 mg tablet 4	105	45	84
Cefixime	Leo Pharmaceuticals	Cefilife 200 mg tablet 4	115.21	49.68	92.17
Cefixime	Micro Labs Ltd	Rite O Cef 200 mg tablet 4	110.67	47.84	88.54
Cefixime	Apex Laboratories Ltd.	Nufix 200 mg tablet 10	195	84.8	156
Cefixime	Kee Pharma	Axim-O 200 mg tablet 4	110	47.84	88
Cefixime	Indswift Laboratories Ltd.	Excef 200 mg tablet 4	102	45	86.55
Cefixime	Neuron Pharma (P) Ltd	Nurocef 200 mg tablet 6	115	50.88	87.62
Cefixime	Cachet Pharmaceuticals Pvt Ltd	Traxol O 200 mg tablet 4	111.33	49.68	89.07
Cefixime	Lupin Ltd	Lupicef-O 200 mg tablet 10	250	112.5	79.38
Cefixime	Lupin Ltd	Ximeceff 200 mg tablet 10	250	112.5	70
Cefixime	Elder Pharmaceuticals Ltd	Zoftax O 200 mg tablet Dt 10	250	112.5	60
Cefixime	Cachet Pharmaceuticals Pvt Ltd	Traxol O 200 mg tablet 4	99.8	45	73.35
Cefixime	Cachet Pharmaceuticals Pvt Ltd	Traxol O 200 mg tablet 6	112.31	50.88	89.85
Cefixime	Indica Laboratories Pvt. Ltd.	Cf Xim 200 mg tablet 4	105	47.84	84
Cefixime	Mapra Laboratories Pvt. Ltd	Taxone O 200 mg tablet 6	109.88	50.88	84.58
Cefixime	Cachet Pharmaceuticals Pvt Ltd	Traxol O 200 mg tablet 4	105.9	49.68	81.39
Cefixime	Cachet Pharmaceuticals Pvt Ltd	Traxol O 200 mg tablet 6	108.33	50.88	86.67

(continued)

Table A.2 (continued)

Medicine	Company	SKU	MRP	Ceiling	PTR
Cefixime	Regalia Pharmaceuticals (I) Pvt Ltd	Receft O 200 mg tablet 10	180	84.8	144
Cefixime	Indica Laboratories Pvt. Ltd.	Cf Xim 200 mg tablet 4	105	49.68	84
Cefixime	Lupin Ltd	Ximeceff 200 mg tablet 10	250	119.6	70
Cefixime	Lupin Ltd	Lupicef-O 200 mg tablet 10	250	119.6	79.38
Cefixime	Zydus Cadila	Raxim O 200 mg tablet 10	235	112.5	40
Cefixime	Zydus Cadila	Raxim O 200 mg tablet 10	235	112.5	188
Cefixime	Zydus Cadila	Ceefix 200 mg tablet 10 X 10	235	112.5	45
Cefixime	Psychotropics India Ltd	Omnapil 200 mg tablet 10	235	112.5	39
Cefixime	Zydus Cadila	Ceefix 200 mg tablet 10 X 10	235	112.5	55
Cefixime	United Biotech (P) Ltd	U Fixim 200 mg tablet 4	98.81	47.84	79.05
Cefixime	Southshourne Corporation(India)	Oncef 200 mg tablet Dt 10	174.63	84.8	139.71
Cefixime	Cachet Pharmaceuticals Pvt Ltd	Traxol O 200 mg tablet 4	101.92	49.68	81.54
Cefixime	United Biotech (P) Ltd	U Fixim 200 mg tablet 4	98	47.84	79.05
Cefixime	Cachet Pharmaceuticals Pvt Ltd	Traxol O 200 mg tablet 4	101.73	49.68	81.39
Cefixime	Cachet Pharmaceuticals Pvt Ltd	Traxol O 200 mg tablet 4	91.68	45	73.35
Cefixime	Pfizer Ltd	Vibazime 200 mg tablet Dt 7	119	59.36	90.66
Cefixime	Pfizer Ltd	Vibazime 200 mg tablet Dt 7	119	59.36	91.59
Cetirizine	Serve Pharmaceuticals	Cetree 10 mg tablet 10	216	18.1	7.99
Cetirizine	Shrinivas Gujarat Laboratories Pvt Ltd	Ceday (Hiquem Lab) 10 mg tablet 10	130	18.1	12.58
Cetirizine	Shrinivas Gujarat Laboratories Pvt Ltd	Ceday (Hiquem Lab) 10 mg tablet 10	130	18.1	14.5
Cetirizine	Shrinivas Gujarat Laboratories Pvt Ltd	Ceday (Hiquem Lab) 10 mg tablet 10	130	19.2	14.5

(continued)

Table A.2 (continued)

Medicine	Company	SKU	MRP	Ceiling	PTR
Cetirizine	Shrinivas Gujarat Laboratories Pvt Ltd	Ceday (Hiquem Lab) 10 mg tablet 10	130	19.2	14.48
Cetirizine	Intas Pharmaceuticals Ltd	Intazin 10 mg tablet 10	125.5	19.2	1.6
Cetirizine	Ramose Laboratories Pvt. Ltd.	Suhit Cold 10 mg tablet 10	49	19.9	38.88
Cetirizine	Ramose Laboratories Pvt. Ltd.	Suhit Cold 10 mg tablet 10	49	19.9	38.89
Cetirizine	Ramose Laboratories Pvt. Ltd.	Suhit Cold 10 mg tablet 10	48.61	19.9	38.89
Cetirizine	Ramose Laboratories Pvt. Ltd.	Suhit Cold 10 mg tablet 10	48.6	19.9	38.88
Cetirizine	Sun Pharma Laboratories Ltd.	Cetrizet 10 mg tablet 10	44	18.1	33.88
Cetirizine	Cipla Ltd.	Alerid 10 mg tablet 10	43	18.1	32.76
Cetirizine	Glaxosmithkline Pharmaceuticals Ltd.	Cetzine 10 mg tablet 100	357.12	153	285.7
Cetirizine	Jenburkt Pharmaceuticals Ltd	Allerzine 10 mg tablet 10	35	15.3	26.67
Cetirizine	Alkem Laboratories Ltd.	Cetiriz 10 mg tablet 10	41.25	18.1	15.61
Cetirizine	Alkem Laboratories Ltd.	Cetiriz 10 mg tablet 10	41.25	18.1	31.76
Cetirizine	Indoco Remedies Ltd	Triz 10 mg tablet 10	39.5	18.1	30.41
Cetirizine	Indoco Remedies Ltd	Triz 10 mg tablet 10	38.01	18.1	15.61
Cetirizine	Cipla Ltd.	Cetcip 10 mg tablet 10	38	18.1	2.35
Cetirizine	Unichem Laboratories Ltd	Zyncet 10 mg tablet 10	38	18.1	28.96
Cetirizine	Cipla Ltd.	Cetcip 10 mg tablet 10	38	18.1	3
Cetirizine	Cipla Ltd.	Cetcip 10 mg tablet 10	38	18.1	2.5
Cetirizine	Cipla Ltd.	Cetcip 10 mg tablet 10	38	18.1	2.25
Cetirizine	An Pharmaceuticals Pvt.Ltd.	Anzin 10 mg tablet 10	32	15.3	24.46
Cetirizine	Cadila Pharmaceuticals Ltd	Cetrizine (Cadila Pharma) 10 mg tablet 10	40	19.2	1.61

(continued)

Table A.2 (continued)

Medicine	Company	SKU	MRP	Ceiling	PTR
Cetirizine	Glaxosmithkline Pharmaceuticals Ltd.	Cetzine 10 mg tablet 10	37.5	18.1	28.57
Cetirizine	Glaxosmithkline Pharmaceuticals Ltd.	Cetzine 10 mg tablet 100	375	181	285.7
Cetirizine	Glaxosmithkline Pharmaceuticals Ltd.	Cetzine 10 mg tablet 100	375	181	156
Cetirizine	Dr. Reddys Laboratories Ltd	Zyrtec 10 mg tablet 10	37.3	18.1	28.72
Cetirizine	Ranbaxy Laboratories Ltd	Hisnofil 10 mg tablet 10	36.92	18.1	29.54
Cetirizine	Bayer Pharmaceuticals Pvt. Ltd.	Incid L 10 mg tablet 10	36.72	18.1	27.98
Cetirizine	Bayer Pharmaceuticals Pvt. Ltd.	Incid L 10 mg tablet 10	36.72	18.1	15.2
Cetirizine	Micro Labs Ltd	Allercet 10 mg tablet 10	36.5	18.1	27.81
Cetirizine	Micro Labs Ltd	Allercet 10 mg tablet 10	36.5	18.1	29.71
Chlorpheniramine	Inga Laboratories Pvt. Ltd.	Ingahist 4 mg tablet 10	27.85	0.8514	22.35
Chlorpheniramine	Inga Laboratories Pvt. Ltd.	Ingahist 4 mg tablet 10	29.5	1	22.72
Chlorpheniramine	Inga Laboratories Pvt. Ltd.	Ingahist 4 mg tablet 10	29.5	1.1	23.12
Chlorpheniramine	Inga Laboratories Pvt. Ltd.	Ingahist 4 mg tablet 10	29.5	1.1	22.72
Chlorpheniramine	Inga Laboratories Pvt. Ltd.	Ingahist 4 mg tablet 10	28.66	1.1	23.12
Chlorpheniramine	Inga Laboratories Pvt. Ltd.	Ingahist 4 mg tablet 10	28.66	1.1423	23.12
Chlorpheniramine	Inga Laboratories Pvt. Ltd.	Ingahist 4 mg tablet 10	28.66	1.1423	23.11
Chlorpheniramine	Inga Laboratories Pvt. Ltd.	Ingahist 4 mg tablet 10	28.66	1.1423	23.08
Chlorpheniramine	Inga Laboratories Pvt. Ltd.	Ingahist 4 mg tablet 10	28.63	1.1423	23.08
Chlorpheniramine	Inga Laboratories Pvt. Ltd.	Ingahist 4 mg tablet 10	27.85	1.1423	22.35
Ciprofloxacin	Shreya Life Sciences Pvt. Ltd	Cipdose 500 mg tablet 10	595	38.6	16.67
Ciprofloxacin	Micro Labs Ltd	Ciptab 500 mg tablet 4	62.16	13.2	49.73
Ciprofloxacin	Stanford Laboratories	Winflox 250 mg tablet 10	52.5	16.2	42

(continued)

Table A.2 (continued)

Medicine	Company	SKU	MRP	Ceiling	PTR
Ciprofloxacin	Ranbaxy Laboratories Ltd	Cifran Od 500 mg tablet 5	50.05	16.5	38.13
Ciprofloxacin	Ranbaxy Laboratories Ltd	Cifran 250 mg tablet 10	59.8	20.2	45.56
Ciprofloxacin	Ranbaxy Laboratories Ltd	Cifran 250 mg tablet 10	59.8	21	45.56
Ciprofloxacin	Cipla Ltd.	Ciplox 250 mg tablet 10	54.79	20.2	42.18
Ciprofloxacin	Leben Laboratories Pvt.Ltd	Ciproleb 500 mg tablet 6	61.79	23.16	30.66
Ciprofloxacin	Ranbaxy Laboratories Ltd	Cifran Od 500 mg tablet 5	50.05	19.3	38.14
Ciprofloxacin	Sh Pharmaceuticals Ltd	Ciprosol 500 mg tablet 10	85.35	33	68.28
Ciprofloxacin	Ranbaxy Laboratories Ltd	Cifran 500 mg tablet 10	99.5	38.6	75.81
Ciprofloxacin	Ranbaxy Laboratories Ltd	Cifran Od 500 mg tablet 5	50.05	20.05	38.14
Ciprofloxacin	Ranbaxy Laboratories Ltd	Cifran 500 mg tablet 10	94.76	38.6	75.81
Ciprofloxacin	Cipla Ltd.	Ciplox 500 mg tablet 10	93.36	38.6	71.88
Ciprofloxacin	Numed	Floxmed 500 mg tablet 5	44.55	19.3	35.64
Ciprofloxacin	Aglowmed Pharmaceuticals Ltd.	Cifomed 250 mg tablet 10	37.34	16.2	29.95
Ciprofloxacin	Numed	Floxmed 500 mg tablet 5	43.68	19.3	35.64
Ciprofloxacin	Dr. Reddys Laboratories Ltd	Ciprolet 250 mg tablet 10	35.35	16.2	29.02
Ciprofloxacin	Leben Laboratories Pvt.Ltd	Ciproleb 500 mg tablet 6	50	23.16	30.66
Ciprofloxacin	Taurus Laboratories Pvt Ltd	Taurcip 250 mg tablet 10	34.42	16.2	27.54
Ciprofloxacin	Biochem Pharmaceutical Inds	Biocip 250 mg tablet 10	33.75	16.2	27.1
Ciprofloxacin	Stadmed Pvt. Ltd	Cfx 500 mg tablet 10	80	38.6	60.32
Ciprofloxacin	Leben Laboratories Pvt.Ltd	Ciproleb 500 mg tablet 6	40.32	19.8	32.26
Ciprofloxacin	Leben Laboratories Pvt.Ltd	Ciproleb 500 mg tablet 6	40.22	19.8	32.18
Ciprofloxacin	Apex Laboratories Ltd.	Ciprobex 250 mg tablet 10	41	20.2	21.68
Ciprofloxacin	Cipla Ltd.	Ciplox Od 500 mg tablet 5	40.53	20.05	8.57

(continued)

Table A.2 (continued)

Medicine	Company	SKU	MRP	Ceiling	PTR
Ciprofloxacin	Bayer Pharmaceuticals Pvt. Ltd.	Baycip 250 mg tablet 10	32.5	16.2	26.21
Ciprofloxacin	Biochem Pharmaceutical Inds	Biocip 500 mg tablet 10	66	33	52.8
Ciprofloxacin	Canvarzys Pharmaceuticals	Cefobang Cv 250 mg tablet 6	186	9.72	143.34
Ciprofloxacin	Canvarzys Pharmaceuticals	Cefobang Cv 250 mg tablet 6	186	12.12	143.34
Ciprofloxacin	Canvarzys Pharmaceuticals	Cefobang Cv 250 mg tablet 6	179.17	12.12	143.34
Ciprofloxacin	Canvarzys Pharmaceuticals	Cefobang Cv 250 mg tablet 6	186	12.6	143.34
Ciprofloxacin	Canvarzys Pharmaceuticals	Cefobang Cv 250 mg tablet 6	179.17	12.6	143.34
Clopidogrel	Sanofi India Ltd.	Plavix 75 mg tablet 28	3231.36	280.84	2461.99
Clopidogrel	Sanofi India Ltd.	Plavix 75 mg tablet 28	3231.36	280.84	242.1
Clopidogrel	Psychotropics India Ltd	Pilogrel 75 mg tablet 10	438.41	64.4	16
Clopidogrel	Usv Ltd	Clopigrel 75 mg tablet 10	235.75	100.3	179.62
Clopidogrel	Usv Ltd	Clopigrel 75 mg tablet 10	235.75	100.3	86.47
Clopidogrel	Zydus Cadila	Clopidogrel 75 mg tablet 10	235.75	100.3	179.62
Dexamethasone	Cadila Pharmaceuticals Ltd	Demisone 0.5 mg tablet 200	578.12	42	462.5
Diazepam	Lupin Ltd	Placidox 5 mg tablet 10	38	13.2	29.26
Diazepam	Micro Labs Ltd	Microdep 5 mg tablet 10	35.5	13.2	28.71
Diazepam	Lupin Ltd	Placidox 5 mg tablet 10	33.75	13.2	29.26
Diazepam	Abbott Healthcare Pvt. Ltd	Valium 5 mg tablet 10	33.21	13.2	11.38
Diazepam	Abbott Healthcare Pvt. Ltd	Valium 5 mg tablet 10	33.21	13.2	25.3
Diazepam	Micro Labs Ltd	Microdep 5 mg tablet 10	32.5	13.2	26.48
Diazepam	Micro Labs Ltd	Microdep 5 mg tablet 10	35.5	14.5	28.71
Diazepam	Abbott Healthcare Pvt. Ltd	Valium 5 mg tablet 10	31.62	13.2	11.38
Diazepam	Micro Labs Ltd	Microdep 5 mg tablet 10	30.97	13.2	24.78

(continued)

Table A.2 (continued)

Medicine	Company	SKU	MRP	Ceiling	PTR
Diazepam	Micro Labs Ltd	Microdep 5 mg tablet 10	32.5	14	26.48
Diazepam	Micro Labs Ltd	Microdep 5 mg tablet 10	33.1	14.5	26.48
Diazepam	Micro Labs Ltd	Microdep 5 mg tablet 10	32.5	14.5	26.48
Diazepam	Ranbaxy Laboratories Ltd	Calmpose 5 mg tablet 10	29	13.2	22.1
Diazepam	Micro Labs Ltd	Microdep 5 mg tablet 10	28.35	13.2	24.78
Diazepam	Micro Labs Ltd	Microdep 5 mg tablet 10	28.35	13.2	22.68
Diazepam	Micro Labs Ltd	Microdep 5 mg tablet 10	28.35	13.2	22.8
Diazepam	Ranbaxy Laboratories Ltd	Calmpose 5 mg tablet 50	138.12	66	110.5
Diclofenac	Ranbaxy Laboratories Ltd	Volini 50 mg tablet 10	118	20.7	11.07
Diclofenac	Novartis India Ltd	Neuroflam 50 mg tablet 10	86.08	17.7	68.87
Diclofenac	Novartis India Ltd	Neuroflam 50 mg tablet 10	99	20.7	75.43
Diclofenac	Kivi Labs Ltd	Topac (Kivi) 50 mg tablet 10	90.2	19.5	16.81
Diclofenac	Kivi Labs Ltd	Topac (Kivi) 50 mg tablet 10	90.2	19.5	69.89
Diclofenac	Kivi Labs Ltd	Topac (Kivi) 50 mg tablet 10	90.2	19.5	17.52
Diclofenac	Novartis India Ltd	Neuroflam 50 mg tablet 10	94.28	20.7	75.43
Diclofenac	Novartis India Ltd	Neuroflam 50 mg tablet 10	94.28	21.5	75.43
Diclofenac	Kivi Labs Ltd	Topac (Kivi) 50 mg tablet 10	90.2	20.7	16.81
Diclofenac	Novartis India Ltd	Neuroflam 50 mg tablet 10	86.08	21.5	68.87
Diclofenac	Lark Laboratories Ltd	Larfen 50 mg tablet 10	80.58	21.5	64.47
Diclofenac	Zydus Cadila	Activa 50 mg tablet 10	60.62	17.7	48.5
Diclofenac	Zydus Cadila	Activa 50 mg tablet 10	61	19.5	42.44
Diclofenac	Zydus Cadila	Activa 50 mg tablet 10	61	19.5	42.81
Diclofenac	Zydus Cadila	Activa 50 mg tablet 10	61	19.5	43.37

(continued)

Table A.2 (continued)

Medicine	Company	SKU	MRP	Ceiling	PTR
Diclofenac	Zydus Cadila	Activa 50 mg tablet 10	60	19.5	42.81
Diclofenac	Zydus Cadila	Activa 50 mg tablet 10	60	19.5	42.66
Diclofenac	Zydus Cadila	Activa 50 mg tablet 10	62	20.7	44.06
Diclofenac	Zydus Cadila	Activa 50 mg tablet 10	62	20.7	44.23
Diclofenac	Zydus Cadila	Activa 50 mg tablet 10	62	20.7	43.84
Diclofenac	Zydus Cadila	Activa 50 mg tablet 10	62	20.7	44.08
Diclofenac	Zydus Cadila	Activa 50 mg tablet 10	61	20.7	43.84
Diclofenac	Zydus Cadila	Activa 50 mg tablet 10	61	20.7	43.3
Diclofenac	Zydus Cadila	Activa 50 mg tablet 10	61	20.7	43.37
Diclofenac	Zydus Cadila	Activa 50 mg tablet 10	61	20.7	43.13
Diclofenac	Zydus Cadila	Activa 50 mg tablet 10	62	21.5	44
Diclofenac	Zydus Cadila	Activa 50 mg tablet 10	62	21.5	44.09
Diclofenac	Zydus Cadila	Activa 50 mg tablet 10	54.21	19.5	43.37
Diclofenac	P &B Laboratories Pvt Ltd	Dilofen 50 mg tablet Sr 10	56.6	21.5	43.2
Diclofenac	Zydus Cadila	Inac 50 mg tablet 4	18.55	7.08	14.43
Diclofenac	P &B Laboratories Pvt Ltd	Dilofen 50 mg tablet Sr 10	54	20.7	41.02
Diclofenac	Zydus Cadila	Activa 50 mg tablet 10	55.11	21.5	44.09
Diclofenac	Zydus Cadila	Activa 50 mg tablet 10	55.07	21.5	44.06
Diclofenac	P &B Laboratories Pvt Ltd	Dilofen 50 mg tablet Sr 10	54	21.5	41.02
Diclofenac	Zydus Cadila	Inac 50 mg tablet 4	17.36	7.08	13.89
Diclofenac	Dr. Reddys Laboratories Ltd	Supanac 50 mg tablet 10	45.5	19.5	35.03
Diclofenac	Dr. Reddys Laboratories Ltd	Supanac 50 mg tablet 10	45.5	19.5	35.26
Diclofenac	Zydus Cadila	Inac 50 mg tablet 4	17.43	7.8	13.95

(continued)

Table A.2 (continued)

Medicine	Company	SKU	MRP	Ceiling	PTR
Diclofenac	Zydus Cadila	Inac 50 mg tablet 4	17.88	8.28	13.89
Diclofenac	Zydus Cadila	Inac 50 mg tablet 4	17.88	8.28	13.77
Diclofenac	Zydus Cadila	Inac 50 mg tablet 4	18.55	8.6	14.43
Diclofenac	Zydus Cadila	Inac 50 mg tablet 4	16.82	7.8	13.74
Diclofenac	Zydus Cadila	Inac 50 mg tablet 4	16.82	7.8	12.95
Diclofenac	Zydus Cadila	Inac 50 mg tablet 4	16.82	7.8	13
Diclofenac	Zydus Cadila	Inac 50 mg tablet 4	16.82	7.8	13.95
Diclofenac	Novartis India Ltd	Voveran 50 mg tablet Dt 10	41.7	19.5	32
Diclofenac	Novartis India Ltd	Voveran 50 mg tablet Dt 10	41.6	19.5	31.7
Diclofenac	Novartis India Ltd	Voveran D 50 mg tablet Dt 10	41.6	19.5	31.7
Diclofenac	Zydus Cadila	Inac 50 mg tablet 4	17.88	8.6	13.91
Diclofenac	Novartis India Ltd	Voveran D 50 mg tablet Dt 10	39.62	19.5	16.81
Diclofenac	Zydus Cadila	Inac 50 mg tablet 4	16.82	8.28	13.81
Diclofenac	Zydus Cadila	Inac 50 mg tablet 4	17.38	8.6	13.91
Diclofenac	Zydus Cadila	Inac 50 mg tablet 4	17.21	8.6	13.77
Diethylcarbamazine	Pfizer Ltd	Hetrazan 50 mg tablet 10	32	5	2.81
Diethylcarbamazine	Glaxosmithkline Pharmaceuticals Ltd.	Banocide 50 mg tablet 100	264.75	47	211.8
Diethylcarbamazine	Glaxosmithkline Pharmaceuticals Ltd.	Banocide 50 mg tablet 100	202.85	47	162.28
Diethylcarbamazine	Glaxosmithkline Pharmaceuticals Ltd.	Banocide 50 mg tablet 100	211.6	50	161.2
Diethylcarbamazine	Glaxosmithkline Pharmaceuticals Ltd.	Banocide 50 mg tablet 100	209.6	50	166.4

(continued)

Table A.2 (continued)

Medicine	Company	SKU	MRP	Ceiling	PTR
Diethylcarbamazine	Glaxosmithkline Pharmaceuticals Ltd.	Banocide 50 mg tablet 100	217.6	52	172.6
Diethylcarbamazine	Glaxosmithkline Pharmaceuticals Ltd.	Banocide 50 mg tablet 100	215.75	52	172.6
Diethylcarbamazine	Glaxosmithkline Pharmaceuticals Ltd.	Banocide 50 mg tablet 100	211.6	52	161.2
Diethylcarbamazine	Glaxosmithkline Pharmaceuticals Ltd.	Banocide 50 mg tablet 100	202.85	50	162.28
Diethylcarbamazine	Glaxosmithkline Pharmaceuticals Ltd.	Banocide 50 mg tablet 100	202.75	50	162.2
Diethylcarbamazine	Glaxosmithkline Pharmaceuticals Ltd.	Banocide 50 mg tablet 100	208	52	166.4
Diethylcarbamazine	Glaxosmithkline Pharmaceuticals Ltd.	Banocide 50 mg tablet 100	197.5	50	162.2
Diethylcarbamazine	Glaxosmithkline Pharmaceuticals Ltd.	Banocide 50 mg tablet 100	197.4	50	162.2
Diethylcarbamazine	Glaxosmithkline Pharmaceuticals Ltd.	Banocide 50 mg tablet 10	12.75	4.7	8.11
Diethylcarbamazine	Glaxosmithkline Pharmaceuticals Ltd.	Banocide 50 mg tablet 10	12.75	4.7	9.71
Diethylcarbamazine	Glaxosmithkline Pharmaceuticals Ltd.	Banocide Forte 50 mg tablet 30	38.74	15	29.51
Diethylcarbamazine	Glaxosmithkline Pharmaceuticals Ltd.	Banocide Forte 50 mg tablet 30	39.7	15.6	30.24
Diethylcarbamazine	Glaxosmithkline Pharmaceuticals Ltd.	Banocide Forte 50 mg tablet 30	38.74	15.6	29.51
Diethylcarbamazine	Glaxosmithkline Pharmaceuticals Ltd.	Banocide Forte 50 mg tablet 30	36.3	15	27.66
Diethylcarbamazine	Glaxosmithkline Pharmaceuticals Ltd.	Banocide Forte 50 mg tablet 30	33.25	14.1	25.33
Diethylcarbamazine	Glaxosmithkline Pharmaceuticals Ltd.	Banocide Forte 50 mg tablet 30	36.3	15.6	27.66

(continued)

Table A.2 (continued)

Medicine	Company	SKU	MRP	Ceiling	PTR
Diethylcarbamazine	Glaxosmithkline Pharmaceuticals Ltd.	Banocide Forte 50 mg tablet 30	33.25	15	25.33
Diethylcarbamazine	Glaxosmithkline Pharmaceuticals Ltd.	Banocide 50 mg tablet 10	10.13	4.7	8.11
Diethylcarbamazine	Glaxosmithkline Pharmaceuticals Ltd.	Banocide 50 mg tablet 10	9.87	4.7	8.11
Digoxin	Novartis India Ltd	Cardioxin 0.25 mg tablet 10	146.94	12.6	5.73
Digoxin	Novartis India Ltd	Cardioxin 0.25 mg tablet 10	146.94	12.6	123.43
Digoxin	Astrum Healthcare Pvt. Ltd.	Zigoxin 0.25 mg tablet 10	71.5	13.4	12
Diltiazem	Modi Mundi Pharma Pvt Ltd	Dilcontin 60 mg tablet 10	101.15	47.9	77.88
Domperidone	Veritaz Healthcare Ltd	Revert 10 mg tablet 10	110	22.4	77.2
Domperidone	Veritaz Healthcare Ltd	Revert 10 mg tablet 10	110	24	79.63
Domperidone	Veritaz Healthcare Ltd	Revert 10 mg tablet 10	96.48	22.4	77.2
Domperidone	Veritaz Healthcare Ltd	Revert 10 mg tablet 10	99.53	24	79.63
Domperidone	Veritaz Healthcare Ltd	Revert 10 mg tablet 10	96.5	24	77.2
Domperidone	Veritaz Healthcare Ltd	Revert 10 mg tablet 10	96.48	24	77.2
Domperidone	Veritaz Healthcare Ltd	Revert 10 mg tablet 10	96.48	24	77.19
Domperidone	Veritaz Healthcare Ltd	Revert 10 mg tablet 10	95.95	24	52.42
Domperidone	Veritaz Healthcare Ltd	Revert 10 mg tablet 10	65.52	22.6	52.42
Domperidone	Veritaz Healthcare Ltd	Revert 10 mg tablet 10	68	24	52.42
Domperidone	Veritaz Healthcare Ltd	Revert 10 mg tablet 10	65.52	24	52.42
Domperidone	Unichem Laboratories Ltd	Unistal 10 mg tablet 10	58	22.4	44.64
Domperidone	Unichem Laboratories Ltd	Unistal 10 mg tablet 10	58	24.9	44.64
Domperidone	Janssen	Motilium M 10 mg tablet 10	51.34	22.6	19.46
Domperidone	Janssen	Gastractiv 10 mg tablet 10	51.34	22.6	19.46

(continued)

Table A.2 (continued)

Medicine	Company	SKU	MRP	Ceiling	PTR
Domperidone	Janssen	Gastractiv 10 mg tablet 10	51.34	22.6	39.53
Domperidone	Janssen	Motilium M 10 mg tablet 10	51.34	22.6	39.53
Domperidone	Unichem Laboratories Ltd	Unistal 10 mg tablet 10	53.85	24	41.47
Domperidone	Unichem Laboratories Ltd	Unistal 10 mg tablet 10	55.8	24.9	44.64
Domperidone	Janssen	Motilium M 10 mg tablet 30	148.23	67.8	118.59
Domperidone	Unichem Laboratories Ltd	Unistal 10 mg tablet 10	49	22.6	37.72
Domperidone	Unichem Laboratories Ltd	Unistal 10 mg tablet 10	53.85	24.9	41.44
Domperidone	Unichem Laboratories Ltd	Unistal 10 mg tablet 10	53.85	24.9	41.47
Domperidone	Unichem Laboratories Ltd	Unistal 10 mg tablet 10	49	24	37.72
Doxycycline	Sun Pharma Laboratories Ltd.	Doxy Plus 100 mg tablet 10	55	9.4	44
Doxycycline	Sun Pharma Laboratories Ltd.	Doxy Plus 100 mg tablet 10	57.75	10	44
Doxycycline	Sun Pharma Laboratories Ltd.	Doxy Plus 100 mg tablet 10	57.75	10.4	44
Doxycycline	Dr. Reddys Laboratories Ltd	Doxt 100 mg tablet 7	35.1	6.58	12.93
Doxycycline	Euphoric Pharmaceuticals (P) Ltd	Doxyric 100 mg tablet 10	49.85	9.4	38.4
Doxycycline	Euphoric Pharmaceuticals (P) Ltd	Doxyric 100 mg tablet 10	49.85	9.4	38.38
Doxycycline	Euphoric Pharmaceuticals (P) Ltd	Doxyric 100 mg tablet 10	55.07	10.4	44.06
Doxycycline	Sun Pharma Laboratories Ltd.	Doxy Plus 100 mg tablet 10	55	10.4	44
Doxycycline	Euphoric Pharmaceuticals (P) Ltd	Doxyric 100 mg tablet 10	50	10	38.38
Doxycycline	Euphoric Pharmaceuticals (P) Ltd	Doxyric 100 mg tablet 10	50	10	38.4
Doxycycline	Euphoric Pharmaceuticals (P) Ltd	Doxyric 100 mg tablet 10	49.85	10	38.38
Doxycycline	Octane Biotech	Doc Dr 100 mg tablet Dr 10	49.5	10	39.6
Doxycycline	Octane Biotech	Doc Dr 100 mg tablet Dr 10	49.5	10	39.66
Doxycycline	Cipla Ltd.	Doxicip 100 mg tablet 8	36	7.52	8.75

(continued)

Table A.2 (continued)

Medicine	Company	SKU	MRP	Ceiling	PTR
Doxycycline	Octane Biotech	Doc Dr 100 mg tablet Dr 10	49.57	10.4	39.66
Doxycycline	Octane Biotech	Doc Dr 100 mg tablet Dr 10	49.5	10.4	39.6
Doxycycline	Euphoric Pharmaceuticals (P) Ltd	Doxyric 100 mg tablet 10	47.97	10.4	38.38
Doxycycline	Intas Pharmaceuticals Ltd	Doxitas 100 mg tablet 8	33.5	8	13.93
Doxycycline	Sun Pharma Laboratories Ltd.	Doxy Plus 100 mg tablet 10	37.75	9.4	36.57
Doxycycline	Bennet Pharmaceuticals Limited	Nab 100 mg tablet 10	34.5	9.4	27.6
Doxycycline	Bennet Pharmaceuticals Limited	Nab 100 mg tablet 10	34.5	10	26.29
Doxycycline	Bennet Pharmaceuticals Limited	Nab 100 mg tablet 10	34.5	10	27.6
Doxycycline	Ronak Labs	R Dox 100 mg tablet 10	34	10	27.2
Doxycycline	Ronak Labs	R Dox 100 mg tablet 10	33.48	10	24.8
Doxycycline	Bennet Pharmaceuticals Limited	Nab 100 mg tablet 10	34.5	10.4	27.65
Doxycycline	Bennet Pharmaceuticals Limited	Nab 100 mg tablet 10	34.5	10.4	27.38
Doxycycline	Bennet Pharmaceuticals Limited	Nab 100 mg tablet 10	34.5	10.4	26.29
Doxycycline	Bennet Pharmaceuticals Limited	Nab 100 mg tablet 10	34.5	10.4	27.6
Doxycycline	Ronak Labs	R Dox 100 mg tablet 10	34	10.4	27.2
Doxycycline	Lancer Pharmaceuticals Pvt. Ltd	Lytedox 100 mg tablet 10	31.76	10.4	25.41
Doxycycline	Dr. Reddys Laboratories Ltd	Doxt 100 mg tablet 7	15.75	6.58	12.93
Doxycycline	Lancer Pharmaceuticals Pvt. Ltd	Lytedox 100 mg tablet 10	24.62	10.4	19.7
Doxycycline	Lancer Pharmaceuticals Pvt. Ltd	Lytedox 100 mg tablet 10	23.33	10.4	19.7
Doxycycline	Intas Pharmaceuticals Ltd	Doxitas 100 mg tablet 8	17.41	8	13.93
Doxycycline	Macleods Pharmaceuticals Pvt.Ltd	Revidox 100 mg tablet 4	7.85	3.76	6.73
Ethinylestradiol	Organon (India) Ltd	Lynoral 0.01 mg tablet 10	44.5	21.2	33.9
Ethinylestradiol	Organon (India) Ltd	Lynoral 0.01 mg tablet 10	44.5	21.2	17.8

(continued)

Table A.2 (continued)

Medicine	Company	SKU	MRP	Ceiling	PTR
Fluconazole	Swiss Pharma Pvt. Ltd	Flucovar 150 mg tablet 1	150	15.36	7.88
Fluconazole	Axon Health Care Ltd	Flz 150 mg tablet 1	100	15.36	24.82
Fluconazole	Pasteur Laboratories Pvt. Ltd.	Floret 150 mg tablet 1	80	14.45	12.81
Fluconazole	Pasteur Laboratories Pvt. Ltd.	Floret 150 mg tablet 1	80	14.45	12.87
Fluconazole	Axon Health Care Ltd	Flz 150 mg tablet 1	31.02	10.99	24.82
Fluconazole	Cipla Ltd.	Fluka 150 mg tablet 1	40	14.45	4.5
Fluconazole	Cipla Ltd.	Fluka 150 mg tablet 1	40	14.45	5
Fluconazole	Zydus Cadila	Fusys 200 mg tablet 4	192.38	69.72	153.91
Fluconazole	Perk Pharma	Hinzole 150 mg tablet 1	29	10.99	21.99
Fluconazole	Biochem Pharmaceutical Inds	Fluzol (Biochem) 150 mg tablet 1	38	14.45	3.7
Fluconazole	Biochem Pharmaceutical Inds	Fluzol (Biochem) 150 mg tablet 1	38	14.45	12
Fluconazole	Windlas Biotech Ltd	Canawar 150 mg tablet 1	40	15.36	9.58
Fluconazole	Axon Health Care Ltd	Flz 150 mg tablet 1	39	15.36	24.82
Fluconazole	Intas Pharmaceuticals Ltd	Fcn 150 mg tablet 1	36.5	14.45	3.5
Fluconazole	Artel Laboratories	Floz 150 mg tablet 1	27.73	10.99	22.19
Fluconazole	Cipla Ltd.	Fungicip 150 mg tablet 1	36.25	14.45	3.3
Fluconazole	Cipla Ltd.	Fungicip 150 mg tablet 1	36.25	14.45	4
Fluconazole	Cipla Ltd.	Fungicip 150 mg tablet 1	36.25	14.45	4.62
Fluconazole	Cipla Ltd.	Fungicip 150 mg tablet 1	36.25	14.45	3.9
Fluconazole	Cadila Pharmaceuticals Ltd	Fluzon 150 mg tablet 1	38	15.36	3.5
Fluconazole	Biochem Pharmaceutical Inds	Fluzol (Biochem) 150 mg tablet 1	38	15.36	3.7
Fluconazole	Prism Lifescience	Odcan 150 mg tablet 1	26.92	10.99	21.54
Fluconazole	Hegde & Hegde	Fzhh 150 mg tablet 1	35	14.45	26.67

(continued)

Table A.2 (continued)

Medicine	Company	SKU	MRP	Ceiling	PTR
Fluconazole	Hegde & Hegde	Fzhh 150 mg tablet 1	35	14.45	11.01
Fluconazole	Elder Pharmaceuticals Ltd	Fluzant 150 mg tablet 1	34.51	14.45	4.77
Fluconazole	Cipla Ltd.	Fungicip 150 mg tablet 1	36.25	15.36	4.25
Fluconazole	Cipla Ltd.	Fungicip 150 mg tablet 1	36.25	15.36	4
Fluconazole	Cipla Ltd.	Fungicip 150 mg tablet 1	36.25	15.36	4.2
Fluconazole	Cipla Ltd.	Fungicip 150 mg tablet 1	36.25	15.36	3.81
Fluconazole	Galpha Laboratories Ltd	Flucan 150 mg tablet 1	34	14.45	6
Fluconazole	Psychotropics India Ltd	Myconorm F 150 mg tablet 1	36	15.36	3
Fluconazole	Lupin Ltd	Flucalup 150 mg tablet 1	33.75	14.45	3.5
Fluconazole	Lupin Ltd	Flucalup 150 mg tablet 1	33.75	14.45	5
Fluconazole	Fdc Ltd.	Zocon 150 mg tablet 1	33.6	14.45	25.87
Fluconazole	Biostrass Health Sciences	Cantras 150 mg tablet 4	100	43.96	76.19
Fluconazole	Elder Pharmaceuticals Ltd	Fluzant 150 mg tablet 1	34.51	15.36	4.77
Fluconazole	Fdc Ltd.	Zocon 150 mg tablet 1	32.33	14.45	12.46
Fluconazole	Maneesh Pharmaceuticals Ltd	Flucofit 150 mg tablet 1	32	14.45	11.9
Fluconazole	Novartis India Ltd	Flucess 150 mg tablet 1	32	14.45	3.95
Fluconazole	Zydus Cadila	Flugee 150 mg tablet 1	32	14.45	5
Fluconazole	Zydus Cadila	Flugee 150 mg tablet 1	32	14.45	4
Fluconazole	Zydus Cadila	Fungo 150 mg tablet 1	32	14.45	12
Fluconazole	Micro Labs Ltd	Nucon 150 mg tablet 1	32	14.45	14.58
Fluconazole	Novartis India Ltd	Flucess 150 mg tablet 1	32	14.45	3.9
Fluconazole	Zydus Cadila	Fungo 150 mg tablet 1	32	14.45	14.5
Fluconazole	Zydus Cadila	Flugee 150 mg tablet 1	32	14.45	3.5

(continued)

Table A.2 (continued)

Medicine	Company	SKU	MRP	Ceiling	PTR
Fluconazole	Novartis India Ltd	Flucess 150 mg tablet 1	32	14.45	4
Fluconazole	Novartis India Ltd	Flucess 150 mg tablet 1	32	14.45	3.81
Fluconazole	Novartis India Ltd	Flucess 150 mg tablet 1	32	14.45	3.92
Fluconazole	Maneesh Pharmaceuticals Ltd	Flucofit 150 mg tablet 1	32	14.45	24.38
Fluconazole	Lupin Ltd	Flucalup 150 mg tablet 1	31.95	14.45	3.6
Fluconazole	Lupin Ltd	Flucalup (Alu/Alu) 150 mg tablet 1	31.95	14.45	4
Fluconazole	Lupin Ltd	Flucalup 150 mg tablet 1	33.75	15.36	3.75
Fluconazole	Alembic Ltd	Alflucoz 150 mg tablet 1	31.75	14.45	4.85
Fluconazole	Alembic Ltd	Alflucoz 150 mg tablet 1	31.75	14.45	3.9
Fluconazole	Alembic Ltd	Alflucoz 150 mg tablet 1	31.75	14.45	4.5
Fluconazole	Serve Pharmaceuticals	Fluco (Serve) 150 mg tablet Dt 2	62.86	28.9	50.29
Fluconazole	Zuventus Healthcare Ltd	Tucanozol 150 mg tablet 1	34.28	15.95	27.43
Fluconazole	Fdc Ltd.	Zocon 100 mg tablet Dt 4	63.5	29.6	50.4
Fluconazole	Dr. Reddys Laboratories Ltd	Flustan 150 mg tablet 1	32.77	15.36	26.22
Fluconazole	Cure Quick Pharmaceuticals	Fulcure 150 mg tablet 1	30.37	14.45	22.4
Fluconazole	Wockhardt Ltd	Funaz 150 mg tablet 1	30.34	14.45	4
Fluconazole	Wockhardt Ltd	Funaz 150 mg tablet 1	30.34	14.45	3
Fluconazole	Zydus Cadila	Fungo 150 mg tablet 1	32	15.36	12
Fluconazole	Zydus Cadila	Flugee 150 mg tablet 1	32	15.36	4
Fluconazole	Maneesh Pharmaceuticals Ltd	Flucofit 150 mg tablet 1	32	15.36	11.9
Fluconazole	Novartis India Ltd	Flucess 150 mg tablet 1	32	15.36	3.81
Fluconazole	Novartis India Ltd	Flucess 150 mg tablet 1	32	15.36	3.95

(continued)

Table A.2 (continued)

Medicine	Company	SKU	MRP	Ceiling	PTR
Fluconazole	Leeford Healthcare	Flumet (Leeford) 150 mg tablet 1	32	15.36	3.38
Fluconazole	Novartis India Ltd	Flucess 150 mg tablet 1	32	15.36	3.5
Fluconazole	Zydus Cadila	Flugee 150 mg tablet 1	32	15.36	5
Fluconazole	Leeford Healthcare	Flumet (Leeford) 150 mg tablet 1	32	15.36	3.63
Fluconazole	Leeford Healthcare	Flumet (Leeford) 150 mg tablet 1	32	15.36	4
Fluconazole	Novartis India Ltd	Flucess 150 mg tablet 1	32	15.36	3.9
Fluconazole	Zydus Cadila	Flugee 150 mg tablet 1	32	15.36	4.5
Fluconazole	Zydus Cadila	Flugee 150 mg tablet 1	32	15.36	3.15
Fluconazole	Novartis India Ltd	Flucess 150 mg tablet 1	32	15.36	4.05
Fluconazole	Ranbaxy Laboratories Ltd	Stefazol 150 mg tablet 1	31.95	15.36	4
Fluconazole	Ranbaxy Laboratories Ltd	Stefazol 150 mg tablet 1	31.95	15.36	3
Fluconazole	Ranbaxy Laboratories Ltd	Stefazol 150 mg tablet 1	31.95	15.36	3.78
Fluconazole	Dr. Reddys Laboratories Ltd	Flustan 150 mg tablet 1	31.95	15.36	26.22
Fluconazole	Alembic Ltd	Alflucoz 150 mg tablet 1	31.75	15.36	4.85
Fluconazole	Alembic Ltd	Alflucoz 150 mg tablet 1	31.75	15.36	5
Fluconazole	Cure Quick Pharmaceuticals	Fulcure 150 mg tablet 1	29.79	14.45	22.4
Fluconazole	Cadila Pharmaceuticals Ltd	Fluzon 150 mg tablet 1	29.64	14.45	3.5
Fluconazole	Cadila Pharmaceuticals Ltd	Fluzon 150 mg tablet 1	29.64	14.45	4
Fluconazole	Serve Pharmaceuticals	Fluco (Serve) 150 mg tablet Dt 2	62.86	30.72	50.29
Fluconazole	Coxswain Healthcare	Fluty 150 mg tablet 1	22.28	10.99	17.83
Fluconazole	Novartis India Ltd	Flucess 150 mg tablet 1	32	15.95	4
Folic Acid	Arvind Remedies Ltd.	Megafit 5 mg tablet 10	255	14.6	10.78
Folic Acid	Arvind Remedies Ltd.	Megafit 5 mg tablet 10	246	14.6	10.78

(continued)

Table A.2 (continued)

Medicine	Company	SKU	MRP	Ceiling	PTR
Folic Acid	Triton Health Care Pvt Ltd	Folistar 5 mg tablet 10	145	11.5	101.75
Folic Acid	Triton Health Care Pvt Ltd	Folistar 5 mg tablet 10	145	11.5	101.31
Folic Acid	Zydus Cadila	Folly 5 mg tablet 10	140	11.5	112
Folic Acid	Triton Health Care Pvt Ltd	Folistar 5 mg tablet 10	128.66	11.5	101.75
Folic Acid	Triton Health Care Pvt Ltd	Folistar 5 mg tablet 10	145	13.7	108.4
Folic Acid	Triton Health Care Pvt Ltd	Folistar 5 mg tablet 10	159.5	15.2	126.54
Folic Acid	Triton Health Care Pvt Ltd	Folistar 5 mg tablet 10	159	15.2	115.67
Folic Acid	Triton Health Care Pvt Ltd	Folistar 5 mg tablet 10	158.17	15.2	126.54
Folic Acid	Triton Health Care Pvt Ltd	Folistar 5 mg tablet 10	149	14.6	108.4
Folic Acid	Triton Health Care Pvt Ltd	Folistar 5 mg tablet 10	145	14.6	108.4
Folic Acid	Triton Health Care Pvt Ltd	Folistar 5 mg tablet 10	135.5	13.7	108.4
Folic Acid	Triton Health Care Pvt Ltd	Folistar 5 mg tablet 10	149	15.2	108.4
Folic Acid	Triton Health Care Pvt Ltd	Folistar 5 mg tablet 10	144.58	15.2	115.67
Folic Acid	Triton Health Care Pvt Ltd	Folistar 5 mg tablet 10	128.66	13.7	101.31
Folic Acid	Triton Health Care Pvt Ltd	Folistar 5 mg tablet 10	135.5	15.2	108.4
Folic Acid	Arvind Remedies Ltd.	Megafit 5 mg tablet 10	122.55	15.2	98.04
Folic Acid	Nouveau Medicament Pvt Ltd	Folmet 5 mg tablet 10	72.5	11.5	58
Folic Acid	Micro Labs Ltd	Folfit 5 mg tablet 10	70	11.5	53.33
Folic Acid	P &B Laboratories Pvt Ltd	F 5 5 mg tablet 10	64.78	11.5	51.84
Folic Acid	P &B Laboratories Pvt Ltd	F 5 5 mg tablet 10	64.78	11.5	51.83
Folic Acid	P &B Laboratories Pvt Ltd	F 5 5 mg tablet 10	64.78	11.5	31.19
Folic Acid	Micro Labs Ltd	Folfit 5 mg tablet 10	83	15.2	63.89
Folic Acid	Micro Labs Ltd	Folfit 5 mg tablet 10	83	15.2	63.24

(continued)

Table A.2 (continued)

Medicine	Company	SKU	MRP	Ceiling	PTR
Folic Acid	Intas Pharmaceuticals Ltd	Folic Acid 5 mg tablet 10	60	11.5	0.97
Folic Acid	Micro Labs Ltd	Folfit 5 mg tablet 10	76	14.6	57.9
Folic Acid	Micro Labs Ltd	Folfit 5 mg tablet 10	70	13.7	53.33
Folic Acid	Micro Labs Ltd	Folfit 5 mg tablet 10	76	15.2	57.9
Folic Acid	Micro Labs Ltd	Folfit 5 mg tablet 10	66.66	13.7	53.33
Folic Acid	Arvind Remedies Ltd.	Megafit 5 mg tablet 10	70	14.6	10.78
Folic Acid	Micro Labs Ltd	Folfit 5 mg tablet 10	70	14.6	57.9
Folic Acid	Alembic Ltd	Folinal 5 mg tablet 10	54.28	11.5	43.43
Folic Acid	Vance & Health Pharmaceuticals Ltd	Trifol 5 mg tablet 10	60	13.7	15.23
Folic Acid	Intas Pharmaceuticals Ltd	Folitas 5 mg tablet 10	56.46	13.7	45.17
Folic Acid	Vance & Health Pharmaceuticals Ltd	Trifol 5 mg tablet 10	60	14.6	15.23
Folic Acid	Intas Pharmaceuticals Ltd	Folitas 5 mg tablet 10	60	14.6	45.17
Folic Acid	Intas Pharmaceuticals Ltd	Folitas 5 mg tablet 10	56.46	14.6	45.17
Folic Acid	P &B Laboratories Pvt Ltd	F 5 5 mg tablet 10	38.98	11.5	31.19
Folic Acid	Alembic Ltd	Folinal 5 mg tablet 10	37.15	11.5	29.72
Folic Acid	Cipla Ltd.	Vitafol(Cip) 5 mg tablet 10	45.85	14.6	9
Folic Acid	Cipla Ltd.	Vitafol(Cip) 5 mg tablet 10	45.85	14.6	3
Folic Acid	Cipla Ltd.	Vitafol(Cip) 5 mg tablet 10	45.85	14.6	2.94
Folic Acid	Nouveau Medicament Pvt Ltd	Folmet 5 mg tablet 10	36	11.5	27.43
Folic Acid	Alembic Ltd	Folinal 5 mg tablet 10	44.39	14.6	32.88
Folic Acid	Cipla Ltd.	Vitafol(Cip) 5 mg tablet 10	45.85	15.2	9.5
Folic Acid	Cipla Ltd.	Vitafol(Cip) 5 mg tablet 10	45.85	15.2	9

(continued)

Table A.2 (continued)

Medicine	Company	SKU	MRP	Ceiling	PTR
Folic Acid	Cipla Ltd.	Vitafol(Cip) 5 mg tablet 10	45.85	15.2	10
Folic Acid	Alembic Ltd	Folinal 5 mg tablet 10	45.8	15.2	36.35
Folic Acid	Alembic Ltd	Folinal 5 mg tablet 10	45.8	15.2	35.26
Folic Acid	Alembic Ltd	Folinal 5 mg tablet 10	43.4	14.6	32.88
Folic Acid	Alembic Ltd	Folinal 5 mg tablet 10	43.15	14.6	32.88
Folic Acid	Alembic Ltd	Folinal 5 mg tablet 10	43.15	14.6	34.25
Folic Acid	Alembic Ltd	Folinal 5 mg tablet 10	44.07	15.2	35.26
Folic Acid	Alembic Ltd	Folinal 5 mg tablet 10	43.62	15.2	34.9
Folic Acid	P &B Laboratories Pvt Ltd	F 5 5 mg tablet 10	38.98	13.7	31.19
Folic Acid	Alembic Ltd	Folinal 5 mg tablet 10	43.15	15.2	34.25
Folic Acid	Alembic Ltd	Folinal 5 mg tablet 10	41.1	14.6	32.88
Folic Acid	P &B Laboratories Pvt Ltd	F 5 5 mg tablet 10	37.75	13.7	31.19
Folic Acid	Vance & Health Pharmaceuticals Ltd	Trifol 5 mg tablet 10	31.5	11.5	15.38
Folic Acid	Alembic Ltd	Folinal 5 mg tablet 10	37.15	13.7	29.72
Folic Acid	Alembic Ltd	Folinal 5 mg tablet 10	37.15	13.7	28.73
Folic Acid	Cipla Ltd.	Vitafol(Cip) 5 mg tablet 10	36.23	13.7	3
Folic Acid	Nouveau Medicament Pvt Ltd	Folmet 5 mg tablet 10	36	13.7	27.43
Folic Acid	Emcure Pharmaceuticals Ltd	Emfolic 5 mg tablet 10	30.15	11.5	22.97
Folic Acid	Alembic Ltd	Folinal 5 mg tablet 10	35.91	13.7	28.73
Folic Acid	Nouveau Medicament Pvt Ltd	Folmet 5 mg tablet 30	90	34.5	68.57
Folic Acid	Nouveau Medicament Pvt Ltd	Folmet 5 mg tablet 30	90	34.5	27.43
Folic Acid	Nouveau Medicament Pvt Ltd	Folmet 5 mg tablet 30	90	34.5	57.14
Folic Acid	Mankind Pharmaceuticals Ltd.	Folimust 5 mg tablet 10	29.9	11.5	9.2

(continued)

Table A.2 (continued)

Medicine	Company	SKU	MRP	Ceiling	PTR
Folic Acid	Mankind Pharmaceuticals Ltd.	Folimust 5 mg tablet 10	29.9	11.5	22.78
Folic Acid	P &B Laboratories Pvt Ltd	F 5 5 mg tablet 10	37.75	14.6	29.95
Folic Acid	P &B Laboratories Pvt Ltd	F 5 5 mg tablet 10	37.75	14.6	29.94
Folic Acid	P &B Laboratories Pvt Ltd	F 5 5 mg tablet 10	37.75	14.6	31.19
Folic Acid	P &B Laboratories Pvt Ltd	F 5 5 mg tablet 10	37.42	14.6	29.94
Folic Acid	Cipla Ltd.	Vitafol(Cip) 5 mg tablet 10	36.23	14.6	3
Folic Acid	Nouveau Medicament Pvt Ltd	Folmet 5 mg tablet 10	36	14.6	27.43
Folic Acid	Vance & Health Pharmaceuticals Ltd	Trifol 5 mg tablet 10	36	14.6	15.23
Folic Acid	Emcure Pharmaceuticals Ltd	Emfolic 5 mg tablet 10	27.45	11.5	9.18
Folic Acid	Emcure Pharmaceuticals Ltd	Emfolic 5 mg tablet 10	27.45	11.5	22.97
Folic Acid	Emcure Pharmaceuticals Ltd	Emfolic 5 mg tablet 10	27.45	11.5	9.89
Folic Acid	Nouveau Medicament Pvt Ltd	Folmet 5 mg tablet 10	36	15.2	27.43
Folic Acid	Pfizer Ltd	Folvite 5 mg tablet 30	80.8	34.5	62.21
Folic Acid	Synokem Pharmaceuticals Ltd	Folik 5 mg tablet 10	26.4	11.5	20.38
Folic Acid	Synokem Pharmaceuticals Ltd	Folik 5 mg tablet 10	26.4	11.5	20.39
Folic Acid	Pfizer Ltd	Folvite 5 mg tablet 30	77.76	34.5	29.27
Folic Acid	Bestochem Formulations (I) Ltd	Fh 12 5 mg tablet 10	25.9	11.5	20
Folic Acid	Bestochem Formulations (I) Ltd	Fh 12 5 mg tablet 10	25.9	11.5	9.2
Folic Acid	Synokem Pharmaceuticals Ltd	Folik 5 mg tablet 10	25.9	11.5	20.39
Folic Acid	Bestochem Formulations (I) Ltd	Fh 12 5 mg tablet 10	25.9	11.5	19.73
Folic Acid	Nouveau Medicament Pvt Ltd	Folmet 5 mg tablet 30	90	41.1	27.43
Folic Acid	Mankind Pharmaceuticals Ltd.	Folimust 5 mg tablet 10	29.9	13.7	9.2
Folic Acid	Nouveau Medicament Pvt Ltd	Folmet 5 mg tablet 30	75	34.5	68.57

(continued)

Table A.2 (continued)

Medicine	Company	SKU	MRP	Ceiling	PTR
Folic Acid	Vance & Health Pharmaceuticals Ltd	Trifol 5 mg tablet 10	31.5	14.6	15.23
Folic Acid	Emcure Pharmaceuticals Ltd	Emfolic 5 mg tablet 10	27.45	13.7	10.94
Folic Acid	Emcure Pharmaceuticals Ltd	Emfolic 5 mg tablet 10	27.45	13.7	9.18
Griseofulvin	Dr. Reddys Laboratories Ltd	Gris Od 250 mg tablet 10	126	14.5	46.69
Griseofulvin	Dr. Reddys Laboratories Ltd	Gris Od 250 mg tablet 10	62.1	14.5	46.69
Hydrochlorothiazide	Ordain Healthcare Pvt. Ltd	Thiazide 12.5 mg tablet 10	21	9.700001	7.81
Hydrochlorothiazide	Ordain Healthcare Pvt. Ltd	Thiazide 12.5 mg tablet 10	21	9.700001	16.15
Hydrochlorothiazide	Ordain Healthcare Pvt. Ltd	Thiazide 12.5 mg tablet 10	21	9.700001	16
Hydrochlorothiazide	Usv Ltd	Xenia 25 mg tablet 15	55	26.4	17.45
Hydroxychloroquine	Maneesh Pharmaceuticals Ltd	Fe Q 200 mg tablet 10	425	56.4	327.22
Hydroxychloroquine	Maneesh Pharmaceuticals Ltd	Fe Q 200 mg tablet 10	425	60	327.22
Hydroxychloroquine	Maneesh Pharmaceuticals Ltd	Fe Q 200 mg tablet 10	425	62.3	327.22
Hydroxychloroquine	Maneesh Pharmaceuticals Ltd	Fe Q 200 mg tablet 10	409.02	62.3	327.22
Hydroxychloroquine	Zydus Cadila	Zy Q 200 mg tablet 10	150.54	55	115.87
Hydroxychloroquine	Zydus Cadila	Zy Q 200 mg tablet 10	140.08	56.4	112.07
Hydroxychloroquine	Zydus Cadila	Zy Q 200 mg tablet 10	145.13	60	111.74
Hydroxychloroquine	Zydus Cadila	Zy Q 200 mg tablet 10	150.54	62.3	115.87
Hydroxychloroquine	Zydus Cadila	Zy Q 200 mg tablet 10	145.13	62.3	111.74
Hydroxychloroquine	Zydus Cadila	Zy Q 200 mg tablet 10	131.37	56.4	105.1
Hydroxychloroquine	Zydus Cadila	Zy Q 200 mg tablet 10	139.67	60	111.74
Hydroxychloroquine	Zydus Cadila	Zy Q 200 mg tablet 10	136.5	60	105.1
Hydroxychloroquine	Zydus Cadila	Zy Q 200 mg tablet 10	136.5	60	111.74
Imatinib Mesylate	Novartis India Ltd	Glivac 400 mg tablet 10	40000	2852.9	2683.3

(continued)

Table A.2 (continued)

Medicine	Company	SKU	MRP	Ceiling	PTR
Isoniazide	Lupin Ltd	Pyzina Kid 300 mg tablet 10	38.5	13.5	29.33
Isoniazide	Lupin Ltd	Pyzina Kid 300 mg tablet 10	35.42	12.7	26.99
Isoniazide	Lupin Ltd	Pyzina Kid 300 mg tablet 10	38.5	14	29.33
Isoniazide	Lupin Ltd	Pyzina Kid 300 mg tablet 10	35.42	13.5	26.99
Isoniazide	Lupin Ltd	Pyzina Kid 300 mg tablet 10	38.5	18.6	29.31
Isosorbide Dinitrate	Troikaa Pharmaceuticals Ltd	Sorbidine 10 mg tablet 10	160.58	6.9	130.55
Isosorbide-5-Mononitrate	Jagsonpal Pharmaceuticals Ltd	Isotrate 20 mg tablet 10	196	36.3	150.15
Isosorbide-5-Mononitrate	Jagsonpal Pharmaceuticals Ltd	Isotrate 20 mg tablet 10	196	36.3	150.86
Isosorbide-5-Mononitrate	Jagsonpal Pharmaceuticals Ltd	Isotrate 20 mg tablet 10	188.57	36.3	150.86
Isosorbide-5-Mononitrate	Jagsonpal Pharmaceuticals Ltd	Isotrate 20 mg tablet 10	180	36.3	138.59
Isosorbide-5-Mononitrate	Jagsonpal Pharmaceuticals Ltd	Isotrate 20 mg tablet 10	173.23	36.3	138.59
Isosorbide-5-Mononitrate	Jagsonpal Pharmaceuticals Ltd	Isotrate 20 mg tablet 10	152.06	36.3	121.65
Leflunomide	Sanofi India Ltd.	Arava 10 mg tablet 30	1560	453	390.52
Leflunomide	Sanofi India Ltd.	Arava 10 mg tablet 30	1560	453	1248
Leflunomide	Sanofi India Ltd.	Arava 20 mg tablet 30	2769.12	858.9	2215.3
Leflunomide	Sanofi India Ltd.	Arava 20 mg tablet 30	2769.12	858.9	740.43
Leflunomide	Zydus Cadila	Rumalef 20 mg tablet 10	436.71	181.3	336.14
Levo-Thyroxine (Synthetic)	Akumentis Healthcare Ltd	Euthyroid 100 mcg tablet 4	99	4.44	75.43
Levo-Thyroxine (Synthetic)	Akumentis Healthcare Ltd	Sunthyroid 100 mcg tablet 4	99	4.44	75.43
Levo-Thyroxine (Synthetic)	Akumentis Healthcare Ltd	Thyroweek 100 mcg tablet 4	99	4.44	75.07
Levo-Thyroxine (Synthetic)	Akumentis Healthcare Ltd	Thyroweek 100 mcg tablet 4	99	4.44	75.43
Levo-Thyroxine (Synthetic)	Akumentis Healthcare Ltd	Euthyroid 50 mcg tablet 4	79	3.64	60.19
Levo-Thyroxine (Synthetic)	Akumentis Healthcare Ltd	Sunthyroid 50 mcg tablet 4	79	3.64	60.19

(continued)

Table A.2 (continued)

Medicine	Company	SKU	MRP	Ceiling	PTR
Levo-Thyroxine (Synthetic)	Akumentis Healthcare Ltd	Thyroweek 50 mcg tablet 4	79	3.64	60.19
Levo-Thyroxine (Synthetic)	Akumentis Healthcare Ltd	Euthyroid 100 mcg tablet 4	99	4.92	75.43
Levo-Thyroxine (Synthetic)	Akumentis Healthcare Ltd	Sunthyroid 100 mcg tablet 4	99	4.92	75.43
Levo-Thyroxine (Synthetic)	Akumentis Healthcare Ltd	Thyroweek 100 mcg tablet 4	99	4.92	75.43
Levo-Thyroxine (Synthetic)	Akumentis Healthcare Ltd	Sunthyroid 50 mcg tablet 4	79	4.44	60.19
Levo-Thyroxine (Synthetic)	Akumentis Healthcare Ltd	Euthyroid 50 mcg tablet 4	79	4.44	60.19
Levo-Thyroxine (Synthetic)	Akumentis Healthcare Ltd	Thyroweek 50 mcg tablet 4	79	4.44	60.19
Levo-Thyroxine (Synthetic)	Alkem Laboratories Ltd.	Thyropil 100 mcg tablet 10	126.5	11.8	88.89
Levo-Thyroxine (Synthetic)	Alkem Laboratories Ltd.	Thyropil 100 mcg tablet 10	111.11	11.8	88.89
Levo-Thyroxine (Synthetic)	Alkem Laboratories Ltd.	Thyropil 100 mcg tablet 10	111.11	12.3	88.89
Levo-Thyroxine (Synthetic)	Macleods Pharmaceuticals Pvt.Ltd	Thyonorm 50 mcg tablet 30	147.84	30.3	112
Levo-Thyroxine (Synthetic)	Macleods Pharmaceuticals Pvt.Ltd	Thyonorm 50 mcg tablet 30	132.3	27.3	105.84
Levo-Thyroxine (Synthetic)	Macleods Pharmaceuticals Pvt.Ltd	Thyonorm 50 mcg tablet 30	144.48	30.3	112
Levo-Thyroxine (Synthetic)	Macleods Pharmaceuticals Pvt.Ltd	Thyonorm 50 mcg tablet 30	143.99	30.3	111.62
Levo-Thyroxine (Synthetic)	Macleods Pharmaceuticals Pvt.Ltd	Thyonorm 50 mcg tablet 30	140.64	30.3	111.62
Levo-Thyroxine (Synthetic)	Macleods Pharmaceuticals Pvt.Ltd	Thyonorm 50 mcg tablet 30	140.64	30.3	112
Levo-Thyroxine (Synthetic)	Macleods Pharmaceuticals Pvt.Ltd	Thyonorm 50 mcg tablet 30	140	32.1	105.84
Levo-Thyroxine (Synthetic)	Macleods Pharmaceuticals Pvt.Ltd	Thyonorm 50 mcg tablet 30	132.3	33.3	105.84
Levo-Thyroxine (Synthetic)	Intas Pharmaceuticals Ltd	Lethyrox 100 mcg tablet 30	118.47	33.3	28.26
Levo-Thyroxine (Synthetic)	Intas Pharmaceuticals Ltd	Lethyrox 50 mcg tablet 30	107.07	30.3	24.1
Levo-Thyroxine (Synthetic)	Macleods Pharmaceuticals Pvt.Ltd	Thyonorm 50 mcg tablet 30	106	30.3	87.17

(continued)

Table A.2 (continued)

Medicine	Company	SKU	MRP	Ceiling	PTR
Levo-Thyroxine (Synthetic)	Intas Pharmaceuticals Ltd	Lethyrox 100 mcg tablet 30	122.74	35.4	28.26
Levo-Thyroxine (Synthetic)	Intas Pharmaceuticals Ltd	Lethyrox 50 mcg tablet 30	110.92	32.1	24.1
Levo-Thyroxine (Synthetic)	Intas Pharmaceuticals Ltd	Lethyrox 100 mcg tablet 30	118.47	35.4	28.26
Levo-Thyroxine (Synthetic)	Intas Pharmaceuticals Ltd	Lethyrox 50 mcg tablet 30	107.07	32.1	24.1
Levo-Thyroxine (Synthetic)	Intas Pharmaceuticals Ltd	Lethyrox 50 mcg tablet 30	110.92	33.3	22.33
Levo-Thyroxine (Synthetic)	Intas Pharmaceuticals Ltd	Lethyrox 100 mcg tablet 30	122.74	36.9	28.26
Levo-Thyroxine (Synthetic)	Intas Pharmaceuticals Ltd	Lethyrox 50 mcg tablet 30	100.41	30.3	24.1
Levo-Thyroxine (Synthetic)	Macleods Pharmaceuticals Pvt.Ltd	Thyonorm 50 mcg tablet 30	106	32.1	105.84
Levo-Thyroxine (Synthetic)	Macleods Pharmaceuticals Pvt.Ltd	Thyonorm 50 mcg tablet 30	106	32.1	87.17
Levo-Thyroxine (Synthetic)	Intas Pharmaceuticals Ltd	Lethyrox 50 mcg tablet 30	104.33	32.1	24.1
Levo-Thyroxine (Synthetic)	Intas Pharmaceuticals Ltd	Lethyrox 100 mcg tablet 30	118.12	36.9	28.26
Levodopa + Carbidopa	Torrent Pharmaceuticals Ltd.	Tidomet 100/25 mg tablet Cr 10	43.37	20	33.04
Levodopa + Carbidopa	Torrent Pharmaceuticals Ltd.	Tidomet 100/25 mg tablet Cr 10	43.07	20	36.18
Levodopa + Carbidopa	Torrent Pharmaceuticals Ltd.	Tidomet 100/25 mg tablet Cr 10	47.49	22.6	36.18
Levodopa + Carbidopa	Torrent Pharmaceuticals Ltd.	Tidomet 100/25 mg tablet Cr 10	47.49	22.6	33.04
Levodopa + Carbidopa	Torrent Pharmaceuticals Ltd.	Tidomet 100/25 mg tablet Cr 10	47.49	23.5	36.18
Lithium	Psychotropics India Ltd	Manicarb 300 mg tablet Sr 10	30	15	13.54
Metformin	Lupin Ltd	Metkin 500 mg tablet 10	118.75	15.6	95
Metformin	Lupin Ltd	Metkin 500 mg tablet 10	118.75	16.6	95

(continued)

Table A.2 (continued)

Medicine	Company	SKU	MRP	Ceiling	PTR
Metformin	Fourrts India Laboratories Pvt. Ltd	Metfil 500 mg tablet 10	67.71	15.6	54.17
Metformin	Fourrts India Laboratories Pvt. Ltd	Metfil 500 mg tablet 10	67.71	16.6	54.17
Metformin	Fourrts India Laboratories Pvt. Ltd	Metfil 500 mg tablet 10	67.71	17.2	54.17
Metformin	Glenmark Pharmaceuticals Ltd.	X-Met 500 mg tablet Sr 10	48	15.6	36.57
Metformin	Glenmark Pharmaceuticals Ltd.	X-Met 500 mg tablet Sr 10	45.71	15.6	36.57
Metformin	Glenmark Pharmaceuticals Ltd.	X-Met 500 mg tablet Sr 10	48	16.6	36.57
Metformin	Abbott India Ltd.	Obimet 500 mg tablet Sr 10	40	13.9	30.48
Metformin	Glenmark Pharmaceuticals Ltd.	X-Met 500 mg tablet Sr 10	44.25	15.6	33.71
Metformin	Abbott India Ltd.	Obimet 500 mg tablet Sr 10	37.5	15.6	28.57
Metformin	Abbott India Ltd.	Obimet 500 mg tablet Sr 10	40	17.2	30.48
Metformin	Abbott India Ltd.	Obimet 500 mg tablet Sr 10	40	17.7	30.48
Metformin	Abbott India Ltd.	Obimet 500 mg tablet Sr 10	37.5	16.6	28.57
Metformin	Abbott India Ltd.	Obimet 500 mg tablet Sr 10	37.5	17.2	28.57
Metformin	Bal Pharma	Diamet 500 mg tablet Sr 10	30	13.9	22.98
Metformin	Sanofi India Ltd.	Cetapin Xr 500 mg tablet Sr 10	33	15.6	25.41
Metformin	Merck Ltd	Carbophage 500 mg tablet Sr 10	33	15.6	25.41
Metformin	Finer Pharmaceuticals Pvt Ltd	Fagomet 500 mg tablet Sr 10	32.56	15.6	26.05
Metformin	Shrinivas Gujarat Laboratories Pvt Ltd	Emline 500 mg tablet 10	32.5	15.6	6.15
Metformin	Glenmark Pharmaceuticals Ltd.	X-Met 500 mg tablet Sr 15	48	23.4	36.57
Metformin	Shreya Life Sciences Pvt. Ltd	Glycifit 500 mg tablet 10	28.18	13.9	21.69
Metformin	Shreya Life Sciences Pvt. Ltd	Glycifit 500 mg tablet 10	28.18	13.9	21.59
Metformin	Intas Pharmaceuticals Ltd	Zomet 500 mg tablet Sr 10	27.88	13.9	21.46

(continued)

Table A.2 (continued)

Medicine	Company	SKU	MRP	Ceiling	PTR
Metformin	Sanofi India Ltd.	Cetapin Xr 500 mg tablet Sr 10	27.88	13.9	21.46
Metformin	Sanofi India Ltd.	Cetapin Xr 500 mg tablet Sr 10	31.23	15.6	24.04
Metformin	Sanofi India Ltd.	Cetapin Xr 500 mg tablet Sr 10	31.23	15.6	25.41
Methotrexate	Zydus Cadila	Mexate 7.5 mg tablet 2	73.2	23.96	38.35
Methotrexate	Zydus Cadila	Mexate 7.5 mg tablet 2	73.2	23.96	51.89
Methotrexate	Zydus Cadila	Mexate 7.5 mg tablet 2	73.2	23.96	38.86
Methotrexate	Zydus Cadila	Mexate 7.5 mg tablet 2	64.86	23.96	51.89
Metoclopramide	Lupin Ltd	Promet 10 mg tablet 10	250.98	10.8	200.79
Metoclopramide	Lupin Ltd	Promet 10 mg tablet 10	250.98	11.5	200.79
Metoclopramide	Adcock Ingram Healthcare Pvt Ltd	Reglan 10 mg tablet 10	23.45	10.8	19.25
Metoclopramide	Adcock Ingram Healthcare Pvt Ltd	Reglan 10 mg tablet 10	21.84	10.4	17.93
Metoclopramide	Adcock Ingram Healthcare Pvt Ltd	Reglan 10 mg tablet 10	21.83	10.4	17.47
Metoclopramide	Adcock Ingram Healthcare Pvt Ltd	Reglan 10 mg tablet 10	23.45	11.5	19.25
Metoclopramide	Adcock Ingram Healthcare Pvt Ltd	Reglan 10 mg tablet 10	23.22	11.5	19.06
Metoprolol	Intas Pharmaceuticals Ltd	Embeta Er 25 mg tablet 10	115	28.8	88.1
Metoprolol	Intas Pharmaceuticals Ltd	Embeta Er 25 mg tablet 10	115	37.3	88.52
Metoprolol	Intas Pharmaceuticals Ltd	Embeta Er 25 mg tablet 10	115	37.3	88.1
Metoprolol	Intas Pharmaceuticals Ltd	Embeta Er 25 mg tablet 10	105.5	37.3	81.2
Metronidazole	Mapra Laboratories Pvt. Ltd	Sprot P 400 mg tablet 10	20.21	7.5	16.17
Metronidazole	Jagsonpal Pharmaceuticals Ltd	Metronidazole (Jag) 200 mg tablet 100	89.51	40	71.61
Misoprostol	Zydus Cadila	Cytolog 100 mcg tablet 4	159.11	37.72	127.29

(continued)

Table A.2 (continued)

Medicine	Company	SKU	MRP	Ceiling	PTR
Nifedipine	Cadila Pharmaceuticals Ltd	Calnif Retard 10 mg tablet 10	126.07	11.3	12.2
Nifedipine	Cadila Pharmaceuticals Ltd	Calnif Retard 10 mg tablet 10	126.07	11.3	11.42
Nifedipine	Merck Ltd	Depicor 10 mg tablet Sr 10	32.5	14.2	12.52
Nitrofurantoin	Bharat Serums & Vaccines Ltd	Nitro F 100 mg tablet 1	76.57	6.88	58.34
Nitrofurantoin	Bharat Serums & Vaccines Ltd	Nitro F 100 mg tablet 1	75	6.88	60
Nitrofurantoin	Bharat Serums & Vaccines Ltd	Nitro F 100 mg tablet 1	75	6.88	58.34
Ondansetron	Sun Pharma Laboratories Ltd.	Zofer 8 mg tablet 4	152.88	36.24	122.31
Ondansetron	Sun Pharma Laboratories Ltd.	Zofer 8 mg tablet 4	152.88	44.28	122.31
Ondansetron	Sun Pharma Laboratories Ltd.	Zofer 8 mg tablet 4	152.88	47.08	122.31
Ondansetron	Sun Pharma Laboratories Ltd.	Zofer 8 mg tablet 4	152.88	48.88	122.31
Ondansetron	Skymax Laboratories Ltd.	Prospect 4 mg tablet 10	142	47.6	113.4
Ondansetron	Skymax Laboratories Ltd.	Prospect 4 mg tablet 10	141.75	47.6	57.54
Ondansetron	Alkem Laboratories Ltd.	Ondem Of 4 mg tablet 6	69	28.56	52.57
Ondansetron	Alkem Laboratories Ltd.	Ondem Of 4 mg tablet 6	65.71	28.56	52.57
Ondansetron	Sun Pharma Laboratories Ltd.	Zofer 4 mg tablet 4	39.67	17.4	31.74
Ondansetron	Alkem Laboratories Ltd.	Ondem Of 4 mg tablet 6	69	30.36	52.57
Ondansetron	Alkem Laboratories Ltd.	Ondem Of 4 mg tablet 6	65.71	30.36	52.57
Ondansetron	Morepen Laboratories Limited	Ondoc 4 mg tablet 10	100	47.6	5.8
Ondansetron	Morepen Laboratories Limited	Ondoc 4 mg tablet 10	100	47.6	20
Ondansetron	Cipla Ltd.	Emeset Od 4 mg tablet 10	100	47.6	21
Ondansetron	Alkem Laboratories Ltd.	Ondem Of 4 mg tablet 6	65.71	31.5	52.57
Ondansetron	Sun Pharma Laboratories Ltd.	Zofer 4 mg tablet 4	39.67	19.04	31.74
Ondansetron	Neon Laboratories Ltd	Neomit 4 mg tablet 10	99	47.6	37

(continued)

Table A.2 (continued)

Medicine	Company	SKU	MRP	Ceiling	PTR
Ondansetron	Neon Laboratories Ltd	Neomit 4 mg tablet 10	99	47.6	53.64
Ondansetron	Cipla Ltd.	Emset 4 mg tablet 10	98.44	47.6	75
Ondansetron	Cipla Ltd.	Emeset 4 mg tablet 10	98.44	47.6	75
Ondansetron	Cipla Ltd.	Emeset Md 4 mg tablet Md 10	97	47.6	20.75
Ondansetron	Cipla Ltd.	Emeset Md 4 mg tablet Md 10	97	47.6	21
Ondansetron	Cipla Ltd.	Emset Md 4 mg tablet 10	97	47.6	79.5
Ondansetron	Cipla Ltd.	Emset Md 4 mg tablet 10	97	47.6	29.73
Ondansetron	Cipla Ltd.	Emeset Md 4 mg tablet Md 10	97	47.6	24
Ondansetron	Cachet Pharmaceuticals Pvt Ltd	Emitino 4 mg tablet Md 6	52.62	26.1	39.9
Paracetamol	Alkem Laboratories Ltd.	Paracetamol (Alkem) 500 mg tablet 10	700	9.4	2.4
Paracetamol	Alkem Laboratories Ltd.	Paracetamol (Alkem) 500 mg tablet 10	700	9.4	2.45
Paracetamol	Syncom Formulations (I) Limited	Fabrimol 500 mg tablet 10	575	9.4	2.65
Paracetamol	Syncom Formulations (I) Limited	Fabrimol 500 mg tablet 10	575	9.4	2.89
Paracetamol	Exotic Laboratories Pvt Ltd	Eboo Plus (Exotic Lab) 500 mg tablet 10	129.92	8.3	103.94
Paracetamol	Exotic Laboratories Pvt Ltd	Eboo Plus (Exotic Lab) 500 mg tablet 10	135	9.4	104.14
Paracetamol	Exotic Laboratories Pvt Ltd	Eboo Plus (Exotic Lab) 500 mg tablet 10	135	9.4	73.29
Paracetamol	Exotic Laboratories Pvt Ltd	Eboo Plus (Exotic Lab) 500 mg tablet 10	135	9.4	104.16
Paracetamol	Unireach Healthcare Pvt Ltd	Primosul 500 mg tablet 10	115.06	8.3	92.05
Paracetamol	Exotic Laboratories Pvt Ltd	Eboo Plus (Exotic Lab) 500 mg tablet 10	130.2	9.4	103.94

(continued)

Table A.2 (continued)

Medicine	Company	SKU	MRP	Ceiling	PTR
Paracetamol	Exotic Laboratories Pvt Ltd	Eboo Plus (Exotic Lab) 500 mg tablet 10	130.2	9.4	104.16
Paracetamol	Exotic Laboratories Pvt Ltd	Eboo Plus (Exotic Lab) 500 mg tablet 10	130.17	9.4	104.14
Paracetamol	Exotic Laboratories Pvt Ltd	Eboo Plus (Exotic Lab) 500 mg tablet 10	135	10	104.16
Paracetamol	Exotic Laboratories Pvt Ltd	Eboo Plus (Exotic Lab) 500 mg tablet 10	135	10.4	103.94
Paracetamol	Exotic Laboratories Pvt Ltd	Eboo Plus (Exotic Lab) 500 mg tablet 10	130.2	10.4	104.16
Paracetamol	Exotic Laboratories Pvt Ltd	Eboo Plus (Exotic Lab) 500 mg tablet 10	129.92	10.4	103.94
Paracetamol	Unireach Healthcare Pvt Ltd	Primosul 500 mg tablet 10	115.06	9.4	92.05
Paracetamol	Bioguard Organics Ltd.	Dolo Sp 500 mg tablet 10	73.15	9.4	55
Paracetamol	Bioguard Organics Ltd.	Dolo Sp 500 mg tablet 10	74.25	10	55
Paracetamol	Bioguard Organics Ltd.	Dolo Sp 500 mg tablet 10	68.75	9.4	52.47
Paracetamol	Bioguard Organics Ltd.	Dolo Sp 500 mg tablet 10	72.6	10	55
Paracetamol	Bioguard Organics Ltd.	Dolo Sp 500 mg tablet 10	68.2	9.4	52.47
Paracetamol	Bioguard Organics Ltd.	Dolo Sp 500 mg tablet 10	68.2	9.4	55
Paracetamol	Bioguard Organics Ltd.	Dolo Sp 500 mg tablet 10	67.69	9.4	52.47
Paracetamol	Bioguard Organics Ltd.	Dolo Sp 500 mg tablet 10	65.06	9.4	52.47
Paracetamol	Bioguard Organics Ltd.	Dolo Sp 500 mg tablet 10	68.75	10	55
Paracetamol	Bioguard Organics Ltd.	Dolo Sp 500 mg tablet 10	64.01	9.4	52.47
Paracetamol	Bioguard Organics Ltd.	Dolo Sp 500 mg tablet 10	68.75	10.4	55
Paracetamol	Dew Drops Lab	Denim P (Dew Drops) 500 mg tablet 10	49.75	8.3	37.9
Paracetamol	Symcox Research Lab P.Ltd	Flupra 500 mg tablet 10	45	8.3	36

(continued)

Table A.2 (continued)

Medicine	Company	SKU	MRP	Ceiling	PTR
Paracetamol	Exotic Laboratories Pvt Ltd	Eboo (Exotic Lab) 500 mg tablet 10	42.5	8.3	32.72
Paracetamol	Symcox Research Lab P.Ltd	Flupra 500 mg tablet 10	50	10	36
Paracetamol	Symcox Research Lab P.Ltd	Flupra 500 mg tablet 10	45.36	9.4	36.29
Paracetamol	Symcox Research Lab P.Ltd	Flupra 500 mg tablet 10	45	9.4	36.29
Paracetamol	Symcox Research Lab P.Ltd	Flupra 500 mg tablet 10	45	9.4	36
Paracetamol	Dew Drops Lab	Denim P (Dew Drops) 500 mg tablet 10	49.75	10.4	37.9
Paracetamol	Ronak Labs	Cetcold 500 mg tablet 10	38	8.3	30.48
Paracetamol	Dew Drops Lab	Denim P (Dew Drops) 500 mg tablet 10	45.25	10	34.48
Paracetamol	Symcox Research Lab P.Ltd	Flupra 500 mg tablet 10	45	10	36
Paracetamol	Dew Drops Lab	Denim P (Dew Drops) 500 mg tablet 10	41.14	9.4	31.34
Paracetamol	Dew Drops Lab	Denim P (Dew Drops) 500 mg tablet 10	41.14	9.4	31.35
Paracetamol	Dew Drops Lab	Denim P (Dew Drops) 500 mg tablet 10	41.14	9.4	34.48
Paracetamol	Dew Drops Lab	Denim P (Dew Drops) 500 mg tablet 10	45.25	10.4	34.48
Paracetamol	Symcox Research Lab P.Ltd	Flupra 500 mg tablet 10	45	10.4	36
Paracetamol	Dew Drops Lab	Denim P (Dew Drops) 500 mg tablet 10	41.14	10	31.34
Paracetamol	Dew Drops Lab	Denim P (Dew Drops) 500 mg tablet 10	41.14	10	34.48
Paracetamol	Exotic Laboratories Pvt Ltd	Eboo (Exotic Lab) 500 mg tablet 10	42.5	10.4	32.72
Paracetamol	Cipla Ltd.	Actiflu 500 mg tablet 10	38	9.4	6.9
Paracetamol	Cipla Ltd.	Actiflu 500 mg tablet 10	38	9.4	8.66

(continued)

Table A.2 (continued)

Medicine	Company	SKU	MRP	Ceiling	PTR
Paracetamol	Cipla Ltd.	Actiflu 500 mg tablet 10	38	9.4	8.42
Paracetamol	Exotic Laboratories Pvt Ltd	Eboo (Exotic Lab) 500 mg tablet 10	42	10.4	32.34
Paracetamol	Exotic Laboratories Pvt Ltd	Eboo (Exotic Lab) 500 mg tablet 10	40.91	10.4	32.73
Paracetamol	Exotic Laboratories Pvt Ltd	Eboo (Exotic Lab) 500 mg tablet 10	39	10	30.03
Paracetamol	Ronak Labs	Cetcold 500 mg tablet 10	40	10.4	30.48
Paracetamol	Exotic Laboratories Pvt Ltd	Eboo (Exotic Lab) 500 mg tablet 10	39	10.4	30.03
Paracetamol	Exotic Laboratories Pvt Ltd	Eboo (Exotic Lab) 500 mg tablet 10	35	9.4	27.01
Paracetamol	Exotic Laboratories Pvt Ltd	Eboo (Exotic Lab) 500 mg tablet 10	35	9.4	26.95
Paracetamol	Ronak Labs	Cetcold 500 mg tablet 10	38.1	10.4	30.48
Paracetamol	Ronak Labs	Cetcold 500 mg tablet 10	38	10.4	30.4
Paracetamol	Ronak Labs	Cetcold 500 mg tablet 10	38	10.4	30.48
Paracetamol	Exotic Laboratories Pvt Ltd	Eboo (Exotic Lab) 500 mg tablet 10	37.53	10.4	30.03
Paracetamol	Ronak Labs	Cetcold 500 mg tablet 10	35	10	30.48
Paracetamol	Ronak Labs	Cetcold 500 mg tablet 10	35	10	28
Paracetamol	Ronak Labs	Cetcold 500 mg tablet 10	35	10	23.6
Paracetamol	Exotic Laboratories Pvt Ltd	Eboo (Exotic Lab) 500 mg tablet 10	35	10	26.95
Paracetamol	Novartis India Ltd	Temfix 500 mg tablet 10	35	10	7
Paracetamol	Ronak Labs	Cetcold 500 mg tablet 10	35	10.4	28
Paracetamol	Exotic Laboratories Pvt Ltd	Eboo Spaz (Exotic Lab) 500 mg tablet 10	27	8.3	21.6

(continued)

Table A.2 (continued)

Medicine	Company	SKU	MRP	Ceiling	PTR
Paracetamol	Dew Drops Lab	Denim P (Dew Drops) 500 mg tablet 10	32.95	10.4	25.11
Paracetamol	Cipla Ltd.	Parafast 500 mg tablet 4	10.47	3.32	8.38
Paracetamol	Cipla Ltd.	Parafast 500 mg tablet 4	11	3.76	8.38
Paracetamol	Ronak Labs	Cetcold 500 mg tablet 10	29.5	10.4	23.6
Paracetamol	Exotic Laboratories Pvt Ltd	Eboo Spaz (Exotic Lab) 500 mg tablet 10	28	10	21.6
Paracetamol	Exotic Laboratories Pvt Ltd	Eboo Spaz (Exotic Lab) 500 mg tablet 10	28	10	22.87
Paracetamol	Cipla Ltd.	Parafast 500 mg tablet 4	10.47	3.76	8.38
Paracetamol	Navil Laboratories	C 37 500 mg tablet 10	23	8.3	17.71
Paracetamol	Cipla Ltd.	Parafast 500 mg tablet 4	11	4	8.38
Paracetamol	Exotic Laboratories Pvt Ltd	Eboo Spaz (Exotic Lab) 500 mg tablet 10	27	10	21.6
Paracetamol	Cipla Ltd.	Parafast 500 mg tablet 4	11.21	4.16	8.97
Paracetamol	Exotic Laboratories Pvt Ltd	Eboo Spaz (Exotic Lab) 500 mg tablet 10	24	9.4	18.51
Paracetamol	Exotic Laboratories Pvt Ltd	Eboo Spaz (Exotic Lab) 500 mg tablet 10	24	9.4	22.87
Paracetamol	Cipla Ltd.	Parafast 500 mg tablet 4	10.48	4.16	8.39
Paracetamol	Cipla Ltd.	Parafast 500 mg tablet 4	10.47	4.16	8.38
Paracetamol	Exotic Laboratories Pvt Ltd	Eboo Spaz (Exotic Lab) 500 mg tablet 10	24	10	22.87
Paracetamol	Thrift Pharmaceuticals	Adwin 500 mg tablet 10	19.75	8.3	15.8
Paracetamol	Adcock Ingram Healthcare Pvt Ltd	Adcopara 500 mg tablet 2	3.8	1.66	2.93
Paracetamol	Navil Laboratories	C 37 500 mg tablet 10	23	10.4	17.71
Paracetamol	Agron Remedies Pvt. Ltd.	37 C 500 mg tablet 10	20.75	9.4	15.6

(continued)

Table A.2 (continued)

Medicine	Company	SKU	MRP	Ceiling	PTR
Paracetamol	Navil Laboratories	C 37 500 mg tablet 10	21.83	10	16.17
Paracetamol	Agron Remedies Pvt. Ltd.	37 C 500 mg tablet 10	20.44	9.4	15.6
Paracetamol	Agron Remedies Pvt. Ltd.	37 C 500 mg tablet 10	20.12	9.4	15.6
Paracetamol	Navil Laboratories	C 37 500 mg tablet 10	17.75	8.3	13.6
Paracetamol	Dial Pharmaceuticals Pvt. Ltd.	Peristop 500 mg tablet 10	20	9.4	15.34
Paracetamol	Glaxosmithkline Pharmaceuticals Ltd.	Crocin Advance 500 mg tablet 15	30	14.1	23.31
Paracetamol	Glaxosmithkline Pharmaceuticals Ltd.	Crocin Advance 500 mg tablet 15	30	14.1	23.81
Paracetamol	Panacea Biotec Ltd	Tecpara 500 mg tablet 10	19.8	9.4	15.09
Paracetamol	Panacea Biotec Ltd	Tecpara 500 mg tablet 10	19.8	9.4	15.71
Paracetamol	Navil Laboratories	C 37 500 mg tablet 10	21	10	16.17
Paracetamol	Agron Remedies Pvt. Ltd.	37 C 500 mg tablet 10	19.5	9.4	15.6
Paracetamol	Navil Laboratories	C 37 500 mg tablet 10	21	10.4	16.17
Paracetamol	Indoco Remedies Ltd	Febrex 500 mg tablet 10	18.87	9.4	14.53
Paracetamol	Indoco Remedies Ltd	Febrex 500 mg tablet 10	18.87	9.4	12.16
Paracetamol	Glaxosmithkline Pharmaceuticals Ltd.	Crocin Advance 500 mg tablet 15	30	15	23.81
Paracetamol	Glaxosmithkline Pharmaceuticals Ltd.	Crocin Advance 500 mg tablet 15	30	15	23.31
Phenobarbitone	Abbott Healthcare Pvt. Ltd	Gardenal 60 mg tablet 20	76.68	32.8	61.35
Phenobarbitone	Abbott Healthcare Pvt. Ltd	Gardenal 30 mg tablet 20	41.08	18.6	31.3
Phenobarbitone	Abbott Healthcare Pvt. Ltd	Gardenal 30 mg tablet 20	41.08	18.6	16.03
Phenobarbitone	Medo Pharma	Emgard 30 mg tablet 10	20	9.3	15.33
Phenobarbitone	Medo Pharma	Emgard 30 mg tablet 10	20	9.3	15.4

(continued)

Table A.2 (continued)

Medicine	Company	SKU	MRP	Ceiling	PTR
Phenobarbitone	Medo Pharma	Emgard 30 mg tablet 10	19.25	9.3	7.84
Phenytoin	Alkem Laboratories Ltd.	Phenykem 100 mg tablet 10	164.85	12.7	125.6
Phenytoin	Mankind Pharmaceuticals Ltd.	Epiforce 100 mg tablet 10	164.08	12.7	125.01
Phenytoin	Mankind Pharmaceuticals Ltd.	Epiforce 100 mg tablet 10	175	14.2	133.33
Phenytoin	Mankind Pharmaceuticals Ltd.	Epiforce 100 mg tablet 10	166.66	14.2	133.33
Phenytoin	Alkem Laboratories Ltd.	Phenykem 100 mg tablet 10	153.01	14.2	122.41
Phenytoin	Alkem Laboratories Ltd.	Phenykem 100 mg tablet 10	153.01	14.2	113.6
Phenytoin	Alkem Laboratories Ltd.	Phenykem 100 mg tablet 10	149.1	14.2	113.6
Phenytoin	Alkem Laboratories Ltd.	Phenykem 100 mg tablet 10	164.85	15.7	125.6
Phenytoin	Alkem Laboratories Ltd.	Phenykem 100 mg tablet 10	158.49	15.1	120.75
Phenytoin	Mankind Pharmaceuticals Ltd.	Epiforce 100 mg tablet 10	158	15.1	113.52
Phenytoin	Mankind Pharmaceuticals Ltd.	Epiforce 100 mg tablet 10	164.08	15.7	125.01
Phenytoin	Alkem Laboratories Ltd.	Phenykem 100 mg tablet 10	143.75	14.2	115
Phenytoin	Alkem Laboratories Ltd.	Phenykem 100 mg tablet 10	158.49	15.7	120.75
Phenytoin	Mankind Pharmaceuticals Ltd.	Epiforce 100 mg tablet 10	158	15.7	120.38
Phenytoin	Alkem Laboratories Ltd.	Phenykem 100 mg tablet 10	142.86	14.2	114.29
Phenytoin	Alkem Laboratories Ltd.	Phenykem 100 mg tablet 10	150.93	15.1	120.75
Phenytoin	Mankind Pharmaceuticals Ltd.	Epiforce 100 mg tablet 10	141.9	14.2	113.52
Phenytoin	Mankind Pharmaceuticals Ltd.	Epiforce 100 mg tablet 10	156.26	15.7	125.01
Phenytoin	Alkem Laboratories Ltd.	Phenykem 100 mg tablet 10	149.1	15.1	120.75
Phenytoin	Alkem Laboratories Ltd.	Phenykem 100 mg tablet 10	149.1	15.1	113.6
Phenytoin	Mankind Pharmaceuticals Ltd.	Epiforce 100 mg tablet 10	149	15.1	113.52
Phenytoin	Alkem Laboratories Ltd.	Phenykem 100 mg tablet 10	150.93	15.7	120.75

(continued)

Table A.2 (continued)

Medicine	Company	SKU	MRP	Ceiling	PTR
Phenytoin	Mankind Pharmaceuticals Ltd.	Epiforce 100 mg tablet 10	150.47	15.7	120.38
Phenytoin	Mankind Pharmaceuticals Ltd.	Epiforce 100 mg tablet 10	149	15.7	113.52
Phenytoin	Mankind Pharmaceuticals Ltd.	Epiforce 100 mg tablet 10	141.9	15.1	113.52
Phenytoin	Mankind Pharmaceuticals Ltd.	Epiforce 100 mg tablet 10	141.9	15.7	113.52
Phenytoin	Zydus Cadila	Epsolin Er 100 mg tablet Er 30	192	47.1	147.83
Phenytoin	Zydus Cadila	Epsolin Er 100 mg tablet Er 30	168.42	42.6	134.74
Phenytoin	Zydus Cadila	Epsolin Er 100 mg tablet Er 30	175	45.3	134.74
Phenytoin	Zydus Cadila	Epsolin Er 100 mg tablet Er 30	168.43	45.3	134.75
Phenytoin	Zydus Cadila	Epsolin Er 100 mg tablet Er 30	168.42	45.3	134.74
Phenytoin	Zydus Cadila	Epsolin Er 100 mg tablet Er 30	144.93	42.6	134.74
Phenytoin	Zydus Cadila	Epsolin Er 100 mg tablet Er 30	144.93	42.6	115.95
Prednisolone	Mankind Pharmaceuticals Ltd.	Nucort 5 mg tablet 10	272.7	5.8	127.43
Prednisolone	Mankind Pharmaceuticals Ltd.	Nucort 5 mg tablet 10	159.28	5.2	127.43
Prednisolone	Mankind Pharmaceuticals Ltd.	Nucort 5 mg tablet 10	159.28	5.5	127.43
Prednisolone	Mankind Pharmaceuticals Ltd.	Nucort 5 mg tablet 10	159.28	5.8	127.43
Prednisolone	Mankind Pharmaceuticals Ltd.	Nucort 5 mg tablet 10	159.28	6	127.43
Prednisolone	Cipla Ltd.	Predone 5 mg tablet 10	36.25	5.5	29
Prednisolone	Mankind Pharmaceuticals Ltd.	Nucort 20 mg tablet 10	85	18.1	64.45
Prednisolone	Mankind Pharmaceuticals Ltd.	Nucort 20 mg tablet 10	85	18.3	64.76
Prednisolone	Mankind Pharmaceuticals Ltd.	Nucort 20 mg tablet 10	85	19	64.46

(continued)

Table A.2 (continued)

Medicine	Company	SKU	MRP	Ceiling	PTR
Prednisolone	Mankind Pharmaceuticals Ltd.	Nucort 20 mg tablet 10	85	19	64.76
Prednisolone	Mankind Pharmaceuticals Ltd.	Nucort 20 mg tablet 10	85	19	64.45
Prednisolone	Mankind Pharmaceuticals Ltd.	Nucort 20 mg tablet 10	80.95	18.3	64.76
Prednisolone	Mankind Pharmaceuticals Ltd.	Nucort 20 mg tablet 10	80.95	19	64.76
Prednisolone	Admac Pharma Ltd.	Adred 20 mg tablet 10	40	18.3	22.3
Primaquine	Leo Pharmaceuticals	Leoprime Forte 7.5 mg tablet 14	72	29.54	52.52
Primaquine	Leo Pharmaceuticals	Leoprime Forte 7.5 mg tablet 14	65	27.72	52
Primaquine	Leo Pharmaceuticals	Leoprime Forte 7.5 mg tablet 14	65	27.72	49.52
Primaquine	Leo Pharmaceuticals	Leoprime Forte 7.5 mg tablet 14	68	29.54	52.52
Primaquine	Leo Pharmaceuticals	Leoprime Forte 7.5 mg tablet 14	65.65	29.54	52.52
Primaquine	Leo Pharmaceuticals	Leoprime Forte 7.5 mg tablet 14	65.65	30.66	52.52
Propranolol	Mova Pharmaceuticals Pvt Ltd	Movalol 40 mg tablet Sr 10	59.9	27.2	30.4
Propranolol	Mova Pharmaceuticals Pvt Ltd	Movalol 40 mg tablet Sr 10	54.9	27.2	30.4
Pyrazinamide	Morepen Laboratories Limited	Pyriza 750 mg tablet 10	258.71	57.3	217.32
Quinine	Troikaa Pharmaceuticals Ltd	Quinax 300 mg tablet 10	699.6	51	530
Quinine	Ipca Laboratories Pvt Ltd.	Cinkona 300 mg tablet 6	69.25	30.6	44.09
Quinine	Ipca Laboratories Pvt Ltd.	Cinkona 300 mg tablet 6	69.25	30.6	52.76
Salbutamol	Raptakos, Brett & Co. Ltd.	Durasal 4 mg tablet 10	6.7	1.7	5.36
Salbutamol	Raptakos, Brett & Co. Ltd.	Durasal 4 mg tablet 10	6.1	1.7	4.52
Salbutamol	Raptakos, Brett & Co. Ltd.	Durasal 4 mg tablet 10	6.7	1.9	5.36
Salbutamol	Cipla Ltd.	Asthalin Sa 4 mg tablet 10	5.9	1.7	4.54
Salbutamol	Raptakos, Brett & Co. Ltd.	Durasal 4 mg tablet 10	6.1	1.8	4.52
Salbutamol	Raptakos, Brett & Co. Ltd.	Durasal 4 mg tablet 10	5.65	1.7	4.52

(continued)

Table A.2 (continued)

Medicine	Company	SKU	MRP	Ceiling	PTR
Salbutamol	Raptakos, Brett & Co. Ltd.	Durasal 4 mg tablet 10	5.97	1.8	4.52
Salbutamol	Cipla Ltd.	Asthalin Sa 4 mg tablet 10	5.9	1.8	4.54
Salbutamol	Raptakos, Brett & Co. Ltd.	Durasal 4 mg tablet 10	6.2	1.9	4.96
Salbutamol	Raptakos, Brett & Co. Ltd.	Durasal 4 mg tablet 10	5.65	1.8	4.52
Salbutamol	Cipla Ltd.	Asthalin Sa 4 mg tablet 10	5.9	1.9	4.54
Salbutamol	Cipla Ltd.	Asthalin 4 mg tablet 30	15.26	5.1	11.75
Salbutamol	Raptakos, Brett & Co. Ltd.	Durasal 4 mg tablet 10	5.65	1.9	4.52
Salbutamol	Cipla Ltd.	Asthalin 4 mg tablet 30	15.26	5.4	11.75
Salbutamol	Cipla Ltd.	Asthalin 4 mg tablet 30	14.68	5.4	11.75
Salbutamol	Cipla Ltd.	Asthalin 4 mg tablet 30	15.26	5.7	11.75
Salbutamol	Cipla Ltd.	Asthalin 4 mg tablet 30	14.68	5.7	11.75
Salbutamol	Cipla Ltd.	Asthalin 2 mg tablet 30	10.1	4.2	7.78
Salbutamol	Cipla Ltd.	Asthalin 2 mg tablet 30	10.1	4.5	7.78
Salbutamol	Cipla Ltd.	Asthalin 2 mg tablet 30	10.1	4.8	7.78
Salbutamol	Cipla Ltd.	Asthalin 2 mg tablet 30	10.1	4.8	8.15
Salbutamol	Cipla Ltd.	Asthalin 2 mg tablet 30	9.72	4.8	7.78
Tamoxifen	Astrazeneca Pharma India Ltd	Nolvadex 10 mg tablet 10	201	43.5	153.14
Tamoxifen	Astrazeneca Pharma India Ltd	Nolvadex 10 mg tablet 10	201	43.5	36.53
Tamoxifen	Astrazeneca Pharma India Ltd	Nolvadex 10 mg tablet 10	201	43.5	36.72
Trihexyphenidyl	Sun Pharma Laboratories Ltd.	Parkitane 2 mg tablet 10	90.43	11.3	72.35
Trihexyphenidyl	Sun Pharma Laboratories Ltd.	Parkitane 2 mg tablet 10	87	11.3	66.96
Trihexyphenidyl	Sun Pharma Laboratories Ltd.	Parkitane 2 mg tablet 10	87	15.1	66.96
Trihexyphenidyl	Sun Pharma Laboratories Ltd.	Parkitane 2 mg tablet 10	83.7	15.1	66.96

(continued)

Table A.2 (continued)

Medicine	Company	SKU	MRP	Ceiling	PTR
Trihexyphenidyl	Sun Pharma Laboratories Ltd.	Parkitane 2 mg tablet 10	77	14.5	61.6
Trihexyphenidyl	Sun Pharma Laboratories Ltd.	Parkitane 2 mg tablet 10	72.18	13.6	57.75
Trihexyphenidyl	Sun Pharma Laboratories Ltd.	Parkitane 2 mg tablet 10	80	15.1	61.58
Trihexyphenidyl	Sun Pharma Laboratories Ltd.	Parkitane 2 mg tablet 10	77	15.1	61.6
Trihexyphenidyl	Sun Pharma Laboratories Ltd.	Parkitane 2 mg tablet 10	76.97	15.1	61.58
Trihexyphenidyl	Sun Pharma Laboratories Ltd.	Parkitane 2 mg tablet 10	69.3	13.6	57.75
Trihexyphenidyl	Sun Pharma Laboratories Ltd.	Parkitane 2 mg tablet 10	69.3	13.6	55.44
Trihexyphenidyl	Sun Pharma Laboratories Ltd.	Parkitane 2 mg tablet 10	72.18	14.5	57.75
Trihexyphenidyl	Sun Pharma Laboratories Ltd.	Parkitane 2 mg tablet 10	63	14.5	61.6
Trihexyphenidyl	Mova Pharmaceuticals Pvt Ltd	Movahexy 2 mg tablet Md 10	33.58	11.3	26.87
Trihexyphenidyl	Pfizer Ltd	Pacitane 2 mg tablet 10	31	13.6	11.53
Trihexyphenidyl	Pfizer Ltd	Pacitane 2 mg tablet 10	31	13.6	23.87
Trihexyphenidyl	Mova Pharmaceuticals Pvt Ltd	Movahexy 2 mg tablet Md 10	33.58	15.1	26.87
Trihexyphenidyl	Pfizer Ltd	Pacitane 2 mg tablet 70	200	95.2	23.87
Trihexyphenidyl	Pfizer Ltd	Pacitane 2 mg tablet 70	200	95.2	29.35
Trihexyphenidyl	Pfizer Ltd	Pacitane 2 mg tablet 70	200	95.2	29.4

Source: NPPA, AIOCD, Author's calculations